For Greta,

with compliments!

All the best, Thomas

(Dec. '15)

CATALYST FOR CHANGE

Chinese Business in Asia

ASIA-PACIFIC BUSINESS SERIES   (ISSN: 1793-3137)

Series Editor
Philippe Lasserre
Emeritus Professor of Strategy and Asian Business
INSEAD

Published

Vol. 1   Guanxi and Business
       by Yadong Luo

Vol. 2   From Adam Smith to Michael Porter: Evolution of Competitiveness Theory
       by Dong-Sung Cho & Hewy-Chang Moon

Vol. 3   Islamic Banking and Finance in South-East Asia: Its Development and Future
       (2nd Edition)
       by Angelo M. Venardos

Vol. 4   Asian Models of Entrepreneurship — From the Indian Union and the
       Kingdom of Nepal to the Japanese Archipelago: Context, Policy and Practice
       by Leo-Paul Dana

Vol. 5   Guanxi and Business (2nd Edition)
       by Yadong Luo

Vol. 6   Islamic Banking and Finance in South-East Asia: Its Development and Future
       (3rd Edition)
       by Angelo M. Venardos

Vol. 7   From Adam Smith to Michael Porter: Evolution of Competitiveness Theory
       (Extended Edition)
       by Dong-Sung Cho & Hwy-Chang Moon

Vol. 8   Catalyst for Change: Chinese Business in Asia
       edited by Thomas Menkhoff, Hans-Dieter Evers, Chay Yue Wah &
       Hoon Chang Yau

Asia-Pacific Business Series – Vol. 8

CATALYST FOR CHANGE

Chinese Business in Asia

Editors

Thomas Menkhoff (Singapore Management University, Singapore)

Chay Yue Wah (SIM University, Singapore)

Hans-Dieter Evers (Institute of Asian Studies, Universiti Brunei Darussalam, Brunei)

Hoon Chang Yau (Singapore Management University, Singapore)

World Scientific

NEW JERSEY · LONDON · SINGAPORE · BEIJING · SHANGHAI · HONG KONG · TAIPEI · CHENNAI

Published by

World Scientific Publishing Co. Pte. Ltd.

5 Toh Tuck Link, Singapore 596224

USA office: 27 Warren Street, Suite 401-402, Hackensack, NJ 07601

UK office: 57 Shelton Street, Covent Garden, London WC2H 9HE

Library of Congress Cataloging-in-Publication Data
Catalyst for change : Chinese business in Asia / edited by Thomas Menkhoff (Singapore Management University, Singapore), Hans-Dieter Evers (Institute of Asian Studies, Universiti Brunei Darussalam, Brunei), Chay Yue Wah (SIM University, Singapore) and Hoon Chang Yau (Singapore Management University, Singapore).
    pages cm
    Includes bibliographical references.
    ISBN-13: 978-9814452410
    ISBN-10: 9814452416
    1. China--Commerce--Asia. 2. Asia--Commerce--China. 3. Chinese diaspora--Economic aspects. 4. Corporations, Chinese--Asia. 5. Chinese--Asia--Economic conditions. 6. Entrepreneurship--China. 7. Entrepreneurship--Asia. I. Menkhoff, Thomas, editor of compilation. II. Evers, Hans-Dieter, editor of compilation. III. Chay, Yue Wah, editor of compilation. IV. Hoon, Chang-Yau, editor of compilation.
    HF3838.A783C38 2013
    382.095105--dc23
                                                    2013023522

British Library Cataloguing-in-Publication Data
A catalogue record for this book is available from the British Library.

In-house Editor: Alisha Nguyen

Typeset by Stallion Press
Email: enquiries@stallionpress.com

Printed in Singapore by B & Jo Enterprise Pte Ltd

Contents

Contributors   ix
Contributors   ix
List of Figures   xvii
List of Tables   xxi

Introduction: Coping with Change — Understanding Ethnic
Chinese Business Behavior   xxiii
*Thomas Menkhoff, Chay Yue Wah, Hans-Dieter Evers
and Hoon Chang Yau*

**Part 1   The Story of the "Chinese Overseas": Implications
for Identity, Business and "Chineseness"**   1

Chapter 1   The Sea as Paddy: The Making of Fujian
as a Transnational Place   3
Jessica Chong

Chapter 2   What Chinese Am I? The Use of Heritage
for Economic Imperatives in Singapore   23
Daphnée HL Lee

Chapter 3   Managing Change in Asian Business:
A Comparison between Chinese-educated
and English-educated Chinese Entrepreneurs
in Singapore   45
*Thomas Menkhoff, Ulrike Badibanga
and Chay Yue Wah*

Chapter 4   Chinese Business in Malaysia:
Ethnicity and Knowledge Management   73
Chin Yee Whah

Chapter 5   Evolving Chineseness, Ethnicity and Business:
             The Making of the Ethnic Chinese as a
             "Market-Dominant Minority" in Indonesia   107
             Hoon Chang Yau

Part 2:   The Management of Business Networks and Change   129

Chapter 6   Trading Networks of Chinese Entrepreneurs
             in Singapore   131
             Thomas Menkhoff and Chalmer E Labig

Chapter 7   Improving Small Firm Performance through
             Collaborative Change Management
             and Outside Learning: Trends in Singapore   155
             Thomas Menkhoff and Chay Yue Wah

Chapter 8   Ethnic Chinese Family-Controlled Firms
             in Singapore: Continuity and Change
             in Corporate Governance   193
             Lai Si Tsui-Auch and Dawn Chow Yi Lin

Chapter 9   Building a Successful Brand: The Story of
             Eu Yan Sang   213
             *Jessica Chong, Willem Smit, Thomas Menkhoff
             and Christopher Clayman (with Richard Eu)*

Chapter 10   Generational Change in Chinese Indonesian SMEs?   231
             Juliette Koning

Chapter 11   The Salim Group: The Art of Strategic Flexibility 251
             Marleen Dieleman

**Part 3:   Leadership, Knowledge and Learning
            in Chinese Business   277**

Chapter 12   In Search of "Asian" Conceptions of Leadership with a
             Focus on Mindfulness   279
             *Chay Yue Wah, Charles Chow, Hans-Dieter Evers,
             Lee Cher Leng, Thomas Menkhoff, Jochen Reb,
             Jayarani Tan and Elfarina Zaid*

Chapter 13   Exploring Lee Kong Chian's Knowledge
              Leadership Style in Nam Aik Company   299
              Dai Shiyan and Zhang Guocai

Chapter 14   Organizational Learning Approaches of Small
              and Medium-sized Enterprises: A Comparative
              Study of Chinese Firms in Singapore   315
              Thomas Menkhoff

Chapter 15   Understanding the Role of Cultural Orientations
              in Students' Predispositions toward Knowledge
              Transfer in Project Teams: Evidence from Singapore   345
              Thomas Menkhoff, Chay Yue Wah
              and Hans-Dieter Evers

Part 4:   Asian Business in Local Contexts   379

Chapter 16   Urban Property Development in Malaysia:
              The Impact of Chinese and Malay Conceptions
              of Space   381
              Hans-Dieter Evers

Chapter 17   Informal Banking and Early International
              Entrepreneurs: The Case of the Chettiars   397
              Jayarani Tan and Tan Wee Liang

Chapter 18   The Internationalization of Mainland Chinese
              Businesses   419
              Hinrich Voss

Index   439

Contributors

Chalmer Labig is Associate Professor at Oklahoma State University, Spears School of Business. His areas of expertise include small business growth and alliance/acquisition activities. E-mail: cel@okstate.edu

Charles Chow received his PhD from University of South Australia and worked for the military, police, and government before undertaking private enterprise. Since 1996, he has been involved as Managing Director (1996–2009) and Owner (since 2009) in the East-West Group to link high potentials between Germany and India for business in education and the environment. Although a Catholic, he is a lifelong student of the Bhagavad Gita, the Hindu gospel that offers great wisdom for efficacy in business management. E-mail: chowhoihee@gmail.com

Chay Yue Wah is Head of Graduate Studies at Singapore Institute of Management University. He obtained his doctoral degree from the University of Oxford and is a registered Chartered Psychologist. Prior to his academic career, he worked in the merchant navy, electronics industry, and as a research psychologist with CASSIM, a simulator based training facility. He has held faculty positions at National University of Singapore, Singapore Management University, and Nanyang Technological University. His research interests are in knowledge systems, citizenship behavior, work commitment and personnel psychology. E-mail: ywchay@unisim.edu.sg

Chin Yee Whah is Associate Professor and Deputy Dean at the Division of Industry and Community Network, School of Social Sciences, Universiti Sains Malaysia, Penang (Malaysia). He received his PhD in Sociology from National University of Malaysia. His research interests include Chinese business, family business, entrepreneurship, ethnic relations in business partnership, ethnicity, knowledge management, Chinese Malaysian investment abroad and SMEs. His publications include *Budaya dan Keusahawanan Cina di Malaysia* (*Culture and Chinese Entrepreneurship in Malaysia*, 2003) and *Community, Identity, Politics, and Healthcare in Malaysia* (co-editor, 2011). E-mail: ywchin@usm.my

Christopher Clayman holds a BA in Political Science and English from University of North Carolina, Chapel Hill. He is currently working in China.

Dai Shiyan is Deputy Director, China Affairs Office, Nanyang Technological University, Singapore. He holds a PhD in Management & Organization and a Master's degree in Business Administration from National University of Singapore. His thirty years of work experiences in China, the United States, and Singapore is spanning academia, journalism, training, and consultancy. Over the past ten years, he has been actively engaged in the training and consulting sector, and his professional expertise falls within the fields of talent assessment, strategic human resource development and management, organizational behavior, effective leadership and communication, organizational change management, and business communication in China. E-mail: sydai@ntu.edu.sg

Daphnée Lee is Research Fellow at the National Institute of Education, Nanyang Technological University, Singapore. She obtained her PhD in Sociology from Australian National University. Her research interests include state ethnic management's impact on business activity, professional learning communities, and organization culture. E-mail: daphnee.lee@nie.edu.sg

Dawn Chow Yi Lin is a PhD student at Nanyang Technological University in Singapore. Her research interests lie in institutional logics and institutional theory, as well as legal sector innovation. In 2012, she presented a paper at the Strategic Management Society's Special Conference, and she has a forthcoming article (written in collaboration with Lai Si Tsui-Auch) to be published in *The Wiley Encyclopedia of Management*, 3rd Edition. E-mail: ylchow1@e.ntu.edu.sg

Elfarina Zaid holds a Bachelor of Business Management degree from Singapore Management University (SMU) and is an Executive and Leadership Coach (CPCC) as well as a life-long learner and practitioner in the fields of organizational behavior and human consciousness. She has lived 8 years in the Middle East, is a faculty at Coaches Training Institute and co-founded Elf Coaching. E-mail: elfarina@elfcoaching.com

Hans-Dieter Evers, Emeritus Professor of Development Planning, is an Eminent Visiting Professor, Institute of Asian Studies, Universiti Brunei Darussalam. He was formerly Visiting Professor, Lee Kong Chian School of Business, Singapore Management University, Universiti Sains Malaysia, Universitas Indonesia and Distinguished Visiting Professor of Sociology, Singapore National University. His research is concerned with knowledge governance and maritime societies in Southeast Asia. Home page: https://sites.google.com/site/hansdieterevers/home. E-mail: hdevers@uni-bonn.de

Hinrich Voss is a Roberts Academic Research Fellow at the Centre for International Business University of Leeds (CIBUL). His research interests concentrate on the internationalization and the international competitiveness of Mainland Chinese companies. This research strand incorporates the influence of China's institutions on the international investment behavior of Chinese firms. Hinrich is also conducting business-related research on climate change policies and future energies. Before joining CIBUL, Hinrich was a Postdoctoral Research Fellow at White Rose East Asia Centre/National Institute for Chinese Studies. Hinrich is Deputy Director of Leeds International Business Confucius Institute and the head of the advisory board of NetImpact Chapter of Leeds University Business School. E-mail: H.Voss@leeds.ac.uk.

Hoon Chang Yau is Assistant Professor of Asian Studies at the School of Social Sciences, Singapore Management University. He obtained his PhD in Asian Studies (with Distinction) from University of Western Australia. His books include *Chinese Identity in Post-Suharto Indonesia: Culture, Media and Politics* (Sussex Academic Press, 2008) and *Chinese Indonesians Reassessed: History, Religion and Belonging* (Routledge, 2012). E-mail: cyhoon.smu.edu.sg

Jayarani Tan is Senior Lecturer at Lee Kong Chian School of Business, Singapore Management University. She received her doctoral degree (Dr rer soc) in Sociology from University of Bielefeld (Germany). She previously worked on the Chettiars of Singapore as part of her doctoral thesis, which is now in the process of being published as a monograph. E-mail: ranitan@smu.edu.sg

Jessica Chong holds a BA in Geography from Vassar College in Poughkeepsie, New York, USA. Her paper on Fujian in this volume is based on her undergraduate thesis, written under the advisorship of Professor Yu Zhou. E-mail: jessicalaurenchong@gmail.com

Jochen Reb is Associate Professor of Organizational Behavior and Human Resources at Lee Kong Chian School of Business, Singapore Management University. Jochen received his PhD in Management from University of Arizona in 2005. His research focuses on three areas: emotion and decision making, the evaluation of dynamic performance, and the role of attention and mindfulness in organizations. Jochen's work has been published in journals such as *Journal of Applied Psychology*, *Journal of Management*, *Organizational Behavior and Human Decision Processes*, and *Personnel Psychology*, among others. He also serves on the editorial board of the *Journal of Management* and the *Journal of Business and Psychology*. E-mail: jochenreb@smu.edu.sg

Juliette Koning is Senior Lecturer in the Department of Business and Management, Oxford Brookes University (UK) and editor of *Asia Matters: Business, Culture and Theory*. Her research focuses on business, leadership, identity, ethnicity, and religion in Southeast Asia, and her work has been published in journals such as *East Asia: An International Quarterly*, *Copenhagen Journal of Asian Studies*, *International Journal of Business Anthropology*, and *Journal of Business Ethics*. She has a PhD in Social Anthropology from University of Amsterdam in The Netherlands. E-mail: j.koning@brookes.ac.uk

Lawrence Chong graduated from University of Singapore with a B. Soc. Sc. Honors degree (Sociology major) in 1971. He is the grandson of Chong Pak Heng and Mdm Wong Siew Chin. Lawrence is a property consultant based in Hong Kong. Email: lawrencechong@gmail.com

Lai Si Tsui-Auch is Associate Professor at Nanyang Business School, Strategy, Management & Organization, Nanyang Technological University. She conducts research on corporate governance reforms, entrepreneurship, and business groups. Her publications have appeared in *Organizational Science*, *International Journal of Business Studies*, *Organization Studies*, *Journal of Management Studies*, *International Sociology*, and *Journal of International Urban and Regional Research*, among others. E-mail: ALSTsui@ntu.edu.sg

Lee Cher Leng is Associate Professor of Chinese Linguistics in the Department of Chinese Studies, National University of Singapore. Two of her recent journal publications include "How is 'philanthropy' represented in Chinese characters, words, and phrases? Towards an etymological interpretation" (*Journal of Asian Business*); and "'Traditional' Chinese conceptions of knowledge (*zhi*,知): A 'modern' interpretation with reference to business" (*Journal of Asian Business*). E-mail: chsleecl@nus.edu.sg

Marleen Dieleman is Senior Researcher and Associate Director of the Centre for Governance, Institutions & Organisations at National University of Singapore, Department of Strategy and Policy. She holds a PhD from Leiden University and a Master's degree in business administration from Rotterdam School of Management, both located in The Netherlands. Marleen's research and teaching interests are in strategy, particularly in emerging market business groups and family business in Southeast Asia. She has published extensively on Southeast Asian family business groups, including articles in leading academic journals, books chapters, books, and teaching cases. E-mail: marleen@nus.edu.sg

Richard Eu is Group Chief Executive Officer of Eu Yan Sang International Ltd. Since 2001, he has been responsible for the overall corporate development and management of the group. Prior to that, he worked in merchant banking, investment management, stock broking, computer distribution and venture capital before becoming the Group General Manager of Eu Yan Sang Holdings Ltd (EYSH) in 1989. EYSH was the owner of the Eu Yan Sang business in Singapore and Malaysia at that time. In 1993, he organized a management buyout of the business, and in 1996 it was merged with the Eu Yan Sang business in Hong Kong, forming the Eu Yan Sang International Group as it is today. Apart from his business interests, Mr Richard Eu is also actively involved in several community projects and non-profit organizations. He has a Bachelor's Degree in Law from London University, UK.

Tan Wee Liang is Associate Professor of Strategic Management at Singapore Management University. He received his PhD from Eindhoven University of Technology in Innovation Sciences and completed his MSc (Management) at MIT and LLM at Cambridge University. His research interests include entrepreneurship, SMEs, family businesses, and strategic alliances. Wee Liang has published numerous journal articles, conference papers, book reviews, books and chapters in books. His family business research includes "Coping with growth transitions: The case of Chinese family businesses in Singapore," published in the *Family Business Review*. He also co-authored *Entrepreneurship and Enterprise Development in Asia* (Prentice-Hall Asia). He currently serves as Editor-in-Chief of the *Journal of Enterprising Culture*. E-mail: wltan@smu.edu.sg

Thomas Menkhoff is Professor of Organizational Behavior and Human Resources (Education) at Lee Kong Chian School of Business, Singapore Management University. He has formerly taught at National University of Singapore, University of Cologne, and University of Bielefeld in Germany. One of his latest publications is *Beyond the Knowledge Trap — Developing Asia's Knowledge-based Economies* (World Scientific, 2011, co-edited with Hans-Dieter Evers, Chay Yue Wah and Pang Eng Fong). E-mail: thomasm@smu.edu.sg

Ulrike Badibanga is a consultant with extensive experience in marketing research and business intelligence consulting. For over twelve years, she has undertaken research and implemented reporting solutions for large international companies. She recently returned to Singapore and launched her own web-service business. E-mail: uli.b@hotmail.com

Willem Smit is Adjunct Professor at Lee Kong Chian School of Business, Singapore Management University, and Affiliated Research Fellow at

IMD (International Institute for Management Development). Willem earned his PhD from Rotterdam School of Management, Erasmus University, The Netherlands. His specializations include strategic marketing, branding, channel collaboration, and new market creation. He has published in *Harvard Business Review* and *Journal of Business Venturing*, among others. Besides traditional print publications, Willem experiments with disseminating his research findings through new social media. His "Which Chinese/South African/Singapore/Indian Brands Are Best for the World?" video clip series on brands from emerging economies can be viewed on YouTube. E-mail: wsmit@smu.edu.sg

Zhang Guocai is a former Associate Professor in the Department of Journalism and Communication, Xiamen University, China. E-mail: luodzgc@sina.com

List of Figures

Chapter 2

Figure 1. Variable interpretations of Chineseness by ambiguity
anxiety scores   37

Chapter 3

Figure 1. Research model: Individual reference framework
and control variables, information and size of
organization as influencing factors of CM behavior   55

Figure 4. Quantity of change measures initiated
by Chinese-educated English-educated SME
owner-managers   59

Figure 2. Age distribution of Chinese-educated and English
educated SME owner-managers   66

Figure 3. Highest attained educational qualification of
Chinese-educated and English-educated business people   66

Figure 5. Significant relationships and trends between
initiation of change and selected variables   67

Figure 6. Significant relationships and trends between
change management approach and selected variables   67

Chapter 6

Figure 1. Extract of Mr Yao's personal trading network   147

Chapter 7

Figure 1. Change leadership styles to incremental
and transformative change   161

Figure 2. Dunphy and Stace's contingency approach
to change implementation   162

Figure 3. Most frequently adopted change measure   166

Figure 4. Nature of organizational change measures   167

Figure 5. Planning of organizational change measure yes/no — 167
Figure 6. Scale of organizational changes initiated by respondents — 168
Figure 7. Change leadership style — 169
Figure 8. Change management scenario — 170
Figure 9. Appropriate change leadership styles for
incremental change — 171
Figure 10. Appropriate change leadership styles
for transformative change — 172
Figure 11. Scenarios of change and adopted change
leadership modes — 173
Figure 12. Scale of benefits obtained by change measure — 175

Chapter 8

Figure 1. Family-controlled business groups in Singapore
groups in 2006 — 198

Chapter 9

Figure 1. Company growth Eu Yan Sang (1996–2012) — 214
Figure 2. Key strategic brand management processes
and brand positioning guidelines — 218

Chapter 12

Figure 1. Components leading to mindfulness — 285
Figure 2. When work becomes worship — 286

Chapter 14

Figure 1. Antecedents of organizational learning capability
and firm performance of Asian SMEs — 317

Chapter 15

Figure 1. Knowledge transfer between cultural patterns — 355
Figure 2. Emerging model of K-transfer in diverse student teams — 356
Figure 3. Relation between explicit knowledge transfer
and horizontal individualism for high and low levels
of vertical collectivism — 365

Chapter 18

Figure 1. Chinese outward foreign direct investment   427
Figure 2. Chinese OFDI stock in ASEAN   429

List of Tables

Chapter 2

Table 1. Optimism toward career trajectory by heritage
         identifications   36

Chapter 3

Table 1. Comparison of "traditional Chinese"
         and "modern Western"   52
Table 2. Frequencies of selected variables   57

Chapter 6

Table 1. Methods of exporting cited   141
Table 2. Preferences for export marketing transactions   141
Table 3. Trading partners of Singaporean Chinese traders   142

Chapter 8

Table 1. Equity holding in the family-controlled firms
         by the largest block shareholder   204
Table 2. Percentage of outside directors on board of the core
         companies of the largest family-controlled firms   204
Table 3. Relationships of Board Chair/President, CEOs/Managing
         Directors to the controlling families of the largest
         family-controlled firms   205
Table 4. OCBC's succession history   207

Chapter 12

Table 1. Benefits of mindfulness   282
Table 2. How mindfulness can be achieved and trained   294

Chapter 14

Table 1. Qian Hu's benchmarking and learning activities   337

Table 2. Mastery of organizational learning in firms A, B and C   339

Chapter 15

Table 1. Interface of vertical-horizontal individualism-collectivism   352
Table 2. Correlations of major study variables (N = 330)   361
Table 3. Regression model of the predictors of explicit knowledge
     transfer (N = 330)   362
Table 4. Regression model of the predictors of tacit knowledge
     transfer (N = 330)   363
Table 5. Regression model of the predictors of explicit
     knowledge transfer (N = 330)   364

Chapter 17

Table 1. Overall population of Chettiars in India and overseas   398
Table 2. Possible lessons from the Chettiars   412

Chapter 18

Table 1. Chinese mergers and acquisitions in ASEAN   430

Introduction: Coping with Change — Understanding Ethnic Chinese Business Behavior

Thomas Menkhoff, Chay Yue Wah, Hans-Dieter Evers and Hoon Chang Yau

Why This Book?

This book features twelve new and six previously published essays on ethnic Chinese entrepreneurs and business management in Asia, written by several reputable scholars on Chinese business. They cover diverse yet closely related topics, such as the role of ethnic identity, Chineseness, *guanxi* ties, change management, leadership, knowledge and learning management in organizations owned and managed by ethnic Chinese as well as related themes such as conceptions of space and internationalization. Conceptualized as a complete reader, the editors' broad intention is to provide students, scholars, business executives, and others interested in understanding Asia's rise with a comprehensive Asian perspective on the organizational peculiarities and changing business practices of ethnic Chinese businesses and their leaders, who continue to form the backbone of Asia's dynamic economies. We hope that after reading this book, readers will be able to explain what makes ethnic Chinese business in Asia tick; to appreciate both the structure and function of Chinese business organization, networks, and their increasingly global reach; to challenge some of the culturally biased misconceptions about the business conduct of ethnic Chinese in Asia, such as their homogeneity, tribal image, and socio-economic exclusivity; and to critically discuss the challenges, which the rapidly progressing integration of the East and Southeast Asian market cultures into the global market system pose, for ethnic Chinese entrepreneurs, their family businesses, conglomerates, and network ties.

An important question in the context of Chinese business studies is whether there is anything unique (and if yes, what is unique) about the business management approaches adopted by Chinese entrepreneurs, for example, *vis-à-vis* their small and medium-size enterprise (SME) counterparts in the West (Wertheim, 1980; Redding, 1993; Tong and Chan, 2001; Yao, 2002; Barney and Shujun, 2009; Cheung and Hamilton, 2009). As Tong (2010, p. 18) has pointed out:

> "Chinese businesses are generally characterized by personalism; a tendency to incorporate personal relationships in decision making. Chinese businessmen prefer to deal with other Chinese as they are deemed to be more 'trustworthy.' Chinese ethnicity becomes cultural capital, and ethnicity is invoked to ensure smooth business transactions. As economic networks are important, ethnic identification takes on practical considerations. It can be argued that the Chinese maintain a coherent sense of ethnic solidarity as it is good for business."

While comparative empirical research that could shed more light on these important issues is still rare, ongoing research on SMEs conducted by some of the editors in Southeast Asia (together with anecdotal evidence gathered during sporadic trips to Europe and the United States) suggests that a contingency (comparative) perspective is perhaps a useful approach to further examine this interesting issue (Menkhoff and Chay, 2008). Let us start with a rather simple (and arguably somewhat stereotypical) dichotomy of "traditional Asian" vs. "modern Western" business management patterns to identify some of the potential differences between the two groups. The features of "traditional Asian" (Chinese) SMEs include family ownership, autocratic leadership, centralized decision-making with minimum participation, little sharing of information and knowledge (which are often considered to be trade secrets) beyond the inner family circle, intuitive planning, as well as an underdeveloped training and development function (due to job hopping concerns), reflecting the absence of a strategic human resource management (HRM) system (Menkhoff and Gerke, 2002).

In contrast, "modern Western" firms feature various ownership forms with professional directors, a more participatory leadership style, strategic planning, decentralization, participation and delegation, as well as greater information and knowledge transfer, together with a more developed training and development function embedded in more or less proper strategic HRM structures, due to the overall importance of talent and staff development.

It would be misleading to compare both approaches and argue that one is more successful than the other (in fact, both systems can sometimes be found in one firm, regardless of whether it is located in Singapore or Stuttgart, due to generational succession dynamics). Historically, both systems developed in different institutional contexts and under the influence of very different environmental factors (Yoshihara, 1988). Asia's family-based SMEs, with their traditional patriarchal structures, should be regarded as effective responses to the overall aversive conditions that prevail(ed) in many Asian countries during the colonial and post-colonial eras, including the need for quick decision-making and firm action (Menkhoff, 1993a). If you can rely on well-trained, trustworthy, and committed organizational members, the legal system, contract enforcement, and so forth, an "autocratic" leadership style based on oral business contracts and word-of-mouth as well as ethnic identification becomes less critical (although good relationships do matter in all business dealings).

While China and India continue to grow steadily, the discussion about ethnic Chinese business in Southeast Asia's emerging markets has quieted down a little during recent years compared to the "hype" in the 1990s as indicated by book titles such as *New Asian Emperors* (Haley *et al.*, 1998), *The New Taipans* (Cragg, 1995) or *Asian Eclipse* (Backman, 1999). During the Asian financial crises, it became clear that essentializing Chinese business culture adds little value to analytical attempts to decipher the true spirit of Chinese capitalism. Searching for common ground amongst the various schools of thought (and their contested issues) about Chinese enterprise management research (Gomez and Hsiao, 2001) such as the "culturalists" (Redding, 1993) or the "revisionists" (Yao, 2002), we argue that both oversocialized and undersocialized perspectives of economic action (Granovetter, 1985) are important to understand the business behavior of ethnic Chinese in Asia (see Menkhoff and Gerke eds., 2002).

A contingent institutional perspective (Clegg, 1990, pp. 150–151; Tong and Yong, 1997) ties both cultural and market forces together and considers the influence of what Tong and Yong have termed "institutional belief systems" as well as individual cognitive reference frameworks on both organizational forms and managerial leadership behavior, which can enable or constrict action depending on circumstances. Such an approach also takes history into consideration, which is often ignored by market and even cultural approaches.

While some academics have turned away from studying (and romanticizing) ethnic Chinese entrepreneurship during the past decade, the "Chinese business ground" in Asia has become much more diverse with more and more Chinese firms from both the Nanyang and Mainland China playing crucial catalyzing roles in connecting markets across the region and beyond. Examples include the acquisitions of Thai conglomerates abroad such as Charoen Pokphand Group Co's US$9.4 billion purchase of a minority stake in China's Ping An Insurance as reported by Reuters (2012), the merger of German cement pump maker Putzmeister with Chinese construction-equipment maker Sany Heavy Industry Co (http://www.putzmeister.com/enu/8681.htm) or the portfolio of Singaporean George Quek's BreadTalk Group which has expanded to Mainland China, Hong Kong and Indonesia. Its outlets in China account for 32 percent of the group's revenue (*China Daily,* January 18–24, 2013). Given this new dynamism, it is obvious that the study of ethnic Chinese business will continue to be of utmost importance for understanding Asia.

While the field of Asian business studies remains challenging, given its diversity and empirical challenges, there is one fact that is hardly debatable, and that is the pace of external change impacting the Asian region in general and SMEs and their leaders in particular (Tsui-Auch, 2004; Yeung, 2006; Wong, 2008). Mega trends, such as demographic shifts (e.g., the emergence of Generation Y; Gen Y), globalization, information and communications technology (ICT), or educational advancements in business and society in general, continue to change how SME owner-managers operate and lead. How are ethnic Chinese business leaders as catalyst for change coping with this changing world?

The various essays in this book (written by researchers from Singapore, Malaysia, Hong Kong, Germany, The Netherlands, Belgium, the People's Republic of China, and the United States) seek to provide some answers to this broad question. The various essays can be roughly categorized according to four themes: (i) the story of the Chinese overseas and its implications for identity, business, and Chineseness; (ii) the management of business networks and change; (iii) leadership, knowledge and learning in Chinese business; and (iv) Asian business in local contexts. In the following, we will contextualize and link all of these topics.

The Story of the Chinese Overseas and Its Implications for Identity, Business and Chineseness

One way of familiarizing both Asian and non-Asian readers with the interesting story of the so-called Chinese overseas is to shed light on the dynamic development of the places and areas in South China from where most of them originated (Wang, 1992, 2000; Benton and Hong, 2004). While a thorough analysis of Guangdong and Fujian provinces is beyond the scope of this introduction, it is interesting to note that Shantou (Guangdong) and Xiamen (Fujian), which were selected by the Chinese Government as test beds in the context of its economic reform policy from 1978 onwards, have performed very differently. Before 1981, when Teochew-speaking Shantou (known as Swatow in Teochew) became a Special Economic Zone (SEZ), it was known as a thriving trading port; however, due to infrastructural bottlenecks and poor governance, it failed to keep up with Xiamen (known to Hokkiens as Amoy). In Xiamen, pro-business policies and increasing economic linkages with Taiwan, as a result of closer cross-strait relations, have led to greater trade, investment, and tourist arrivals in recent years. Famous entrepreneurial Teochews, Hokkiens, and Hokchias include Hong Kong property tycoon Li Ka Shing, the boss of food giant Xiamen Yinlu Chen Qingyuan, and Sudono Salim (Chinese: 林绍良, Liem Swie Liong or Lim Sioe Liong; 1916–2012), an Indonesian ethnic Chinese of Hokchia origin who founded the well-known Salim Group, now headed by his son, Anthony Salim.

Shantou, Xiamen, and Fuqing are known for their enterprising diasporas of Teochews, Hokkiens, and Hokchias (Wang, 1992; Jacobson, 2007). In the early days, different dialect groups specialized in different occupational areas in the Nanyang, such as the Hokchias, who established a business niche in the transport sector. An illustrative example is the Green Bus Company in Singapore which ceased to exist in the early 1970s when the Government undertook a major rationalization exercise aimed at enhancing efficiency and service for commuters.

History of Chong Pak Heng Family and Green Bus Company

Chong Pak Heng founded the Green Bus Company in 1945, after the three-year Japanese Occupation of Singapore and Malaya, along with partners from the Fujian — Fuqing — HingHua migrant community. Mr. Chong came from West Hill Village, in Fuqing County, Fujian Province. In West Hill Village, a large family size commanded respect and prestige. His father sent him and his two younger brothers to Singapore in the mid-1910s to earn a living, as well as to produce as many children as possible. Initially, he eked out a living by operating a bicycle repair shop along Jalan Besar. He demonstrated flashes of marketing savvy when he began importing British-made Raleigh bicycle frames, and assembling them with locally-made wheels and working parts. The complete chariot was sold as a Raleigh-brand product, commanding a premium price. He made a small fortune from this endeavour. Mr. Chong was also a founding member of the Singapore Hockchia (Fuqing) Association in 1924, one of the earliest clan associations in Singapore.

When he saved enough capital from his bicycle shop, he invested in a small taxi fleet, and thereafter expanded his fleet by investing in mini buses. However, this operation was halted during the Japanese rule of Singapore (1942–1945). When the Japanese surrendered in September 1945, the British resumed the colonial administration of Singapore. Mr. Chong, being fluent in Malay, succeeded in getting the exclusive bus-operating license for the northern zone. He quickly founded the Green Bus Company and became the Founding Director and General Manager. The license was for the long-haul Bukit Timah trunk route, including a terminal in Johore Bahru (JB), which was then part of Malaya. There were no customs and immigration checkpoints on either side of the causeway, as both territories were administered by the British Administration. At the time, the fare to JB was S$0.60. Other routes covered were Lim Chu Kang (S$0.80), Jurong, Mandai and Queen Elizabeth (Opera) Estate.

Mr. Chong passed away in 1949, after a few years of being bed-ridden with paralysis. In recognition for his pioneering leadership in the Chinese business community, each of the 9 competitor bus companies assigned a bus to form a motorcade known, in those days, as "The Nine Dragons," for his funeral. All ten of the independent bus companies were owned by fellow compatriots from Fujian, and the motorcade was a reflection of their close ties in their newly adopted home.

Upon his passing, his wife Madam Wong Siew Chin, sent from his village to be his wife in Singapore, became a company Director. Within the next eight years, all three of the original male partners passed away, leaving their respective widows as Directors. The four-member "handbag brigade" — as they were referred to by working-class Singaporeans — formed the Board of Directors. They were the first all-female board of directors in Singapore (circa 1950–1964). The most qualified from the next generation was Madam Wong's second son, Chong Wee Ling, who took over the position of general manager during the mid-1950s. Mr. Chong left behind 16 children (11 boys and 5 girls). All the males worked for the Green Bus Company. His second son served as General Manager; his third son was Operations Superintendent. His fourth son handled labour relations, while his fifth son was a route inspector. His sixth son was a traffic license manager, seventh son garage manager, eighth son a planner, ninth son in charge of accounts, tenth son a route inspector, and the eleventh son a scheduling supervisor. Madam Wong and her fellow directors were joint cashiers and treasurers; no other employees were allowed to touch the daily cash count.

The Green Bus Company had the largest fleet among the private bus company franchises. Other franchises included Tay Koh Yat Bus (red — Thompson–Serangoon); Ponggol Bus (blue — Ponggol — Tampines); Easy Bus (yellow — Pasir Panjang); Hock Lee Bus (red — Tanjong Pagar); Paya Lebar Bus (blue); Changi Bus (red) and Singapore Traction Company (white/red — downtown routes mostly powered by overhead electric cables). Green Bus owned the property at the southwest junction of Bukit Timah/Clementi Road. This six-acre footprint was the headquarters and nerve centre for the company — providing facilities such as garage, repair, maintenance, fueling station, stores, canteen, training and accounts. All Green Bus routes began at downtown Queens Road terminal, with the Green Bus town office located nearby at 2 Angulia St. The one-hour ride to JB was 16 miles. Passengers would pay their bus fares in cash to the onboard bus conductor. Fares were charged based on the distance travelled starting from 5 cents. The Chong family also owned Pontian Bus (operating the JB – Pontian route) covering the western shores of Johore State.

Mr. Chong groomed his second son Wee Ling and third son Chok Ling for key positions in the company. Wee Ling was appointed General Manager. He was a flamboyant and charismatic gentleman who graduated from Anglo–Chinese School — making him one of the rare English-speaking managers in the 1950s. He was well respected in the business community, having sat on the board of the Chinese Chamber of Commerce and clan associations. He had diversified investments in property, motor services, fueling stations and entertainment. Being the leader of the Liberal Socialist political party, he contested, and lost, against a young firebrand lawyer Lee Kuan Yew of the People's Action Party in Tanjong Pagar, during the first general election of Singapore in 1959. He passed away in 2006 and is survived by five children.

Chok Ling was appointed Operations Superintendent. He graduated from Hwa Chong Secondary School. His eloquence in Chinese endeared him to the Chinese scholar community, and he was active in the committee that helped establish the Singapore Chinese University in Jurong. He married the daughter of Tan SiewAik, the founding director of OCBC. They had nine children.

In the early 1970s the government forced the merger of all the private bus companies as part of the rationalization plan. Three regional bus groups were formed: Associated Bus, United Bus and Amalgamated Bus. In the late 1970s, all the bus companies were further amalgamated as one national bus company — the Singapore Bus Service.

Madam Wong and most of her sons retired during the initial merger in early 1970s. At the age of 100 years in 1995, she sustained an unfortunate fall and was prematurely called to heaven. By Chinese tradition, three "bonus" years are added for those who attain the age of 100 years. At the time of her passing, she had outlived four of her 16 children. She was survived by 50 sons/daughters-in-law, 70 grandchildren, 86 great grandchildren and 4 greatgreat grandchildren. A total count of 222 surviving relatives over five generations are scattered around the world, making the Chong family one of the largest families in Singapore's history.

Background Info about West Hill Village

The Fuqing village of West Hill is bordered on the east side by the sea. It is about a two-hour drive south of Fuzhou, the capital of Fujian Province. Villagers of past generations made a living harvesting salt and oysters. The village subsists on farming as well. There are 6,000 families in the village and everyone is related by the surname Chong. This is a patriarchal community as illustrated by the 30-metre long marble wall, which has engraved on it the Chinese names of all male offsprings predicated by the surname Chong. This acts as a registry of all Chongs that can trace their lineage to this village, regardless of where in the world they were born. During her active working life in Singapore, Madam Wong sent money, food, and clothing back to the less fortunate in the village. She would also make regular visits, thereby keeping in close touch with her village.

Some of the most well-known overseas Fuzhou — Fuqing Chinese from the sister village include Liem Sioe Leong of the Salim Group of Indonesia and Robert Kuok of Kerry-Shangrila Group of Singapore-Malaysia. The late Ng Teng Fong's family came from the HingHua city of Putian, one hour south of Fuqing.

Mr. Chong Pak Heng's Old House

This private 100-year-old two-storey house is preserved as a family museum, with original furnitures and old family portraits adorning the walls. Mr. Chong's new three-storey house was built in 1995 by his Singapore-born children. His final resting place is in his tomb shared with his wife who outlived him by 46 years — almost a lifetime by 19th-century standards. The generous-sized tomb lies 50 meters from the house compound. The top floor of the three-storey house is home to the family's mascot called Tai Chi Ba — a boy guardian angel worshipped to protect the entire family (narrative by Lawrence Chong).

Many members of the Hokchia diaspora in Southeast Asia can trace their origin to Fuqing county (population: approx. 1.3 million), with its county-level city of Fuzhou located in the eastern part of Fujian province near the East China Sea. Fuqing's dialect (Hokchia) is closely related to the Fuzhou dialect. Fuzhou and Xiamen are the two largest cities in

Fujian Province. Due to good governance, a pro-investment climate, visionary leadership, and the sound infrastructural planning of new highways and port facilities, the regional economy is thriving. Nevertheless, migration to countries such as Japan, Australia, Canada, and the United States continues. However, a fairly new trend is migration to countries on the African continent, as elaborated in Chapter 1 by Jessica Chong, entitled "The Sea as Paddy — The Making of Fujian as Transnational Place." In her chapter, Chong reviews the transnationalization of Fujian Province, which has been known to be the main source of illegal Chinese migrants in the United States since the 1980s. In recent years, the destinations of these migrants have become increasingly varied, with some embarking on transnational activities in South Africa. While most narratives about Fujianese migration sensationalize the role of human smugglers and use economic theory to try to make sense of this large-scale movement of people, Chong's chapter emphasizes the fact that Fujianese transnationalism has a history dating back (at least) 500 years (Wang, 2004). Based on extensive fieldwork in Fujian and documental research, she argues that a long historical perspective is crucial for deducing why Fujian continues to be a transnational hub with a vast and dynamic global reach. Like Jessica Chong, an increasing number of "young ethnic Chinese" in the East and West are interested in understanding and visiting their ancestral homes in southern China as part of their search for their roots and identity or driven by the desire to revive their dialect (Kuah, 1998; Liu, 1998; Rae and Witzel, 2008).

Who Are the Chinese Overseas?

The process of globalization provides interesting food for thought when it comes to defining who the Chinese overseas are, including their identity patterns (Wang, 1998; Pan, 2006). Within China, the term *zhongguoren* 中國人 refers to a person holding the citizenship of the People's Republic of China or the Republic of China, sometimes known as "Chinese nationals or citizens." From a central Chinese perspective, terms such as *huaren*, *huaqiao*, or *huayi* point to the fact that China has often laid claim to ethnic Chinese worldwide to serve her own national interests. From the historical perspective, Chinese nationals or citizens living outside of China as a

Chinese abroad

result of migration during the period between 1850s and 1950 are regarded *huaqiao* 華僑 (i.e., citizens of the People's Republic of China residing abroad). This term (also known as "Chinese sojourner" in English) was often used before the founding of the People's Republic of China in 1949, when China provided citizenship to these so-called "overseas Chinese," who were seen as politically loyal and culturally orientated toward China. As the number of locally born Chinese overseas grew between 1950 and 1980, the new term *huaren* 華人 emerged to classify those ethnic Chinese as well as Chinese overseas communities who had settled permanently abroad and had renounced their Chinese citizenship, while maintaining Chinese cultural values and selected practices. Another label that has been used for the Chinese overseas is *huayi* 華裔, which refers to overseas Chinese as "foreign" citizens of Chinese origin/descent born overseas (outside China). Since people of Chinese descent in their (new) adopted home countries are unlikely to subject themselves to the authority of the Chinese government, the term is arguably outdated (Kwok, 2006).

huaqiao 1850-1950
huaren 1950-1980
huayi

In the context of this book, we refer to the Chinese overseas as "people who are Chinese by descent, but whose non-Chinese citizenship and political allegiance collapse ancestral loyalties" (Pan, 2006, p. 15). This implies that they are loyal to their respective country of citizenship (a foreign country from China's perspective) rather than China, in contrast to what is often wrongfully assumed by non-Chinese. Due to China's rise, the issue of the overseas Chinese (rather than the Chinese overseas) remains an interesting socio-political phenomenon. As Ching points out:

Overseas Chinese vs Chinese overseas

> "China isn't shy about demonstrating how ethnic Chinese communities are currently serving its political purposes. For example, in Beijing's dispute with Japan over the Diaoyu islands — known to Japan as the Senkakus — the state news agency Xinhua reported that overseas Chinese around the world are supporting China's position... Ethnic Chinese can easily be seen as a fifth column, loyal not to their country of citizenship but to a foreign power" (*Business Times*, November 7, 2012).

The definitory and terminological complexity of the issue of overseas Chinese identity is arguably best illustrated in the exhibition, "Chinese

More or Less: An Exhibition on Overseas Chinese Identity," at the Chinese Heritage Centre (Nanyang Technological University; NTU) in Singapore. It was organized by the editor of *The Encyclopedia of the Chinese Overseas*, Lynn Pan, and confronts visitors with questions such as "How Chinese am I?" "In what sense am I Chinese?" or "What does it mean to be Chinese?" By showcasing different portraits of Chinese men and women from various historical eras and in different attires and localities, visitors can assess their Chineseness and appreciate how it has changed continually throughout history. The exhibition enables students of Chinese culture to understand how Chinese self-identities are constructed (ascribed, internalized, and/or rejected) and to appreciate the influence of historical, social, and political forces in this process. It also sheds light on the complex distinctiveness of the Straits Chinese in Malaysia and Singapore, the Peranakan Chinese in the Netherlands Indies, and the Chinese Mestizo in the Spanish Philippines and how these groups absorbed local, Chinese, and European influences in their self-identifications (Tong, 2010).

Chinese More or Less

Issues of Chineseness continue to be of great importance in all Southeast Asian nations where ethnic Chinese form a sizable proportion of the population (Suryadinata, 1997; Jacobson, 2007). Singapore is an interesting case in this context, given the national desire to leverage China's growth and the need to maintain a robust Singaporean identity amidst diversity and increasing foreign immigration. As former President of NTU Su Guaning stressed in the *Straits Times* article "Being Chinese and Singaporean" (December, 29, 2010, A22), "As Singaporeans, we need to be able to chart our own path. Often, this is a middle path between the super-power (United States) and the rising power (China)." The city-state is facing a very volatile business environment, falling birth rates, an aging workforce, and an increasingly heterogeneous Chinese ground due to foreign immigration. How do Chinese Singaporeans (who represent more than two thirds of Singapore's multi-cultural population) perceive their own Chinese heritage connections, which are currently seen as an important element in facilitating transnational commercial relationships?

This question is taken up by Daphnée HL Lee in Chapter 2 ("What Chinese Am I? The Use of Heritage for Economic Imperatives in Developmental State Singapore"), based on a comprehensive study of a group of Chinese Singaporeans (born during the first two decades of Singapore's independence between 1960 and 1979) who, as employees of a Western multinational corporation (MNC), are in charge of liaising with the company's clientele in China. The study examines their individual heritage identifications and their approach toward work ambiguity, i.e., circumstances where there is no clear path, in cross-cultural work contexts *vis-à-vis* the level of their ambiguity anxiety measured with the help of both interview and survey data. As Lee points out, there are different ways in which Chinese Singaporeans are dealing with these issues and how they make sense of their own Chineseness at work, which she typifies as "situational Chineseness," "born-again Chineseness," "integrated Chineseness," and "resolute Chineseness." The study underlines the cultural complexity and ongoing transformation of the Chinese ground in Singapore *vis-à-vis* the rapid change in the business environment. As Lee concludes, Singapore is ever ready to adapt to new figurations in business and politics out of geo-political, socio-cultural, and historical necessity.

Chapter 3 by Thomas Menkhoff, Ulrike Badibanga, and Chay Yue Wah entitled "Managing Change in Asian Business — A Comparison between Chinese-educated and English-educated Chinese Entrepreneurs in Singapore" (a reprint of an article published in 2007 in the *Copenhagen Journal of Asian Studies*) provides deeper insight into the intra-cultural diversity of Singapore's Chinese small-scale business sector, which outside observers often overlook. SMEs owned and managed by ethnic Chinese continue to form the backbone of most economies in high-growth Asia. Given their collective value added to the local economy, business dynamism, and the volatile environment, an interesting question that has received minimal attention is whether there are any significant differences between Chinese-educated and English-educated small-scale ethnic Chinese businessmen in terms of their managerial strategies, corporate governance, leadership styles, and so forth. The dichotomy of the Chinese-educated and English-educated ethnic Chinese is of great historical and politico-cultural significance in Singapore (Lee and Zhou, 2006), as further elaborated in the article. The survey data compiled by the authors show that there are indeed differences between both subgroups (e.g., with regard to the initiation of a more participatory people management style), but these variations are less pronounced than the authors had expected. Access to information and actionable managerial competency appears to be decisive when it comes to the mastery of change management approaches, which take centre stage in their study. English-educated Chinese businessmen in particular seem to have an advantage over their Chinese-educated counterparts, as the modern change management literature is largely published in English.

Across the causeway, attempts to leverage the proximity to Singapore with fresh initiatives continue. In the late 1980s, Singapore, Malaysia, and Indonesia jointly embarked on creating the "SIJORI Growth Triangle" to leverage the competitive strengths of Singapore's infrastructure, capital, and technological know-how as well as Johor's (Malaysia) and Riau's (Riau Islands, Indonesia) labor and land resources in order to attract more foreign and regional investment. Its spill-over effects have been rather limited, despite ongoing sub-regional cooperation in globalizing Asia with its weak foundations (Razeen, 2010). While other, perhaps more competitive, centers of economic integration have been established in Asia since then, Malaysia is currently going ahead with its grand vision of further developing the South-Johor Economic Region (in short: Iskandar Malaysia) as a corridor for economic development, based on a sophisticated development plan. A key objective is to transform the physical and economic landscapes of the Johor Bahru metropolitan area and to realize its cluster vision with the help of foreign investors from neighboring Singapore and elsewhere.

Iskandar Malaysia has been designated by the Malaysian Government as a prime hub for nine economic clusters emphasizing services (Financial Advisory & Consulting, Creative Industries, Logistics, Tourism, Education, and Healthcare) and manufacturing (Electrical & Electronics, Petrochemical & Oleochemical, Food & Agro Processing). "The main thrust is the transformation of truncated and embryonic clusters into a dynamic set of clusters able to generate its own innovation and increase productivity" (http://www.iskandarmalaysia.com.my/what-is-iskandar-malaysia-industry-cluster). A key strategic element is the enhancement of the network cohesion in each cluster to ensure smooth connectivity and coordination between all participating firms and institutions in the private and public sectors with regard to their demand and supply requirements. To achieve the desired systemic cohesion, policy-makers proactively support the formation of cluster associations for each of the major industrial clusters. Whether there is long-term synergy between Singapore's and Malaysia's petrochemical cluster, for example, remains to be seen. What is undisputable, however, is the increasing attractiveness of Johor as an alternative business location for Singaporean SMEs that are affected by rising operational costs and other issues, such as a shrinking workforce. So, how is Malaysia's small business sector dealing with external challenges?

This question is taken up by Chin Yee Whah in Chapter 4 ("Malaysian Chinese Business: Ethnicity and Knowledge Management"), in which he reflects on the resilience of Malaysian Chinese businesses *vis-à-vis* numerous economic crises and how they adapted to the extended pro-Bumiputera affirmative policy (1971–2013). Of utmost importance is the capability of Malaysian SMEs to manage the knowing-doing gap on the basis of healthy ties with stakeholders in business, government, and society, as well as the need to manage talent and innovation capacity effectively. The five case studies featured in the chapter show how Malaysian Chinese business groups and SMEs have conformed to the affirmative policy by engaging Bumiputeras from both the elite and the middle class as one of their business strategies to push for their companies' growth within the domestic market. By leveraging "actionable knowledge," fueled by a strong sense of morality and humanity, Malaysian Chinese businessmen have demonstrated their benevolence by contributing to nation building through employment creation, contribution to economic growth and revenue for the country, and the provision of assistance to the government to achieve its policies, especially to facilitate the emergence of a Bumiputera Commercial and Industrial Community (BCIC). As his study suggests, a Confucian perspective with an emphasis on moral action and humanity represents an enlightening source of ancient wisdom for owner-managers of businesses, whether small or large, especially in times of increased cynicism about "good" business behavior and corporate scandals.

In both the East and the West, the search for the roots of "good leadership" is ongoing if one uses the numerous publications on leadership

Chinese in Indonesia

published each year as an indicator. Recently, the argument was put forward that Asia's own socio-ethical traditions could become the basis for an alternative model of "Asian leadership." As Ho Kwon Ping, Chairman of Singapore Management University (SMU) and Executive Chairman of the Banyan Tree Group, stressed:

> "Asia needs to delve into its own history and culture for inspiration in creating an Asian variant of capitalism. One such source can be the webs of mutual obligations which serve as a common, recurring socio-ethical tradition of Asia. This communitarian characteristic of Asian culture can, if thoughtfully enhanced, nurtured and developed, replace the highly individualistic, Darwinian ethos of American capitalism" (Ho, 2012).

Ho Kwon Ping:
Communitarian
Capitalism

For Mr Ho, communitarian capitalism as "an Asian form of ethical wealth creation" gives priority to the collective interests of enterprise owners, employees, customers and suppliers, and the larger community, rather than return on capital per se. "Real" communitarian capitalism must be stakeholder-driven on the basis of strong corporate social responsibility integrated into the business model. Banyan Tree's company leaders walk the talk when it comes to corporate social responsibility (CSR). Banyan Tree is one of a growing number of businesses releasing CSR reports on a regular basis.

Such a paradigmatic change to real stakeholder-driven, communitarian capitalism, one may add, could arguably also help to correct widespread stereotypes and prejudices about ethnic Chinese and their business behavior in countries such as Indonesia, which forms the regional backdrop of Chapter 5, "Evolving Chineseness, Ethnicity and Business: The Making of the Ethnic Chinese as a 'Market-Dominant Minority' in Indonesia." This chapter, written by Hoon Chang Yau, deals with the ethnic Chinese in Indonesia, who constitute about 8.8 million (3.7 percent) of Indonesia's population of 237 million (2010 Census) and thus play an important role in the nation's economy (Hoon, 2008). Their economic power is often regarded as disproportionate to their numbers, as reflected in the popular assertion that "the Chinese constitute only 3.5 percent of the population but control 70 percent of Indonesia's economy," put forward by the *Far Eastern Economic Review* some time ago (May 28,1998, cited in Chua, 2008). In the *New York Times* bestseller *World on Fire: How Exporting Free Market Democracy Breeds Ethnic Hatred and Global Instability*, Chua (2002) identifies Chinese Indonesians as one of the "market-dominant minorities" of the world. Her book highlights the double bind of free market democracy: it privileges certain ethnic minorities to dominate the market and accumulate wealth on the one hand, and allows a frustrated indigenous majority to pit against the wealthy ethnic minority on the other. The book, which became phenomenally popular among the Chinese Indonesians in Indonesia, cited the May 1998 anti-Chinese riots in Indonesia as a prime example to support its thesis. Although it does not offer any solution to their predicament, to many Chinese Indonesians, the book provides a logical explanation of the vulnerable position of the Chinese minority in Indonesia (Hoon, 2010).

There are many poor Chinese in Indonesia, and there is enormous heterogeneity among the ethnic Chinese Indonesians. This shows that the characterization of Chinese Indonesians as a "market-dominated minority" is not applicable to all. Nevertheless, politicians, academics, popular literature, the press, and other media have repeatedly reinforced this stereotype, making it pervasive and entrenched in the consciousness of many Indonesians. As Hoon argues, the country's regimes have homogenized Chinese ethnicity — a manipulation that somehow perpetuates the prejudices and arguably prevents the development of strong system trust, which is a key precondition for Indonesia's continuous development process.

The Management of Business Networks and Change

In all multi-racial societies, issues of inter-ethnic trust and system trust are of paramount importance to ensuring peaceful co-existence and collective prosperity (Chan and Ng, 2000). In business, distrust often prevents the development of cooperative relationships. Hence, strong personal relationships and relentless networking (*guanxi*) are competitive weapons in the day-to-day war for profitability and stakeholder gains, not only in big business but also in Chinese small-scale businesses (Menkhoff, 1993a).

The Rise and Fall of Singapore's Shark Fins Cluster at Boat Quay

In order to assess the level of modernity of the trade in traditional products, such as shark fins, Menkhoff interviewed dozens of owner-managers of Chinese family-based trading firms dealing in shark fins in 1988–1989 in Singapore's Boat Quay district, examining their unique business management patterns and entrepreneurial strategies (Menkhoff, 1993a). The results suggest that the traders, who once operated their far-flung networks from Singapore's Boat Quay district, are certainly not antiquated in their business operations. Among the various strategies adopted by the traders to cope with the risks of international trade, such as the eventuality that mutual agreements on the quality of goods or payment methods would not be upheld, is to establish long-standing trade relations, where positive or negative sanctions could be used to enforce the fulfillment of obligations. Trust is costly because it takes time to develop and nurture it, but a lack of trust is costlier if one considers foregone business deals. International business trust and trustworthiness are built up in successive stages and are constantly tested. They depend on the length of a relationship, long-term communicative interaction, mutual dependency, (more or less) prompt payment terms, the past behavior of business partners, and so on. Both personal trust in the integrity of a trading partner and system trust in the economic system are essential preconditions for trade and investment and the evolution of international business networks.

Singapore's Boat Quay district is the historic center of Singapore's trade and maritime commerce. Long before German scholar Alfred Weber discussed the phenomenon of spatial clustering in his 1929 "Theory of the Location of Industries," Singapore's shark fin traders had already congregated geographically in the area around the Singapore River. For decades, bumboats transported rice, tin, rubber, or dried seafood from the ships to the shop houses and godowns along the river. Good business prospects attracted more traders and shopkeepers, until the district's decline in the early 1980s, triggered by the introduction of Singapore's new container port and modern cargo facilities in Pasir Panjang. Dried goods — including shark's fin — moved out of Boat Quay because of the massive conservation efforts of the Urban Redevelopment Authority (URA) along Boat

Quay and Clarke Quay, which transformed these areas into leisure hubs with pubs and restaurants. Dried goods traders congregated temporarily at the Victoria Wholesale Centre.

Today, as in the past, shark fin traders know exactly what it takes to be profitable: trustworthiness (Menkhoff, 1993b). Without mutual trust, suppliers would send inferior fins ("stones") instead of the requested first grade fins, one trader explained. They were early "clusterers" long before Michael Porter came up with the notion of clusters as strategic management tools. While many businesses along North Canal Road or Tew Chew Street made way for the modernization of the Singapore River district during the past few years, some of the old shops where we conducted interviews long ago are still there. Why do companies congregate at one place? The answer is simple: it makes good business sense.

Being close to competitors enables traders to watch price developments or new customer service arrangements. It also helps customers to compare quality and prices. Such proximity to rival companies also allows workers to compare various employers and pay rates. An initial concentration of firms, talent, and other related businesses can attract new dependent businesses and experienced workers, creating a virtuous circle as these new clusters encourage others to join in. This, in turn, increases the cluster's efficiency and potential hub function. While rising business costs can lead to a cluster's erosion, good cluster management (by business associations) can work against such trends. Through clustering, businesses can benefit from specialized services. For a Boat Quay shark fin trader, that might be a Teochew restaurant that serves seafood. The location of restaurants in that area could explain the spatial clustering of shark fin firms there. Proximity to the Singapore River is also a key factor in explaining the early agglomeration of dried goods shops in this area.

Looking back at the Boat Quay district almost 25 years after our initial field visits, it seems that the old business logic, with its emphasis on trust and relationships, still prevails. However, the business model itself, with its focus on the shark fin trade, seems to be in grave danger. What some shark fin traders arguably overlook is the power of open innovation. Industry watchers are less concerned with processing or product development innovations, such as canned fins (soup), ready-to-eat products, or technology, and more concerned about using outside ideas generated by stakeholders, such as customers, relevant knowledge partners (scientists), or even their business opponents. Can innovation help Singapore's shark fin traders cope with and even profit from the "ban the fin movement" efforts? Already back in the 1980s, Japanese food processing companies were developing artificial shark fins made out of gelatin. Rising prices and increasing demand in Asia for fins suggest that the trade in these "fake fins" could be very profitable, provided there are no issues with regulators, and local businessmen and consumers are open to such revolutionary change. This might also help those remaining in Singapore's shark fin trading cluster cope with the demands of environmentalists, and avoid the final stage of the cluster life cycle: decline (and going bust). This might be a wise move, given the current threats to the business, including the collapse of shark populations around the world. During a recent walk through the Boat Quay district, we counted three shops selling shark fins and a number of seafood restaurants. As the numerous bars and hairdressing salons in this area suggest, the old maritime cluster strength is long gone. More restaurants refuse to serve shark fins. Times are changing. The traders know this, but they need to embrace the next step of looking beyond their cluster for innovative ways to survive (Menkhoff 2012).

One way to combat notions of strong ethnic in-group orientations and the exclusion of "others" in the context of ethnic business, such as the Chinese case (Carney and Dieleman, 2008), is to study empirically how particular ethnic business networks are actually structured. While plenty of literature about *ties* in modern business exists, empirical studies about the structure and function of "Chinese" business ties are still hard to come by. In "Chinese Business Networks — A Hypothetical Dialogue" (Menkhoff, 2006), we addressed this knowledge gap. It features a hypothetical dialogue between a culturalist, who argues that Chinese business networks derive their strength from their Chineseness, and a more critical analyst, who believes that intra-ethnic business networking does not pay in an era of global market expansion and increased diversity in business and society. The way that business is done in "Chinese" contexts reflects the institutional reality in which corporate actors are embedded. Under certain conditions, ethnic networking may be worthwhile, but to argue that it is a typically and uniquely Chinese phenomenon is incorrect, given that networking is a universal social phenomenon practiced by many social groups.

In November 2012, Singapore hosted the 7th World Fujian Convention. According to the President of the Singapore Hokkien Huay Kuan, Mr Chua Thian Poh, a key objective of the convention was to allow Hokkien people from all over the world to network and re-establish ties (*Straits Times*, October 7, 2012). How significant such ties really are in the context of Asian business is an important topic for further research. To illustrate the wide range of possible ties (weak or strong) and their roles in business, we included an empirical study by Thomas Menkhoff and Chalmer Labig (Chapter 6) entitled "Trading Networks of Chinese Entrepreneurs in Singapore" (first published by the *Journal of Social Issues in Southeast Asia* in 1996), which tries to explore the nature and social foundations of Chinese business networking with reference to Singaporean trading firms. In this study, the authors challenge the notion that the entrenchment of entrepreneurs in local, regional, or global business networks based on kinship, clanship, territorial, or ethnic ties is a typical characteristic of Chinese business communities in Southeast Asia. A key proposition put forward based on empirical data collected in Singapore's small business sector is that there is a clear trend among Chinese entrepreneurs in Singapore of reliance on external commercial relationships with outsiders and friends rather than with those related by blood or marriage. It is suggested that kinship reciprocity may, under some circumstances, curb the autonomy and freedom of the transacting actors, thus limiting their ability to make decisions in the regional and international marketplaces. Doing business via kinship is costly and limits one's options in an era of international market expansion as well as in an era of social media-enabled e-commerce. As Singapore's SME sector is increasingly becoming more international in its outlook, establishments are increasingly embracing the professionalization of management structures in order to better cope with the turbulent times and winds of change (Tsui-Auch, 2004; Hornidge, 2004).

Managing strategic change processes in an enterprise and leveraging new ideas as well as existing knowledge resources is a challenge for many entrepreneurs. What type of change management approach do ethnic Chinese business leaders typically adopt? In a change leadership survey of local SMEs, we found that a very large number of respondents used *collaborative-consultative leadership modes* (70.3 percent), contrary to our initial proposition that directive-coercive modes of change leadership styles would (still) prevail. The results of this study are discussed in Chapter 7 by Thomas Menkhoff and Chay Yue Wah ("Improving Small Firm Performance through Collaborative Change Management and Outside Learning: Trends in Singapore"), a reprint of the article published in the *International Journal of Asian Business and Information Management* in 2011. They argue that there is indeed a great diversity amongst small firm owners in Singapore and beyond with regard to their change leadership practices and that the respective change implementation approaches are contingent on both demographic variables and situational forces, such as the urgency of change, the degree of resistance to change, and/or the dynamics of the environment in which the firms operate.

How can the shift from more autocratic toward more collaborative change leadership styles be explained? One possible reason is that the sampled SME owner-managers (many of whom are tertiary educated) are more consensus-seeking than the previous generation. In addition, in the present work generation, directive-coercive leadership approaches may not be the best way to effect change. The fact that we found reversed trends with regard to the traditional image of Asian business management approaches, as indicated in the dichotomy above, is perhaps an indicator of the convergence of Asian and Western leadership styles, as argued by Harvard scholar Quinn Mills some time ago, or simply the result of good governance, as reflected by the fact that Singaporean SME owner-managers as well as their followers operate in an environment that puts a premium on skills upgrading, staff engagement, and lifelong learning.

In Chapter 8 ("Continuity and Change in Corporate Governance among Ethnic Chinese Family Firms in Singapore"), Lai Si Tsui-Auch and Dawn Chow Yi Lin examine the changing corporate governance approaches used by ethnic Chinese businesses in Singapore. The authors provide an overview of how these businesses have adapted to undertake corporate governance reforms while adhering to certain core values and norms. Their aim is to shift the current discourse on the management structure of ethnic Chinese businesses from stasis to a more dynamic, nuanced conceptualization. The authors chose the context of Singapore because most of the ethnic Chinese enterprises are family-controlled, which makes it a highly relevant case for studying corporate governance change. At the same time, the openness of Singapore's economy and its state agencies' role in mediating pressures for corporate governance reforms provide readers with an interesting case on how ethnic Chinese firms exercise strategic choice in response to institutional change that is shaped largely by global capital market forces and the developmental state.

One Chinese family firm in Singapore that has successfully globalized is Eu Yan Sang (EYS), under the leadership of Richard Eu and his team, who continue to leverage modern brand management and innovation concepts in line with Asian (Chinese) customer needs and wants, as elaborated by Jessica Chong, Willem Smit, Thomas Menkhoff and Christopher Clayman (with Richard Eu) in Chapter 9 ("Building a Successful Brand: The Story of Eu Yan Sang"). EYS was founded in 1879 and represents a fine example of a dynamic enterprise that can serve as a role model for other family-based firms in Asia and beyond, due to its capability of remaining relevant, agile, and profitable despite a volatile business environment. The company started out as a simple herbal medicine shop and has become a leading innovator in traditional Chinese medicine (TCM). With in-depth herbal knowledge and hundreds of proprietary products under its name, EYS has become a strong and, for customers, very attractive brand. Since 1989, Group CEO Richard Eu and his team have been creating value on the basis of effective brand management processes. Like EYS, Asian firms are increasingly realizing that their brands represent key elements of sustained competitiveness. What sets EYS apart from others is its firm belief that future growth can be further enhanced through scientific innovation in collaboration with external knowledge providers. An example is its support of the scientific study conducted by the Chinese University of Hong Kong, "Bak Foong Pills Bio-active Research and Clinical Research," which investigated the pharmacological actions and bio-active ingredients of Bak Foong pills, one of EYS's flagship products. The study findings led to the development of a new TCM formula (Menoease) for the treatment of postmenopausal syndrome. Besides the importance of good brand management in general, the case underlines the benefits that SMEs can derive from strategic research and development as well as science and technology.

The study also points to the importance of succession planning and generational shifts, whose impact upon the continuity of Chinese business is still poorly understood. Specific insight into generational changes in

Indonesia's corporate sector with special emphasis on SMEs is provided
in Chapter 10 by Juliette Koning: "Generational Change in Chinese
Indonesian SMEs?" In her chapter, Koning examines how notions of
Chinese business conduct differ among both older and younger small-
scale ethnic Chinese entrepreneurs in Indonesia. Her study is based on a
discursive, contextual, and generational approach that enables her to provide a more nuanced understanding of ethnic Chinese business acumen in
an Indonesian setting. As she argues, there are differences between the
different generations represented by the members of business families in
terms of, for example, ethnic self-identification, business acumen, and
Chineseness in relation to business conduct, due to the different historical-
cultural contexts in which they grew up. While members of the older
generation lament over the erosion of traditional Chinese business practices, such as the role of reputation via word of mouth and the fact that the
younger generation seems to be strongly influenced by the local culture
(and thereby possibly becoming less Chinese), the latter appreciates
Chineseness when it comes to doing business (while both groups consider
themselves to be superior businessmen compared to non-Chinese). As the
interview extracts indicate, the younger generation has seemingly internalized ascribed stereotypes and prejudices, such as the exclusivity of the
Chinese, because non-Chinese stakeholders are hardly mentioned in the
interview extracts. As the author concludes, the emphasis on intra-ethnic
networks by both the older and younger generations of ethnic entrepreneurs reflects the challenging business environment in which many
Chinese Indonesian SMEs operate.

How external pressures can force businessmen to quickly redirect
their firms' vision and strategic thrusts is taken up again in Chapter 11 by
Marleen Dieleman ("The Salim Group: The Art of Strategic Flexibility"),
first published in the *Asian Case Research Journal* in 2006. The case
examines the story of the Salim Group, a large ethnic Chinese family-
based business conglomerate in Indonesia that had a turnover of US$20
billion before the Asian financial crisis hit. As a consequence of the Asian
crisis, which almost led to the collapse of this diversified and globalized
firm, Salim's current CEO and President, Anthony Salim, was forced to
quickly re-strategize the group's focus to ensure long-term sustainability.
The case reconstructs the path that the firm took until about 2005 and

provides interesting insights into the management of strategic choices by ethnic Chinese entrepreneurs in Asia's rapidly changing business environment (Dieleman, 2010). Anthony Salim, who has maintained a low profile in Indonesia, carefully avoiding media coverage or linkages to politicians, has led the Salim Group since 2006. He has rebuilt many of the businesses and invested substantially in and outside of Indonesia (e.g., in China and the Philippines). Currently, Anthony Salim remains one of Indonesia's most influential businessmen. Some of the companies that were sold during the Asian Crisis of 1998 were re-purchased by the group. Some parts of the group, including palm oil, food, and property, are now listed on the Singapore Exchange (SGX), and some on other stock exchanges. Soedono Salim, the founder, passed away in Singapore in 2012. Indofood, Salim's flagship company, has performed well in an increasingly competitive environment in Indonesia. One of Anthony Salim's sons joined the Indofood Board as Executive Director in 2009, bringing in the third generation of Salim family leaders. The recent developments show that the Salim Group has been able to operate without relying on strong political ties, and that it remains one of the most important players in Indonesia and more broadly in Asia.

Leadership, Knowledge and Learning in Chinese Business

Given the volatility in current global markets, highly capable leadership in both the public and private sectors is a key requirement to steer emerging Asia to greater heights. While there are still many MNCs whose CEOs are reluctant to empower local (Asian) managers as bosses, an increasing number of firms located in Asia are keen to implement strategic leadership development (LD) programs to ensure a sustainable talent pipeline. However, this is easier said than done. While substantial research has been conducted to identify the required attributes of effective leaders, such as visionary thinking, courage, or resilience, there is still widespread confusion with regard to defining what is "Asian" in Asian leadership. When asked about this, executives sometimes construct a simple dichotomy between the "assertive Western" and the "risk-averse Asian" corporate leaders. Asian leadership traits arguably include humility and collectivism. Humility refers to the quality of being modest, reverential, and politely submissive, which is in stark contrast to being arrogant, rude, or self-abasing. Collectivism implies that group goals have priority over individual goals. In everyday corporate life, which is increasingly complex, such traits can sometimes be in conflict with competing value systems imported through foreign talents. Therefore, what are the challenges when it comes to developing global leaders with an Asian focus?

A key challenge is to decipher what is meant by Asian leadership and to incorporate that into needs-based leadership development programs to ensure effective leadership across cultures.

The still nascent Asian leadership research suggests that there is an urgent need for aspiring corporate leaders in the East and the West who want to succeed in Asia to develop a broader range of skills in line with the increasingly diverse and globalizing business environment. This may include the need to be (more) collaborative, assertive, or focused, depending on the particular leadership moment and situational demands.

One source of inspiration for discussions about effective leadership development with an Asian focus is mindfulness, as argued in Chapter 12, entitled "In Search of 'Asian' Conceptions of Leadership with a Focus on Mindfulness," by Chay Yue Wah, Charles Chow, Hans-Dieter Evers, Lee Cher Leng, Thomas Menkhoff, Jochen Reb, Jayarani Tan and Elfarina Zaid. "Mindfulness" can be defined as a sort of enlightened state of being in which greed, hatred, and delusion are absent from the mind. Coupled with clear comprehension of what is taking place now and here, that is, present moment-awareness, mindfulness can help leaders transform other people's fears and anxieties into hope, which some consider to be the hallmark of good leadership. Research conducted by Reb *et al.* (2012) showed that a leader's mindfulness is associated with higher well-being and performance of subordinates. Some of the strengths of mindful leaders include being fully aware of current activities (i.e., not "running on autopilot") or paying full attention to the problems that a follower brings up during an unplanned conversation without being preoccupied with thoughts about the next appointment.

While there is still a dearth of empirical studies aimed at uncovering what exactly makes the mindful, ethnic Chinese leader tick, the available studies suggest that the mastery of mindful leadership can enhance effectiveness at the individual, team, and organizational levels. This arguably will also enrich the development of global leaders with an Asian focus and ensure that more Asians successfully claim leadership roles in the East and the West.

A local case study on an influential and visionary leader is presented in Chapter 13 by Dai Shiyan and Zhang Guocai ("Exploring Lee Kong Chian's Knowledge Leadership Style in Nam Aik Company"). It was first published in a triple issue of the *Journal of Asian Business* in 2008. The chapter explores and examines Lee Kong Chian's leadership and management style and practices, which are considered by the authors to contain features of knowledge leadership for modern enterprises. The chapter primarily discusses the management and operation philosophy, human resource policies, motivation system, and practices of Nam Aik Rubber Company, of which Lee Kong Chian is the founder and leader. The communication approaches and practices adopted by Lee Kong Chian as well as his belief in the power of knowledge and his pursuit of and great contribution to education for the society are also presented and discussed.

Business leaders who leverage new sources of learning, whether in the form of scientific advice to support product development efforts or intellectual property-related know-how to create value through franchising, and contribute to organizational effectiveness and growth. While the positive effects of strategic learning on business performance are well documented, many owner-managers of local SMEs remain unconvinced that learning pays. Small firms must confront numerous challenges, such as rising business costs or succession planning. While it is understandable that these problems can sometimes prevent SMEs from proactively pursuing learning opportunities, the rapid changes in the business environment coupled with the influx of new technologies suggest that there is an urgent need to change such mindsets. Thus, what can SMEs do to enhance their learning capability to improve growth prospects, which is so crucial for sustaining success and survival?

As discussed in Chapter 14 by Thomas Menkhoff ("Organizational Learning Approaches of Small and Medium-Sized Enterprises: A Comparative Study of Chinese Firms in Singapore"), the essential building blocks of a learning-oriented SME include clarity of mission/vision, supportive leadership, experimenting culture, ability to transfer knowledge, and teamwork. We refer to the first two blocks as purposeful knowledge leadership, which is essential for creating new value-added knowledge outcomes, for example, by combining knowledge, ideas, and concepts from various contexts into something new. This includes the ability to use knowledge management solutions, such as knowledge portals to make knowledge available on a shared platform, external experts, or the formation of temporary network alliances in order to innovate. A local example is tropical fish exporter Qian Hu, under the leadership of Kenny Yap, who is successfully engaged in both open and networked innovation, for example, in collaboration with reputable life sciences labs to scale up some of its main products in support of its internationalization strategy (Menkhoff, 2008). The point is that the deployment of relevant learning tools, whether low cost approaches such as mentoring schemes or the systematic mining of particular science and technology journals, must be initiated by the SME owner-manager as the knowledge leader in order to facilitate knowledge conversion and creation processes. It is the leader's responsibility to enhance and nurture the absorptive capacity of the organization so that relevant external information can be acquired and transformed into a competitive advantage through routines and processes.

The learning orientation of any organization is shaped by its culture. Hence, the attitude of the SME owner-manager toward life-long learning and development is crucial in nurturing the firm's experimenting culture with an emphasis on intense cooperation, willingness to share (not hoard) knowledge and power, innovation, relentless networking, and team learning. Our own organizational research has shown that the spirit of knowledge creation and openness to new possibilities is essential for achieving operational excellence and business success. A strategic knowledge combination, for example, enables the cross-fertilization of ideas that often lead to product and/or service innovations, as illustrated by the story of the sushi conveyor belt in local restaurants such as Sakae Sushi, Osim's exercise gadget iGallop, or the popularity of the fish spa pedicure in Asia via the toothless Garra rufa fish from the river basins of Turkey, Syria, Iraq, and Iran. The key is to start with the humble attitude that one's knowledge is not enough and the conviction that continuous learning embedded in a strategic human capital management framework pays.

Learning can be facilitated by tapping the expertise of others via the set-up of so-called communities of practice (COPs). COPs are groups of people who share a passion for something they do, and they learn how to do it better through regular interaction with each other. In Germany, Chambers of Commerce & Industry act as enablers of SME-COPs that actively support both the productivity growth and innovation potential of the country's Mittelstand. COPs flourish in collaborative organizational cultures characterized by care and trust. As the US network scholar R Burt has stressed, organizations with management and collaboration networks that bridge structural holes in their markets learn faster and are more creative. This means that small business leaders who, through networking and various network ties, combine expertise from two or more otherwise disconnected fields are able to create novel products and services. While many Asian SMEs have traditionally acted as brokers (via knowledge arbitrage) between various regional communities, the rapid influx of new communication technologies in conjunction with ASEAN's market integration suggests that respective business models are not sustainable. Research and development as well as science and technology are the new frontiers that SMEs cannot ignore.

SMEs can reap tangible benefits from proactive learning, such as improved productivity and skills, enhanced customer relations, or greater flexibility in production and innovation. Relevant are broad issues of strategy and how newly acquired know-how resources are used to reinforce core competencies. Besides the need for a strong business case, a shared vision, and so forth, personality traits such as openness (e.g., to outside learning opportunities) and a participative, mindful leadership style are important. The fact that an increasing number of SME owner-managers are tertiary educated suggests that SMEs continue to move away from the traditional paternalistic *towkay* (boss) image.

Employer brand conscious SMEs that manage to nurture a climate of continuous team learning through regular dialogue with "the boss" and consensus building will be more attractive for younger (Gen Y) talent, who have ample employment opportunities in the MNC sector. Like talent elsewhere, they expect operational excellence, fairness, and a convincing employee value proposition based on best practice performance management structures and operating procedures. If all of this is in place, SME employees will be motivated to fully utilize externally acquired learning resources in a sustainable manner, which, in turn, will benefit the business and its growth prospects.

The role of knowledge transfer as a conduit for collaborative learning in cross-cultural contexts is further discussed in Chapter 15 by Thomas Menkhoff, Chay Yue Wah and Hans-Dieter Evers: "The Role of Cultural Orientations in Students' Predispositions toward Knowledge Transfer in Project Teams: Evidence from Singapore." The study empirically examines the effects of cultural patterns of undergraduate business management students in Singapore based on a typology developed by Triandis as well as other factors, such as capability, credibility, cohesion, communication, and the type of knowledge (explicit vs. implicit) shared in knowledge transfer activities in a project-based leadership and team-building (LTB) course. Besides exploring the complex relationship between these factors and knowledge transfer, which is derived by combining theories of knowledge transfer, teams, and cross-cultural behavior, the study provides an in-depth look at transferring team member knowledge in student project teams, which represents a critical element of pedagogical peer learning approaches in institutions of higher education. Survey data from a sample of individuals working in undergraduate LTB project teams at a Singaporean university provide support for several of the hypotheses, indicating that highly credible collectivists with strong project related capabilities that belong to a cohesive group with frequent communication are able to effectively transfer knowledge to their peers. Overall, the study underlines the critical role of cultural orientations in students' differing predispositions toward knowledge transfer in team contexts. The implications for managing the potential fault line between collectivists and individualists are discussed.

Asian Business in Local Contexts

To contextualize the material on ethnic Chinese business presented in this book *vis-à-vis* the region's diverse cultural landscapes and other ethnic groups that have engaged in trade and commerce, we have added three papers to shed light on the local dimension of Asian business. In Chapter 16 ("Urban Property Development in Malaysia: The Impact of Chinese and

Malay Conceptions of Space"), Hans-Dieter Evers argues that Malays and Chinese differ in their cultural values concerning space. Whereas the Malay conception of space is centrifocal, the Chinese conception of space is bounded. The consistency of this cultural pattern is demonstrated by examples drawn from conceptions of geographical, social, religious, and political spaces and their combination in an image of the city. As Malaysian towns and housing developments are built according to a Chinese conception of space, the absorption of Malay rural-urban migrants has a detrimental effect on the maintenance of Malay culture, while Chinese control over urban space is maintained. Attempts by the Malay dominated government to create new Malay cities in Malaysia, like Putrajaya and Cyberjaya, have led to a marriage of Middle Eastern architecture and Chinese and Western town planning, rather than a true Malay or Nusantara urbanism.

In "Informal Banking and Early International Entrepreneurs: The Case of the Chettiars" (Chapter 17), Jayarani Tan and Tan Wee Liang review the important role of the Chettiars as moneylenders and informal bankers during the nineteenth century colonial period in Asia. They began as communal entrepreneurs in their clan, but quickly grew beyond their domestic borders. Despite their smallness and limited resources, the Chettiars were able to internationalize. External factors, such as the British protectorate, and internal factors, such as their unique socio-cultural institutions, norms, and values, served as enabling factors for their internationalization. Essential propellants included a strong family culture of training the sons for the business, embracing business best practices, replicating domestic social structures overseas, and the Chettiar community abroad. The social structures extended overseas provided a robust social support network for the Chettiars leaving their homes, while the overseas Chettiar community provided a network for international expansion.

The last chapter by Hinrich Voss ("The Internationalization of Chinese Firms — Evidence from the People's Republic of China") focuses on an exciting new development that will have a profound impact on the international business landscape, namely, the internationalization of Mainland Chinese firms through direct investment in foreign markets. As the author points out, these firms acquire established firms, brand names, technologies, and distribution channels in industrialized and developing countries to strengthen their international competitiveness and to catch up with the incumbents. Another motive is to secure urgently required resources, such as oil, minerals, timber, and food for domestic needs. Due to the rapid growth of Chinese outward foreign direct investment (FDI) flows, competition in markets previously thought to be the domain of Western firms and underdeveloped countries has significantly increased. As the study suggests, Chinese outward investment is likely to grow further, which will have to be sensitively managed by all stakeholders.

Conclusion

As the essays compiled in this book suggest, firms and corporations owned and managed by ethnic Chinese continue to play key roles in the ongoing development of Asia. The story of the Chinese overseas continues, albeit with a different set of actors embedded in a different institutional environment compared to the first generation of ethnic Chinese who ventured into the Nanyang. One takeaway from the various studies featured in this publication is the fact that the Chinese entrepreneurial ground in Asia and beyond is becoming increasingly complex and diverse, which renders notions of "Chinese business" as a sort of homogeneous group obsolete. Several groups make up the changed ground: entrepreneurs from Mainland China, young, middle-class businessmen venturing into new markets, female businesswomen who run start-ups or who joined their family firms upon return from overseas study stints, Chinese educated entrepreneurs, or those who are rediscovering their roots, driven by economic opportunities. Empirical studies which would allow us to typify these groups, their strategies, business ideologies, etc., are scarce. In our classes, we sometimes ask students to describe the unique features of these types. As one student argued with regard to the dichotomy of Chinese-educated and English-educated Chinese businessmen, one key difference arguably lies in their approaches to conducting business:

> "The Chinese-educated puts more emphasis on *guanxi* rather than government, Confucianism principles, and traditional methods (rather than the ways of the modern world), working with family members rather

than outsiders; he/she thus limits the range of opportunities that come his/her way. An example is George Quek, who went on against all odds to become successful in Singapore, an Asian nation. On the other hand, the English-educated combines the knowledge of both the traditional as well as modern worlds, bringing that competitive edge to the business that the Chinese-educated might lack. He/she networks with other cultural groups and integrates into the global market, rather than just the Chinese or Asian market. He/she is more modern in outlook, and all this works to his/her advantage. Though, the disadvantage of this is that by becoming more Westernized in his/her approach, he/she risks losing his/her Chinese values, which are also important for his/her success" (undergraduate business management student).

This summarizes quite nicely the tension between tradition and modernity as well as the fact that Chinese culture represents a potentially lucrative resource for sustainable business models, as the cases of Breadtalk, Eu Yan Sang, or Qian Hu suggest (something that young Asian business management students often overlook). It also points to the ongoing process of hybridization of local and non-Asian business cultures, as stressed by the proponents of the convergence-divergence debate, whose implications with regard to Chinese business, networks and management patterns are still poorly understood. An exciting area where more research is necessary concerns the structure, functionality, and associated challenges of traditional (boundary-spanning) Chinese knowledge networks (e.g., in comparison with the more location-specific networks of indigenous traders) as well as associated collaborative opportunities and threats in an era of regional integration (ASEAN), globalization, digital knowledge traps, and science and technology as new value creators. As argued in another edited volume on Chinese management patterns (Menkhoff *et al.*, 2008), there is a rather strong sense of knowledge as territory in Chinese business and society that can prevent value added qua inter-ethnic knowledge transfer processes between ethnic Chinese and non-Chinese partners (outgroups). If left unchecked, this can lead to foregone business opportunities and win-win outcomes. The relevancy of traditional Asian conceptions of leadership and management in terms of learning effectiveness and morally sound, ethical wealth creation (e.g., based on humility, mindfulness or CSR concepts) represents another promising topic for further investigation. As the studies in this book indicate, a key challenge for business leaders in the East and the West is to achieve a healthy balance with respect to leveraging both global knowledge and local wisdom for sustainable growth. We hope that this book will be useful in the ongoing discourse about the theory and practice of Chinese business that continues to have a very profound impact on development and change in Asia.

References

Backman, M (1999). *Asian Eclipse — Exposing the Dark Side of Business in Asia*. Singapore: Wiley.

Barney, JB and Z Shujun (2009). The future of Chinese management research: A theory of Chinese management versus a Chinese theory of management. *Management & Organization Review*, 5(1), 15–28.

Benton, G and L Hong (eds.) (2004). *Diasporic Chinese Ventures: The Life and Work of Wang Gungwu*. London and New York: Routledge Curzon.

Burt, RS (1995). Structural Holes: The Social Structure of Competition. Boston, MA: Harvard University Press.

Carney, M and M Dieleman (2008). Heroes and villains: Ethnic Chinese family business in Southeast Asia. In *Theoretical Developments and Future Research in Family Business*, P Phan and JE Butler (eds.), pp. 49–73. Greenwich: Information Age Publishing.

Chan, KB and BK Ng (2000). Myths and misperceptions of ethnic Chinese capitalism. In *Chinese Business Networks — State, Economy and Culture*, Chan KB (ed.), pp. 261–284. Singapore: Prentice Hall.

Cheung, WK and GG Hamilton (2009). Getting rich and staying connected: The organizational medium of Chinese capitalists. *Journal of Contemporary China*, 18(58), 47–67.

China Daily (2013). Cakewalk to success. January 18–24, p. 24.

Chua, A (2002). *World on Fire: How Exporting Free Market Democracy Breeds Ethnic Hatred and Global Instability*. New York: Doubleday.

Chua, C (2008). *Chinese Big Business in Indonesia: The State of Capital*. London and New York: Routledge.

Clegg, S (1990). *Modern Organisations: Organisation Studies in the Postmodern World*. London: Sage Publications.

Cragg, C (1996). *The New Taipans*. London: Cox & Wyman.

Dieleman, M (2010). Shock-imprinting: External shocks and ethnic Chinese business groups in Indonesia. *Asia Pacific Journal of Management*, 27(3), 481–502.

Gomez, ET and H-HM Hsiao (eds.) (2001). *Chinese Business in Southeast Asia: Contesting Cultural Explanations, Researching Entrepreneurship*. Surrey: Curzon Press.

Granovetter, M (1985). Economic action and social structure: The problem of embeddedness. *American Journal of Sociology*, 91(3), 481–510.

Haley, GT, TT Chin and UCV Haley (1998). *New Asian Emperors*. Oxford: Butterworth-Heinemann.

House, RJ, PW, Hanges, P, Javidan, Dorfman and V Gupta (eds.) (2004). *Culture, Leadership, and Organizations: The GLOBE Study of 62 Societies*. Thousand Oaks, CA: Sage Publications.

Ho, KP (2012). Asia as global leader? Not so fast. *Asia Sentinel*. Available at http://accountabilitywww.asiasentinel.com/index.php?option=com_content &task=view&id=4504&Itemid=612.

Hoon, CY (2008). *Chinese Identity in Post-Suharto Indonesia: Culture, Politics and Media*. East Sussex: The Sussex Library of Asian Studies.

Hoon, CY (2010). Face, faith, and forgiveness: Elite Chinese philanthropy in Indonesia. *Journal of Asian Business*, 24(1–2), 51–66.

Hornidge, AK (2004). When the younger generation takes over — Singaporean Chinese family businesses in change. *Internationales Asienforum*, 35(1–2), 101–131.

Jacobsen, M (2007). Re-conceptualising notions of Chineseness in a Southeast Asian context. From diasporic networking to grounded cosmopolitanism. *East Asia*, 24(2), 213–227.

Jacobsen, M (2009). Navigating between disaggregating nation states and entrenching processes of globalisation: Reconceptualising the Chinese diaspora in Southeast Asia. *Journal of Contemporary China*, 18(58), 69–91.

Javidan, M, P, Dorfman, M Sully de Luque and RJ House (2006). In the eye of beholder: Cross cultural lessons in leadership from project GLOBE. *Academy of Management Perspectives*, 20(1), 67–91.

Kuah, KE (1998). Rebuilding their ancestral villages: The moral economy of the Singapore Chinese. In *China's Political Economy*, G Wang and J Wong (eds.), pp. 249–276. Singapore: Singapore University Press.

Lee, GK and Z Zhou (2006). The split of the ethnic Chinese and their separate goals of nation-building: Contest for the establishment of Nanyang University. In *Demarcating Ethnicity in New Nations: Case of the Chinese in Singapore, Malaysia and Indonesia*, GK Lee (ed.), pp. 39–67. Singapore: Konrad-Adenauer-Stiftung and Singapore Society of Asian Studies.

Liu, H (1998). Old linkages, new networks: The globalisation of overseas Chinese voluntary associations and its implications. *China Quarterly*, 155, 104–131.

Kwok, KW (2006). Being Chinese in the modern world. In *The Encyclopedia of the Chinese Overseas*, L Pan (ed.), pp. 121–126. Singapore: Archipelago Press and Landmark Books.

Menkhoff, T (1993a). *Trade Routes, Trust and Trading Networks — Chinese Small Enterprises in Singapore*. Saarbruecken, Fort Lauderdale: Breitenbach Publishers.

Menkhoff, T (1993b). Trade routes, trust and tactics: Chinese traders in Singapore. In *The Moral Economy of Trade — Ethnicity and Developing Markets*, H-D Evers and H Schrader (eds.). London: Routledge.

Menkhoff, T (2006). Chinese business networks — A hypothetical dialogue. In *The Encyclopedia of the Chinese Overseas*, L Pan (ed.), pp. 94–95. Singapore: Archipelago Press and Landmark Books.

Menkhoff, T (2008). Case study knowledge management at Qian Hu Corporation Ltd. In *Knowledge Management in Asia: Experience and Lessons*. Report of the APO Survey on the Status of Knowledge Management in Member Countries, Asia Productivity Organization (ed.), pp. 177–192. Tokyo: APO.

Menkhoff, T and S Gerke (eds). (2002). *Chinese Entrepreneurship and Asian Business Networks*. London and New York: Routledge Curzon.

Menkhoff, T and YW Chay (2008). Technological change management strategies in Asian small-scale businesses. *International Quarterly for Asian Studies*, 39(3–4), 305–324.

Menkhoff, T, EF Pang, and H-D Evers (2008). The power of knowing: Studies of Chinese business in Asia. *Journal of Asian Business*, 22–23.

Menkhoff, T (2012). The cluster effect and shark's fin trade. *Straits Times*, May 30, A25.

Pan, L (2006). Definitions. In *The Encyclopedia of the Chinese Overseas*, L Pan (ed.), 14–19. Singapore: Archipelago Press and Landmark Books.

Rae, I and M Witzel (2008). The ancestral country: Changing fast. In *Overseas Chinese of South East Asia: History, Culture, Business*, I Rae and M Witzel (eds.). Hampshire: Palgrave Macmillan.

Razeen, S (2010). Regional economic integration in Asia: The track record and prospects. European Centre for International Political Economy (ECIPE), Occasional Paper No. 2/2010.

Reb, J, J Narayanan and S Chaturvedi (2012). Leading mindfully: Two studies on the influence of supervisor trait mindfulness on employee well-being and performance. *Mindfulness*, September 4.

Redding, SG (1993). *The Spirit of Chinese Capitalism*. Berlin and New York: Walter de Gruyter.

Reuters (2012). Thai group buys $9.4 billion Ping An stake from HSBC. Available at http://www.reuters.com/article/2012/12/05/us-hsbc-pingan-idUSBRE8B400V20121205.

Guaning, S (2010). Being Chinese and Singaporean. *Straits Times*, December 12, A22.

Suryadinata, L (ed.) (1997). *Ethnic Chinese as Southeast Asians*. Singapore: Institute of Southeast Asian Studies.

The Business Times (2012). China staking claim to ethnic Chinese worldwide (by Frank Ching)? November 7, p. 20

The Sunday Times (2012). S'pore to host World Fujian Convention. October 7, p. 24.

Tong, C-K (2010). *Identity and Ethnic Relations in Southeast Asia — Racializing Chineseness*. Singapore: Springer.

Tong, C-K and K-B Chan (2001). One face, many masks: The singularity and plurality of Chinese identity. *Diaspora: A Journal of Transnational Studies*, 10(3), 316–389.

Tong, C-K and PK Yong (1997). Personalism and paternalism in Chinese business. In *Konfuzianischer Kapitalismus in Ost- und Suedostasien*, T Menkhoff (compiler). Schriftenreihe der Zentralstelle für Auslandskunde (ZA), Deutsche Stiftung für Internationale Entwicklung (DSE), Vol. 25. DSE-ZA, Bad Honnef.

Tsui-Auch, LS (2004). The professionally managed family-ruled enterprise: Ethnic Chinese business in Singapore. *Journal of Management Studies*, 41(4), 693–723.

Wang, G (1998). Upgrading the migrant: Neither huaqiao nor huaren. In *The Last Half Century of Chinese Overseas*, E Sinn (ed.), pp. 15–33. Hong Kong: Hong Kong University Press.

Wang, G (1992). A short history of the Nanyang Chinese. In *Community and Nation*, G Wang (ed.). Sydney: Allen and Unwin.

Wang, G (2000). *The Chinese Overseas: From Earthbound China to the Quest for Autonomy*. Boston, MA: Harvard University Press.

Wang, G (2004). Maritime China in transition. In *Maritime China and Overseas Chinese Communities in Transition, 1750–1850*, CK Ng and G Wang (eds.), pp. 3–16. Wiesbaden: Harrassowitz Verlag.

Weber, A (1929). *Theory of the Location of Industries* (trans. Carl J. Friedrich). Chicago, Ill: University of Chicago Press.

Wertheim, WF (1980). The trading minorities in Southeast Asia. In *Sociology of Southeast Asia*, H-D Evers (ed.). Singapore: Oxford University Press.

Wong, R (2008). A new breed of Chinese entrepreneurs? Critical reflections. In *Chinese Entrepreneurship in Global Era*, R Wong (ed.), pp. 3–22. London: Routledge.

Yao, S (2002). *Confucian Capitalism: Discourse, Practice and the Myth of Chinese Enterprise*. Richmond: Routledge Curzon.

Yeung, H (2006). Change and continuity in Southeast Asian ethnic Chinese business. *Asia Pacific Journal of Management*, 23(3), 229–254.

Yoshihara, K (1988). *The Rise of Ersatz Capitalism in Southeast Asia*. Singapore: Oxford University Press.

Part 1

The Story of the "Chinese Overseas": Implications for Identity, Business and "Chineseness"

Chapter 1

The Sea as Paddy: The Making of Fujian as a Transnational Place[*]

Jessica Chong

Since the 1980s, Fujian Province in China has been known as the main source of Chinese illegal migrants in the United States. In recent years, Fujianese immigrants' destinations have become increasingly varied, with some embarking on transnational entrepreneurial activities in Africa. While most narratives about Fujianese migration sensationalize the role of human smugglers and use economic theory to try to make sense of this large-scale movement of people, this chapter emphasizes that Fujianese transnationalism has had at least 500 years of history. Through fieldwork in Fujian and documental research, this chapter shows that a long histori-cal perspective is needed to explain why Fujian is a transnational hub with a vast and dynamic global reach.

1. Introduction

In June 1993, a ship named the *Golden Venture* ran aground on Rockaway Beach in Queens, New York. The ship carried 286 illegal Chinese migrants, mostly from Fujian province. Passengers evacuated the ship and tried to swim through frigid waters to shore; sadly, ten drowned. Televisions across the country broadcasted dramatic images of Coast Guard members dragging the Chinese migrants to safety. Shivering,

[*]An earlier version of this chapter appeared in 2009 in Vol. 2 of the *Columbia East Asia Review* (CEAR), a multidisciplinary academic journal of East and Southeast Asian Studies published by an all-undergraduate editorial team based at Columbia University (New York City). The editors gratefully acknowledge the support of CEAR.

naked, and dwarfed by their rescuers, some clung to small grocery bags that held their belongings (Smith, 1997). This incident fits neatly into the stereotypical image of impoverished people from the "third world" coming to the "promised land" in search of the "American dream," effectively crystallizing what Americans thought about Chinese migrants. Media coverage of the *Golden Venture* also fanned the flames of resentment toward snakeheads, the notorious human smugglers generally depicted as indifferent and cruel profiteers who treat humans as cargo (Kwong, 1998).

Today, Fujianese migrants account for 43 percent of illegal Chinese migration. But Fujianese migration is much more than simply a story of snakeheads and desperate migrants. Nearly 15 years after the *Golden Venture* incident, I found myself in my father's ancestral village Xishancun, in Fuqing County the county from which most of the *Golden Venture* migrants had originated. The people in the village were not as impoverished as the *Golden Venture* migrants had appeared in the media, and their migration trajectories were not singularly motivated by desperation and necessity. Furthermore, the villagers had mobilized their social capital to move to places as far flung as South Africa, Lesotho, and Nigeria to pursue opportunity. Their destinations were not confined to the "promised land" of the United States. In fact, for centuries, sizeable populations of ethnic Fujianese have lived in Southeast Asian countries like the Philippines, Singapore, and Malaysia (*The Taipei Times*, 2007).

One of my initial observations was that Xishancun had been literally emptied of young people. Over the last decade or so, many Xishancun villagers had migrated to countries in Africa on family support, opening shops of their own. With the remittances that these entrepreneurs sent home, their families had built opulent four or five-storey houses in Xishancun. The buzz was thick in the humid July air: Africa had become *the* place to go.

In recent years, scholars have tried to understand Fujianese migration using several conventional theories, some of which provide better explanations than others. The theory of cumulative causation stipulates, for instance, that migration sustains itself by creating *more* migration, forming what Massey describes as "migration networks" (Massey *et al.*, 1998). These networks link previous migrants in a particular destination to potential migrants in their communities of origin. In Fujian, these migration networks were even arguably native to the social structure.

Pieke and Thuno (2005) posit that "emigration from [Fujian] is strongly embedded in local political, sociocultural and economic institutions and histories" (p. 485). In order to move away from a Eurocentric vantage point to explain this movement, they use the term "Chinese globalization," which they conceptualize as "multiple, transnational social spaces straddling and embedded in diversifying smaller regional or national systems [... and] part of a unifying global system" (Pieke *et al.*, 2004, p. 11). They also note that migration is "as much about the details of local places and communities as it is about the networks and connections linking these places to a transnational social space" (p. 6). These are important insights.

Other theories, moreover, are less effective. The economics-based neoclassical migration theory maintains that individuals choose to emigrate based on income differentials, moving from low-wage countries to high-wage countries (Massey *et al.*, 1993). Unfortunately, this theory fails to explain both the recent Fujianese migration to countries whose currencies have less purchasing power than the Chinese *renminbi* (RMB), and the observation that economic development tends to actually *increase* the impetus for emigration (Massey *et al.*, 1998). Meanwhile, proponents of world-systems theory suggest that transnational migration is a result of industrialization in China's reform period, a product of "Western capitalism," wherein farmers have been forced from their land and the increased competition for factory jobs has become an impetus for emigration (Chin, 1999, p. 16). This argument, however, fails to take into account the long history of the Fujianese transnational experience, which goes back several centuries.

Indeed, while Pieke and Thuno provide a critical foundation for understanding the composition of the transnational social space, the long historical creation of this transnational social space lacks mention within their work. Thus, my own research is guided by the question of how past Fujianese migrations and current Fujianese migrations are linked.

In this chapter, I argue that Fujian's history contributes to the "embeddedness" of transnationalism in its people. While I do not wish to paint Fujianese emigration as a uniform phenomenon, I argue that it has been sustained over the centuries in three main ways: one, it has been largely entrepreneurial in nature; two, it has occurred outside of official control; and three, it is sustained by regional and kinship networks. In doing so,

I hope to establish the local context for Fujianese migration, both in terms of history and institutions.

This chapter is primarily informed through documental research and my own fieldwork in Xishancun village, Fuqing County, Fujian province. With regard to Fujian's maritime history, I draw on Carolyn Cartier (2001), who argues that the South China coast is a "historic maritime cultural economy whose conditions in many ways challenged the orthodoxies of agrarian Han society" (p. 31). She also argues for the importance of regional identity in China. Wang Gungwu (1992) provides much of the historical background on Hokkien merchants. Both Cartier and Wang emphasize the "otherness" of southern China and particularly Fujian, and how this has been conducive to an entrepreneurial spirit.

In the next section, I discuss the historical background of Fujian with an emphasis on its entrepreneurial maritime activities and the beginnings of Fujian's transnational existence. In particular, I look at tribute trade and the growth of commercial (illegal) trade in Fujian. I also examine why these trade networks emerged in Fujian rather than elsewhere. In the third section, I discuss the origins of Fujianese transnationalism in Southeast Asia. In the fourth section, I discuss social practices in the village of Xishancun, particularly as they relate to contemporary China and "Chinese globalization." I look at the mechanisms that facilitate their transnational trajectories to such varied places. Finally, in the conclusion, I explore how this project is related to the broader geopolitical climate and provide some commentary about the importance and implications of a long historical perspective.

2. The Sea as Paddy

Mounds of discarded oyster shells dot the paths in Xishancun. Today, oysters are farmed by men in waters about half an hour away by motorcycle. Once the oysters are hauled back to the village, women spend their days shelling them in the shade. These oysters are a small piece of evidence of Fujian's long maritime history, and are emblematic of the Chinese adage that the "sea is paddy to the Fujianese" (Pan, 1999, p. 30). In this chapter, I discuss Fujian's geography and the beginnings of its trade history, the importance of Zheng He and his legacy, and the origins of an overseas Chinese trade network dominated by the Fujianese.

Located on China's southeast coast, Fujian is encircled by mountains and girded by seas (*jinshan dahai*, 近山达海) (Pan, 1999, p. 30). Roughly 95 percent of Fujian's total area is occupied by mountains, while the remaining area consists of generally infertile coastal plains and river valleys. Only eight percent of Fujian, including terrace farms on mountains, is arable (Clark, 1991, p. 9). Before the arrival of Han Chinese settlers from the north, the Fujian region was inhabited by indigenous peoples, who, according to Clark, likely lived in the mountains and depended on hunting and gathering for subsistence. It was during the fall of the Han dynasty in the late second century that many Chinese flooded to the south from the north — not because it was a prosperous region, but because it provided "refuge from chaos" (So, 2000, p. 15). Overpopulation on limited and infertile lands has been a recurrent theme in the province's history. It was natural, therefore, that the Fujianese turned to the sea as their paddy.

During the Yuan Dynasty (1271–1368), the Fujianese city of Quanzhou became a major port for foreign merchants, supplanting Guangdong province's hub of Guangzhou as the empire's largest port. Quanzhou boasted connections to Japan, Korea, the Philippines, Indonesia, the Arabian Peninsula and even the coast of Africa. Marco Polo and Ibn Battuta are said to have remarked that it was the greatest port in the world (Abu-Lughod, 1989, p. 336). While Fujianese merchants were able to develop their maritime skills in a "relatively free, officially backed trading atmosphere" during this period, this policy changed with the fall of the Yuan (Wang, 1992, p. 83). At the beginning of the Ming Dynasty (1368–1644), Emperor Hongwu banned private trade as part of a policy of isolation aimed at self-sufficiency, while allowing the continuation of tribute trade under which mutual gifts were exchanged for no commercial gain. It was in this context that Zheng He embarked on his seven famous voyages between 1405 and 1433. It is widely assumed that Zheng He's voyages were for the sole purpose of exploration, but at least one historian, Edward Dreyer (2007) argues otherwise. During the first voyage, Zheng He's armada, boasting 27,000 "mostly military personnel," destroyed a Palembang-based fleet of pirate ships which had been preying on merchant ships (p. 31). His fourth voyage took him to Hormuz, the great trading center of its region. These events lead Dreyer to suggest that Zheng He's voyages may, in fact, have been commercial in nature.

Whether or not Zheng He's voyages were for trade or exploration, they "educated many more Chinese about the trading opportunities at a time when private trade was being destroyed and future generations of those who were drawn to trade privately overseas were being intimidated" (Wang, 1992, p. 85). Additionally, economic growth from newly discovered cash crops, such as hemp, silk, sugarcane, litchi, and cotton (So, 2000, pp. 28–29) fostered population growth, straining the land area and leading the Fujianese to turn to the seas for profit. Shipbuilding and navigation techniques improved, and an organized private (and thus illicit) trade network flourished. Moreover, Fujianese merchants recognized growing overseas demand for items like cloth, silk, and pottery and were eager to fill it (ter Haar 1990, p. 176). Private trade also flourished because of the acquiescence of nearby state officials. As Pan (1994) notes, "many of the mandarins in the southern ports were persuaded to turn a blind eye — how else were people to live?" (p. 6). As a result, large numbers of Fujianese merchants migrated all over the globe and started to dominate overseas trade, establishing particularly noteworthy presences in Taiwan and the Philippines.

Even as the Ming state turned inward once again in the mid-fifteenth century, imposing a series of bans on international trade, private sea trade showed few signs of stopping. In 1580, the Spanish Governor-General established a trading post for the Chinese in Alcayceria, Manila, permitting them to settle there permanently. Official Spanish authorization of Chinese settlement aimed to strengthen Spanish wealth; the Spanish wanted the ability to ship fine Chinese goods to the European market via Acapulco (Gambe, 2000). The Spanish also saw that they could gain from using established Chinese trading networks, which connected the Malay Archipelago, the Indo-Chinese coasts, China, and Japan, and they wished to capitalize upon the Fujianese's willingness to bring porcelain and silk to the market. Many Dutch-supported merchant communities also came into being (Wang, 1992). However, the presence of a "well-organized, dynamic, and apparently prosperous alien group" proved at times to be a threat to the Europeans, so measures were taken to control the Chinese populations (Gambe, 2000, p. 13). In Manila, all Chinese were ordered to live outside the city walls in an area called the Parian and what is now the city's Chinatown. The Spanish also repeatedly massacred the Chinese in Manila, and "a major bloodletting occurred" in Dutch Batavia in 1740 (Wang, 1992, p. 88).

Significantly, Ming officials "showed no interest in the Chinese overseas merchant communities, in part because trade and profit-seeking went against the Confucian tenets to which the Chinese polity adhered. Chinese trading abroad were on their own" (Wang, 1992, p. 90). The entrepreneurship of the Fujianese was distinctly homegrown and sustained by a well-established tradition of social networks.

Why was such a complex and successful system of overseas trade able to emerge out of Fujian? As Cartier (2001) notes, "it is important to see China how it sees itself — as a country of regions — and to ask questions about processes that create regional meaning and stitch China together as a coherent whole" (p. 38). Most of the knowledge we have inherited about southern China preserves the worldviews of the Chinese literati, who judged the south China coast in terms of the north. The coast, for example, "was not a landscape of desirability in traditional Chinese imagination" (p. 41), and in old Chinese maps, the South China Sea was depicted as especially fearsome. Furthermore, "strangeness about south China has been a type of otherness... that reminded imperial rulers and northern Han Chinese of the extent of the ordered world and the need to secure that world on its margins" (p. 45).

Becoming an independent kingdom during the tenth century was also a "major turning point" in Fujian's history; its cities of Quanzhou and Zhangzhou were in frontier territories, with relative autonomy away from direct interference by court and provincial mandarins (Wang, 1992). It is therefore arguable that China's isolationist policies through the centuries have had a negligible impact on Fujianese commercial activities. As a result, as Wang succinctly puts it, the Hokkien comprised "the majority of the overseas traders between the thirteenth and eighteenth centuries. They were also the most successful" (p. 97).

3. Fujianese Transnationalism in Southeast Asia

While China has volumes of historical records, few tell of the people involved in overseas trade, indicating the "low esteem in which traders were held within Confucian society" (Blussé, 2001, p. 148). Yet because of their marginalization, the Fujianese people were able to cultivate what Bert Hoselitz (1964) has called "genuine innovations in social behavior" (p. 157).

Once in Southeast Asia, the Fujianese engaged in a variety of activities. Some traded rice in the Chaophraya Valley; others were employees of China-based merchants at a port in a Malay trading state. By the nineteenth century, many had become agents for labor recruitment from China, revenue farm bosses, and local leaders (Wang, 1992, p. 5).

How were Fujianese entrepreneurial projects sustained through the years? Their success and predominance overseas relied on a kinship-based system of social organization that characterizes Fujianese transnationalism today:

> "They needed the skills of Hokkien shipbuilders and captains, the capital of wealthy clansmen who had made their fortunes in China's internal trade, and their literati relatives to speak for them and even protect some of their illegal activities. And they needed their families and village networks to provide the personnel. They also had to bribe corrupt officials at home and co-operate with foreign officials and merchants overseas" (Wang, 1992, p. 97).

For example, when the British established Singapore as a free port in 1819, many people from the southern villages of Fujian came to take advantage of the tax-free markets, but most of them already had pre-existing connections with relatives who had been trading in the region for decades (Wang, 1992, p. 167).

The term that is most often used to refer to the Chinese overseas is *huaqiao* (华侨), where "*hua*" means Chinese, and "*qiao*" signifies a short-term visitor, or a sojourner (Redding, 1993). Eventually, the individual will return home. In effect, the word *huaqiao* has helped to maintain the pretense that the "sojourning" is temporary and unrelated to permanent settlement (Wang, 1992). Indeed, Redding argues that "many of the Overseas Chinese do genuinely still feel bound to China even after centuries of family settlement elsewhere, and the flow of movements of *nanyang* (南洋, Southeast Asia) visitors to China is enormous" (p. 23). Is this so surprising? After all, according to Pan (1994), "an intense preoccupation with origins and identity is typical of people who live on the edge of things, away from the cultural or national center; and Chinese emigrants, whether they ended up in Southeast Asia or America, came overwhelmingly from Fukien and Kwangtung, both peripheral areas" (p. 12).

Importantly, "belonging" is not inborn; the awareness of one's native region is created and sustained through institutions such as dialect and clan links, as well as the building of ancestral halls, temples, and a *huiguan* (会馆, dialect association) (Frost, 2005). These institutions connect those abroad on the basis of a common origin, but they also serve to facilitate the entry of new transnational migrants. Indeed, according to Frost, for new migrants, "access to [the clique of the Straits Chinese] was securable through dialect and clan links." Once in their new areas of settlement, Fujianese migrants created what Frost calls "diasporic spaces," which helped a settler population divided by mutually unintelligible dialects to establish "cultural authenticity and political authority" (p. 43).

For example, temples were important gathering places where settlers could share news, continue their social practices and celebrate their patron deities. Singapore's oldest Fujianese temple, Thian Hock Keng, is notable for its patron deity *Mazu* [or *Tianhou* (天后), meaning "Empress of Heaven"]. According to the myth, Mazu was a fisherman's daughter who protected fishermen and seafarers. The temple served as a transit point for new immigrants: upon arrival in Singapore, passengers and crew thanked Mazu for their safe arrival. Other temples celebrated, among others, the god Sam Po (Sanbao), whom Frost hypothesizes as "possibly the deification of the Eunuch admiral (Zheng He), and was worshipped in temples in Java, Singapore and Malaya" (p. 46).

Furthermore, newly built diasporic spaces in the home village — such as temples, ancestral halls, and schools constructed with money from ex-villagers — serve as visual reminders that a life overseas is one to which to aspire. Indeed, "social practices related to former migration not only celebrate the village's identity as part of a transnational community, but[...] reaffirm the importance of international migration as the avenue and marker of success, regardless of the actual destination and presence or absence of other villagers there" (Pieke and Thuno, 2005, p. 497).

In fieldwork conducted in a village in central Fujian, Pieke and Thuno (2005) discovered that ongoing connections with former villagers in Southeast Asia and Japan had a strong influence on current transnational practices, largely informed by "patrilineal ancestor worship and the desire to perpetuate patrilateral kinship ties between villagers and former villagers overseas" (pp. 497–498). Of course, over time, many generations of overseas

Chinese populations around the world have settled and become nationals and political actors in their countries of residence. As Frost (2005) notes, "cultural ties with homelands were often more easily imagined than enjoyed in practice" (p. 31), especially during times of political unrest in China. Thus, there is a myth-making component to this sense of belonging that is negotiated multi-locally and over time; it is not fixed, static, natural, or given.

4. Fujianese Transnationalism during Chinese Globalization: Case Studies in "Peripheral" Countries

In this section, I draw on my own fieldwork and the empirical research of others to examine the climate surrounding the recent trend toward migration to Africa. I contend that the current emigration climate in Fujian, coupled with China's foreign policy in Africa, creates the necessary conditions for their movement.

4.1. *Thinking beyond the constraints of the nation-state*

"It was never possible to understand Chinese migration to Europe solely at the level of the individual European states... Chinese migrants have always shown scant regard for lines drawn quickly and apparently at random across Asia's European promontory. In that respect, they were Europeans before the Europeans" (Benton, 1998, p. viii).

In many ways, Fujianese migrants can be said to be truly transnational, as their transnational journey is not guided by the idea of unidirectional migration and permanent settlement. Rather, the core objective is to "generate savings and remittances for the migrant's natal and/or nuclear family" (Pieke *et al.*, 2004, p. 32). It is generally understood that most migrants wish to go to the United States, Canada, the United Kingdom, or Australia — traditional migratory destinations. However, the new migration paths out of Xishancun are consistent with Pieke's notion that "Chinese emigration no longer simply is the move to the centers of a world system fully dominated by the West, but is just as much an aspect of the outward extension of a world system centered on China itself" (Pieke, 2002, p. 6).

In Xishancun, I spoke with three brothers whose lives were deeply enmeshed in transnational Fujianese practices. The brothers were the wealthiest in the village; they drove cars on newly paved roads still populated mostly by putt-putt motorcycles. They had toothpicks lodged between their gold teeth and wore flashy watches. They spoke on cell phones with their wives, who were looking after their grandchildren at home. Furthermore, their children were scattered around the Southern Hemisphere. Each expressed regret that they had not sent their children to Canada, admitting that if Fujianese people had the resources, they would probably send their children to North America. But just because the United States and Canada are constructed as first choices does not make countries like South Africa and Argentina mere consolation prizes; the brothers were certainly tasting the fruits of success.

4.2. *Factors that enable Fujianese migration*

China lacks a unified emigration policy "beyond the acknowledgement in the 1985 emigration law that allows Chinese citizens who have legitimate reasons to leave to do just that" (Pieke, 2002, p. 20). Passports are available to those who have been invited by relatives abroad; after this, it is up to the migrants to either obtain a valid visa themselves, or to hire a smuggler to help them through the process (Pieke, 2002). However, one cannot privilege the availability of passports too much: after the July 2000 Dover incident — wherein 58 Fujianese migrants (twenty-eight of whom were from Fuqing) were found suffocated in a cargo truck in Dover, England — the Chinese government banned the issuance of passports to any male under 35 years of age in Fuzhou prefecture (Pieke *et al.*, 2004). However, as was the case during trade bans and isolationist policy, little could be done to stop transmigratory activities. Furthermore, local governments have little incentive to stop emigrants. They tolerate it because of the high volume of remittances. In fact, corruption "has reached dimensions unprecedented during Communist rule and bolsters migrant smuggling in [several] ways" (Hood, 1997, p. 80). Snakeheads (or human smugglers) are also crucial to the process of emigration; they are perceived as professional service providers, a source of information and advice, and a gateway to prosperity. Many migrants use several smugglers to reach their destinations. To migrants, at the end of the day, smuggling is "merely their way to get where they want to go" (Pieke, 2002, p. 23).

The potential for legal status is another attractive reason for Fujianese migration. The people whom Pieke interviewed were eager to garner legal permanent residence for its perks. After all, this would enable return visits, finding wives, and benefits including salaries and job opportunities, as well as onward migration to other countries through legal means (notably the United States, Japan, or Western Europe). In sum, "permanent residence makes the migrant a real person again, instead of someone merely in transit" (Pieke, 2002, p. 35). The children of transmigrants who are growing up in Fujianese villages may wind up benefiting from the rights accorded to, for example, citizens of Argentina. Therefore, while reaching their destination country often involves illegal means at one point or another (i.e., using a fake official's passport, flying in legally on a tourist visa but being smuggled across a border illegally), eventual attainment of legal status is a pragmatic concern of Fujianese transnationals.

4.3. *Impact of China's Africa policy on potential transmigrants*

In the last few decades, China has sought to play a more active role in the international arena. The push toward active international participation exists, as Tull (2006) argues, in response to fiercely negative Western reactions to the Tiananmen Square massacre; recently, Chinese foreign policy has become "more dynamic, constructive, flexible, and self confident than was the case during the preceding decades" (p. 460). Following the backlash to the Tiananmen Square massacre, China shielded Beijing from Western criticism by building coalitions with developing countries. Indeed, after the incident, foreign minister Qian Qichan visited no fewer than fourteen African countries, where China "continues to portray itself as a developing nation" (p. 462).

China's strategic networking over the past two decades has enabled it to meet an increased need for resources with a boom in Chinese-African trade. By 2006, there were some 700 Chinese enterprises with a total investment of $1.5 billion in Africa (Tull, 2006). China offers low-price export goods such as textiles, clothing, and electronics. China has also become involved through increased aid, debt cancellation, and Sino-African trade. Tull cautions that China's involvement may prove, economically, to be "mixed at best," and that the political consequences are "bound to prove deleterious" as China supports authoritarian governments (p. 459). Regardless, the Chinese penetration into Africa poses a unique opportunity to Fujianese people, as it offers an attractively affordable migration path.

4.4. *Xishancun's transnational connections to Africa*

Xishancun is a single-surname clan village in Fuqing County, Fujian Province. In the early 1900s, members of the Chong clan immigrated to Singapore; remittances helped to build a primary school, an ancestral hall, and a temple. This kind of family narrative occurred broadly over the Fuqing/Fuzhou area, which sent many of its kin to Southeast Asia. In Xishancun, conditions allow families to grow peanuts, maize, potatoes, rice, and corn. They rent cows from an entrepreneurial villager to plough their rice paddies. Only a decade or so ago, there was no plumbing in the village, and only dirt paths upon which to drive. Today, the roads are paved, and houses have flushing toilets. These changes are the result of a combination of state investment as well as remittance payments from the past decade.

For the villagers of Xishancun, migration is a viable and respectable way of making a living. They consider factories jobs beneath them; such employment is reserved for people from poorer rural provinces. Instead, there is a thriving business that supports the mass migration of people. As one villager explained to me, "Someone will say, 'You want to go to Cameroon? Okay, 50,000 RMB!' and then you pay, then go, and open a mini supermarket. Usually your neighbors from home are there, or you have family connections."

When asked to justify the dangers of the long journey and of cooperating with snakeheads, villagers scoff. For them, paying smugglers is a wise investment with abundant returns, and Africa has become the cheapest and most profitable place to which to go. Why pay 70,000RMB to go to New York, only to wash dishes? In Lesotho, Fujianese immigrants can open their own shops and be the boss of others, and pay back all their debts within two years. Even more of an impetus: the journey cost only 12,000RMB, a fraction of the price.

One villager suggested that one could "try [one's] luck and sneak in somewhere for free, or [one] could invest in a visa and enter legally, which could cost an additional 20,000RMB." This particular villager has two sons and a daughter. His daughter is in South Africa with her husband, where they own a shop selling clothes, shoes, and strollers imported from China. It cost the villager 25,000RMB to send his daughter to Johannesburg. There, she was connected to a "superman" who sells things at wholesale prices. They set up their shop in a Chinatown community that had around 40 Chinese-owned shops, according to the villager's estimates. The daughter has lived there for five to six years. In this time, she has given birth to two sons, both of whom live in Xishancun with their grandparents. The journey and arrangements were financed with borrowed money; luckily, the woman's father was able to borrow interest-free from relatives. It cost between 500,000 and 600,000RMB to open the shop. The family made 100,000RMB in their first year, and by the end of the third year, they had cleared their debts and begun to build a family home on their allotted plot of land in Xishancun.

Three brothers in the same community had all sent their children abroad as well. At the time, it cost 25,000RMB to go to South Africa, and 80,000 to 90,000RMB to go to Argentina. The destinations of their other children included Mozambique, Zimbabwe, and Lesotho.

Brother A has two sons and one daughter, all of whom are in Argentina. His decision to send his children to Argentina was based on the idea that there were "no prospects in China" and the fact that he had connections to Buenos Aires through other villagers who had already migrated there. The original journey cost 150,000RMB for all three children and took thirty hours. They flew from Hong Kong to Bolivia, and then snuck into Argentina. His children have spent eight years in Buenos Aires and now are fluent in Spanish. Currently, his oldest son has three children; two were born in Argentina, and one was born in China. All three are citizens of Argentina. At the time of the interview, the six-year-old had to go back to renew his passport. The children will have to go back to China every five years if they wish to keep their citizenship.

In Buenos Aires, Brother A's first son owns a mini-supermarket with his wife, employing five or six employees as well as security guards. They live upstairs of the shop and pay about 6,000 Argentinean pesos a month in rent. Brother A's second son was a policeman when he lived in China and had the opportunity to go to Canada but refused, to Brother A's chagrin. Now he owns a similar store in a smaller neighborhood in Buenos Aires, paying half in rent. Brother A had hoped that they would go to Canada, where he believed they would face less racial discrimination. But to go to Canada, villagers needed considerable assets before they could borrow. So they settled on Argentina. It took about two and a half years to make back the initial capital; the extra money was used to build a house in Xishancun. Right now Brother A has one million RMB and is planning to spend it on an apartment in Fuqing city. Brother A's children send their money directly home; none of it is invested in Buenos Aires, where they live simply and frugally in small apartments above or adjacent to their shops. In fact, none of the subjects interviewed had invested in homes abroad.

Brother B's children are scattered all over the world, with one in Argentina, another in Ecuador, and three more in South Africa. He admits, "I'm not sure where they are... I don't know where, I've never been... I don't really care as long as they're making money." It cost 22,000 RMB to send each of them abroad. They are all married to villagers from Xishancun. Brother B's daughters in South Africa own clothing stores selling clothing from China. Brother B says, "My children are lucky because I did all the work." Like Brother A, Brother B expressed regret at not being able to send his children to Canada. His son refused because he was not interested in working his way up in a business; he wanted to be a boss. Brother B has a cousin who lives in Toronto and views life in Canada as something to which to aspire. Even so, his son's refusal was so great (he recalls that his son *sidoubuqu* (死都不去) — "would rather die" than go to Toronto) that nothing could be done. Aware that Canada needs a higher birth rate to sustain its population, Brother B told me, "My dream was to have my son move to Canada and have lots of children there."

Brother C's daughter is in Durban, South Africa. He sent his daughter there in 2003, into a community with a rather substantial Chinese population. According to him, in Durban, "all the Chinese are bosses." There, his daughter and her husband live with their son. Travelling to Johannesburg to buy stock, they support themselves by selling clothing, shoes, and strollers.

All three brothers had in common the desire to send their children to Canada, but none had the means to do so. Still, the migrants have found success in their new destinations. They have amassed considerable wealth in a relatively short period of time, and construction projects under way back home are testaments to their new wealth.

Moving to non-traditional "peripheral" regions is thus not without its perks: with the right connections and some capital, it is relatively easy to open a shop. Another respondent had a son who went to Durban, South Africa; it cost 22,000 RMB in a lump sum to go. The family borrowed from relatives on a 1.5 percent interest. On top of that, it cost 500,000 to 600,000 RMB to open a shop. It took about three years to make back the money; once the debt had cleared, they used the money to build a home in Xishancun. On average, homes cost 500,000 or 600,000 RMB to build, and it's not strange to see a house that has three and a half floors. The concept of "face" is not far from the minds of the villagers of Xishancun; one respondent explained to me that if his neighbor added a floor to his house, then he would do the same.

For the villagers, the elevated status that one might acquire from making it to the Western "center" is undeniable. In that regard, Pieke's (2002) hypothesis that "Chinese emigration no longer simply is the move to the center of a world system fully dominated by the West" actually obscures the powerful pull that Western "center" have on migrants, and the limitations that they face in attaining this goal. Indeed, if they had the choice, capital, and connections, most would be there right now. In the meantime, the villagers' transnational networks are anchored in places within reach, representing perhaps only a "step" toward a better life, as one respondent put it. For now, the immediate goal of enriching the family back home has been met.

5. Conclusion: The Implications of a Historical Perspective and Further Directions in Exploring Fujianese and Chinese Transnationalism(s)

In contextualizing and challenging existing models of international migration, which posit that people move from "peripheral" (poor) countries to "core" (rich) countries, we find that current Fujianese transnationalisms in the US and Africa are part of a much longer history of Fujianese transnationalism. This Fujianese transnationalism has often been entrepreneurial in nature, and has largely occurred outside of official sanction. Indeed, Fujian's geography, trade-based economy, and historical ties to other regions have created a transnational people. In looking at the life trajectories of the contemporary villagers of Xishancun in Fuqing County, we can see that migration has grown to be an inevitable option. Such a reframing of Fujianese transnationalism is important if we are to understand the factors that contribute to mobility and settlement strategies. Thus we can reimagine Fujianese migrants not as victims at the hands of vicious snakeheads and moneylenders, but as agents who use their knowledge and networking skills to carve out new lives, navigating the potentials of a globalized world.

My concluding thoughts relate my project to the broader geopolitical climate of today. What are the implications of China's growing footprint in Africa, in which Fujianese merchants play a role? As manifestations of Chinese globalization, how might they be interpreted by scholars and by the global community at large? Are the Fujianese merchants agents of global capitalism? Can they be divorced from perceptions of China as an encroaching giant? And to what extent can and should geographers reconcile the goals of the Chinese government with the continued transmigratory experiences of Fujianese people, and, increasingly, other Chinese people? As Howard French (2007) wrote in a Letter from Africa in *The New York Times*, "Chinese people today look at Africa and see opportunity, promise and a fertile field upon which their energies, mercantile and otherwise, can be given full play."

Indeed, the fear of China's rise as a colonial power is palpable in the mainstream media, particularly as China becomes more prominent in Africa. Yet this continuous scapegoating of China obfuscates the neocolonial and capitalistic projects of the West, both past and present, and the racist tendencies of both governments and mainstream media outlets. In locating the story of Fujianese transnationalism *within* Fujian, I strive to clarify the motives of people who have come to be symbols of China's rise, but who, like anyone, are just trying to make a go at life. It is just that, thanks to 500 years of sustained history, transnationalism is in their bones.

References

Abu-Lughod, JL (1989). *Before European Hegemony: The World System A.D. 1250–1350*. Oxford, UK: Oxford University Press.

Benton, G (1998). Preface. In *The Chinese in Europe*, G Benton and FN Pieke (eds.), pp. vii–xi. London and New York: MacMillan and St. Martin's Press.

Blussé, L (2001). The vicissitudes of maritime trade: Letters from the ocean Hang merchant, Li Kunhe, to the Dutch authorities in Batavia (1803–1808). In *Sojourners and Settlers: Histories of Southeast Asia and the Chinese*, A Reid (ed.), pp. 148–163. Honolulu, HI: University of Hawaii Press.

Cartier, C (2001). *Globalizing South China*. Oxford, UK: Blackwell.

Chin, KL (1999). *Smuggled Chinese: Clandestine Immigration to the United States*. Philadelphia: Temple University Press.

Clark, HR (1991). *Community, Trade, and Networks: Southern Fujian Province from the Third to the Thirteenth Century*. Cambridge, UK: Cambridge University Press.

Dreyer, EL (2007). *Zheng He: China and the Oceans in the Early Ming Dynasty*. New York, NY: Pearson Education.

French, HW (2007). Letter from Africa: The Chinese footprint growing across Africa. *New York Times,* June 14.

Frost, MR (2005). Emporium in imperio: Nanyang networks and the Straits Chinese in Singapore, 1819–1914. *Journal of Southeast Asian Studies*, 36 (1), 29–66.

Gambe, AR (2000). *Overseas Chinese Entrepreneurship and Capital Development in Southeast Asia*. New York, NY: St. Martin's Press.

Guest, K (2002). Religion across borders: Transnational immigrant networks. In *Transnational Religious Networks Among New York's Fuzhou Immigrants*, HR Ebaugh and J Chafetz (eds.), pp. 149–163. Walnut Creek: Altamira Press.

Hood, M (1997). Human smuggling: Chinese migrant trafficking and the challenge to America's immigration tradition. In *Sourcing the Problem: Why Fuzhou?* PJ Smith (ed.), pp. 76–92. Washington DC: The Center for Strategic and International Studies.

Hoselitz, BF (1964). Development and society. In *A Sociological Approach to Economic Development*, D Novack and R Lekachman (eds.). New York, NY: St. Martin's Press.

Kwong, P (1998). *Forbidden Workers: Illegal Chinese Immigrants and American Labor*. New York: New Press.

Massey, D (1988). Economic development and international migration in comparative perspective. *Population and Development Review*, 14(4), 383–413.

Massey, D, J Arango, G Hugo, A Kouaouci, A Pellegrino and JE Taylor (1993). Theories of international migration: A review and appraisal. *Population and Development Review* 19(3), 431–466.

Massey, D, J Arango, G Hugo, A, Kouaouci, A Pellegrino and JE Taylor (1998). *Worlds in Motion: Understanding International Migration at the End of the Millennium*. Oxford, UK: Oxford University Press.

Pan, L (1994). *Sons of the Yellow Emperor*. New York, NY: Kodansha America.

Pan, L (1999). *The Encyclopedia of the Chinese Overseas*. Singapore: Landmark Books.

Pieke, F (2002). *Recent Trends in Chinese Migration to Europe: Fujianese Migration in Perspective*. Geneva: International Organization for Migration.

Pieke, F and M Thuno (2005). Institutionalizing recent rural emigration from China to Europe: New transnational villages in Fujian. *International Migration Review*, 39(2), 485–514.

Pieke, F, P Nyiri, M Thuno and A Ceccagno (2004). *Transnational Chinese: Fujianese Migrants in Europe*. Stanford, CA: Stanford University Press.

Redding, G (1993). *The Spirit of Chinese Capitalism*. Berlin: Walter de Gruyter.

Smith, PJ (1997). Human smuggling: Chinese migrant trafficking and the challenge to America's immigration tradition. In *Chinese Migrant Trafficking: A Global Challenge*, PJ Smith (ed.), pp. 1–22. Washington DC: The Center for Strategic and International Studies.

So, BKL (2000). *Prosperity, Region, and Institutions in Maritime China: The South Fukien Pattern, 946–1368*. Cambridge, MA: Harvard University Asia Center.

The Taipei Times (2007). Smuggling of US-bound Chinese growing in Peru. February 21, p. 3.

Ter Haar, BJ (1990). Development and decline of Fukien province in the 17th and 18th centuries. In *Fukien's Private Sea Trade in the 16th and 17th Centuries*, EB Vermeer (ed.), pp. 163–214 (translation of Lin Renchuan). Leiden: E. J. Brill.

Tull, DM (2006). China's engagement in Africa: Scope, significance, and consequences. *Journal of Modern Africa Studies*, 44(3), 459–479.

Wang, G (1992). *China and the Overseas Chinese*. Singapore: Times Academic Press.

Chapter 2

What Chinese Am I? The Use of Heritage for Economic Imperatives in Singapore

Daphnée HL Lee

1. Introduction

Singapore state leaders now emphasize the economic utility of heritage connections for lubricating transnational commercial relationships. During the early years of the nation's independence, heritage identity had been derided as anti-modernity. Pre-emptive to China's economic ascendency, efforts in the 1980s to revive Chinese heritage were accompanied by remarks of state leaders about the West as being separate and opposite of the East. How do Chinese Singaporean executives perceive their own heritage identifications? How do they make sense of their "Chinese heritage"? What, if any, are the differences in interpreting one's Chineseness when it comes to individual approaches to cross-cultural work scenarios? What are the broader political, economic and social implications of the use of heritage for economic imperatives? This chapter aims to shed light on these questions based on an empirical study of corporate (Chinese Singaporeans) respondents born during the first two decades of Singapore's independence (1960–1979). The respondents were employed by a Western multinational corporation (MNC) located in Singapore to liaise with the company's clientele in China.

2. Whose Chineseness?

If one's Chinese identity needs confirmation through living the ways of Chinese ancestors, then our Chinese ancestors in Singapore would have illustrated how heritage is much inspired by business motivations.

A Chinese business tycoon, for instance, has a highly adaptable ethnic identity that adapts as situation demands (Chan and Chiang, 1994). To the colonial administrators, he is an ethnic comprador entrusted to ensure the orderliness of the Chinese community. To the corvée labor *sinkeh* or new-comers, he is an authoritative figurehead presiding over administrative functions ranging from marriage solemnization to leadership of secret societies. Most importantly, Chinese identification was contested by regimes from the "Mainland," rooting for support of overseas Chinese, with the most controversial being the Chinese Communist Party. Chinese heritage in Singapore, or what is believed to have been cultural importa-tions from China, is in reality the situational identity adaptations of earlier (pre-independence) Chinese immigrants to the region. The adapted identi-ties then came to be selectively preserved for posterity by the later descendants of those who came to be identified with "Chinese heritage". One of the most active usages of Chinese heritage, as with the early Chinese business community, is for the fulfillment of economic objectives.

Postcolonial Singapore emerged as one nation through active state engineering of racial identities. The ethnic landscape has been type-casted to be race-based, diverse, but finite; expressed through what is commonly known as the CMIO (Chinese, Malays, Indians and Others) multicultural model. As this version of ethnic identity is an over-simplified representation of the wide varieties of ethnic identifications of most Singaporeans, the actualization of this model is reinforced by the encouragement of state-approved ethnic identifications, while simultane-ously discouraging state-disapproved varieties. In the early decades of Singapore's independence (1965), the state-initiated acquisition of English proficiency, especially for Chinese Singaporean students, was tempered by the imperative to quash "Chinese chauvinism." The threat of Singapore becoming the "Third China" (Fitzgerald, 1969) made students from Mandarin instruction Chinese schools suspect for left-wing activi-ties, resulting in state persecutions using disciplinary instruments such as the Internal Security Act.

While political sensitivities associated with "Chineseness" had much abated by the 1970s, the spillover effects of overly suppressive policies may persist, for instance, with the enduring belief that one's ethnic identity is under siege (Lazarus, 1991). Individuals finding it a challenge to renounce strong ethnic attachments may devise strategies to cushion the impact of these repercussions.

By the 1980s, the Speak Mandarin Campaign partnered the decade when China sought reintegration into the global economy. The refrain by state leaders on the importance of "bringing Chinese Singaporeans closer to our ethnic and cultural roots" (Lee, 2003) seeks to abate earlier state initiatives:

> "[Goh Chok Tong, former Prime Minister]: If we are proficient in English and Chinese, if we understand China as well as we understand the West, we will be in a strong position to benefit from China's growth" (Goh, 2002).

> "[George Yeo, former Minister for Trade and Industry]: The Chinese Singaporean should always know that he too is a son of the Yellow Emperor and an inheritor of an ancient civilization which is becoming ascendant again" (Yeo, 2004).

The prioritization of heritage does not preclude economic motivations. Where heritage is antithetical to modernization, it is to be actively suppressed. Where China becomes the predominant market for global investors, the heritage imperative regains its position (in relation to China). The imperative of re-piecing lost heritage was principally buttressed by the renewed commercial interest of Western MNCs toward China. Most importantly, state social engineering efforts may bear unintended consequences in the way the use of Chinese heritage unfolds at the individual level. The enduring consequences of past policies on individual dispositions form the issue of discussion in this chapter.

3. The Case

Located in Singapore, the ECI (pseudonym) is the Asia Pacific subsidiary of a multinational corporation (MNC). This case study is engaged within an area of business that is identified by the Economic Development Board (EDB) of Singapore as one of the stronghold industries that bolsters the economic wealth of the country. The regional commercial interest of the ECI encompasses the Pacific (Sydney), South Asia (Mumbai and New Delhi), Southeast Asia (Indonesia, Malaysia and Singapore) and East Asia (Beijing, Guangzhou, Hainan, Hong Kong, Japan, Shanghai and South Korea). While China poses a strong commercial attraction for the ECI due to the rapid growth of the industry in the port cities and the huge market potential, Singapore remains the stronghold where ECI's established business clients are located.

Hosted in Singapore, the ECI regional headquarters deploys a group of corporate representatives, which at the time of the study predominantly comprised Europeans deployed from the corporate headquarters and ethnic Chinese Singaporeans as the faces of the organization. Among corporate representatives, the former group is commonly referred to as "expatriates," and the latter as "locals." As the frontline personnel representing the ECI in commercial negotiations with its clientele, the corporate representatives represent only less than 20 percent of the human resource pool of the organization, but play strategic roles as the key breadwinners. The intentional engagement of profile-matching via ethnic associations is underpinned by the assumption that ethnic Chinese Singaporeans will possess better rapport with the key regional clientele based on common "Chinese heritage."

At the time of this study, the ECI was experiencing a strong drive toward localization, deployed under the motto of "multidomesticism." That is, the corporate headquarters of ECI in Europe had pledged greater representation of local corporate representatives in top management ranks at their regional subsidiaries. This was inspired by the belief that ECI needs top managers who are closer to the culture of the region, so as to reach out to regional clients more effectively. The commitment was explicitly demonstrated through the relocation of all top manager offices to a centralized location within the office building, so as to showcase the diverse cultural profiles of ECI top managers. This move inspired a tongue-in-cheek comment by a newly promoted ECI top manager, "I am moved here for *racial* harmony; a statistic of Singaporean against Europeans." The use of familiar terms in the state ethnic management discourse, such as racial harmony, is prevalent among ECI corporate representatives. However, different respondents selectively echo the state ethnic management discourse, suggesting that certain dimensions of these social engineering efforts tend to stand out more than others. Altogether, I identified four distinct groups of respondents in our research whose sense-making ways were shaped by these discourses as far as their Chinese identity is concerned. Before I deal with these issues in greater detail, let us review the methodology employed in this study.

3.1 *Methodology*

This inquiry employs a mixed-method approach to gain insights on how ECI Chinese Singaporean corporate representatives make sense of their own Chineseness to lubricate commercial relationships with their clients in China.

Participant observation formed the initial part of fieldwork. Everyday events at the ECI ("ongoing action") were observed and recorded alongside how they were understood by the participants ("mediated action") (Daniels *et al.*, 2007, pp. 51–59). That is, analytical insights were obtained via the meanings that participants infused to events, as informed by the positions they occupied within the organizational hierarchy (Daniels *et al.*, 2007, p. 51).

Having obtained a sense of the implicit ground sentiments from participant observation, a scored survey questionnaire was introduced to explore the profile of personal value-orientations held by the corporate representatives. Hofstede's concept of Uncertainty Avoidance was adapted to facilitate this discussion (2001). Uncertainty Avoidance (UA) refers to the tendency to avoid exposure to situations of ambiguity in order to minimize the level of anxiety toward the unknown. In the survey of the IBM international offices, Hofstede found variable scores of Uncertainty Avoidance across 50 countries, and attributed the score differences to cultural ones (2001). While the ranked scores provided an extensive baseline for cross-cultural comparisons, Hofstede's analysis stopped short at extending the findings on Uncertainty Avoidance beyond the surface cultural associations. In order to shed insights of the concept's associations with structural factors, I adapted its indicators to form an independent survey measurement of UA. Therefore, UA indicators were constructed based on Hofstede's elaboration of the construct. The indicators include rule orientation, resistance to change, rejection/avoidance of ambiguity, intolerance of diversity and negative attitudes toward the whims of youth at the workplace. However, as much of Hofstede's analytical approach differs from the one adopted in this study, a reconceptualization of the concept is needed.

For the sake of conceptual clarity, I will refer to the reconceptualized construct as Ambiguity Anxiety (AA). A survey questionnaire measured the degree of AA by means of respondents' self-reports. I sought to compare respondents' AA scores with the way they frame the perceptions of their own Chinese identity during the in-depth interviews. This was done in order to explore possible relationships between the two constructs.

In Hofstede's report on the UA index of 50 countries across three regions, Singapore possesses the lowest score in UA. Upon examination of Hofstede's questionnaire items, it has been found that scenarios of uncertainty constructed by Hofstede are the ones that Singaporeans are generally amenable toward; namely, openness to adaptation insofar as supervision is made available. Questions in this survey (AA) differ from Hofstede's in that it measures anxiety toward uncertainty when individual adaptability is required in the absence of supervision. With this revision, it has been found that the ECI corporate representatives possessed significantly lower AA scores than non-corporate representatives in the case study. Apart from the 30 corporate representatives, the measurement was also applied upon ECI non-corporate representatives. In addition, to ensure that the non-corporate representatives are representative of the "typical Chinese Singaporean working adult," a control group of 130 non-ECI respondents were also recruited. In all, a total of 190 respondents were sampled. Out of a 24-point scale, ECI corporate representatives scored an average of 14.67; ECI non-corporate representatives 16.81; and the control group 16.86. Due to job demands requiring intensive travel in the Asia Pacific, exposure to frequent uncertainties may have resulted in significantly lower scores among corporate representatives. It was also found that AA scores correspond with identification styles toward one's Chinese identity. Respondents with similar identification styles were grouped together, and their average AA score was compared with that of the non-corporate representatives. Groups with average AA scores lower than that of the non-corporate representatives were seen to be characterized by low AA, while groups with higher average AA scores relative to non-corporate representatives were seen to be characterized by high AA.

Given that AA question items relate to non-ethnicity related work scenarios, the relationship between respondent ethnic identifications and AA needs to be further compared with specific profiles of the respondents to shed light on how the construct could be related to respondent personal identifications toward Chinese ethnicity. AA scores were found to be lower among respondents who had used English to communicate with their parents during childhood, in contrast to the non-English users. Differences also emerged in the way the two groups of respondents make sense of the use of Chinese ethnic affiliations to lubricate commercial relationships with their clients in China. For the sake of convenience, I shall refer to this medium as *linguistic primacy*. The dominant language medium symbolically represents the power of the social group associated with the language (Bourdieu, 1979). In Singapore, the English language holds significant influence. Today, the language is the nation's lingua franca, medium of teaching instruction and business language. In the era of 1960–1979, it was the language of the power elite. Then, few Singaporeans possessed the same proficiency of the language as did the power elite. One may eventually acquire English proficiency from years of study since English is the medium of teaching instruction, but this need not equate with English-primacy. Since linguistic primacy is acquired from parents and hence precedes language acquisition at school, its role in shaping value-orientation and behavior is more critical and enduring. The eventual use of the English language as a primary medium of communication by an individual does not override the linguistic primacy effect. The ECI sample suggests that respondents are identifiable by three types of linguistic primacies: "English-primacy," "(Chinese) Dialect-primacy" and "Mandarin-primacy." The further comparison of respondent in-depth interview responses by their linguistic primacy points to the English-primacy being more confident of their ability to harness Chinese heritage for commercial negotiations, more so than the non-English primacy corporate representatives.

30 corporate representatives participated in the in-depth interviews, where they were queried on their perceptions of the expectation of them at the ECI toward the use of Chineseness to bridge commercial

relationships. Each interview session spanned between 3–6 hours. The responses were coded with NVivo, a qualitative data analysis software, for the emergent patterns of responses, and these patterns were compared with the AA scores and linguistic primacy profile. Further confirmation of the response patterns emergent from the in-depth interview was consolidated through a follow-up questionnaire.

4. State Discourse on the Use of Heritage for Economic Imperatives: Echoes, Partial Resonances, Medleys and Silence

Singapore has been hailed as the ideal springboard for Western MNCs to launch commercial operations in Asia (Kraar, 1996). It is believed, that Anglicized Singapore is pro-Western by nurture, and Chinese by nature. Yet, it may be overly simplistic to believe that all Chinese Singaporeans can be consistently and concurrently both pro-Western and pro-Chinese. This expectation becomes doubly challenging when state leaders had promoted one view about culture while deriding alternative views. For instance, the Speak Mandarin Campaign had occurred alongside strident derogations of "Western decadence" by its state leaders. This sends mixed messages of not just encouraging one set of values, beliefs and practices on the one hand, but also the discouragement of a (real or perceived) competing set of values, beliefs and practices on the other hand.

In the ideal situation, some in the workforce may echo heritage identifications as desired by changing social engineering efforts. In this, one takes a pragmatically economic approach, represented by the statements made by the state leaders, presented earlier in the opening paragraphs of this discussion. Out of the 30 respondents interviewed, 6 respondents echoed the stand that Chineseness is *situational,* as inspired by this strand of state discourse:

> "Race and everything else will go out through the window when I am with the customer. For me, when I go through the door, and I am in for the kill to close the deal, all my senses are heightened. It's how I connect with the customer that matters, and I will do all I can to connect with the customer" (Carlos, respondent).

Others found a *born-again* zeal toward one's "Chinese heritage" (5 respondents), along with the derogation of "Western decadence":

> "I am not a local (China) Chinese, but I maintain the same Chinese culture as them. The mentality that they have when I went into China about 10 over years ago is still there: the foreigner (Westerner) disadvantage is that you are 老外 (Mandarin: foreigner). You (Westerner) only know how to drink beer and you don't like our food. But we don't like your sausages either. Most importantly, they don't trust them. The feeling is you (Westerner) came here to make money and after 2–3 years, you go" (Joseph, respondent).

In contrast to the echoes of pragmatism, statements in state discourse that stood out to them are those that profess an affiliation with being Chinese, accompanied by the derogation of the West, such as the following statements made by Singapore state leaders:

> "[Lee Kuan Yew, former Senior Minister]: Lim Boon Keng (Straits Chinese elite) was not taught Chinese... He realized during his stay in UK that whatever his accomplishments, the British would always treat him as a British subject of Chinese origin, not as their equal. He resolved to connect with his cultural roots" (Lee, 2004).

> "[Lee Hsien Loong, Prime Minister]: Deng Xiaoping (Chinese Communist Party Leader) said, 'When you open the windows, the flies will fly in'... When Michael Fay (US citizen in Singapore) was sentenced to caning for vandalism, Bill Clinton as President wrote to our President on his behalf. But we couldn't remit his sentence of caning... And people in Asia noted our stand" (H. L. Lee, 2004).

Then, there are those who seek to reconcile all perspectives for a more balanced stand. They *integrate* diverse views into a common platform of dialogue (10 respondents):

> "There are three types of local employees who will break the ice with the expatriates (Westerners). One, the type who do not see themselves as inferior to the expatriates, so they don't see a problem with speaking up and voicing their opinions, too, as they feel that their ideas are also

worth consideration. Two, those ostracized by local colleagues (Chinese Singaporeans) and hence attempt to build friendship with expatriates in the company. Three, the type who has no choice as they need to work very closely with superiors (Westerners) and subordinates (Chinese Mainland and Singaporeans) and eventually, the rapport is built when both parties are open to establish relationships... The problems of integrating with the corporate headquarters becomes real because there is no effort from all parties to break the ice. Especially in times of conflict, the expatriates will tend to cut off communication by speaking amongst themselves to the meeting chair (in a foreign language incomprehensible to the locals), usually an expatriate. The locals will then do the same and speak amongst themselves in dialects or Mandarin" (Bernard, respondent).

The remaining have simply given up, and sought to remain *resolute* toward their personal moral order by the conscious exclusion of heritage concerns (9 respondents):

"If not life will be very difficult if you bring everything in and restrict yourself: you don't like this, you don't like the person and you don't like the color. It will be very difficult. At the end of the day you achieve nothing" (Norman, respondent).

Furthermore, it appears, according to the average AA scores of the four groups that, the interpretation of state ethnic management discourse mirrors the level of anxiety one experiences in general, non-culture related work scenarios.

5. Ambiguity Anxiety

Ethnic management had guaranteed an early head-start for Singapore in establishing an economic stronghold in the region. Indeed, Singapore's aggressive engineering of the English language as the de facto language in the country (Rubdy *et al.*, 2008) had much to do with the influx of foreign direct investments from Western MNCs. However, the ardent efforts also precipitated what Hu describes as the "accelerated monolingualism" of the nation (2008, p. 207), manifested in the dramatic demographical shift of home language use in Singaporean households to English (Kwan-Terry, 1991; Silver, Hu and Iino, 2002). The 1980s Speak Mandarin Campaigns were inspired by the previous state social engineering efforts, but with an agenda to re-engineer a different orientation to heritage from the previous initiative. With China's ascendency in the international economic arena, the need for a common Chinese heritage linking the Chinese populations of China and Singapore was then driven with the same fervor as the previous emphasis on the need to temper with one's heritage affiliations in favor of Anglicization.

However, not all Chinese Singaporeans are equally adept at managing the mixed messages at as to whether Chinese heritage is to be or not to be cherished. In the examination of AA scores of the corporate representatives to work situations that are unrelated to the cultural dimension, I found corresponding patterns in the level of AA with the willingness to adapt one's heritage identification in accordance to state discourse on the matter.

As presented in the previous section, not all corporate representatives at the ECI had echoed the messages communicated by the state ethnic management discourse. Their interpretation of the state discourse, in addition, corresponded with the level of anxiety felt toward ambiguous work scenarios. The 6 respondents who adopted a highly pragmatic stance to the *situational* use of Chinese heritage (represented earlier by respondent, Carlos) had the lowest average AA scores (10.67). In general, their scores are significantly lower in comparison to the non-corporate representatives. This group was found to be exclusively English-primacy.

Most non-English primacy ECI corporate representatives had higher AA scores than their English-primacy peers, and their average scores were somewhat closer to those of the non-corporate representatives, although still slightly lower in comparison. Among non-English primacy corporate representatives, AA scores appear to correspond with perceptions of whether one's heritage was not favored/disfavored by pre-1980s ethnic management initiatives, and hence the interpretation of one's heritage identification. Those who did not perceive themselves as disadvantaged by previous ethnic management initiatives may be more inclined to echo these initiatives. The group of 5 corporate representatives with a *born-again* enthusiasm of their heritage identification (represented earlier by respondent, Joseph) echoed state discourse in their favor. They reiterated the importance of establishing heritage affinities with China, alongside beliefs that this affinity necessitated the rejection of the West. The group scored an average of 15.6 in Ambiguity Anxiety. While the average score of this *born-again* group was higher than that of the *situational* group, the score average remained lower than that of the non-corporate representatives (16.81).

Another group who similarly did not perceive themselves as "not favored/disfavored" by past ethnic management initiatives enacted a different identification with heritage that appeared much more lukewarm and measured than their "born-again" compatriots. They sought an *integrated* perception of their own heritage as a blend of East (Chinese/Asian/ Singaporean) and West (Anglicized/Westernized/Singaporean) as represented earlier by respondent Bernard. This group of corporate representatives scored a slightly higher AA average of 16.6 than their *born-again* peers. The score was close to the average score of the non-corporate representatives (16.81) and just slightly lower. AA scores and the style of identification with heritage of this group suggests a higher anxiety toward work ambiguity, which resulted in greater exertion of efforts in the attempt to balance all interests of the stakeholders (i.e., both Chinese clients and one's European expatriate colleagues) involved in commercial negotiations.

Respondents who believed their heritage identity was not favored, or was disfavored prior to the Speak Mandarin Campaigns were found to be least optimistic about the potential of the use of heritage, or were the most *resolute* against the use of heritage to lubricate commercial relationships (represented earlier by respondent, Norman). This group also possessed the highest AA scores, which suggests that respondents in this group experienced high levels of anxiety in ambiguous situations. The average AA score of this group was 18.11. The average score of this group was not only the highest in average in this cohort of ECI corporate representatives. This average score was also significantly higher than that of the ECI non-corporate representatives (16.81) and the control group (16.86).

Two factors stood out among this group of corporate representatives. Firstly, AA scores were unusually high, suggesting that respondents in this group preferred the most conservative approaches when faced with ambiguous work scenarios. Secondly, the group unanimously and exclusively expressed the belief that their heritage identity was neglected or negatively stigmatized pre-1980. When asked about the potential of helming leadership positions in either ECI Singapore or the China subsidiary office, optimism was also significantly lower. While respondents in the other groups tended to express optimism in their own upward mobility within the ECI, respondents in this group clustered in the expression of an opposing belief.

The last group of corporate representatives are distinguished in their belief that when intangible elements, such as culture, are allowed to intervene with work, such interventions will most probably work against their favor. For instance, when queried on the reason for the pessimism toward his own career prospects at the ECI, one respondent said:

> "I imagine if I were the senior management in the corporate headquarters, I will be concerned about losing control so it's better to put some of my guys here in the subsidiary" (Shane, respondent).

According to Shane, as the ECI is a Western multinational corporation, trusted senior management can only be Western employees, who were believed to be entitled with the greater right to manage. Here, this perceived "entitlement to manage" was based on the sharing of common cultural heritage among "Westerners." Local employees convinced of their inherent marginality due to distorted notions of "entitlement to manage" tended to feel they possess little stake or control (Li, John and Richter, 2002). One of the commonly employed coping strategies toward marginalization is through the defense mechanism of reversing this disadvantage by likewise excluding Western peers in activities that are believed to be advantageous to locals (Li *et al.*, 2002). Yet, for the *resolute* group (whose respondents had articulated the belief in the follow-up questionnaire that their non-English linguistic primacy had been disfavored/not favored prior to the 1980s Speak Mandarin Campaigns) pessimism pervaded when they encountered situations where the issue of heritage emerged. When expected to make use of their Chinese "advantage" as cultural insiders, the belief that this advantage may be contrived and misconceived seem to haunt the corporate representative who is privately convinced of the disadvantage of being Chinese. For instance, when queried upon their personal efficacy as the arbiters of commercial negotiations between ECI and the Chinese clientele during the in-depth interviews, respondents of this group were convinced that their Western colleagues are more highly valued than themselves when meeting the clients. The pessimism toward their personal efficacy as the cross-cultural arbiters at the ECI extends to views of non-culture related dimensions at work. When asked about their promotion prospects at the ECI, most of them replied that they are not optimistic about their own chances (see Table 1).

As the AA scores demonstrate, corporate representatives who possessed lower inhibitions at tackling intangible, ambiguous issues experienced less challenges at coping with the past state ethnic management discourse. For instance, Joseph, who could be identifiable by the *born-again* enthusiasm toward Chinese heritage, constantly reiterated that he possessed greater customer commitment as a corporate representative than his Western counterparts, as he was operating within his "home-ground." Henry, as with his peers who adopted a *situational* view toward heritage, acknowledged his lack of familiarity with Chinese history, but remained positive that later efforts to "brush up all this knowledge by myself" had allowed him to catch up with the lost time. Kelvin believed

Table 1.   Optimism toward career trajectory by heritage identifications

| | Are you optimistic toward your promotion prospects to top leadership positions at either the ECI (Singapore) or its China subsidiary? | | |
	Yes	No	Total
Situational	6	0	6
Born-again	4	1	5
Integrated	9	1	10
Resolute	3	6	9
Total	22	8	30

that sharing the same Chinese face had already helped him place a foot in the door, and will be helpful for bringing the *integrated* interests of the Western ECI and Chinese clients within a common platform for dialogue. These examples illustrate how coping mechanisms can help to generate positive self-images, in contrast to the *resolute* avoidance of the heritage dimension within the work environment. The next section discusses how race-ethnic identities are reinterpreted with the revival of commercial interest in China.

6. Chineseness Reinterpreted

While ethnic management advertises re-engagement with China through the cultural connection, individual definitions on what comprises heritage affinity vary. In the following we present four typologies of how Chinese-ness is constructed to illustrate how respondents variably interpret their roles as Chinese Singaporean corporate representatives of a Western MNC. It is important to highlight at this point that the illustrations serve only as ideal types. Hence, the profile of corporate representatives that each typol-ogy tends to characterize will be inferred but not specified to avoid deter-ministic associations of a typology with specific profiles. The typologies are termed "Chineseness" as opposed to "Chinese," to express the

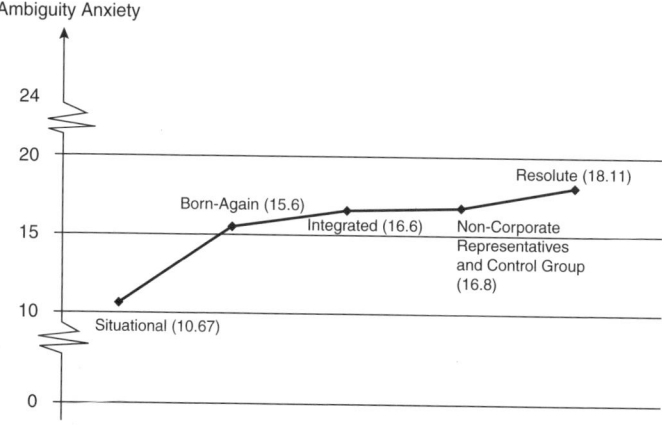

Figure 1. Variable interpretations of Chineseness by ambiguity anxiety scores

situational character of these identifications. The term identification, as opposed to identity, is employed to emphasize the situational manner in which individuals express their perception of what comprises race-ethnic kindred and non-kindred (Wang, 2008). By gaining awareness of how heritage identification is influenced by state ethnic management, the potential for one to fine-tune one's approach is initiated.

Out of 30 corporate representatives, a group of 9 experienced high Ambiguity Anxiety. Their approach was characterized by uncertainty minimization strategies in the resolute resolve to overcome real/perceived discrimination. This form of identification is hence termed *resolute Chineseness*. Professional skills do the talking, and is prioritized over personal concerns toward heritage attachments:

> "Initially when I started, they look at Asians, especially in China, they look at you just like Chinese, the local guys there (i.e., privilege is given to the Westerner). After certain years of dealing with them, in a way, you earn your respect because you really go out all the way to be upfront with them and help them resolve problems, then it's a different story" (Norman, respondent).

On the other end of the continuum is where heritage identification is a matter of *situational Chineseness*. With little appreciation for pre-scribed notions of Chinese heritage, identification with this heritage is a useful commercial tool, free from burdens of heritage fidelity, as with their *situational Englishness*. This group of 6 English-primacy corporate representatives readied themselves to cheer simultaneously for the ingenuity of the Western MNC and/or the buoyancy of the Chinese market. Though their commitment to relationship-building at work is restricted to business, they appeared to be smooth negotiators with the motivation to deliver insofar as there are commercial objectives to achieve:

> "Each company wants to do certain things and they want to do things a certain way. Now if you're in tune with that, by all means, you can be whoever you want — Chinese, Indian — nah, it doesn't matter. You're working for the company, and the company is paying you to push their agenda correct?" (Peter, respondent).

Non-English primacy corporate representatives had higher AA scores across the board than their English-primacy peers. For the English-primacy, an intuitive confidence characterized their responses toward the questions posed to them in this study. The favorable statements made about Anglophones in state discourse, especially during the period where Anglicization policies were instituted in Singapore, may have forged this disposition of confidence. Therefore, the belief that most circumstances, however unpredictable, will unfold in their favor, may be the underpinning factor for the significantly lower AA scores. For the Non-English primacy, scores (although still slightly lower) prevalently converged with those of the non-corporate representatives when compared to the English-primacy. The two groups that fell along this range are the *born-again Chineseness* (5 respondents) and the *integrated Chineseness* (10 respondents). Born to Mandarin/dialect linguistic background families, respondents here adapted to Anglicization imperatives without feeling their race-ethnic identities disfavored. This adaptation-ready attitude had carried them through earlier imperatives, and had proven useful again a decade later with Chinese commercial revivalism. After more than a decade of aggressive Anglicization, the importance of Chinese heritage was broached upon once again by Singapore state leaders, alongside the Speak Mandarin Campaign. For the *born-again Chineseness* group, this change in the nature of state discourse created an enthusiasm to catch up with the lost time. Their strong subscription to Chinese heritage may have raised the ire of the expatriate management, but appeared desired by the Chinese customers:

> "Just recently, I went through so much trouble to get a deal closed and I was calling the China office to reassure them that I have already told the expatriates not to mess up. I told them [the expatriates], 'You mess this one up, you will never make it in China; 100% guarantee'" (Joseph).

The *integrated Chineseness* corporate representatives took to a safer route by refraining from putting all their eggs in one basket. This group actively bridged the multiple interests at work. They bank on their ability to balance multicultural commercial settings without choosing sides. Meantime, as they find themselves caught between cultural cross-fires, they marvel at their own ability to be a part, yet apart:

> "A team from Europe, two Europeans and one China Chinese went to the customer site in China. They [the team] were [onsite] troubleshooting, and suddenly, the Chinese [technical representative from the clientele] decided to delay the progress of the troubleshooting. He told the team, 'You can go back to the hotel and rest. There's a power failure, and when we solve that power failure, we will invite you back.' Even when the China Chinese [representative from ECI] tried to negotiate, they were asked to go back. Then the team called me. I called my contact in China and I told him very specifically, 'We have a problem to deal with, and ECI will deal with it. We cannot agree to such a delay. Our agreement is that we are there for one week, and we have to work. If your people are not prepared to work to solve this problem, I will pull out the whole team immediately.' Then immediately, the problem was solved... I understood later that there were a lot of problems between the Chinese [China] and the Europeans. To solve the [technical] problem was not an issue. As a Singaporean Chinese, I could do it (i.e., not something to be pushed by the European or Chinese corporate representatives)" (Kelvin).

7. Conclusion

This chapter focused on the ethnic management efforts by the Singapore state in the era of 1965–1979, and subsequently from 1980 onwards. In both eras, state ethnic management discourses were characterized by the zealous promotion of one way of cultural identification and conversely, the derogation of alternative worldviews. In 1965–1979, the dichotomous depictions of a modern, rational West and outmoded, irrational East animated specific language policies that sought to establish the English language as the lingua franca. In the 1980s, negative imageries of a strange and exogenous West, and a once estranged yet now re-conjugated China, shaped the approach toward how ECI Chinese Singaporean corporate representatives came to identify themselves with being Chinese. Consequently, heritage identifications came to influence the way the corporate representatives surveyed in our study negotiate(d) the economic landscape. However, the variety of selective re-enactments of the previous state ethnic management discourse suggests that the influence of these state efforts is far from uniform in their effects, with some outcomes that are unintended and enduring.

While it may be argued that most Chinese Singaporeans nevertheless benefitted from these state efforts, the question remains whether there is a need to consider moral justice as a key indicator of success in assessing policy implementations. While outdated policies can always be re-engineered to suit new contexts, the onus of re-adjustment rests upon the individual. Individuals who developed enduring perceptions of marginality may find themselves in a limbo that may be much harder to extricate from than expected. Previous ethnic management initiatives may serve the nation better if promoted without the accompanying punitive undertones.

The four typologies of Chineseness developed and featured in this chapter illustrate the possible varieties emergent from individual interpretations of the imagery presented in the state ethnic management discourse. With this, I hope to bring to attention the political, economic and social implications of social engineering efforts at externally imposing the reinvention of heritage identity for economic objectives.

Firstly, concerted efforts at intervening with the personal cultural identifications of the population may not bear the desired outcomes. Real contexts have too many factors contravening social engineering efforts. This may result in unintended consequences with social costs that need to be borne decades later by the state and/or the society.

Secondly, companies seeking a monolithic Chinese identity to be used to lubricate commercial relationships in the one way they believe these relationships should be conducted are likely going to be disappointed most of the time. Perhaps in their efforts to tap into the regional awareness of their "local managers," Western MNCs should trust more in the ability of their local scouts at negotiating the commercial terrain in a variety of ways that may or may not conform to stereotypical expectations.

Thirdly, social engineering policies tend to prioritize economic imperatives over the individual will to construct social identifications that may be more personally meaningful. When identities are externally imposed and changed at the whim of economic fads, the individual becomes estranged from one's sense of self. As demonstrated in this study, an estranged social self not only affects the way one engages socially, but also economically. Top decision-makers may appear to succeed at re-inventing ethnic identifications according to economic imperatives on the surface. In the process, the divestment of the individual will to social identifications by the state may also create a weakened human capital, with limited capacity to produce the desired economic returns. The problem may be resolved by relying on imported talent, which of course, creates more social problems that will require attention in yet another few decades to come.

References

Bourdieu, P (1979). Symbolic power. *Critique of Anthropology,* 13(14), 77–85.

Chan, KB and C Chiang (1994). *Stepping out: The Making of Chinese Entrepreneurs.* Singapore: Prentice Hall.

Daniels, H, J Leadbetter, A Soares and N MacNab (2007). Learning in and for cross-school working. CHAT Technical Reports 1, pp. 45–72.

Fitzgerald, CP (1969). *The Third China: The Chinese Communists in Southeast Asia.* Australia: Donald Moore Press.

Goh, CT (2002). Prime Minister's National Day Rally: Speech in English.

Hofstede, G (2001). *Culture's Consequences: Comparing Values, Behaviors, Institutions, and Organizations across Nations.* Thousand Oaks, CA: Sage Publications.

Hu, G (2008). The misleading academic discourse on Chinese–English bilingual education in China. *Review of Educational Research,* 78(2), 195–231.

Kraar, L (1996). Need a friend in Asia? Try the Singapore connection. *Fortune,* 4, 86–95.

Kwan-Terry, A (1991). Child language development in Singapore and Malaysia. In *Home Language and School Language: A Study of Children's Language Use in Singapore,* A Kwan-Terry (ed.). Singapore: Singapore University Press.

Lazarus, RS (1991). Cognition and motivation in emotion. *American Psychologist,* 46(4), 352–367.

Lee, BY (2003). Speech by Dr Lee Boon Yang, Minister for Information, Communications and the Arts, Official Launch of the Speak Mandarin Campaign, September 23, 2003.

Lee, HL (2004). Prime Minister's National Day Rally: Speech in English.

Lee, KY (2004). Speech by Senior Minister Mr Lee Kuan Yew, International Conference on National Boundaries and Cultural Configurations, 10th Anniversary Celebration of the Center for Chinese Language and Culture, Nanyang Technological University, June 23, 2004.

Li, XK, B John and F-J Richter (2002). The realization of meanings: Understanding expatriates' needs in the Asian post-crisis environment. In *Asian Post-crisis Management: Corporate and Government Strategies for Sustainable Competitive Advantage,* UCV Haley and F-J Richter (eds.), pp. 102–134. New York: Palgrave.

Rubdy, R, SL McKay, L Alsagoff and WD Bokhorst-Heng (2008). Enacting English language ownership in the outer circle: A study of Singaporean Indians' orientations to English norms. *World Englishes,* 27(1), 40–67.

Silver, RE, G Hu and M Iino (2002). *English Language Education in China, Japan, and Singapore.* Singapore: National Institute of Education.

Wang, G (2008). Chinese history paradigms. Paper presented at the International Conference "Chineseness Unbound: Boundaries, Burdens and Belongings of Chineseness Outside China," Asia Research Institute (ARI), National University of Singapore.

Yeo, G (2004). Speech by George Yeo, Minister for Trade and Industry, The Singapore Business Awards, March 25, 2004.

Chapter 3

Managing Change in Asian Business: A Comparison between Chinese-Educated and English-Educated Chinese Entrepreneurs in Singapore

Thomas Menkhoff, Ulrike Badibanga and Chay Yue Wah

1. Introduction

Most enterprises operating in Asia are small and medium-sized (family) firms (Chong, 1987; Buchholt and Menkhoff, 1996; Tsui-Auch, 2004; Menkhoff and Chay, 2006). Their economic success has often been attributed to the so-called "Chinese cultural heritage."

> "There is a worldwide recognition that ethnic Chinese, wherever they have sunk new roots, have contributed significantly to the wealth of their adoptive lands and in the process, to nation-building. They were able to overcome severe odds and difficulties through thrift, hard work, perseverance, tolerance, and above all, their entrepreneurial spirit — which constitute part of the core values of the Chinese cultural heritage." (Encounter, Singapore Chinese Chamber of Commerce and Industry). Since the Asian economic crisis, culture-centric explanations of Chinese business behavior have been replaced by an alternative proposition according to which cultural factors alone are inadequate in

This is a reprint of an article originally published in 2007 in *The Copenhagen Journal of Asian Studies* (Special Issue "In the Shadow of Mainland China: Changing Ethnic Chinese Business Practices in Southeast Asia"), 25, 50–73. The editors gratefully acknowledge the permission to reprint the essay in this edition.

understanding the organizational peculiarities and economic (success) patterns of Chinese business. The 1997–1999 crisis served as a reminder that the economic behavior of these entrepreneurs, is also determined to a large extent by social, economical and political factors in each of their respective host countries as well as external factors (Lasserre, 1988, p. 117; Vasil, 1995; Menkhoff, 1998, p. 253; Chan and Ng, 2001; Menkhoff and Gerke eds., 2002; Tsui-Auch and Lee, 2003; Tan ed., 2006).

Previous explanations to this situation, which highlight the cultural traits of ethnic Chinese in Asia, arguably imply that ethnic Chinese entrepreneurs are members of a homogenous group of people. This is clearly not the case as evidenced by the dichotomy of "Chinese-educated" and "English-educated" Chinese. The implications of the above will be spelled out in this chapter with reference to the Republic of Singapore (Kwok, 1998). In the case of Singapore with its Chinese majority, it is interesting to note that Chinese small and medium sized enterprises arguably played a secondary role in the city-state's rapid economic development after it had become independent in 1965. The success of Singapore has mainly been attributed to the strategy of the leading People's Action Party (PAP), whose aim was to develop the country with the help of multi-national corporations (MNCs) based on export-led growth (Low, 1999).

British colonial rule represented a strong pull factor for the migration of ethnic Chinese to Singapore. At the end of the 20th century, the percentage of Chinese descendants represented over 70 percent of the total population. Due to the structure of the colonial school system, a certain section of the Chinese population attended schools where English was used as the main medium of instruction. The rest, initially the majority but subsequently the minority, attended Chinese schools at least till the late 1980s (Pakir, 1991). This situation led to internal challenges. The government, the majority of which were English-educated intellectuals and professionals, focused its post-independence (1965) economic development strategies on the demands of MNCs and government-linked companies (GLCs). At least until the recession in the mid 1980s, the small indigenous private business sector — of which the majority was Chinese-educated — did not gain much prominence (Low, 1999; Ng, 2002). However, this situation changed drastically after the recession in the 1990s, when numerous SME friendly initiatives and policies were introduced to encourage the development of local enterprises (Bjerke, 1998).

Policymakers have realized that local SMEs represent the backbone of the national economy and that they need help to master the transition to a knowledge-based economy, a key strategic goal of Singapore's government. All this requires the modernization of traditional structures and mindsets which explains why the topic of this chapter, namely organizational change management, is so important in Singapore's business and society (MTI, 1998; Tsui-Auch, 2003; Hussey, 2005; Pfeffer, 2005).

Against the background of a very dynamic business environment and rapid external change, the study is aimed at analyzing how local SMEs cope with these demands and requirements. The core objective is to ascertain empirically whether there is a difference between the change management (CM) behavior of Chinese and English-educated (Chinese) business people in Singapore or not, and to examine possible reasons. Theoretically, the study is informed by (i) Child's strategic choice theory (1972, 1997) which puts primary importance on the ability of business managers and leaders to embrace change proactively, relating differences in managerial decision-making processes and approaches to individual cognitive reference frameworks and (ii) the emerging theory of Chinese enterprise management (Tong and Yong, 1997; Gomez and Hsiao eds., 2001; Menkhoff and Gerke eds., 2002; Yao, 2002; Yeung, 2004) that postulates more or less substantial differences between "traditional Chinese" and "modern Western" management methods. In the context of Singapore, differences that have developed historically between Chinese and English-educated businessmen within the Chinese community with regard to their management behavior (Chong, 1987; Lau, 1999; Ng, 2001), are also theoretically important.

From this, it is perhaps necessary to ask what the social-cultural and political implications and dimensions of the difference between Chinese and English-educated Chinese people are in Singapore (Badibanga, 2002). As far as Singapore is concerned, there is the widespread perception that Chinese and English-educated Chinese have different cultural values and world views which is often explained with reference to their different upbringings and educational paths. As has been stated:

> "Generally, the Chinese-educated regarded the English-educated as arrogant, open, modern, Westernized and easygoing. The English-educated thought of the Chinese-educated as conservative, parochial, chauvinistic, politicized (as in the 1940s and 1950s) and hard-working" (Lau, 1999, p. 201).

Despite mutual stereotypes and prejudices, hardly any empirical evidence can be found about the differences between the two groups. In fact, there is a dearth of empirical research studies on the subject, which is somewhat surprising given the latent interest conflicts between both groups as evidenced by historical reflections and the renewed interest in Singapore's "Chinese ground" (*Straits Times*). Possibly a key factor in this respect is the heritage of the insufficiently integrated colonial school system with its different language orientations.

Since Singapore's early days, English and Chinese-educated Chinese developed certain (often contrary) stereotypical perceptions of each other, which was arguably manifested in different lifestyles and consumption habits caused by different cultural programmings (Lau, 1999; Siddique, 2004). Subsequently, diverging political interests and social class disparities emerged. In the 1920s, this mental divide became even bigger and politically disruptive, due to the rise of nationalism that ignited an intense interest in Chinese education. At the same time, there was a steep increase in the dissemination of communist ideologies and political movements in several Chinese schools (i.e., those where Chinese was used the main medium of instruction), which resulted in discriminating sanctions imposed by the ruling British colonial government. Social class differences along language lines began to harden, as it was easier for the English-educated to secure a job in the civil service (and later in MNCs) due to their language competence (Tan, 1996). Consequently, many Chinese-educated Chinese found employment in independent micro-enterprises and SMEs. They were also known as the "reluctant entrepreneurs." In 1965 when Singapore became independent, the ruling elite consisted primarily of English-educated professionals, yet a large proportion of Singapore's Chinese population was Chinese-educated.

As far as the current situation in Singapore's SME sector is concerned (Tan, Tan and Young, 2000), the research was guided by the following broad assumptions: (a) Chinese-educated entrepreneurs form the majority of all SME managers; (b) they are generally older and have a lower educational level than English-educated entrepreneurs; (c) as argued by some key informants, Chinese and English-educated Chinese entrepreneurs can be differentiated according to their "traditional Chinese" (i.e., Chinese-educated) and "modern-Western" (i.e., English-educated) managerial behavior (see Table 1).

Exploratory research questions included:

1. Are there differences between Chinese and English-educated businessmen when it comes to strategic decisions on whether or not to initiate organizational change measures? If yes, in what ways? If not, why not? What is the implication of this dichotomy with regard to change management approaches (see Section 3.4)?
2. What is the implication of this dichotomy with regard to change management approaches in general?
3. Do Chinese-educated businessmen adopt more traditional (Chinese) management and organizational practices when it comes to change management (e.g., unsystematic, muddling through approaches) while English-educated businessmen use more modern, Western change management methods? If yes, how can such differences (if any) be explained?

2. Methodology

There is hardly any empirical material available in Singapore, which can shed light on the change management behavior of small firms and possible differences between Chinese and English-educated business people. There is also limited literature concerning the socio-economic dynamics and specifics of Chinese and English-educated ethnic Chinese (Pakir, 1991; Kwok, 1998; Lau, 1999). To tackle these issues, the research was focused on firstly literature reviews and secondly, qualitative interviews with entrepreneurs, management consultants and representatives from monetary institutions and academics. Through these interviews, some general hypotheses were generated. The majority of the interviewees were identified with the help of the Singapore Chinese Chamber of Commerce & Industry (SCCCI) and the Singapore Institute of Management Consultants. The study employed a questionnaire survey of a population of Singapore SMEs found on the register of membership in the Singapore Chinese Chamber of Commerce and Industry and across industries and business type. As Singapore SMEs are reluctant to respond to surveys, the authors employed both postal and face-to-face interviews to secure completion of the research. The SMEs were randomly selected from the membership data-base. A team of research assistants then followed up this initial research with phone calls to secure their cooperation.

The final survey form (questionnaire) was divided into the following sections: (i) demographics of respondent, (ii) business characteristics, (iii) organizational change (iv) personality traits, (v) firm performance, and (vi) external management consultants. Two versions of the survey questionnaire (English and Chinese) with mostly closed questions were developed. To ensure the survey was easy to understand, different pilot tests were conducted. As indicated above, the initial response rate was very disappointing. We finally managed to obtain a sample of 101 SMEs. This is a notable sample size considering the disclosure reservations of Chinese entrepreneurs.

The SMEs surveyed were represented by the following sectors: manufacturing (28.7 percent), commerce (23.8 percent), professional services (20.8 percent), retail (8.9 percent) and other sectors (17.6 percent). The SME criterion used in the study corresponds to the definition used by Singapore's Economic Development Board (EDB):

- 30 percent local ownership;
- fixed assets investments (FAI) of less than S$15 million;
- employment size of less than 200 (less than 500 in manufacturing)

Quantitative data analyses were conducted with the help of SPSS based on descriptive analyses, using Chi-Square tests and correlation measures such as Cramer's V-coefficient.

3. Theoretical Framework

In view of the contested issue of Chinese enterprise management (Gomez and Hsiao, 2001) with its various schools of thought such as the so-called "culturalists" (Redding, 1993) or the "revisionists" (Yao, 2002), it is perhaps pertinent to stress that both "oversocialized" and "undersocialized" perspectives of economic action (Granovetter, 1985) are important business behavior of ethnic Chinese in Asia (see Menkhoff and Gerke eds., 2002). In terms of theorizing Chinese change management behavior, this chapter attempts to build a case for a contingent institutional perspective (Clegg, 1990, pp. 150–151; Tong and Yong, 1997) which ties both cultural and market forces together. Such an approach rests on the belief that both organizational forms and management behavior reflect what Tong and Yong have termed "institutional belief systems" and individual cognitive reference frameworks, which can enable or constrict action (Child, 1972, 1997). Such an approach also considers the importance of history, which is often ignored by market and even cultural approaches.

Tong (1996) has compared the "typical" centralized organizational characteristics of Chinese enterprises with the concept of "centripetal authority." Often, the company founder is also the owner and manager. The decision process is centralized around the owner and a core group of family members. There is a low degree of delegation of authority or responsibility because information pertaining to the company is usually considered a trade secret and distributed solely among the close employees (usually the family members). The organization structure is informal. The management of Chinese family enterprise has been described as — in analogy to the traditional Chinese family system — as paternalistic, personal and authoritative (Tong and Yong, 1997; Chong, 1987, p. 136). The employer has obligations *vis-à-vis* his or her employees in return for their respect and loyalty. For example, he/she will ensure the well-being of employees, which could include influencing aspects of their private lives. Selective (paternalistic) remunerations in the form of certain privileges or monetary gifts are used as management instruments, which may lead to vast internal differences between employees and negative group dynamics (Herrmann-Pillath, 1997, p. 116). Chinese entrepreneurs typically believe that they are well informed. This over-confidence (Herrmann-Pillath, 1997, p. 117) may explain why decisions are often made intuitively and why systematic strategic planning is sometimes neglected. Relationships (*guanxi*) are paramount for business initiations as the trustworthiness of a business partner is of the highest priority. Oral

Table 1.   Comparison of "traditional Chinese" and "modern Western"

Organization and Management	Traditional Chinese	Modern Western
	Family-owned	Various forms of ownership
Ownership Structure	Owner is usually director of company	Professional management/ directors
Leadership Style	Authoritative	Participative
Planning	Intuitive	Strategic
Decision Making	Centralized with minimum participation	Decentralized, participation and delegation
Information Management	Information is considered as a secret/little information and knowledge sharing	More systematic information sharing
Staff Development/ Training	No proper staff development/concern that "well-trained" employees might leave the company Low budget for training	Training is seen as a form of investment into human capital Relatively large budget for training and development
Change Management	Not handled systematically as it is not seen as an area of great concern (muddling through)	More awareness that change is imperative and that CM should be based on a systematic approach

Sources: Lassere (1988); Redding (1993); Menkhoff (1993); Tong (1996); Hermann-Pillath (1997); Anderson Consulting & Economist Intelligence Unit (2000); Menkhoff and Gerke (2002).

agreements are seen as equivalent to contractual ones, particularly among the older generation.

   This partly explains the important role of middlemen and networks as well as (in)formal interest groups in the Chinese business community, as this guarantees, more or less, a "moral" code of business behavior and the honouring of business deals (Chan and Ng, 2000, p. 291). Another reason for the importance of trust, middlemen and networks, is the hostile (institutional) environment in Asia in which Chinese entrepreneurs traditionally had to do business (Redding, 1993; Menkhoff, 1993; Tan, 2000; Menkhoff and Gerke eds., 2002).

3.1 *Organizational and management characteristics*

Table 1 illustrates potential differences between a typical "traditional Chinese organization and management style" compared to a more "modern Western corporate approach." It can be argued that these characteristics have implications for the respective change management practices of Chinese and English-educated entrepreneurs.

Child's (1972, 1997) strategic choice theory represents a suitable analytical framework for the study for two reasons: (i) it complements the theory of Chinese business as it puts an emphasis on the role of the organization's top decision-maker(s) in change processes and their network contacts; (ii) it highlights the cognitive framework of individual actors *vis-à-vis* the historical dimension and dichotomy of Chinese and English-educated Chinese business people and their potentially different CM approaches.

A key proposition of the Strategic Choice perspective is that top organizational decision-makers have a significant influence on the strategic direction and associated change/adaptation processes of their organization. Respective individual decision processes are influenced by several factors such as action determinism and the individual cognitive reference framework, access to relevant, distinct and complete information and internal political processes.

While political processes within organizations are difficult to examine, it is relatively easier to examine the cognitive reference frameworks of corporate decision-makers that represent potential core antecedents (or barriers) of organizational change measures. According to Child, the cognitive reference framework also influences the interpretation of information as well as competence in information processing (provided that information is accessible at all in adequate form). Important cognitive variables include one's own ideology and demographic traits:

"... that decision-makers' cognitive evaluations of the situation would be shaped by their 'prior ideology,' and this drew attention to the ways that class, occupational and national socialization may shape managerial beliefs about action choices" (Child, 1997, p. 51).

"The 'demography' of top management teams, such as the age and educational level of their members, has also been found to exert an influence on the extent to which companies initiate strategic change […]. Age and education, although they locate people within social categories which can generate common identities and beliefs, are likely to affect action determinism not only though the medium of ideology but also through competence. Thus, other things being equal, one would expect a young, highly educated person to be more aware of and/or to seek out a wider range of action alternatives than would an older, poorly educated person" (Child, 1997, p. 51).

Regarding the meaning of the information used in the decision making process, Child said:

"Action determinism can lead to an unwillingness to consider information that does not fit preconceived ideas, but the scarcity of information as a resource can also inhibit the range of choices considered. There are two issues to note here. The first concerns the problem of securing relevant information that is timely, in an analyzable form and not prohibitively expensive. The second concerns the problem of coping with information that is ambiguous, of questionable reliability and incomplete. Decision making, especially of the non-routine kind considered within strategic choice analysis, is thus liable to be conducted with uncertainty" (Child, 1997, p. 52).

Both Chinese business theory and strategic choice theory provide conceptual tools for addressing the primary concerns of the study as specified above (see Research Questions) and in form of the model below.

4. Research Model

As illustrated in the research model (see Figure 1), the individual cognitive reference framework of managers was put into operation as follows. The variable Chinese versus English-educated is regarded as a sort of proxy for the overriding ideology in line with Child's ideas while the variables age and educational level represent key demographic characteristics. In addition, two control variables were looked at in relation to the CM behavior of the surveyed managers, namely information measured by examining whether research subjects participated in a CM training and the size of the organization in terms of number of employees. These

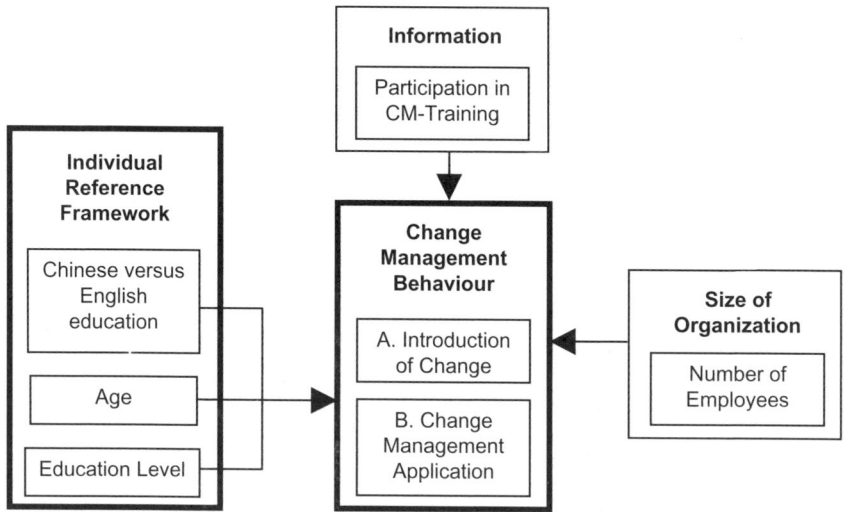

Figure 1. Research model: Individual reference framework and control variables, information and size of organization as influencing factors of CM behavior

5 variables were also investigated with regard to their relationship to the CM behavior of the surveyed managers. As far as the CM behavior is concerned, the research distinguishes between two factors.

(A) Initiation of Change — with the independent variables introduction of change (yes/no) as well as the targets (or objects) of change measures: organizational structure, systems and work processes, technology, people (including task behaviors), organization culture, and organizational strategy.

(B) CM Approach — with the corresponding variables as well as scale of change measure (e.g., reactive vs. anticipative change), degree of planning the change measure before the start of implementation, resistance toward change, urgency of change, change leadership style, evaluation of change benefits and ability to overcome resistance to change.

The study tried to understand and evaluate the relationship between the variables Chinese versus English-educated and the actual change measures (in terms of number, scale of change and so on) adopted by the SME owner-managers as well as internal and external forces of change.

4.1 *Hypotheses*

H1: There is a significant relationship between the variable Chinese versus English-educated and the initiation of organizational change in ethnic Chinese small- and medium-sized enterprises (SMEs) in Singapore.

The chapter argues that English-educated Chinese SME owner-managers are more likely to initiate change measures than their Chinese-educated counterparts (H1a), that they do this with regard to a larger number of change targets (H1b), and that there is a clear difference between both groups with regard to the actual change measures (H1c) implemented.

H2: Chinese- and English-educated Chinese SME owner-managers differ in terms of their Change Management approaches.

The research expected significant differences between both groups with regard to *people-oriented* change initiatives. In particular, it was expected that Chinese-educated SME owner-managers hardly ever initiate changes concerning (enhanced) training and development measures, (improved) information flows as well as (greater) participation. Furthermore, the research expected differences with regard to the assessment of the forces of change, resistance to change initiatives and success in overcoming these barriers.

H3: Chinese-educated Chinese SME owner-managers have a tendency to adhere to "traditional Chinese" management and organization techniques, while English-educated managers tend to adopt "modern-Western" ones.

It was expected that there is a *positive* association between being English-educated and change management related variables such as the number of people-related organizational changes, the scale of such changes in terms of (enhanced) training and development, (improved) information flows and (greater) participation, a larger degree of planning and control, a higher perceived urgency for change, a larger magnitude of change, and a more participatory leadership style. Consequently, *negative* associations between being Chinese-educated and the variables above were expected. Furthermore, it can be argued that being Chinese-educated is positively associated with *reactive* change, while English-educated business people embrace change more *proactively*.

5. Research Findings

5.1 *Demographic characteristics of SME owner-managers*

The average Chinese-educated businessman surveyed was 47 years old, male and tended to have a secondary or tertiary education. English-educated business people averaged 41 years old, male and tended to have a tertiary education (see Table 2 as well as Figures 2 and 3 in the Appendix). As expected, the Chinese-educated businessmen in the sample were older and significantly lower educated than their English-educated counterparts.

5.2 *Control variables*

Only a fifth of the managers in both groups had participated in a CM-related training measure. The majority of the surveyed businessmen had less than 50 employees (see Table 2).

Table 2. Frequencies of selected variables

	Frequencies of selected independent variables	Frequencies of control variables for Chinese- vs. English educated owner-managers	
Chinese- vs. English educated	Chinese educated: 40 percent English educated: 60 percent	Chinese-educated	English-educated
Age	≤42 years: 49 percent >42 years: 51 percent	≤42 years: 34 percent >42 years: 66 percent	≤42 years: 60 percent >42 years: 40 percent
Educational Level	Primary/Secondary: 30 percent Junior College/University 70 percent	Pr/Sec: 40 percent JC/Uni: 60 percent	Pr/Sec: 20 percent JC/Uni: 80 percent
CM-Training	Participated: 20 percent Not participated: 80 percent	Yes: 20 percent No: 80 percent	Yes: 20 percent No: 80 percent
Size of Enterprise	≤50 employees: 75 percent >50 employees: 25 percent	≤50 employees: 70 percent >50 employees: 30 percent	≤50 employees: 80 percent >50 employees: 20 percent

5.3 Typical characteristics of SMEs

Except for the year the company was founded, there were hardly any differences between both groups as far as company characteristics are concerned. The typical SME in the sample was a private limited company (Pte Ltd) in which 90 percent of the managers had stakes. External investors beyond the family circle were almost non-existent. The majority of the SMEs employed less than 50 employees. In almost two-thirds of all cases, the annual income in the reporting year was more than five (5) million Singapore dollars. Chinese-educated business people had typically established their own enterprises in the mid 1970s. The main activity, which accounted for almost a third of the enterprises, was manufacturing, followed by trade or professional services. English-educated Chinese businessmen had typically established their firms in the early 1980s. Main activities, comprising almost a third of the businesses, were professional service provision, followed by manufacturing and trade.

5.4 Frequency distribution for initiation of change

The data indicate that English-educated Chinese SME owner-managers initiate change more often than their Chinese-educated counterparts.

In total, 89 percent of the English-educated SME owner-managers had initiated change measures compared to 77 percent of the Chinese-educated ones. However, significant differences emerged only in terms of the quantity of change initiatives. 76 percent of the English-educated SME owner-managers reported that they had implemented 4–6 percent change initiatives compared to 49 percent of their Chinese-educated counterparts (see Figure 4).

5.5 Frequency distribution for CM-approach

With regard to the type of change, 19 percent of the Chinese-educated and 10 percent of the English-educated SME owner-managers, stated that their change measures were of a reactive nature. The rest claimed that they had

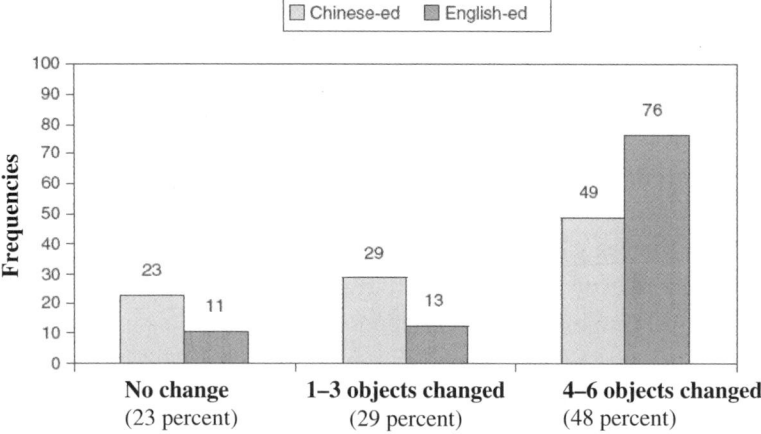

Figure 4. Quantity of change measures initiated by Chinese-educated vs. English-educated SME owner-managers

implemented proactive as well as reactive change management practices in anticipation of future prospects or risks.

About 60 percent of the Chinese-educated businessmen had embarked on a detailed planning exercise before the start of the implementation, compared to 70 percent of the English-educated respondents. 70 percent of the Chinese-educated SME had experienced little resistance, as compared to 63 percent of the English-educated ones. Both groups rated the urgency of change as high (70 percent).

60 percent of the surveyed Chinese-educated businessmen assessed the nature of the change measures implemented as incremental, as opposed to 40 percent who felt that it was radical in nature (the percentages were 80 percent and 20 percent for the English-educated subjects respectively).

Surprisingly, 74 percent of the Chinese-educated SME owner-managers stated that they had adopted a participatory leadership style and 80 percent of them felt that they had been successful in their change efforts (compared to 65 percent and 70 percent respectively of the English-educated business people).

About 60 percent of the interviewed SME owner-managers in both groups felt that they had been successful in overcoming barriers to change.

5.6 *People-related change measures and forces of change*

Almost 90 percent of the surveyed entrepreneurs in both groups reported that they had introduced between 7 and 9 people-related changes. The majority (70 percent in each group) initiated change measures such as *more intense consultation with employees, stronger participation of employees in decision-making and wage increases*. However, other potential change measures, such as the introduction of a stock option scheme and profit sharing, turned out to be irrelevant. There was one important difference between both groups: English-educated Chinese SME owner-managers felt very strongly that more consultation with employees is critical. As the survey data show they had implemented respective measures significantly more often (Cramer's $V = 0.3$; $p = 0.04$) than their Chinese-educated counterparts.

Both groups assessed the internal forces of change impacting upon their businesses as important and critical, but showed pronounced differences with regard to the evaluation of the magnitude of external forces of change.

5.7 *Key results*

H1: partially verified

English-educated Chinese SME owner-managers turned out to be more active initiators of change measures compared to their Chinese-educated counterparts (Cramer's $V = 0.16$; $p = 0.13$) as they had implemented significantly more change measures (Cramer's $V = 0.29$; $p = 0.03$).

H2: partially verified

People-related change measures initiated by both groups turned out to be quite similar in terms of quantity and type. However, English-educated managers perceived stronger consultation with employees as a critical change measure in contrast to Chinese-educated business people (Cramer's $V = 0.3$; $p = 0.04$). While the surveyed managers viewed the impact of the internal forces of change on their businesses in a similar way, external forces of change were evaluated differently, especially with regard to the changing economic and trading conditions as well as distribution patterns.

No important differences were found regarding the barriers to change and the degree of success in overcoming such hurdles.

H3: not supported

Statistically relevant differences between both groups with regard to their respective CM approaches could not be established. The change management data indicate, that there is no empirical support for the argument that Chinese-educated Chinese SME owner-managers adhere to more "traditional Chinese" management and organizational techniques, while English-educated managers employ "modern Western" ones when it comes to people-related change, the scale of change, planning intensity or the magnitude of change.

5.8 Central results for demographic and control variables

A strong (anticipated) relationship between age and the initiation of change measures could not be established. Regarding the CM approach, however, age mattered as older managers, in particular, had developed a detailed plan before the implementation of the change measure (Cramer's $V = 0.35$, $p \leq 0.01$). They also rated the urgency of change higher than younger businessmen. In addition, the more experienced businessmen stated that they were more successful in overcoming barriers to change compared with their younger counterparts.

There was also no significant correlation between the educational levels of the surveyed SME owner-managers and the initiation of change variable. With respect to the actual change measures implemented, however, the data analysis revealed that entrepreneurs with higher educational levels had more often initiated changes in the area of employees and their task performance than managers with lower educational levels. With regard to the CM approach, the survey showed that managers with lower educational levels had initiated a significantly higher extent of change measures in their organizations (Cramer's $V = 0.29$; $p \leq 0.01$). The data also suggest that managers with higher educational levels exercise a more participatory style of change leadership.

As far as the relationship between the size of the enterprise and the initiation of change is concerned, managers of large enterprises turned out to be more active initiators of change measures than leaders of smaller firms. Moreover, there were differences concerning the actual change targets and initiatives implemented. In large enterprises, people-related change measures were more profound (Cramer's $V = 0.3$, $p \leq 0.01$).

No statistically relevant relationship could be established between any participation in CM training and the initiation of change. However, there were significant relationships as far as the actual change targets and measures are concerned. Participants of CM training measures had initiated significantly more change measures with regard to organizational structures (Cramer's $V = 0.22$, $p \leq 0.05$), systems and work processes (Cramer's $V = 0.24$, $p \leq 0.05$) as well as employees and their task performance (Cramer's $V = 0.27$, $p \leq 0.025$) than non-participants. A similar trend could be established with regard to technology related change measures.

Up-to-date and clear-cut information, i.e., formal knowledge of CM, turned out to be very crucial for the chosen CM approach. Participation in CM training was related to almost all CM approach variables, except for urgency of change and extent of change. Participants of CM training measures had conducted significantly more change impact studies than non-participants (Cramer's $V = 0.29$, $p \leq 0.01$). They were also significantly more successful in overcoming barriers to change (Cramer's $V = 0.32$, $p \leq 0.01$). With regard to the nature and type of change initiatives, the study revealed that CM participants in particular had initiated proactive, anticipative change measures based on detailed plans and a more participatory change leadership style. Contrary to non-participants, they also experienced fewer barriers to change and claimed to be more successful in overcoming barriers to change.

6. Summary and Conclusions

The assumption that English-educated Chinese SME owner-managers are more likely to initiate change measures than Chinese-educated (H1) was partially verified. The same is true for H2, i.e., the assumption that there are differences between both groups with regard to their CM approach. In contrast, H3, i.e., the assumption that potential differences between both groups with regard to their CM behavior can be traced back to cultural specifics (e.g., in terms of their "traditional Chinese" and/or more "modern-Western" managerial orientation), could not be ascertained. In fact, the study found contradictory statistical trends and percentage differences for some variables, e.g., in the form of Chinese-educated Chinese business leaders with (for us surprisingly) democratic change leadership styles.

With regard to the research model, the results of the study can be summarized as follows. There is a relationship between the individual cognitive frame of reference of SME owner-managers and the initiation of change. The variable Chinese versus English-educated does play a central role, and more empirical research is needed to examine its business implications. As far as the CM approach related variables are concerned, age and education turned out to be of significant importance (they mattered less in terms of the initiation of change). There were also close connections between the control variables and the initiation of change with company size playing a key role. Information and participation in CM training measures were closely related to all CM-approach related variables.

The difficulty still lies in explaining why H3 was not supported. One reason might be the biased sample structure with regard to age (one-sided age distribution; 70 percent of the participants were in the age group 35–45 years), the high education and language proficiency of the respondents; many of the younger entrepreneurs sampled are probably bilingual due to the implementation of bilingualism in Singapore's education system a few years ago. Another possibility is that time contingencies may have reduced possible differences between both groups and that there is a convergence of styles (Triandis and Gelfand, 1998; Hornidge, 2004; Quinn Mills, 2005; Yeung, 2006).

Due to the significant relationship between the variable participation in CM training and the CM behavior of the survey participants, as well as their different assessments of the external forces of change, it can be argued that differentiating Chinese and English-educated SMEs is less relevant as a result of an overriding ideology which influences their individual frames of reference. However, it does matter when it comes to getting access to crucial information resources, depending on the dominant language used. In the context of change management and business, access to modern English business media, the integration in regional/global network relations and/or professional change management expertise from consultants are crucial. Further research is necessary to substantiate this argument. With regard to this, future research would expand the analytical range of Strategic Choice Theory in the area of CM by incorporating group-specific information gathering strategies and their effects.

Due to the lack of representative data and comparison opportunities with other research, the survey has the character of an explorative baseline study. A generalization of the results is not possible without further research. One tentative conclusion is that there are differences in the CM-behavior of Chinese and English-educated Chinese business people in Singapore. In firms owned and managed by Chinese-educated business individuals, the type of change seems to be more reactive; the planning of change is at times rather unsystematic; the nature of change more incremental and the change leadership approach surprisingly participatory. Despite this, all these differences are less pronounced than commonly expected. Cultural specifics of the two groups play — at least statistically — no visible role in their CM-behavior. While the results contradict the perceptions of many local interviewees, businessmen and academics, they are in line with the arguments of contemporary Chinese management researchers who contend that culturally based explanations are insufficient in accounting for the business practices of ethnic Chinese entrepreneurs (Tong and Yong, 1997; Chan and Ng, 2000; Menkhoff and Gerke eds., 2002; Yao, 2002; Yeung, 2006). The data emphasize the dynamics and rapid modernization of SMEs in Singapore.

Most important for a better understanding of sub-ethnic dimensions in the CM-behavior of Singapore's ethnic Chinese SMEs, appears to be the role and meaning of information. The survey data suggest that both groups have different sources of retrieving information and that English-educated entrepreneurs possess an advantage over Chinese-educated businessmen through their relatively easier access to international media and networks. Therefore, future "CM studies in the Chinese business world" that intend to utilize Child's strategic choice framework should expand the analytical scope beyond the cognitive reference framework of actors by examining structure and function of "Chinese" information and knowledge management approaches (Menkhoff, Evers and Chay eds., 2005; Menkhoff, Pang and Evers, 2007). China's rise and its implications for the competitive edge of Singapore's new Chinese ground whether they are bilingual and passionate about Chinese culture or "fair-weather Chinese" (i.e., English speakers who are rediscovering their roots, including speaking Mandarin and often driven by economic motives) represent other interesting topics for future research.

Appendix

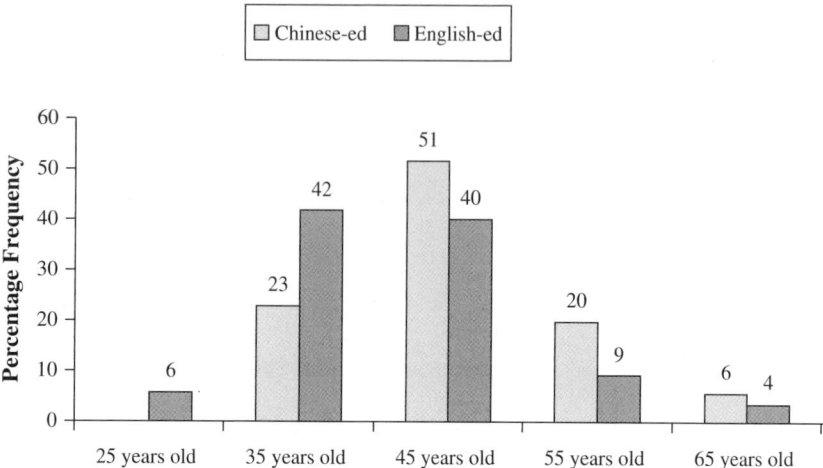

Figure 2. Age distribution of Chinese-educated and English-educated SME owner-managers

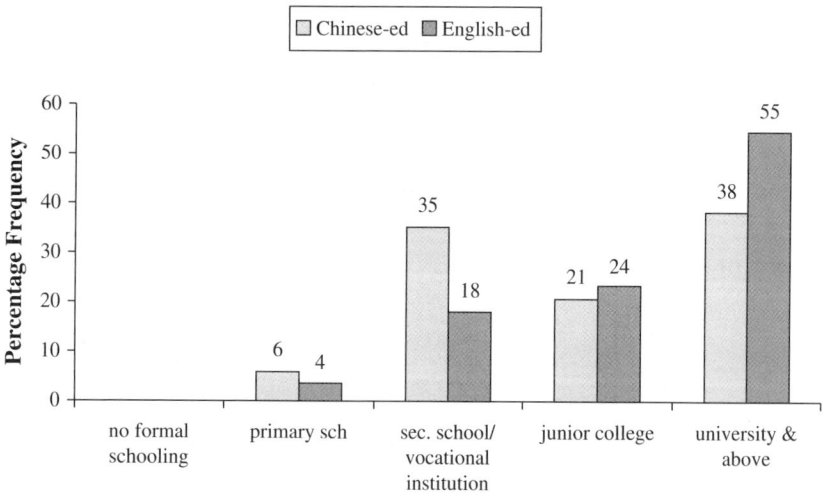

Figure 3. Highest attained educational qualification of Chinese-educated and English-educated business people

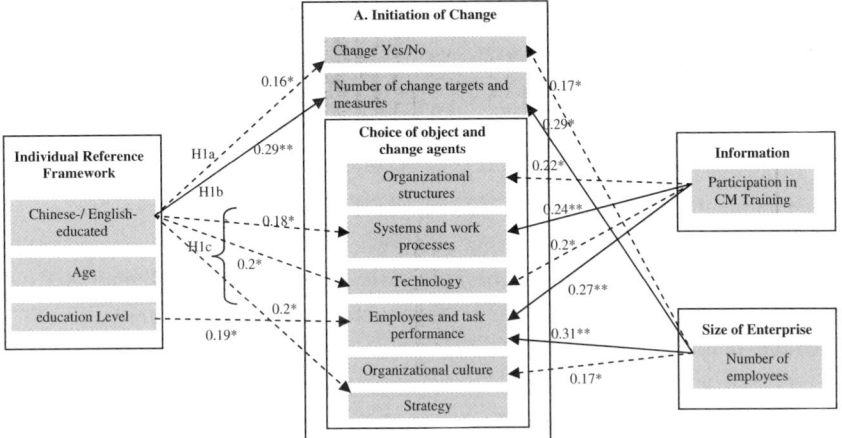

Figure 5. Significant relationships and trends between initiation of change and selected variables

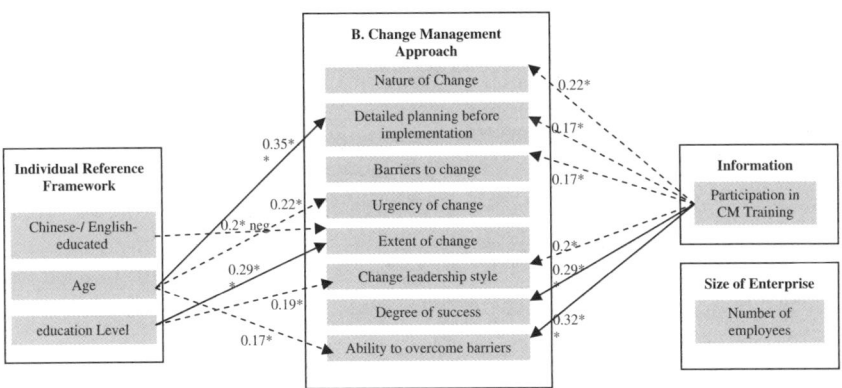

Figure 6. Significant relationships and trends between change management approach and selected variables

References

Badibanga, U (2002). Subethnische Dimensionen im Management des wirtschaftlichen Wandels in Singapur — Eine theoretische und empirische Analyse des Change Management Verhaltens von, "Chinese-educated vs. English-educated" Managern in Singapurs kleinen und mittelständischen Unternehmen. Diplomarbeit, TU-Darmstadt und National University of Singapore.

Bjerke, B (1998). Entrepreneurship and SMEs in the Singaporean context. In *Competitiveness of the Singapore Economy: A Strategic Perspective*, MH Toh and KY Tan (eds.), pp. 249–293. Singapore: Singapore University Press.

Bucholt, H and T Menkhoff (Hrsg) (1996). *Vom Wanderkraemer zum Towkay. Ethnische Chinesen und die Modernisierung der asiatisch-pazifischen Region.* Schriftenreihe Internationales Asienforum, Bd. 8, Weltforum Verlag, Koeln.

Chan, KB and BK Ng (2000). Myths and misperceptions of ethnic Chinese capitalism. In *Chinese Business Networks, State Economy and Culture*, KW Chan (ed.), pp. 285–303. Singapore: Prentice Hall.

Chan, KB and BK Ng (2001). Singapore. In *Chinese Business in Southeast Asia: Contesting Cultural Explanations, Researching Entrepreneurship*, ET Gomez and H-HM Hsiao (eds.), pp. 38–61. Surrey: Curzon Press.

Child, J (1972). Organizational structure, environment and performance: The role of strategic choice. *Journal of Sociology*, 6, 1–22.

Child, J (1997). Strategic choice in the analysis of action, structure, organizations and environment: Retrospect and prospect. *Journal of Organization Studies*, 8(1), 43–76.

Chong, LC (1987). History and managerial culture in Singapore: Pragmatism, openess and paternalism. *Asia Pacific Journal of Management*, 4(3).

Clegg, S (1990). *Modern Organisations: Organisation Studies in the Postmodern World*. London: Sage Publications.

Economist Intelligence Unit (EIU) and Andersen Consulting (2000). Beyond the bamboo network — Successful strategies for change in Asia. Research Report, EIU, Wanchai, Hong Kong.

Gomez, ET and H-HM Hsiao (eds.) (2001). *Chinese Business in Southeast Asia: Contesting Cultural Explanations, Researching Entrepreneurship*. Surrey: Curzon Press.

Granovetter, M (1985). Economic action and social structure: The problem of embeddedness. *American Journal of Sociology*, 91(3), 481–510.

Herrmann-Pillath, C (1997). Unternehmensführung im chinesischen Kulturraum. In *Internationales Personalmanagement*, A Clermont and W Schmeisser (Hrsg.). München: Verlag Franz Vahlen.

Hornidge, A-K (2004). When the yunger generation takes over — Singaporean Chinese family businesses in change. *Internationales Asienforum*, 35(1), 101–131.

Hussey, D (1995). *How to Manage Organisational Change*. London: Kogan Page.

Kwok, KW (1998). Singapore. In *The Encyclopedia of the Chinese Overseas*, L Pan (ed.), pp. 200–217. Singapore: Archipelago Press and Landmark Books.

Lassere, P (1988). Corporate strategic management and the overseas Chinese groups. *Asia Pacific Journal of Management*, 5(2), 115–131.

Lau, WH (1999). Bridging the gap between the two worlds — The Chinese educated and the English educated. In *Our Place in Time: Exploring Heritage and Memory in Singapore,* KW Kwok (ed.), pp. 199–207. Singapore: Ngai Heng Book Binders.

Low, L (ed.) (1999). *Singapore, towards a Developed Status*. New York, NY: Oxford University Press.

Menkhoff, T (1993). *Trade Routes, Trust and Trading Networks — Chinese Small Enterprises in Singapore*. Saarbruecken, Fort Lauderdale, Breitenbach Publishers.

Menkhoff, T (1998). Singapur zwischen Staat, Markt und Modernisierung. In *Länderbericht China. Politik, Wirtschaft und Gesellschaft im chinesischen Kulturraum,* C Herrmann-Pillath and M Lackner (Hrsg.), pp. 240–258. Bonn: BpB.

Menkhoff, T and S Gerke (eds.) (2002). *Chinese Entrepreneurship and Asian Business Networks*. London: Routledge Curzon.

Menkhoff, T, H-D Evers and YW Chay (eds.) (2005). *Governing and Managing Knowledge in Asia*. New Jersey: World Scientific.

Menkhoff, T and YW Chay (2006). Change leadership in small enterprises: Evidence from Singapore (in German: Die Durchfuehrung von Veraenderun gsprozessen in Kleinunternehmen: Anhaltspunkte aus Singapur). *Zeitschrift für KMU und Entrepreneurship*, 54(2), 116–140.

Menkhoff, T, EF Pang and H-D Evers (2007). What makes Chinese knowledge cultures tick? In *The Power of Knowing: Studies of Chinese Business in Asia,* T Menkhoff, Pang EF and H-D Evers (eds.). Special Issue of the *Journal of Asian Business*.

Ministry of Trade & Industry (1998). *Committee on Singapore's Competitiveness*.

Ng, BK (2002). The changing role of ethnic Chinese SMEs in economic restructuring in Singapore. In *The Chinese in Singapore and Malaysia: A Dialogue Between Tradition and Modernity*, L Surydinata (ed.), pp. 255–275. Singapore: Times Books.

Pakir, A (1991). Bilingualism in Singapore: Tradition and change among the Chinese. *Journal of the Institute for Asian Studies*, 18, 316–404.

Pfeffer, J (2005). Changing mental models. In *The Future of HR: 50 Thought Leaders Call for Change*, M Losey, S Meisinger and D Ulrich (eds.), pp. 163–171. New York: John Wiley.

Quinn Mills (2005). Asian and American leadership styles: How are they unique? *Harvard Business School Working Knowledge*, June.

Redding, G (1993). *The Spirit of Chinese Capitalism*. Berlin: Walter de Gruiter & Co. Lee, GK (2005). Three men, three models, the Chinese divide. Available at http://www.wspc.com.sg/chinese/bookshop/59_61d.html Accessed 10.08.2005.

Siddique, S (2004). An outsider looking in at Chinese Singaporeans. In *Ethnic Relations and Nation-Building in SEA*, L Suryadinata (ed.), pp. 220–229. Singapore.

The Straits Times (1998). SME's can turn to 60 schemes. April 15.

The Straits Times (2001). New Strategy for a New Singapore. August 20, pp. H2 and H4.

The Straits Times (2001). In search of global champs in backyard. August 25, pp. H12–H13.

The Straits Times (2005). Who is afraid of Chinese poetry? September 3, p. S8.

Tan, C-B (ed.) (2006). *Chinese Transnational Networks*. Richmond: Routledge Curzon.

Tan, H (1996). State capitalism, multinational corporations and Chinese entrepreneurship in Singapore. In *Asian Business Networks*, G Hamilton (ed.), pp. 157–170. Berlin: Walter de Gruiter.

Tan, K-B (2000). Success amidst prejudice: Guanxi networks in Chinese business. *Journal of Asian Business*, 16(1), 65–84.

Tan, TM, WL Tan and JE Young (2000). Entrepreneurial infrastructure in Singapore: Developing a model and mapping participation. *Journal of Entrepreneurship*, 9(1), 1–25.

Tong, CK and PK Yong (1997). Personalism and paternalism in Chinese business. In *Konfuzianischer Kapitalismus in Ost- und Suedostasien*, T Menkhoff (compiler). Schriftenreihe der Zentralstelle für Auslandskunde (ZA), Deutsche Stiftung für Internationale Entwicklung (DSE), Vol. 25. DSE-ZA, Bad Honnef.

Tsui-Auch, LS (2003). Learning strategies of small and medium-sized Chinese family firms — A comparative study of two suppliers in Singapore. *Management Learning*, 34(2), 201–220.

Tsui-Auch, LS and Y-J Lee (2003). The state matters: Management models of Singaporean Chinese and Korean business groups. *Organization Studies*, 24(4), 507–534.

Tsui-Auch, LS (2004). The professionally managed family-ruled enterprise: Ethnic Chinese business in Singapore. *Journal of Management Studies*, 41(4), 693–723.

Triandis, HC and MJ Gelfand (1998). Converging measurement of horizontal and vertical individualism and collectivism. *Journal of Personality and Social Psychology*, 74(1), 118–128.

USSU Education Project, Singapore Undergrad 1979. History of Education in Singapore. In *Education in Singapore*, Singapore, pp. 7–10.

USSU Education Project, Singapore Undergrad 1979. Teaching Values in the School. In *Education in Singapore,* Singapore, pp. 57–60.

Vasil, R (1995). *Asianising Singapore: The PAP's Management of Ethnicity.* Singapore: Heinemann Asia.

Yao, S (2002). *Confucian Capitalism: Discourse, Practice and the Myth of Chinese Enterprise.* Richmond: Routledge Curzon.

Yeung, HWC (2004). *Chinese Capitalism in a Global Era — Towards Hybrid Capitalism.* London: Routledge.

Yeung, HWC (2006). Change and continuity in Southeast Asian ethnic Chinese business. *Asia Pacific Journal of Management*, 23, 229–254.

Chapter 4

Chinese Business in Malaysia: Ethnicity and Knowledge Management

Chin Yee Whah

1. Introduction

In the past four decades, Malaysian Chinese businesses have survived not only economic and financial crises but also adapted to the extended pro-Bumiputera affirmative policy (1971–2013). This chapter relates how the power of knowing (business, market, government policy and people) has helped Chinese businessmen in Malaysia develop and expand their businesses locally and abroad. The notion of knowledge is broadly defined and implies the ability to innovate, to identify business opportunity, to deploy business strategies and to know people. In regard to knowledge of people, the notion of knowledge is derived from the Confucian tradition that emphasizes moral action and to "know man" (Lee, 2008). We refer to knowledge as moral action that is not merely an external entity to know and to understand. It involves taking action and implies change that brings about solutions to everyday issues. To "know man" is to understand others; it requires the knowledge of the person that is associated with humanity or benevolence. In business, besides having knowledge of a business, "understanding and knowing man" is important to bring about good and prosperous solutions (Lee, 2008, pp. 27–29). One should know how to behave as a person, as a member of a business community and as a citizen of a country of a particular political and socio-economic context to act to extend the goodness to the community and the nation. In knowledge management terminology, knowledge of knowing man fits in well with Zeleny's (2005) concept of knowledge management, especially the concept of "purposeful coordination of action," which also involves the importance of "know-who" as one of the components of knowledge. This notion of knowledge is also consistent with the definition of knowledge management by Menkhoff *et al.* (2004, p. 88) which emphasizes both the tangible and intangible knowledge resources of an organization.

The chapter is based on empirical studies drawn from five case studies. It aims to provide a broad description of Chinese business in Malaysia that includes large Chinese business groups and also small and medium enterprises (SMEs). The chapter argues that having knowledge of business and people (their character, credibility and potential), working harmoniously with others and through seizing opportunities, Chinese Malaysian have managed to maintain their significant presence in various sectors of the Malaysian economy.

Externally, by having knowledge of the market and taking advantage of opportunities, many large and medium Malaysian Chinese companies have managed to expand regionally. Internally, having knowledge of people, their talent, credibility and connection; by involving them as part of a business venture and by going along with them in good working and business relationships are vital for company growth in the long-term; especially in a context of affirmative policy that does not favor the Chinese. The selected cases in this chapter also highlight how Malaysian Chinese business groups and SMEs conformed to the affirmative policy by engaging Bumiputeras (basically Malays) from both the elite and middle class as one of their business strategies to push for their companies' growth at the domestic market. By referring to knowledge as moral action and associating it with humanity, Malaysian Chinese businessmen have demonstrated their benevolence. They contributed to nation building by providing employment to people, contributing to economic growth and revenue for the country and by assisting the government to achieve its policy goals, especially to facilitate the emergence of a Bumiputera Commercial and Industrial Community (BCIC).

2. An Overview of Chinese Business in Malaysia

In the 18th century, Chinese merchants in Southeast Asia already possessed knowledge of trade, supply chains, movement of goods and ways to finance these businesses. "They understood the nature and limitations of local economies and were adept at exploiting them" (Trocki, 2008, p. 36). Their knowledge of business and ability to adapt to the local socio-economy and politics remain thriving in Malaysia today. The significant presence of Chinese business in Malaysia can be traced back to British Malaya. In fact, some of the present Malaysian Chinese companies can trace the roots of their history to the early 20th century. Before the mid-19th century, Chinese immigrants, especially Straits-born Chinese in Malaya, already had an efficient system of financing and supplying Chinese labor in plantation agriculture and tin mining activities (Jomo, 1986, p. 151; Tan, 1982, p. 267; Yip, 1969, pp. 89–94). A few prominent Chinese planters and tin miners emerged successfully in the early to mid-20th century. During this same period, Chinese involvement in trading and retail activities also grew tremendously. For instance, in 1954, of the 85,120 registered small enterprises in Malaya, 75 percent were Chinese-owned, mostly as retail shops (Ling, 1989, p. 59). With the accumulation of capital from commerce and tin mining, the Chinese started some cottage industries. The Chinese were able to acquire the know-how and experience on their own initiative to start simple processing and fabrication in rubber, rice and coconut milling, and the production of simple consumer items especially foodstuff, building materials and metal goods (Huff, 1994, pp. 212–214). As the economy grew, especially with rubber, tin production and trade in general pushed up the demand for monetary and financial services. In the first half of the 20th century, a total of 14 Chinese banks were established to meet this demand (Chin, 2008, pp. 209–210).

In the post-independence period, the plantation sector underwent a major change in ethnic ownership. During the 1950s–1970s, Western and Chinese enterprises in the plantations sector were taken over by Bumiputera interests (Drabble, 2000, pp. 216–217). However, several enterprising small-timers seized the opportunity to acquire estates from the foreigners. The late Loy Hean Heong, founder of Malayan Borneo Finance (MBF Berhad), made a fortune from the subdivision and resale of these estates to smallholders (Loy and Crofts, 1997). Another principal buyer was the late Lee Loy Seng, founder of today's Kuala Lumpur–Kepong Bhd (KLK), a top 15th company listed on the Kuala Lumpur Stock Exchange (KLSE). In the late 1960s, after the Malaysian government backed the plan of export-oriented industrialization with incentives to promote employment and investment, some prominent leading families ventured into large scale manufacturing. Robert Kuok (Malaysia's richest man) partnered a government agency and Japan's Nissan Sugar Manufacturing to establish Malayan Sugar. Later, he established Federal Flour Mills (Ling, 1989, p. 63). The late Loy acquired a fledging carbide company that made adhesive tapes, rubber bands and aluminium foil lamination (Jesudason, 1989, p. 62). The late Loh Boon Siew (founder of Boon Siew Sdn Bhd and Oriental Holdings Berhad) acquired the sole distributorship for Honda motorbikes in 1957 and subsequently set up the first-ever Malaysian motorcycle manufacturing company in 1968 (Flower, Lim and Loh 2006, pp. 72–74). The Singapore-based Hong Leong group had a strong presence in the manufacture of construction raw materials (Yohsihara, 1988; Tan, 1982). William Cheng, who owned and controlled the Lion Group, was involved in steel manufacturing (Gomez, 1999). The Chinese also acquired know-how in construction and property development. According to Snodgrass (1980), the "Chinese had the most modernized employment structure... and... supplied most of the rather modest skilled and educated labor inputs." One of the earlier contractor and property developers was the late Lim Goh Tong. Through his company, Kien Huat, he was involved in building a number of public infrastructure projects and buildings (Lim, 2004). Tan Chin Nam, another well known entrepreneur and founder of Petaling Garden (1959) and Ipoh Garden (1964), built several major housing estates in Malaysia (Tan, 2006).

Before the race riots of May 13, 1969 and the onset of affirmative action, Malaya had, at that time, a Chinese Finance Minister who could help to promote the interests of the Chinese community. For instance, seven Chinese banks and a finance company were incorporated in the 1960s (Chin, 2008). Following the communal riots, a pro-Bumiputera affirmative action policy dubbed the New Economic Policy (NEP) was implemented in 1971 by the Malaysian government. The ultimate goal of the NEP was to facilitate "the emergence of a full-fledged Malay entrepreneurial community within one generation," and to achieve a 30-percent Bumiputera ownership of the corporate sector by 1990. In accordance with the affirmative action policy, ethnic quotas were introduced. Consequently, Bumiputera were favored when it came to the award of government contracts, tender, loans and credit. Bumiputera interests, mostly linked to "rentier activities," occupied an increasingly important role in the economy. Chinese businesses of all sizes were challenged and driven to re-position themselves in response to the NEP and the changing economic climate. Within this political and economic context, Chinese companies that sought to participate in government projects took a pro-active approach in complying with the NEP regulation by incorporating Bumiputera as business partners. One of the lasting effects of this political and economic scenario was the weakening of the old intra-ethnic and family-based Chinese businesses and the formation of inter-ethnic companies involving Bumiputera partners. Some Chinese businesses protected their interests by forming alliances with Malay "sleeping partners." However, large Chinese business corporations responded by relocating their capital overseas as a form of protest and as a way of "escap[ing] the domestic constraints and spread[ing] economic and political risks more widely" (Jesudason, 1989).

The NEP had successfully restructured the ownership of the Bumiputeras and Chinese in the banking industry and the construction sector. The central bank took over Malayan Banking in December 1969 when it was put under government protection (Ranjit, 1987). Following that action, Bumiputera capital ownership in Chinese-run banks had increased to 77 percent for the whole Malaysian banking industry by early 1982 (Hara, 1991). Whenever a Chinese bank got into management or succession problems, it disappeared from the corporate scene. By 1990, another six Chinese-controlled banks had been taken over by the state or by Bumiputera when the government moved to consolidate the Malaysian banks by limiting local commercial banks to ten anchor banks. In the process, small Chinese-controlled banks were absorbed into bigger banks and vanished from the corporate scene. The latest, hostile take-over of a small but profitable Chinese-owned bank (Southern Bank) by Bumiputera Commerce Bank (now CIMB Bank) took place in late 2006. Today, only two Chinese-controlled banks remain, namely, Public Bank and Hong Leong Bank. In the banking sector, the Chinese have lost control, their ownership declining from 24.3 percent (1970) to 10.2 percent in 2004 (Chin, 2008). In the construction sector, Bumiputera penetration is very significant, expanding from merely 2.5 percent in 1970 to 35.2 percent in 2004. At the same time,

Chinese ownership in the construction sector fell from 52.8 percent to
42.6 percent during the same period. Bumiputera also made inroads in the
wholesale and retail trade, successfully increasing their interest from
2.2 percent to 20.4 percent during the same period. The Bumiputera also
encroached into the manufacturing sector, increasing from 2.5 percent in
1970 to 8.1 percent in 2004. During the same period, Chinese ownership
in the manufacturing sector also increased but by a meagre 2.5 percent to
24.5 percent (Malaysia, 1973, 2006).

3. Case Studies on Knowledge Management of Chinese Business Groups in Malaysia

Corporate ownership by Chinese business groups in the Malaysian economy has remained fairly substantial and significant. In 1990, the Chinese
held approximately 45.5 percent of the total share capital of Malaysian
limited companies compared to 22.5 percent in 1970 (Malaysia, 1973,
1999). This increase of corporate wealth in the 20-year period was
achieved largely at the expense of declining foreign ownership on the one
hand and the expansion of the private sector following the adoption of
strategies to accommodate new state policies on the other. However,
Chinese ownership of corporate wealth slipped to 40.9 percent in 1995
and 34.9 percent in 2008. During the same period, Bumiputera ownership
rose from 20.6 percent in 1995 to 21.9 percent (Malaysia, 2006, 2010).
However, an independent think-tank reported that Bumiputera had
achieved 45 percent equity share in 2008 (CPPS, 2005).

Major large Chinese business groups that formed a substantial por-
tion of the Malaysian corporate equity include the Genting Group (gaming and leisure), Public Bank Group (banking), IGB Group (construction
and property), Kuala-Lumpur Kepong Group (plantation), IOI Group
(plantation), Sunway Group (construction and property), Berjaya Group
(diversified), Hong Leong Group (diversified), YTL Group (diversified),
Lion Group (diversified), Rimbunan Hijau Group (plantation), Kerry
Group/Kuok Group (diversified) and the Oriental Group (diversified),
among others. In the following section, three selected cases describe the
importance of knowledge management for Chinese business groups operating in Malaysia. These three cases were chosen because of their long

company history, quality of leadership, quality of management, and market capitalization. However, it should be noted that this does not imply that other business groups lack such qualities.

Case study 1: Genting Group — From Lim Goh Tong to Lim Kok Thay

Genting Berhad has grown from a single company to several large listed companies namely, Genting Berhad, Genting Malaysia Berhad and Genting Plantations Berhad being listed on the Malaysian Stock Exchange (KLSE). As of August 31, 2012, these three companies had a combined market capital of RM61.66 billion, bigger than Malayan Banking, the largest government-link company listed on the KLSE in terms of market capitalization. Together with Genting Singapore PLC which is listed on the Singapore Stock Exchange and Genting Hong Kong Limited, listed on the Hong Kong Stock Exchange, the multinational conglomerate has a combined market capitalization of RM110.49 billion and employs more than 50,000 employees worldwide (www.Genting.com).

Stimulated by the success of his cousin who ventured out to Malaya in 1934, Genting Group founder, the late Tan Sri Lim Goh Tong set off for Malaya in 1937. He was born in 1918 in Anxi, China. Lim joined his fourth uncle who came to Malaya many years ago who was already a successful Class A contractor[1] in Kuala Lumpur. Lim started working with his uncle as a carpenter and accumulated knowledge of the building trade by doing heavy manual work. With the knowledge and experience he gained after a two-year stint with his uncle, Lim stepped out on his own as a building contractor. Later, Lim switched from construction work to petty trading because of the Japanese occupation of Malaya. Through a network of used hardware traders in Kuala Lumpur and Selangor who were from Anxi, Lim accumulated knowledge of this business and joined their ranks after he acquired sufficient capital. He created a niche in his hardware business by taking up scrap-metal and new hardware trading. With proper management, his business grew and he managed to accumulate substantial capital (Lim, 2004).

---

[1]A Class A contractor is qualified to undertake public projects of any size.

When the British returned to Malaya after the Second World War many abandoned mines and rubber plantations resumed operations and there was an urgent demand for heavy machinery. Lim seized this golden opportunity to buy many used-machines on offer. He was innovative. He reconditioned the machines and resold them at double or triple the purchase price, and he made huge profits. Lim invested time to acquire an intimate knowledge of the market and its operations (Lim, 2004, pp. 23–25).

With help and guidance from his uncle, Lim set up his family construction company, Kien Huat Private Limited, in 1951 to spearhead his construction business (Lim, 2004, p. 27). In the early 1950s, Kien Huat built several roads in Petaling Jaya and contributed to the early development of the township which was a satellite town of Kuala Lumpur and is a major residential area today. In 1954, Kien Huat was awarded a project by the Kuala Lumpur Municipal government. Kien Huat was the third company that took up a challenging project to construct part of a four-mile sewer from the Kuala Lumpur Railway Station to Klang Road. Earlier, two contractors took on this project but failed to complete it. The first contractor was a local and the second contractor was a reputable British firm. There were two major difficulties to overcome. The first was the soil structure which comprised 80 percent of rock overlaid with sand and a high water table. Working through the rock was tough and time consuming. The second was related to water because as soon as the trenches were pumped dry for concrete laying, water would ooze from all sides to fill them again. The greatest challenge was to deal with the ground water. Lim, who possessed no engineering qualification, used his experience and common sense by using the gravel pump to replace the water pump that could not offload the ground water. The gravel pump, widely used in tin mining amongst the Chinese, was able to solve the ground water problem and enable the concrete work to be carried out. Kien Huat, a new player with no track record of competency, proved its capabilities within four years by successfully completing many major projects. The Public Works Department recognized its achievements and upgraded Kien Huat to a Class A contractor in 1955. This recognition brought Kien Huat bigger projects. Kien Huat successfully completed building the Ayer Item Dam in Penang (1962), the Yahya Putra Bridge in Kelantan (1963), and became subcontractor to a German firm to build a RM20 million hydroelectric project in the Cameron highlands in 1964 (Lim, 2004, pp. 51–61).

In 1968, Kien Huat won a contract of RM54 million to build the Kemubu irrigation Scheme, the second largest in Malaysia after the Muda Irrigation Scheme in Kedah. The project was to construct a network of some 570km of criss-crossing irrigation canals; 2,000 reinforced concrete structures fabricated for diverting water into paddy fields; and more than 200 bridges that used up some 20,000 feet of concrete pipes of diameters ranging from three to six feet. The project ran into a host of problems: delay in the Government's acquisition of land; theft of equipment and materials from work sites; severe flooding due to monsoons and the May 13, 1969 race riot. Work delays caused about RM5 million in losses. At the end of the first year, Kien Huat had managed to complete only five percent of the project and was in a serious cash crunch. The French consultant held Kien Huat responsible for the consequences of the delay and threatened to take action to terminate his contract. Lim had a meeting with the consultant's chief engineers, its general managers and government officials to find a solution to the problem. Lim asked for a six-month extension period. He pledged that if he could not finish more than 5–6 percent of the project within this period he was ready to be sued and made a bankrupt. Lim was smart to apply his knowledge and experience. He demonstrated his innovative ideas by redesigning the 2,000 80 tonne concrete structures. Based on his knowledge and experience in the construction line, he felt that these structures were over-designed to handle the flow of only two feet of water. He proposed to redesign these concrete structures weighting 12 tonnes and eight tonnes respectively. Lim also proposed to scale down the thickness of the 200 bridges from seven feet each to three feet because there were no heavy vehicles in the area. Lim also pointed out to the consultant engineers that switching to the smaller design could help to save a huge cost and time. The consultant engineers were convinced and approved his proposals. The new designs were adequate for on-site fabrication, required smaller equipment, convenient for installation and speeded up the project. It also saved the Government RM11 million in total material cost. Within four months of the grace period, Lim completed 320km of canals, some 1,000 bifurcation gates and 100 bridges, which was about 60 percent of the entire project. Lim completed the project on schedule and made a profit of RM4 million (Lim, 2004).

Besides his innovative ideas of reconditioning used-bulldozers and re-selling them for profit, switching to smaller designs for the bifurcation gates and bridges, Lim demonstrated his knowledge of government policies, markets, management of finance and people that eventually earned him and his partners good profits in their new ventures. In 1953, Lim forayed into the mining industry when he came into contact with an iron mining company in Johor that had cash issues. Lim was invited to be a partner. He took the offer and went to Japan to find a buyer for the iron ore. Initially, the general manager of the Japanese iron-mining company refused to see him. Waiting everyday outside the general manager's office, he was eventually given an opportunity to present and discuss his business proposal. He persuaded the iron-mining company to offer him a business opportunity although he spoke very little Japanese, In the initial deal, Lim was asked to bear the airfares and monthly wages of each of four Japanese mining engineers who would be carrying out a three-month study at Lim's iron mine. The Japanese also verbally promised to give Lim a ¥400 million loan to support the mining operations. Having knowledge of strict foreign exchange controls imposed by the Japanese government at that time, Lim foresaw that it was clearly impossible for the Japanese to arrange such a loan. He counter proposed that the Japanese pay the airfares and wages of the engineers up front and he would take care of their board and lodging in Malaya. Also, upon signing an agreement on the sale and purchase of iron ore, Lim would reimburse them for the sundry expenses. A deal was finally approved. To finance the mining business, he tried to raise funds from his fellow council members of the Selangor Hardware Dealers' Association but was branded a fool as no one believed that an investment of $300,000 would receive an annual return of $4 million at a profit margin of $10 per ton for an estimated annual output of 400,000 tons of iron ore. Lim then persuaded Mr Fang Yen San, one of the major shareholders of the iron mining company not to withdraw from the company. Mr Fang had earlier signed a contract with Lim to sell Lim his stake in the company. Lim proposed to cancel the contract between him and Mr Fang and form a new company (Malayan Mining Limited) and Mr Fang agreed. In restructuring the company, both Lim and Mr. Fang increased their stakes in the company. Lim became the largest shareholder and Mr. Fang the second largest shareholder. At the completion of the restructuring exercise, Malayan Mining Limited boasted a paid up capital of $800,000 after incorporating 31 other shareholders that a Singapore rice merchant recruited. Each subscribed a fraction of the 300,000 shares with a value of $200,000. This venture yielded an annual profit in excess of $3 million for the first two years. In the following years, its annual profit hovered between $4 million to $5 million. Lim made further investments in iron mining by acquiring two more companies in 1962. By 1967, Lim had made more than $10 million in profit from iron mining. Later, he was offered a joint-venture in tin mining. It happened that he acquired a set of used dredging machinery and equipment when he was in hardware trading. He reconditioned them for this new venture. Seng Kee Dredging, the joint-venture company between Lim and his friend, emerged as the first Chinese-owned tin mining company to break the tradition of using gravel pump in tin mining (Lim, 2004).

In 1963, Lim had an idea of venturing into developing a holiday resort at Genting Ulu Kali Mountain, in a remote area about an hour's drive from Kuala Lumpur. In April 1965, Lim and his good friend, Mohamad Noah Omar incorporated a private company, Genting Highlands Hotel Sdn Bhd, with Lim as its managing director and Noah as the chairman. Noah was an important person then. He was Assistant District Officer in Batu Pahat, Johor, and later became a Johor state assemblyman and Speaker of the Dewan Rakyat (House of Representative). Noah was the father-in-law of two future Prime Ministers, Abdul Razak (1971–1976) and Hussein Onn (1976–1981) (Lim 2004; Gomez, 1999). With Tunku Abdul Rahman's (Malaysia's First Prime Ministers) recommendation, the Pahang Government promptly approved their application for freehold land. Lim manoeuvred to secure freehold land from the Selangor government as Genting is situated on the border of Pahang and Selangor (Lim, 2004). To help expedite the development of tourism in Genting and to ensure profitability of the resort, Lim was given a licence on April 28, 1969. The casino licence had to be paid in advance before the issue of the licence and on subsequent renewals. Since Genting was only a start-up company and to ease the cash flow burden, Lim appealed to the Finance Minister to allow him to pay in instalments for the high licence fee. The outcome of this was that the casino licence was awarded for three months with a quarterly renewal requirement. With no experience in the gaming business, Lim engaged a casino operator from Seoul (Korea) to provide the expertise in managing the Genting casino for only nine months (Lim, 2004). As the business grew, Lim engaged more professional managers to oversee the operations. Genting Highlands Hotel Sdn Bhd changed its name to Genting Highlands Hotel Berhad upon listing on the Kuala Lumpur Stock Exchange in July 1970 (Genting.com/groupprofile/gent.htm) and was renamed Genting in June 1978.

As the business grew and diversified, Genting went through a major restructuring exercise. The purpose was to focus on the management of its other growing businesses in plantations, property, paper mills, power generation, oil and gas exploration, and the cruise industry. A major restructuring involving shares-for-assets swap was initiated in August 1989. The Resort World Berhad (RWB) was set up to manage all tourism activities of the Genting Group. RWB was subsequently listed on the KLSE in late 1989 and fulfilled the NEP policy by allocating 30 percent of its shares for Bumiputeras (Gomez, 1999, p. 51; Lim, 2004, p. 103). RWB was later renamed Genting Malaysia Berhad in 2010. Lim Kok Thay, the patriarch's second son, was given the task of expanding the family business overseas in the later 1980s. This was probably intended to prepare him for taking over the business. The overseas expansion strategy should be viewed in the context where it was not likely that the Genting Group could expand its casino operation in Malaysia at that time. To maintain the group's casino operation in Malaysia and to expand its business, the group endeavoured to become a major international casino operator, through Genting International (Gomez, 1999, p. 55).

In the gaming industry, the Genting Group is riding on the liberalization trend in the global casino business to expand into Macau, Singapore, Britain and the United States. Genting is now into the second generation managed by Tan Sri Dato' Lim Kok Thay. Kok Thay has successfully transformed the group from a Malaysia-based casino into an international gaming group. Genting Berhad's subsidiary, Genting International Ltd (GIL), has taken over Stanley Leisure Ltd. for £640 million (RM4.3 billion). With this acquisition, Genting is now the biggest casino operator in Britain with 46 casinos. The competitiveness of the Genting Group is demonstrated by GIL's success in securing Singapore's Sentosa Integrated Resorts (IR) project in late 2006 (*The Edge*, December 28, 2009).

Under Kok Thay's leadership, the Genting Group acquired Lucayan Beach Resort and Casino venture in the Bahamas. However, it was a loss-making partnership with the Bahamas government (*Far Eastern Economic Review*, January 5, 1989). Nevertheless, Genting has bounced back partnering RAV Bahamas in June 2012 to open the USD24 million Resort World Bimini Bay (*The Star*, July 3, 2012). Kok Thay also set up the Adelaide Casino and the Bursewood Island Resort in Perth, Australia. His first year operations in Australia earned him a profit of RM100 million. After operating in Australia for 18 months, he sold the entire Australia venture to a Japanese company. The proceeds from the sale, if deposited in banks, would generate the same level of income in the form of interest. Moreover, he foresaw stiff competition and profit erosion when the Australian State Governments were expected to issue more casino licences upon the expiry of the casino's 15-year exclusivity (Lim, 2004, pp. 171–172).

Lim's family and the Genting Group have over 20 years experience of operating business in the United States. They have strong ties with some Indian tribal gaming groups in the United States that include the Native American tribe of Mashantucket Pequot in Connecticut and the Native American tribe of the Mashpee Wampanoag in Massachusetts. It was reported that some of the Pequot people attended Lim Goh Tong's funeral in October 2007 (*The Edge*, December 30, 2011). These ties are intangible knowledge resources for the Genting Group to later expand their casino empire in the Unites States. In the early 1990s, the Pequot proposed to establish Foxwoods Casino on their reservation and tried to secure a loan for it. However, their loan proposal was rejected by about 30 US and foreign banks. The project was perceived to be risky as the tribe was very poor, had no financial track record and the proposed location was in an economically depressed and rural part of the state of Connecticut. Kok Thay knew about this and visited the site. He understood the challenges faced by the Pequot. His vision of great opportunities for the Foxwoods projects surpassed the economic concerns and was translated into action to provide a loan to the Pequot for initial funding of the project despite the tribe not having secured the casino licence from the state. Eventually, Kok

Thay became a close friend of the Pequot. Foxwoods Resort Casino is today the largest resort casino in the world, providing jobs to more than 11,000 people and a major economic driving force in the State of Connecticut. In late 2002, Kok Thay extended financial assistance to another US-based Native American tribe, the Seneca Nation of Indians, to build their casino in the Niagara Falls location (Lim, 2004, pp. 172–173). In May 2010, the Lim family's private vehicle partnered with the Mashpee Wampanoag to finance a proposed casino resort in Massachusetts (*Bloomberg*, June 15, 2010). Some observers think that Genting will eventually get what they want because of their ties with some native tribes in the Unites States (*The Edge*, October 5, 2011; December 30, 2011). Recently, Genting's plan to build a USD3.8 billion casino resort in Miami is facing competition from Las Vegas Sands Corp (LVS).

Kok Thay has demonstrated his ability to blend together his experience and knowledge of operating family recreation and entertainment. He seized the opportunity to enter the cruise industry in the 1990s. He used the proceeds from the assets sold in Australia and the Bahamas in 1986 to acquire two Swedish cruise ships that were on auction. In August 1993, Genting Group bought two cruise ships for USD165 million, each with passenger capacity of 1,700. Star Cruises Limited was incorporated in September 1993 and listed on the Hong Kong Stock Exchange in November 2000. Star Cruises' fleet had 20 cruise ships then (Lim, 2004). Today, Star Cruise has grown to become the third largest cruise line in the world and continues to be the leading cruise line in Asia-Pacific (Starcruises.com). Kok Thay's success in spearheading Star Cruises has proven his leadership and capability as the successor of Genting.

Besides gaming, entertainment and cruise industries, the Genting Group diversified into the plantation business (Asiatic Development Sdn Bhd) in 1980. Lim seized the opportunity when the stock markets plummeted due to high oil prices. This forced many British-controlled companies to sell off their large Malaysian plantation holdings at bargain prices. The group took advantage of the opportunities to accumulate significant stakes in a number of listed plantation companies between 1974 and 1979. The group also established a paper mill (Genting Sanyen Industrial Paper Sdn Bhd) in 1990, businesses in the power supply sector (Genting Sanyen Power Sdn Bhd) in 1996 and newsprint industry (Genting Sanyen

Newsprint Sdn Bhd) in 1997 (Gomez, 1999). In the gas and oil industry, the group has investment in China and in Indonesia.

Case study 2: IGB Group, Tan Chin Nam and his family business

The IGB Group comprises of five listed entities in the KLSE, namely IGB Corporation Berhad, Goldis Berhad, Ipmuda Berhad, KrisAssets Holdings Berhad, and Wah Seong Corportion. IGB Corporation is a developer and real estate giant in Malaysia. It is a top-50 company listed on the KLSE. IGB is scheduled to list its retail assets, IGB REIT by end of September 2012. It will become the largest Real Estate Investment Trust (REIT) in Malaysia with an estimated market capitalization of over RM4.3 billion (*The Edge Malaysia*, August 13, 2012). Following this new listing, the IGB Group will have six listed entities.

IGB Group founder Tan Chin Nam was born in Kuala Lumpur in 1926. Chin Nam, together with his brother Kim Yeow, established their family-owned company Wah Seong in 1948 trading rice, fish, chicken and other perishables in Malaya. Chin Nam founded a few major companies, Sino-Thai Rice (1951), Petaling Garden (1959), Ipoh Garden (1964) and Tan & Tan Development (1971). He, his family and many business partners have developed and managed low-cost housing, apartment buildings, office buildings, shopping centres and resorts in Malaysia (Tan, 2006, pp. 74–75). His Perak-based housing development company, Ipoh Garden, expanded to other major cities in the peninsula in the 1970s. In the 1980s, Ipoh Garden changed its name to IGB Corporation Berhad and expanded aggressively. IGB moved into the manufacture and supply of building materials and is known as a property giant in Malaysia. The group has expanded to the United States, Australia, UK, Italy, Chile, Argentina, Pakistan, Bangladesh, Hong Kong, China, Singapore and Vietnam (Gomez, 1999, p. 118). In Australia, he is known for the high-profile restoration and development projects of the Queen Victoria Building and Capitol Theatre in Sydney, and the Como Hotel in Melbourne. In Singapore, he built the Gleneagles Hospitals, Shangri-La Hotel and Parkway Parade. In Kuala Lumpur, he built Malaysia's first condominium (Kudalari) in 1983, and the first service apartments (MiCasa Hotel Apartment and Desa Angkasa).

In 1999, IGB group completed building a major landmark in Kuala Lumpur, the Mid-Valley City, which now stands as one of the half-dozen largest shopping malls in the world (Tan, 2006, p. 75, pp. 129–136).

The period of the construction of the Mid-Valley City, from April 1996–November 1999, took place during the Asian financial crisis in 1997–1998. During this crisis, while other property companies were slowing down, IGB speeded up the project so that it would be ready for business when the crisis was over and thus ahead of its competitors (Tan, 2006). This was not the only business strategy. All the properties the group developed were to ensure a fixed income derived from property investment and management. What enabled IGB to complete the mega project during the Asian financial crisis were two main assets its founder possessed, *jian* and *jinqian*. *Jian* (thrift) as Chinese proverbs put it, refers to "frugality as source of abundance." *Jinqian* (cash or capital), in essence, implies that one should not overtrade, i.e., "do not bite off more than your resources have the teeth to chew." Both words imply the need to watch cash flow vigilantly and not borrowing short on a long-term project (Tan, 2006, pp. 8–9). A few Malaysian banks were in deep trouble during the Asian financial crisis because they violated these two basic precepts.

The group's strategies are for long-term recurring income and to continuously identify and invest in sectors with high growth potential and to build businesses within those sectors. Today, IGB has the earning power and a creative pool of property development and construction talent within a single company in Southeast Asia (Tan, 2006). In 2000, the group set up Goldis Berhad, a cash rich investment company that positioned itself strategically to take advantage of important and promising investments in the new-economy as Malaysia and the region grow wealthier. Goldis has private equity investment in Malaysia and China. It focuses on life sciences, healthcare, water/wastewater treatment, information communication technology and organic aquaculture. Goldis is owned and managed by the Tan family (Goldis.com; Tan, 2006, p. 121) and it is the major substantial shareholder of IGB Corporation. With the listing of IGB REIT by end September 2012, this new listed entity will enable the group to have stable and long-term cash inflow. IGB also ventured into the energy sector, seen as Asia's engine of economic growth. Wah Seong, Tan's family-owned company that originally traded in rice, fish and chicken has expanded into a major oil service provider. The group set up Wah Seong Corporation Berhad in 1994 to be involved in the provision of highly specialized pipe-coating services, and is a major Asian oil and gas service provider today. Although IGB is controlled by the Tan family it engages foreign expertise for its oil and gas ventures (*The Star*, September 4, 2007).

Knowledge of people and managing them is an intangible knowledge resource for Tan Chin Nam and the group. In his biography, Tan said, "All true enough — though not nearly enough. For business is *above all* about people. Managers who work hard and give credit understand that in spite of the value of modern business learning, business still boils down to people problems... Whilst recognizing the usefulness of the methods and systems taught in Western business schools, the Chinese businessman has an unshakeable belief... that when all is said and done the successful conduct of business depends, not on methods and systems, but on human relations. A network of systematic contacts is worth a library of glossy brochures sent to cold-call potential investors; ten minutes on the phone with the right people are worth a dozen volumes of working papers by technocrats" (Tan, 2006, p. 2). Tan also said, "Try to learn about people and forget about their weak spots... Look for something special in everybody because it can be put to good use" (Tan, 2006, p. 3–4). Business is people — people who know and who can do. With regard to the importance of knowing men, Tan mentioned in his biography his 30 years of friendship with the first Prime Minister of Malaysia. A confidant of Malaysia's first two Prime Ministers, Tan was also Tun Abdul Razak's (Malaysia's second Prime Minister) regular golfing partner. Tan was invited to be a member of the Institute of Strategic and International Studies (ISIS) by Malaysia's third Prime Minister, Tun Hussein Onn. In 1991, Tan was appointed to the Malaysian Business Council by Tun Dr. Mahathir Mohamad, who was then Malaysia's fourth Prime Minister. In the same year, Tan was appointed as a panel member of the Ministry of International Trade and Industries.

In business, Tan knew that to build Ipoh Garden, he needed someone with experience in government to handle the political side of business as well as a dynamic personality. Tan recruited Yap Lim Sen who worked in town planning in the government service and who had just resigned. Tan played an important role in building the Mid-Valley City (Tan, 2006). In building the 24-floor Shangri-La Hotel in Singapore, Tan hired the first hotel landscape consultants ever to come to Southeast Asia and to build the first hotel that was environmentally-friendly. He also engaged Bailieu Myer, Australia's premier merchandising family and Coles-Myer, Australia's leading retail store chain. Tan was possibly the first local businessman to employ a Westerner (Tan, 2006, p. 123).

In his business ventures Tan encountered a few failures. One of them was in a multi-million dollar sky resort business in Australia in 1981. Tan regarded this as "human failure" because he invested in something he did not understand and which he did not attend to personally. He relates this failure to his violation of several basic precepts. He blamed himself for not being hardworking and diligent (*qin*) enough. He felt incompetent because he was distinctly uninformed about the technical and professional expertise required to run the business. Tan related it to *ren* (recognize, know, make out or identify). What is important behind the quest for knowledge is not merely to master necessary technical and professional expertise to run a business; it is to be hungry for knowledge and to satisfy that hunger by constantly learning from life, books, newspaper and magazines (Tan, 2006, p. 10). He also blamed himself for not acquiring the technical and professional expertise in advance of making the investment, and he did not assess carefully the limits of his knowledge. He associates this to *zhi* (wisdom or resourcefulness). For Tan, *zhi* is related to *ren*, which is the commitment to learning, because the leader with *zhi* must renew himself everyday (Tan, 2006, pp. 11, 16).

Case study 3: Public Bank Group and the Public Bank family

Public Bank (PB) is the largest non-Governmental linked company, and the fourth largest (after Malayan Banking, Sime Darby and CIMB Bank) company listed on the KLSE in terms of market capitalization. The Public Bank Group has two listed entities on the KLSE, namely Public Bank Berhad and Loanpac Insurance Bhd. Its founder, Tan Sri Teh Hong Piow, is ranked by Forbes Asia as Malaysia's fourth richest man in 2012 after Robert Kuok, Ananda Krishnan, and the late Tan Sri Lim Goh Tong's spouse and family.

PB is a well-managed bank. It survived the 1986–1987 recession that led to the liberalization of the New Economic Policy. It also survived the ten critical anchor banks consolidation of the domestic banking system in post 1997–1998 Asian financial crisis. It was the least affected among other local banks when the Asian financial crisis occurred. PB emerged relatively unscathed whilst two government-link banks received bail-outs and other banks were nursing their wounds (some took ten years to recover, some were absorbed by other banks). PB's non-performing loan ratio was well below industry average. Its management quality of being prudent and conservative saved the bank from crises. PB actually added 17 bank branches and 18 finance company branches during the crisis years' 1997–1998 (Bowie, 2006, p. 219). PB's emergence from the crisis proved Teh's able leadership in banking. He could foresee future risks and took precaution by managing prudently. In knowledge management terminology, PB had avoided 'the growth of ignorance' that reflects the growth of knowledge (Evers and Menkhoff, 2004, p. 124). PB under Teh's leadership again remained strong during the 2008–2012 Global Financial Crises.

Born in Singapore in 1930, a "typical Chinese," Teh learned the virtue of hard work, thrift and diligence very early on in his life. He was brought up in a family of nine siblings and only managed to complete the Cambridge Overseas School Certificate. According to his protégé, Dato' Sri Tay Ah Lek, "… paternalistic attitude to his people has helped create a unique PB family" (Bowie, 2006, p. 42). He set up a "family" business but with no nepotism in his case as the founder and patriarch of the PB "family" (Bowie, 2006, p. 77). PB is not run as a family business like YTL, Genting, IGB and Kuok's business group. Instead the bank is run as a corporate family. PB is still being led by Teh as the Chairman.

At age 20, Teh joined Overseas Chinese Banking Corporation (OCBC) as a clerk in 1950 and later became an officer. His 16 years of banking knowledge and work experience with OCBC and Malayan Banking helped to develop him to venture on his own to set up PB in 1966. He had six years at managerial level at Mayan Banking. At 39, Teh became Managing Director of PB and moved aggressively to open three branches within five months (August, 1966 – January, 1967) and listed PB on the KLSE on April 6, 1967 with a paid-up capital of Ringgit 16 million, a record then for a commercial bank (Bowie, 2006, pp. 34–35).

In the early years of his venture, Teh lacked the management and resources to compete with established banks. It was very difficult for him to compete, especially with foreign banks to recruit graduates aspiring to a banking career. Established banking giants already captured elite, talented individuals and multinational markets. Teh, however, identified his niche and strategized to focus on retail banking, targeting wage earners on the street, the middle income groups and small scale enterprises (Bowie, 2006, pp. 204, 207). To overcome the lack of management talent, he recruited many school leavers who joined the bank and provided them opportunities for self-development.

Knowledge of people and to include them as leader to drive the organization's growth is an intangible knowledge resource for PB. Teh is always on the lookout for talent, working to identify their strengths and grooming them to achieve their full potential. Teh's management style is people-oriented, and he selects the best talents. Teh chooses people he knows well and they are thoroughly tested before they are selected as key trusted leaders in the bank. For instance, Teh recognized Dato' Sri Tay Ah Lek's determination and honesty when he was recruited in 1966 to start PB (Bowie, 2006, p. 51). Tay has been with PB from day one — 51 years in total as of 2012 and is Managing Director of PB. Teh also looks for compatibility and people with an accredited career and reputation. Teh handpicked Dato' Lee Kong Lam from the Central Bank of Malaysia and Tan Sri Dato' Thong Yaw Hong, a distinguished civil servant of high repute from the Ministry of Finance and the Economic Planning Unit (Bowie, 2006, pp. 86, 103). Thong first joined PB as a member of the Board in 1986 upon his retirement. Four months later, Thong became Chairman of the Board in October 1986. Age is not seen as a barrier to capability, but character is a crucial factor. Thong served as Secretary-General of the Finance Ministry for seven years. Given his background, he was made Chairman of the Audit Committee of the bank (Bowie, 2006, pp. 192–193, p. 326). Thong became co-Chairman of Public Finance in July 2006 and presently co-Chairman of PB. Teh's dedicated, knowledgeable and people-oriented leadership as well as his astute management give PB its extra competitive edge.

PB's strategically powered growth is supported with a strong technical proficiency that determins its policy, structure, and financial strategy.

Teh took great trouble to acquire technical proficiency and learned how to handle the human side of the enterprise (Bowie, 2006, p. 104). For the bank to progress in the information age and knowledge era where knowledge is evolving at a breathtaking pace, Teh has created a learning environment, providing incentives for staff to develop the right set of competencies. The bank has set up its own Knowledge and Learning Centre for continuous human capital development (Bowie, 2006, p. 374).

Besides technical proficiency, Teh understands the importance of networks and cultivates good relations with key people critical to PB's future. Approval for PB to open branches in the 1970s were at first slow in coming because of the NEP. Teh also knew how to sustain the necessary contacts with the relevant Government departments. He also pursued serious business networking by cultivating good relations (*guanxi*) with the public sector and all the decision makers such as political leaders, government officials and the business community. During the NEP period, PB implemented a Bumiputera policy in the bank. PB was the first Malaysian local bank to have a Malay Chairman — Tan Sri Nik Ahmed Kamil, an influential member of the United Malay National Organization (UMNO) ruling party. PB also fulfilled its social responsibility and its contribution to the socio-economic development of the country (Bowie, 2006, p. 78; Tan, 1982, p. 282). PB collaborated with the public sector in the post independent economy and for nation building.

Teh has a great ability to perceive and recognize opportunity. Many non-Bumiputeras regarded the NEP as a disincentive but Teh recognized it's potential. He conformed to the NEP staffing requirements by providing scholarships and college places for Bumiputeras who were then bonded to serve the bank. PB was accordingly granted "Approved Status" by the Finance Minister for meeting all of the Central Bank's priority lending guideline and for fulfilling the NEP's Bumiputera ownership and employment quotas. The "Approved Status" also enables PB to accept government deposits (Gomez, 1999, p. 39; Bowie, 2006, p. 107). An important component of PB's Five Year Plan was to align with the NEP. The bank had always supported the government's affirmative action. As early as 1980, it attained the prescribed goal, reaching a 31.2 percent equity stake in the bank, consistent with the national agenda. By abiding with the affirmative policy, PB was given licences. By 1987, the bank had

61 bank branches and 49 finance company branches in the 1980s. By 1990, the bank had 90 bank branches and 78 finance company branches (Bowie, 2006, pp. 211–215). Teh is not politically-aligned but politically-savvy. The greatest setback Teh encountered was during the 1970s when he was unable to expand the banks' network and branches as quickly as he would have liked. This was in the context of the early period of the affirmative policy (Bowie, 2006, p. 371). By growing PB as one of the largest banks in Malaysia, managing it with integrity and conforming to NEP regulations, Teh has managed to retain control of the bank. Other Chinese-owned banks that encountered management issues (e.g., Malayan Banking in 1969) were taken over by the Central Bank and put under government protection (Ranjit, 1987). Teh's strategy has helped to avoid PB being forced to merge with larger banks. Smaller Chinese banks such as Ban Hin Lee Bank, Wah Tat Bank, and Hock Hua Bank were forced to merge with larger banks (Cook, 2008, p. 93). PB also managed to avoid a hostile take-over which had happened to other Chinese-owned banks such as Southern Bank (*The Star*, August 4, 2012).

Since the 1990s, PB operates as a regional bank, ahead of Malaysia's two other two largest Government-linked banks. On January 1990, PB made a significant move to acquire Public Finance Limited, Hong Kong (formerly known as JCG Finance Company Limited) as the banks' first overseas subsidiary. Since early 1992, PB entered Sri Lanka and Vietnam. Later in mid-1992 it opened a branch in Cambodia. In late 1992, it became Malaysia's first bank to open a branch each in Myanmar and Laos. In June 2006, PB achieved another milestone when it acquired Hong Kong's Asia Commercial Bank (ABC) for HK4.5 billion. ABC was renamed Public Bank (Hong Kong) Limited with 32 branches, operating in Shenzhen and with representative offices in Shanghai and Shenyang. The acquisition of ABC and JCG Finance reflects Teh's vision and strategy; he thinks long-term — 10–20 years ahead (Bowie, 2006, pp. 186, 215). At the domestic front, PB acquired a 55% equity in KL Mutual Fund Berhad in 1993 and renamed it Public Mutual. On July 12, 2006, Public Mutual became a 100 percent-owned subsidiary of PB. It merged with Hock Hua Bank in 2001 and acquired Sime Merchant Bank in 2000 (Bowie, 2006, pp. 218, 266). As of 2011, the Public Bank Group expanded its regional network to 120, with 83 branches in Hong Kong, 3 branches in China, 23 branches in

Cambodia, 7 branches in Vietnam, 3 branches in Laos, a branch in Sri Lanka and 3 representative offices in Shanghai, Shenyang and Taipei (pbebank.com/corporate/).

4. Case Studies on Knowledge Management of Small and Medium Enterprise (SMEs) in Malaysia

The affirmative policy also led to the breaking of the old intra-ethnic and family based Chinese SMEs[2] and their transformation to inter-ethnic ones, involving especially Bumiputera partners. Necessarily, this transformation requires new operating structures, strategies, skills, capability and knowledge amongst Chinese entrepreneurs. The large Chinese business groups responded to the affirmative policy in different ways compared to Chinese SMEs. Amongst Chinese SMEs, a 'new' modus operandi to access not only lucrative government projects but also to manage both the projects and their Bumiputera partners was needed. The collection of processes that had been created amongst Chinese entrepreneurs and disseminated throughout their networks as the realm of "knowledge development" was exploited to fulfill their new business objectives. The creation of a "smart partnership" with Bumiputera has become a common practice amongst Chinese SMEs (Chin, 2004, 2006, 2007, 2010; Heng, 1992; Jesudason, 1989; Nonini, 1983; Rugayah Mohamed, 1994; Sia, 1994).

I have mentioned elsewhere (Chin, 2008) that in 68 Sino–Bumiputera partnerships in manufacturing, several case studies clearly indicate that Bumiputera partners possess technical and technological knowledge which they brought into the partnerships with Chinese partners. The selection process of a Bumiputera partner is pivotal. Knowledge of the potential partner, not only about his/her knowledge and qualification but also

---

[2] According to the Census of Establishments and Enterprises (2005), SMEs in Malaysia accounted for 99.2 percent or 518,996 of total establishments. In terms of employment, Malaysia's SMEs generated jobs for approximately three million workers (65.1 percent of the total employment of 4.6 million engaged in these three main sectors) in 2003 (Normah, 2006, p. 5). In 1998, nine out of ten manufacturing establishments in the country were SMEs and more than four-fifths were Chinese-owned. Lee and Lee (2003) estimated the number of Chinese SMEs at around 200,000.

his/her character as a "genuine" entrepreneur, is critical to success. These Bumiputeras represent the new Malay middle class which emerged as a result of the NEP. They are now part of a productive knowledge force forming new strategic partnerships with the Chinese in technology-based industries. As Evers (2005, p. 106) has noted, in an emerging knowledge-based economy new strategic groups emerge that will compete in "structuring society to maximize their chance for appropriating wealth and power…"

Two interviews in the semiconductor manufacturing sector provide insights that the transfer of knowledge in the electronics sector usually takes place in three stages as far as SMEs are concerned. The first stage unfolds when sub-contractors are used to carry out the "back-end" manufacturing, which is labor intensive and without the use of machineries to assemble parts and components provided by the customers. The second is the taking on of "front-end" manufacturing, which involves the use of machinery to assemble all the parts and components provided by the customers. The third stage is a more advanced stage where the sub-contractors, either SMEs or large companies are usually awarded a turnkey project. In this stage, sub-contractors handle the supply chain and need to acquire knowledge of the electronic commodities and be able to source and assemble them. This stage also involves the re-engineering of new products to complement or provide more value-added products to the transnational (TNC) companies. Research and development take place at this stage, which involves the research team from TNC companies working together with the local companies. Throughout the three stages, knowledge is created and transferred (Chin, 2008, pp. 195–196). As indicated by Kogut and Zander (1993, p. 631), "through repeated interactions, individuals and groups in a firm develop a common understanding by which to transfer knowledge from ideas into production and markets."

The following section presents two case studies, one in the manufacturing sector and one in the construction sector. The case study on ABCD Electronics Sdn Bhd describes how close relationships help to promote trust. The case study also provides detailed information about the process of knowledge sharing and creation in a Sino–Bumiputera partnership as a result of their trust. The case study on XYZ Construction Sdn Bhd describes the importance of knowing the quality of the Bumiputera partner in an Ali-Baba partnership. Hence, successful knowledge sharing involves determining the modus operandi of the partnership, and managing the partnership, which includes managing good working relationship and the *Alis*.

Case study 4: ABCD electronics Sdn Bhd[3]

ABCD Electronics Sdn Bhd is a company that specializes in the manufacture of electronics and computer parts, and providing advanced engineering services. This company was established in April 2001 with, amongst others, four partners: Ahmad, Kong, Tan and Yam (not their real names). The company was established as an offshoot of Hitachi Metals Electronics (M) Sdn Bhd (HMEM) to capitalize on HMEM's skilled workforce and modern equipment and to provide product and services to regional and international companies.

The four partners were long time colleagues in Hitachi, a Japanese company. Ahmad was General Manager (GM) of the human resource department at Hitachi in Penang from 1988–2001. Tan was GM and Kong a senior manager, and both were in charge of production. Yam, a senior manager, was in charge of accounting and finance in the same company. In 2001, when Hitachi Metal in Penang decided to shut down its branch, Ahmad was called in to discuss this matter with his Japanese boss. Ahmad saw this as an opportunity and proposed to Hitachi to close and sell the company to a team of local managers. Ahmad and his three colleagues drafted a working paper and managed to convince Hitachi to allow them to take over the business with a "very generous price, plus with all the machineries" as Ahmad informed us. Ahmad had the experience of managing 4,300 workers. He had plans to recruit three qualified and experienced Chinese partners in the industry whom he trusted. Together they ventured into this business. He selected 60 people from the existing Hitachi branch: the best managers, supervisors and other supporting staff all with experience in the industry. Hence, Ahmad and his partners set out

---

[3]This case study is derived from my previous research works published in the *Journal of Asian Business* in 2008: Chin Yee Whah (2008). Knowledge management: Business development in Chinese–Bumiputera partnerships in Malaysia. *Journal of Asian Business*, 22(2)/22(3)/23(1), 189–212.

with both physical and human capital. In 2006, they had 150 workers, including six engineer managers.

In terms of division of labor in this partnership, Ahmad assumed the position of a managing director while the other three Chinese partners become company directors. Since he had vast experience as GM in human resource, Ahmad was responsible for the company's administration. He also takes pride in his important role of securing business for the company. He emphasized that with his long years of service in the business, especially with Japanese companies, he could easily clinch business for his new company. He stressed:

> "I can influence and appeal to customers especially Japanese companies due to my previous seniority at Hitachi. I know people and am recognized by many in this industry. I also have extensive networks."

It is very natural for other partners to make use of the knowledge and experience they acquired while working with Hitachi, and to then assume equally important tasks in their new venture. In this case, Tan is responsible for the production of the company's products while Yam as financial controller, takes charge of managing salaries, employee provident funds, bank loans, products pricing and purchase.

In terms of research and development (R&D) and staff training, ABCD Electronics collaborates with their clients, which includes two Japanese TNCs, a Dutch TNC and an American TNC. Because ABCD played the supporting role for these TNCs, they had joint training and R&D activities locally and abroad. The cost is shared by both parties. Meanwhile ABCD has developed its own small internal R&D program. With support from TNCs, especially in the R&D area, this company has remained competitive in terms of innovations and product development.

This partnership was successful not only because of the individuals' knowledge of business and the division of labor but it was also a result of the trust amongst the key personnel. Ahmad was very confident that his partners would not bypass him to secure business and that they would not intrude into each other's area of responsibility. On occasion, conflicts did arise but these were overcome through discussions.

Case study 5: XYZ construction Sdn Bhd[4]

XYZ Construction Sdn Bhd is a medium-sized company that employs 80 workers, including five Bumiputera supervisors. Meng, Managing Director of XYZ construction Sdn Bhd has 23 years of experience in the construction industry and he stressed that all the Bumiputera partners he came across in the previous projects were all sleeping partners. From his accumulated experience and knowledge of how Bumiputera sleeping partners work, he deals with the Bumiputeras on a "consignment" basis to reduce risks. A consignment refers to an agreement, where a government project is awarded to a company, scheduled payments from the government are paid to a joined account of the company (not to the individual Bumiputera or Chinese partner), and the company will then pay the Chinese and Bumiputera partners based on work completed. This is to avoid payment being absconded by the Bumiputera partners which had happened to some Chinese partners before in "Ali-Baba partnerships."

In an Ali-Baba partnership, *Ali*, or the Malay partner, is often regarded as the less active or "sleeping partner" who basically brought his political influence and connections into the partnership. *Baba*, or the Chinese partner, is typically seen as the more active half of the alliance who brought into the partnership his capital, skills and technical know-how. This kind of partnership enabled the Chinese to get access to licenses and lucrative government contracts that are reserved for the Bumiputera.

In these partnerships, *Ali* only needs to have the knowledge of "know-who" while the *Baba* partner also needs to know whom to work with. Knowing who, especially their character, matters in an Ali-Baba partnership. Chinese partners have to find out the background of their potential Bumiputera partners. This implies the notion of knowledge with regard to the importance of "knowing man." For instance, Meng always checks out the past performance of the Bumiputeras he intends to work with. It is a know-who game and finding a workable solution to achieve business goals is critical. Meng always reinvents his modus operandi to meet the demands of the government to ensure that his company would continue to

---

[4]This case study is derived from Chin (2008).

secure government projects. The logic of employing Bumiputera as supervisors in his company is that it "looks nice" as a Chinese-Bumiputera company. In Meng's company, the Bumiputera partners are put under the business development section with the rationale that they will use their marketing strategy to meet with clients from government departments. On the other hand, the Bumiputera partners can perform well on stage shows, especially during press conferences. Meng said that though the Malay CEOs often appear in front as capable directors and managing directors of large construction companies, in reality, most of their work is done by Chinese contractors.

Managing Ali-Baba partnerships is challenging. Maintaining good working and "partnership" relations is important to safeguard sustainable partnerships. The pure type of an Ali-Baba partnership is when the Bumiputera partners have no interest at all to learn but simply capitalize on their status as Bumiputera and therein take advantage of the affirmative action policy. In other words, they simply assist to secure the necessary licenses and to gain access to government tenders. "They don't even provide capital" (an informant) whereas the Chinese have to bring in money and expertise while undertaking risks. Meng asserted that:

> "... the Bumiputera partners do not know the operational and technical details because it is hard work at the construction side, and very few of them are involved in the day-to-day operation. Instead, most of them do their own thing."

Moreover, it can be very expensive to manage the *Alis*. Having knowledge of the Ali-Baba partnership, the Chinese have learned to be very careful in the selection of *Ali* as partners because once the *Alis* are appointed as partners, they usually assume a director's post and the Chinese have to begin spending money on them. All these practices are already an open secret among most Chinese entrepreneurs in the construction sector. Knowing their history of job delivery is very important. On average, Meng's company spends RM15,000 a month for one Bumiputera director, which usually includes providing him with a luxurious car. Moreover, the *Alis* also expect other benefits. Although they do not interfere in the daily operation of the business, the Chinese have to pay them a salary. The worst thing that could happen to the Chinese partners is to have their Bumiputera partners run away — abscond — with the project money which is sometimes deposited into the Bumiputera partners' bank account. However, experienced and knowledgeable contractors like Meng take several precautions; for instance, payment from the government is credited into the company's account which is under the control of the Chinese partners. Meng emphasized that there is no legal contract with subcontractors and the job is usually delayed if there is no progress payment. In this case, both the company and the contractors need money and if the project is abandoned the company will be black-listed. To avoid these potential risks, the Chinese must be able to control everything, the cash flow, the side operation and the Bumiputera partners as well. Since Meng's partnership is conducted on a consignment basis, the company opened an "exco account" so that payment goes to the company and the company pays the Bumiputera partners according to scheduled payments as agreed upon. The terms and conditions are clearly spelt out in black and white.

The major challenge for Meng is that the Bumiputera partners may ask for more money. In this case, Meng has to consider how to deal with them. Meng will always try to keep good partners who can deliver and who can get contracts from the government. If Meng does not keep them, they might take the contracts and pass them to other businesses. The solution to this is to advise them to take a long-term perspective so that they can work together on a "win-win" basis to ensure that both of them could deliver their projects. If the Bumiputera partners want to pass on work to other contractors, there is no guarantee that other contractors can deliver it if they cannot control the finance, administration and side operations well. Many Bumiputeras have obtained contracts for themselves but failed to complete the work. This meant that the Bumiputeras might not be able to make a profit. Some were persuaded to accept Meng's "win-win" rationale, while others have tended to take the short-term view of maximizing their gains.

According to Meng, most Bumiputera construction companies fail because they face cash-flow and management problems. It is difficult for them to put up capital due to a lack of networking with sub-contractors and suppliers, almost all of whom are Chinese. Some Bumiputeras have also failed to prove themselves capable and therefore were unable to earn the trust of Chinese contractors and suppliers. The affirmative action policy adds on to this dilemma, since they can earn money by simply being a middleman.

5. Conclusion

"Know-who" or "know man" is an important component of knowledge. It is also an intangible knowledge resource of an organization. Knowing, understanding and building good relationships with people in powerful positions, particularly policy makers, to act and to provide solutions will have a great bearing on the development and future direction of a business group. This is reality in the context of affirmative policy that is biased toward a particular ethnic group. This is evident in the development of the Genting Group and the IGB Group, and in the early development of the Pubic Bank Group. As for the SMEs, without "know-who" the Chinese are unable to obtain access to lucrative government projects. Forming strategic partnerships with Bumiputera partners they know well helps promote trust and sustains business partnerships. Such practices led to the transformation from intra-ethnic ownership to inter-ethnic ownership in Chinese business groups and Chinese-owned SMEs.

A number of Malaysian Chinese business groups are now managed by the second generation. Some of the older founders of Chinese business groups who "knew the wrong man" in the political economy scenario were not able to sustain their businesses. Some Chinese business groups that lacked entrepreneurial drive when the second or third generation took over, or failed to make adjustments to the NEP-induced changes, stagnated or even declined during the periods of the NEP (1971–1990) and the National Development Policy (1991–2000).

Know-who is an important knowledge asset or as Zeleny (2005, p. 29) has put it: "Who knows what and who knows how to do what is a critical resource." The Bumiputeras have access to government projects due to their knowledge of who, where, when and how to lobby for projects. The affirmative action policy, which led to the development of Ali-Baba partnerships, especially in the construction sector, has created opportunities for the Bumiputeras to make gains via entry into partnerships with Chinese businessmen. In my view, such politically expedient partnerships should be regarded as "smart"; they represent real business practices in the context of the Malaysian political economy. The combination of know-how and know-who in smart partnerships that involved knowledge transfer in expediting the formation of a Bumiputera Commercial and Industrial Community (BCIC) is associated with the knowledge element of humanity or benevolence. Interpret this as an act by the Chinese business community to extend the goodwill to the nation. Know-who and having strong ties is also important beyond national borders where business interest is involved. The Genting Groups and Lim's family have strong ties with a few native tribes in the United States, an important intangible knowledge resource of the group.

In terms of leadership and management, knowing people of noble character and compatibility; recruiting, training, and placing them in key positions; trusting and empowering them — these practices will result in exponential growth for a business organization. The Public Bank Group exhibits such phenomena by putting people with noble character in top positions. In the case of the Genting Group and IGB Group, consultants were recruited to help plan and execute projects and business ventures in which the group did not have sufficient experience. The founder of the Genting Group was very innovative and seized business opportunities in his early business ventures. In terms of business strategy, the group rides on the trend in the global casino business to expand abroad and to reduce risk. The cash rich IGB Group sped up the construction of one of Asia's largest shopping mall during the 1997–1998 Asian financial crisis whilst others were slowing down. IGB positions itself for strong broad-base fixed income returns and financial stability. Its strong cash flow enabled the group to keep investing in potentially promising business sectors. The PB Group keeps its focus on banking, finance and share trading businesses, prudence in management, identifies, trains and retains talent. PB's knowledge of the financial sector and its prudence management led to minimized risk and protected itself from financial crises. As for smart partnerships, the strategy is to look for genuine partners for a long-term partnership.

References

Aris, NM (2006). SMEs: Building blocks for economic growth. Working Paper.

Bloomberg (2012). Genting "aggressively" seeks US casino stakes with $1.7 billion of cash. June 15. Available at http://www.bloomberg.com/news/2010-06-14/genting-aggressively-seeks-u-s-casino-stakes-with-1-7-billion-of-cash.html.

Bowie, P (2006). *The Hong Piow: A Banking Thoroughbred*. Kuala Lumpur: Public Bank Berhad.

Cheong, S (1992). *Chinese Controlled Companies in the KLSE Industrial Counter*. Kuala Lumpur: Corporate Resourse Service Sdn Bhd.

Chin, YW (2004). Ethnicity and the transformation of the Ali-Baba partnership in the Chinese business culture in Malaysia. In *The Challenge of Ethnicity: Building a Nation in Malaysia*, BK Cheah (ed.), pp. 54–88. Singapore: Marshall Cavendish International.

Chin, YW (2008). Knowledge management: Business development in Chinese–Bumiputera partnerships in Malaysia. *Journal of Asian Business*, 22(2)/22(3)/23(1), 189–212.

Chin, YW (2008). The evolution of Malaysian Chinese entrepreneurship: From British Colonial rule to post new economic policy. *Journal of Chinese Overseas*, 4(2), 203–237.

Chin, YW (2010). Toward inter-ethnic business development and national unity in Malaysia. CRISE Working Paper No. 73, January. UK: Queen Elizabeth House, University of Oxford.

Cook, M (2008). *Banking Reform in Southeast Asia: The Region's Decisive Decade*. Abingdon, UK: Routledge.

CPPS (Centre for Public Policy Studies) (2005) Corporate equity distribution: Past trends and future policy. Available at http://www.cpps.org.my/downloads/D_%20Corporate_Equity_Distribution. pdf.

Drabble, JH (2000). *An Economic History of Malaysia, c. 1800–1990: The Transition to Modern Economic Growth*. London: McMillan Press.

Evers, H-D (2005). Transition towards a knowledge society: Malaysia and Indonesia in global perspective. In *Governing and Managing Knowledge in Asia*, In T Menkhoff *et al.* (eds.), pp. 99–110. Singapore: World Scientific.

Evers, H-D and T Menkhoff (2004). Expert knowledge and the role of consultants in an emerging knowledge-based economy. *Human System Management*, 23, 123–135.

Far Eastern Economic Review (1989). January 5.

Flower, R, W Lim and CY Loh (2006). *Tan Sri Loh Boon Siew: The Life and Times of a Fire Dragon*. Singapore: SNP Edition.

Gomez, ET (1999). *Chinese Business in Malaysia: Accumulation, Accommodation and Ascendance*. Surrey: Curzon.

Hara, F (1991). Malaysia's new economic policy and the Chinese business community. *The Developing Economie*, 29(4), 350–370.

Heng, PK (1992). The Chinese business elite of Malaysia. In *Southeast Asian Capitalists*, R McVey (ed.), pp. 127–144. New York: Southeast Asia Program.

Huff, WG (1994). *The Economic Growth of Singapore: Trade and Development in the Twentieth Century*. Cambridge, UK: Cambridge University Press.

Jesudason, JV (1989). *Ethnicity and the Economy: The States, Chinese Business, and Multinationals in Malaysia*. Singapore: Oxford University Press.

Jomo, KS (1986). *A Question of Class: Capital, the State and Uneven Development in Malaya*. Kuala Lumpur: Oxford University Press.

Kogut, B and U Zander (1993). Knowledge of the firm and the evolutionary theory of the multinational corporation. *Journal of International Business Studies,* 24(4), 625–645.

Lee, CL (2008). Traditional Chinese conceptions of knowledge (zhi, 知): A "modern" interpretation with reference to Business. *Journal of Asian Business*, 22(2)/22(3)/23(1), 25–32.

Lee, KH and PP Lee (2003). Malaysian Chinese business: Who survived the crisis? *Kyoto Review*. Available at http://kyotoreview.cseas.kyoto-u.ac.jp/issue/issue3/article_280.html.

Lim, GT (2004). *My Story*. Subang Jaya: Pelanduk Publications.

Ling, W (1989). The Chinese in post-war Malaysia, economic development and current conditions. In *The Economy of the Chinese in Southeast Asia*, M Jiang (ed.). Fuzhou: Fujian Renmin Chubanshe.

Loy, HH and A Crofts (1997). *Against All Odds: The Making of a Billionaire*. Singapore: Times Books International.

Malaysia (1973). *Mid-Term Review of the Second Malaysia Plan, 1971–1975*. Kuala Lumpur: Malaysia Government Press.

———(1999). Mid-Term Review of the Seventh Malaysia Plan, 1996–2000. Kuala Lumpur: National Printing Department.

——— (2006). *Ninth Malaysia Plan, 2006–2010*. Putrajaya: Economic Planning Unit.

——— (2010). *Tenth Malaysia Plan, 2011–2015*. Putrajaya: Economic Planning Unit.

Nonini, DM (1983). The Chinese truck transport "industry" of a Peninsular Malaysia market town. In *The Chinese in Southeast Asia*, Vol. 1, LYC Lim and LAP Gosling (eds.), pp. 171–206. Singapore: Maruzen Asia.

Menkhoff, T, YW Chay, and B Loh (2004). Notes from an "intelligent island": Towards strategic knowledge management in Singapore's small business sector. *Internationales Asienforum*, 35(1-2), 85–99.

NSDC (National SME Development Council) (2005). SME Annual Report. Kuala Lumpur: Percetakan Nasional Berhad.

Gill, R (1987). *Khoo Teck Puat: Tycoon on a Tightrope*. Singapore: Sterling Corporate Services.

Rugayah, M (1994). Sino–Bumiputera cooperation. In *The Development of Bumiputera Enterprises and Sino–Malay Economic Cooperation in Malaysia*, H Fujio (ed.), pp. 73–90. Tokyo: Institute of Developing Economics.

Sia, I (1994). The Yeos — In search of markets. In *The Development of Bumiputera Enterprises and Sino–Malay Economic Cooperation in Malaysia*, H Fujio (ed.), pp. 91–108. Tokyo: Institute of Developing Economics.

Searle, P (1999). *The Riddle of Malaysian Capitalism: Rent-seekers or Real Capitalism?* St. Leonards: Allen and Unwin.

Snodgrass, DR (1980). *Inequality and Economic Development in Malaysia*. Kuala Lumpur: Oxford University Press.

Starcruises.com. Available at http://www.starcruises.com/en/home/aboutus.aspx.

Singh, S (1984). *The First 25 Years: 1959–1984*. Kuala Lumpur: Bank Negara Malaysia.

Tan, CN (2006). *Tan Chin Nam: Never Say I Assume!* Petaling Jaya: MPH Group Publishing Sdn Bhd.

Tan, TW (1982). *Income Distribution and Determination in West Malaysia*. Kuala Lumpur: Oxford University Press.

The Edge Malaysia (2008). Special focus: Genting group bets big on Singapore. Available at http://www.theedgemalaysia.com/features/158007—special-focus-genting.

The Edge Malaysia (2012). IGB REIT feeds into thirst for yield, August 13.

The Star (2012). Genting expands into the Bahamas, July 3.

The Star (2012). Nazir talks about CIMB as a regional bank, August 4.

Trocki, CA (2008). Knowledge management in the world of eighteen century Chinese business. *Journal of Asian Business*, 22(2)/22(3)/23(1), 33–45.

Yip, YH (1969). *The Development of the Tin Mining Industry of Malaya*. Kuala Lumpur: University of Malaya Press.

Yoshihara, K (1988). *The Rise of Ersatz Capitalism in Southeast Asia*. Singapore: Oxford University Press.

Zeleny, M (2005). Knowledge of enterprise: Knowledge management or knowledge technology? In *Governing and Managing Knowledge in Asia*, T Menkhoff *et al.* (eds.), pp. 23–57. Singapore: World Scientific.

Chapter 5

Evolving Chineseness, Ethnicity and Business: The Making of the Ethnic Chinese as a "Market-Dominant Minority" in Indonesia

Hoon Chang Yau

1. Introduction

The ethnic Chinese in Indonesia play a very significant role in the nation's economy. Their dominance in the Indonesian economy is often seen as disproportionate to their numbers, as reflected in the popular assertion that "the Chinese constitute only 3.5 percent of the population but control 70 percent of Indonesia's economy" (*Far Eastern Economic Review*, May 28, 1998, cited in Chua, 2008). In the *New York Times* bestseller, *World on Fire: How Exporting Free Market Democracy Breeds Ethnic Hatred and Global Instability*, Amy Chua (2004) identified Chinese Indonesians as one of the "market-dominant minorities" in the world. Her book highlights the double bind of free market democracy: it privileges certain ethnic minorities to dominate the market and accumulate wealth on the one hand, and also allows a frustrated indigenous majority to pit against the wealthy ethnic minority on the other. The book, which became phenomenally popular among the Chinese Indonesians in Indonesia, cited the May 1998 anti-Chinese riots in Indonesia as a prime example of its thesis. Although it does not offer any solution to their predicament, to many Chinese Indonesians, the book has provided a logical explanation to the vulnerable position of the Chinese minority in Indonesia.

The ethnic Chinese have been stereotypically portrayed in Indonesia's public sphere as economic creatures and wealthy business people. While it is true that a large proportion of Indonesia's *private* economy pre-1998 was dominated by a *handful* of Chinese conglomerates, the characterization of

Chinese Indonesians as "market-dominated minority" is not applicable to all — there are many poor Chinese in Tangerang and Singkawang, for instance. Nevertheless, politicians, academics, popular literature, presses and media have repeatedly reinforced such stereotype making it pervasive and entrenched in the popular imagination of many Indonesians. Against such generalization, Christian Chua argues that Chinese tycoons and Chinese minority "do not share more than the same ethnic ascription," as he sought to "analytically de-link" the two in his book (Chua, 2008, p. 3). Gilman reminds us that stereotypes are "the product of history and of a culture that perpetuates them" (Gilman, 1985, p. 20). This chapter addresses how the Chinese have been constructed and constituted as a "market-dominant minority" through an examination of the changes in the identity and societal and economic role of the Chinese in Indonesian history.

Ethnicity can be used (or misused) to serve the interests of power holders. Under the pretext of nation building, governments can manipulate ethnicity by developing cultural policies to suit this objective. The state often appeals to common paradigms of "race," culture, nation, blood and soil when promoting nationalism for most people still regard identities based on culture, society and nation-state as absolute, essential and substantial. To them, "culture is organic, territory bound, and normative; a society is a bounded community; a nation-state has only one cultural system which eventually leads to the assimilation of people with different cultures" (Wu, 1997, pp. 142–143). Such paradigm is problematic not least because it homogenizes culture and identity, and ignores the possibility of multiple identities that people may assert at different times or even at the same time. As different regimes in Indonesia homogenized and manipulated the Chinese ethnicity, the heterogeneity within this ethnicity was disregarded and denied. This is one of the reasons why Chinese Indonesians persist to be a distinct ethnic group, which becomes a ready target of violence and attacks during times of social unrests and regime changes.

2. The Heterogeneous and Evolving Chinese Identity

The ethnic Chinese in Indonesia have been flexible, responsive and ingenious in their adaptation to change. Their identity has been multiplied in accord with their degrees of adaptation and acculturation to their local circumstances. The different manifestations of Chineseness in different political periods in Indonesia indicate that identities are not static, but are dynamic and can be transformed and redefined. The ethnic Chinese in Indonesia have never been a homogeneous group. Regional and class diversity partly account for their heterogeneous self-identification. Chineseness in Medan, for instance, is different from Chineseness in Jakarta, Pontianak, Bangka, Semarang, Sukabumi or Malang.

The ethnic Chinese are culturally heterogeneous and can be grouped differently in different periods. Conventionally, scholars have divided them into two main groups, the China-oriented *totok* (China-born, pure blood) and the acculturated *peranakan* (local-born or mixed blood). Although centuries of residence in Indonesia caused *peranakan* men (most immigrants being male) to intermarry with local women, to adopt local culture and to lose many of the features of their Chineseness, by 1900, they were still unable to fully assimilate into the native population. The main obstacles to assimilation include colonial racial policy, religion, economic position and the Chinese sense of cultural superiority. The identity of the *peranakan* was by no means unified, though it is worth noting that it was racially and patrilineally defined, i.e., the group was defined and constituted by the race and gender of immigrants.

In contrast to the earlier, predominantly male migrations, the immigrants who arrived in Indonesia at the end of the 19th century included a significant number of women. As a result, it became possible for Chinese men to take a China-born wife rather than a native or *peranakan*, and these immigrants formed the distinct *totok* community. The *totok* community, nevertheless, was not a unified group as they came from different parts of China and spoke in different Chinese dialects. The *totok* were generally more politically orientated to China. The *totok-peranakan* distinction, however, is not fixed and has been subject to change. The traditional distinction based on "race" and birthplace became unrealistic after the Great Depression when migration of Chinese from China into Indonesia halted. Scholars subsequently used a socio-cultural definition to replace the previous definition of *totok* and *peranakan*. According to this distinction, a *totok* refers to a Chinese who had a Chinese-orientated upbringing and who use the Chinese language as the medium of communication even though he/she was born in Indonesia. Similarly, a *peranakan* refers not only to the Chinese with mixed ancestry, but also to those pure-blood Chinese who were born locally and who could not speak Chinese.

To understand the complex identities that the ethnic Chinese in Indonesia have assumed at different times and the multiple identities that they assert at the same time, it is necessary to understand how the Chinese have perceived themselves and others, and the extent to which they have been willing to identify with their Chineseness. It is also necessary to understand how they have been regarded and how their ethnicity has been constructed by indigenous Indonesians (hereafter, *pribumi*), and the willingness of the *pribumi* to accept them as one of their own. In order to achieve such understanding, it will be useful to examine the common stereotypical identities portrayed and perceived by the Chinese themselves and by the *pribumi*.

Stereotyping is a method of processing information that involves a reduction of images and ideas to a simple and manageable form. As there is no real line between the "self" and the "other," stereotypes function as an imaginary line that serves to set "them" apart from "us" (Gilman, 1985). *Pribumi* have commonly perceived the Chinese in these stereotypes: *They* are a homogeneous and changeless group. *They* exploit our economy and are rich. *They* feel superior and exclusive. *Their* loyalty to Indonesia is questionable. *They* are reluctant to assimilate (Coppel, 1983, pp. 5–27). The next section will explore the constructions of these stereotypes in Indonesian history.

3. The Making of the "Market-Dominant Minority" in Indonesian History

The journey of the ethnic Chinese in becoming a "market-dominating minority" began during the Dutch colonial period when they played the role of economic middlemen. Chinese immigrants in the 19th and early 20th century in Dutch East Indies found assimilation into native society virtually impossible. This was largely due to the Dutch "divide-and-rule" policies and the structure of colonial society. The population in colonial

Dutch colonial rule: different policies for different races (= hierarchical) [handwritten annotation]

Indonesia was divided into three racial groups with different legal rights and privileges: the Europeans were at the top, the Foreign Orientals (mainly Chinese) were in the middle and the natives were at the bottom. The economic activities of the Chinese were circumscribed by the Dutch administration: the Agrarian Law of 1860 prohibited them from owning land, thereby preventing them from engaging in agriculture; and they were excluded from becoming civil servants as they were not allowed from taking the civil servant examination. These restrictions left them with few options but to engage in trade and retail activities (Diao and Tan, 2004).

Before the end of the 19th century, the Dutch granted a small number of Chinese monopoly privileges to engage in profitable but "immoral" activities (read: revenue farming), such as the selling of opium and the operation of gambling establishments and pawnshops. The Chinese were also involved in the much hated enterprise of tax and debt collection. In granting the Chinese these licences, the government collected licence fees in return. This proved to be an inexpensive and simple means of raising official revenues. The privileges given to these Chinese, and their dominance in the retail market, contributed to the construction of the stereotype that the Chinese dominated the economy. [handwritten: note the sb ke - Pawnshop early 20th century]

Under these conditions, for the Chinese to assimilate into indigenous society would have meant a drop in social status and the loss of some of the business privileges. The *pribumi* resented the revenue farmers and perceived the Chinese as "natural enemies of the indigenous, sucking their blood and exploiting them, thwarting their economic development" (Phoa, 1992, p. 14). In 1900, in order to protect the natives' rights, the Dutch implemented the Ethical Policy for "native betterment," but it came at Chinese expense. The grievances of the Chinese at that time include the ban on revenue farming; paying higher taxes; and the restrictions resulting from the pass and zoning systems, which required them to live in specific urban ghettos and to obtain visas if they wanted to travel. The Ethical Policy discriminated against the Chinese, destroyed assimilation processes and changed the Chinese position from being the "protégés of the rulers to becoming the foremost enemy of the state" (Phoa, 1992, p. 14). [handwritten: 1900 Ethical Policy: for benefit of indig. But increasing discrimination of Chinese]

The widespread resentment caused by Dutch "apartheid" policies and the inability to attain European or local identity catalyzed many *peranakan* Chinese to move in a direction which enhanced their Chinese identity.

Around 1900, partly through mass immigration of the Chinese to Southeast Asia, sentiments of Chinese nationalism were spread to the region, causing diverse Chinese communities in the Dutch Indies to mobilize and identify with a greater "imagined community" of a pan-Chinese nation. The rise of pan-Chinese nationalism in Java was manifest in the emergence of the Tiong Hoa Hwe Koan (THHK or the Chinese Organization) which fostered educational and cultural nationalism; the Sianghwee (Chinese Chamber of Commerce) which encouraged commercial nationalism; and a *peranakan* Chinese newspaper, *Sin Po*, which promoted political nationalism.

3.1 *Contested citizenship in post-colonial Indonesia*

"They have been here since the time of our ancestors. In fact, they are real Indonesians who live and die in Indonesia. However, because of a political sleight of hand, they have suddenly become foreigners who are not foreign" (Pramoedya Ananta Toer, famous Indonesian writer, 1998, p. 54).

After Indonesia gained Independence, the ethnic Chinese were faced with the quandary of citizenship. A Citizenship Act that aimed at a demonstration of loyalty to Indonesia was introduced in 1958. This Act adopts an "active system" by which Indonesian citizens of Chinese descent would lose their citizenship if they failed to make an official declaration to reject Chinese citizenship. When this Act was fully implemented in 1960, there were two main categories of Chinese in Indonesia: the *Warga Negara Indonesia* (or Indonesian citizens, WNI) who were mainly *peranakan*, and the *Warga Negara Asing* (or foreign citizens, WNA) who were mainly *totok*. The WNA Chinese were further divided into citizens of the People's Republic of China (PRC) and "stateless" Chinese who were either Taiwan nationals or those who dissociated themselves from PRC and Taiwan. However, as a result of the historic division and prejudices between the *pribumi* and Chinese, many government officials and *pribumi* considered both *totok* and *peranakan* alike, regardless of their nationality, as undesirable "aliens" by and discriminated against them.

Postcolonial Indonesia's economic policies show evidence of discriminations against the Chinese, irrespective of their nationality. The move to

"Indonesianize" the economy by the Sukarno administration should more accurately be described as the "indigenization" of the economy. Many discriminatory measures that were implemented against the WNA equally affected the WNI Chinese. The Othering of the Chinese as a whole became clear when the government introduced the "Benteng" (Fortress) Program in 1950 to promote the development of an indigenous business class (Thee, 2006). The program gave priority and special privileges for *pribumi* Indonesians to participate in the economy, which drew a line between *pribumi* and non-*pribumi* instead of between Indonesians and foreigners. The program, which proved to be a failure, gave rise to the "Ali Baba" practice where business licenses issued to indigenous Indonesians were channeled into companies financed and managed by the ethnic Chinese. *Pribumi* licence holders would receive remuneration as directors of the company with little or no participation in the business (Diao and Tan, 2004). Another anti-Chinese campaign known as the "Assaat Movement" was launched in 1956 to urge the government to give preferential economic treatment to *pribumi* rather than to WNI Chinese, in order to compensate the *pribumi* for their weak positions created by colonial Dutch policy.

The regulation that hit the Chinese the hardest was the law prohibiting retail trade by WNA in rural areas. This regulation known as the Presidential Decree No.10 (PP-10) was enacted in November 1959. Since the Citizenship Act of 1958 was only fully implemented in 1960, the nationality of most Chinese was still ambiguous when the PP-10 was promulgated. Thus, although the PP-10 was only officially directed at WNA, the WNI Chinese experienced similar distress and insecurity as the line of distinction between foreigners and citizens was still unclear. Some WNI Chinese, especially the *peranakan*, supported the PP-10 to show their loyalty to Indonesia and their separateness from the *totok* (Suryadinata, 1978). The wash from PP-10 was dramatic: the dissociation of some *peranakan* from the *totok*; a general increase in consciousness of their problematic identity among the ethnic Chinese; and more than a hundred thousand Chinese (mostly WNA) left for China.

The Chinese in Indonesia have been rendered scapegoats or convenient targets of social hostility at times of regime change or when established authority is shaken. They have suffered a long history of persecution since the first ethnic cleansing carried out by the Dutch in Java in 1740. One of the most brutal forms of this phenomenon was manifest when President Sukarno's regime collapsed in 1965 as a result of an abortive coup attempt known as the 30th September Movement (G30S). This coup attempt provided the legitimacy for a military offensive against the Indonesian Communist Party (PKI). After the coup, a surge of anti-Communist and anti-Chinese sentiment swept through the country as Communists and Chinese were held responsible for the alleged role of the PRC in the abortive coup. In the process, many Chinese suffered great loss of property and lives. Even though this number is relatively small compared to the number of *pribumi* that were slain at that time, what cannot be overlooked is the mass hysteria that followed the crisis. Anti-Chinese episodes occurred in different parts of Indonesia until 1967 when anti-Chinese sentiments finally began to subside. However, oppression of Chinese identity increased after 1967 under the pretext of "anti-Communism," as part of the Suharto regime's "paranoia."

3.2 *Being the "minor-wives" of Suharto's New Order regime*

> "He [Suharto] used them [the Chinese] but he did not want to acknowledge that because it could become a political liability for him. Never once did he give us [Chinese] a decent place within the New Order because he wanted to keep things — including the credit for what his government achieved — for himself. It was sadly fitting that the New Order should later collapse amid the rubble of anti-Chinese riots. We [Chinese] were treated as minor wives, enjoyed but not recognized" (Jusuf Wanandi, prominent Chinese Indonesian, 2012, pp. 126–127).

The allegations that the ethnic Chinese in Indonesia were linked to the People's Republic of China (PRC) and that both parties were involved in the September 1965 abortive coup determined the fate of the Chinese in New Order Indonesia. After assuming power in 1966, Suharto systematically repressed any expression of Chinese ethnic, cultural and religious identities. Chineseness during the New Order was an imposed rather than a self-identified identity. Chinese identity was artificially constructed by the regime and juxtaposed as an internal and hostile "other" to the "true" indigenous Indonesian (Aguilar Jr., 2001). The dominant society and state institutions persisted in viewing as outsiders, and imposed discriminatory policies on them.

In the process of making the ethnic Chinese an internal outsider, the New Order imposed a social stigma on the Chinese as exclusive, asocial, rich and China (hence, Communist) -oriented. This stigmatization of the ethnic Chinese was manifest in the reformulation and institutionalization of the "Chinese problem" in Indonesia. The ethnic Chinese — their culture, their religion, their role in the nation's economy, and their very existence — were labeled by New Order politicians as a national problem. The government legitimized its policies, which marginalized the ethnic Chinese in all social, educational, political and religious arenas, in an attempt to solve the "problem."

During the Cold War period, suspicions that the Chinese Indonesians were a potential "fifth column" of China were strongly felt. The suspicious climate resulted in local governments' and *pribumi*'s distrust of ethnic Chinese and justified their discrimination and cultural oppression. The New Order viewed anything related to Chineseness as linked to the Communists and thus as threatening to national interests. Even though this paranoia faded after the Cold War and Sino–Indonesian relations were normalized in the early 1990s, it never disappeared completely.

In 1991, Siswono, then State Minister for People's Housing, issued a paper listing nine "sins" of the ethnic Chinese which he thought had "marred their image" (cited in Tan, 1995, pp. 16–17). The nine "sins" of the ethnic Chinese which he listed are:

1. They live exclusively in their own area;
2. Some companies have a preference to recruit people of Chinese descent;
3. Some companies discriminate in salary in favor of the ethnic Chinese workers;
4. There are some who discriminate between ethnic Chinese and ethnic Indonesians in their behavior toward clients, in their business relations;
5. They do not show social solidarity and togetherness with the ethnic Indonesians in their neighborhood;

6. There are those whose sense of national identity is still very weak, and who treat Indonesia solely as a place to live and earn a living;

7. There are those who in their daily life still speak Chinese and who adhere to their traditions, and do not even know Indonesian customs, and who make no effort to speak Indonesian well;

8. There are those who view their Indonesian citizenship as a legality only;

9. There are those who feel superior toward other population groups.

Three of these "sins" are related to the business practices of this ethnic group. The prominent role of the ethnic Chinese in Indonesia's economy contributed to negative stereotyping. This is also due to the fact that a disproportionate number of Chinese became very wealthy under the New Order and some of them seemed to flaunt their wealth in extravagant life-styles — a circumstance that was perceived as a problem by the *pribumi* when juxtaposed to the poverty of many Indonesians.

The New Order did not follow in the footsteps of Sukarno's policy in indigenizing Indonesia's economy. Instead, the development-oriented Suharto government utilized Chinese business skills to recover the sinking economy. The government's embarkation on a market-oriented economic strategy could not have succeeded without opening the way for the Chinese to participate as fully as possible in economic life because they alone had the commercial experience and ready access to foreign capital. Mackie notes that, "Their contribution to the economic transformation of the country since 1966–1967 has far exceeded that of the *pribumi* businessmen and state enterprises" (1991, p. 91). The New Order government, however, had never acknowledged the economic and other contributions of the Chinese to the nation. This prompted Jusuf Wanandi — a prominent Chinese who had worked closely with the New Order regime — to lament, "We [Chinese Indonesians] were treated as minor wives, enjoyed but not recognized" (2012, p. 127).

Privileges and opportunities provided by the New Order bolstered the positions of Chinese business interests, contributing to the rapid growth of Chinese economic power. However, in restricting the conception of the Chinese to that of players in the economic arena, state policies in Indonesia fostered an image of the Chinese as "economic creatures." Commercial success unwittingly demonized the Chinese and stirred up anti-Chinese sentiments as they were identified with greed and other negative values, and as villains who secured their gains through exploitation, corruption and collusion to the detriment of the *pribumi*.

A small group of Chinese, referred to as the *cukong*, became very wealthy through cooperation with the Indonesian power elite — usually members of the military. Some of them were cronies of Suharto. The close ties that the ethnic Chinese business community developed with the military regime were known collectively as the *cukong* system. The *cukong* provides skills and capital in running the business while the *pribumi* partner gives protection and various facilities to the *cukong*. These personal ties served to protect the Chinese from potential harassment as a non-*pribumi* ethnic minority identified with commercial monopoly power. The logic was this: since the Chinese had a weak political base and were in a vulnerable position, allowing them to dominate the economy would not pose a political threat to the military's rule in the way an independent indigenous business class might. With this arrangement, the ruling regime could ensure that they had a certain degree of control over the private sector (Lim and Gosling, 1997).

The unfair advantage provided by the *cukong* system created resentment among some *pribumi*, particularly among the less successful businessmen who were supported by Islamic groups and among the opponents of the Suharto administration. This could be seen in the well-known anti-*cukong* campaign staged by these people in 1971 (Suryadinata, 1988). One common criticism was that the *pribumi* felt that they were not the masters in their own nation (*bukan tuan di negeri sendiri*) because they perceived their economy as being controlled by the Chinese who were (and, to some extent, still are) regarded as foreigners.

On many occasions, Chinese Indonesian conglomerates were criticized for "capital flight" because of their reportedly massive investments in China, especially in infrastructure, which Indonesia also desperately needed. It has not helped that the most prominent Indonesian businessmen investing in China were *totok* Chinese. In fact, most of the *cukong* or conglomerates were *totok*. Mackie (1991) notes that *totok* were almost solely responsible for the expansion of Chinese businesses across Indonesia in the early 20th century, when they carried out small business in the more remote rural areas where *peranakan* had been reluctant to operate. Few *peranakan* were attracted toward the risks and discomforts of such activities; their greater access to education and more settled lifestyle inclined them toward salaried and professional jobs. Also, only *totok* still had a good command of the Chinese language and hence were able to communicate with other Chinese in the region. The expression of Chinese culture, use of the Chinese language and lavish celebrations at Chinese New Year by some rich *totok* had inadvertently heightened doubts about the "loyalty" of the Chinese community as a whole, since the *pribumi* often viewed the Chinese as a homogeneous group. Many *pribumi* do not distinguish the acts of Chinese conglomerates from those of small shopkeepers. The behavior of these big business *totok* conglomerates even caused apprehension among the *peranakan*, who feared that, being less politically protected and more confined to the Indonesian home economy, they were the ones who would bear the brunt of any violent anti-Chinese backlash.

Although Indonesia needed the skills and business networks of the Chinese for national development, paradoxically, the dominant position of the ethnic Chinese in the nation's economy was widely perceived to be a national problem. The result was the government's endorsement and implementation of a military-backed assimilationist policy, directed specifically against the ethnic Chinese and aimed to repress any expression of Chinese identity. Suharto's government considered that Chineseness was incompatible with the national personality and was problematic for national integration and unity. The general assumption was that identity is singular rather than plural, and that one could *either* be an Indonesian *or* a Chinese. To be completely Indonesian, the Chinese were expected to give up all their Chineseness (Hoon, 2006). Hence, a host of harsh measures was introduced to coercively assimilate the ethnic Chinese into the wider Indonesian population and to make them lose their Chineseness and "exclusiveness."

Because their loyalty to the country was under suspicion, the ethnic Chinese were not allowed to form their own political party during Suharto's rule, and no Chinese were appointed to high state positions (with the exception of Bob Hasan in the last years of the regime). Also, entry to public service, the armed forces and state-run educational institutions was made extremely difficult. The use of Chinese language in public places was strongly discouraged. Printed matter in Chinese characters fell under the category of prohibited imports like narcotics, pornography and explosives, when entering Indonesia (Heryanto, 1999). The government-sponsored "Indonesia Daily," which aimed to convey the official voice of the government, was the only permitted Chinese language press. The government also introduced the name-changing regulation in 1966 to encourage the ethnic Chinese to change their Chinese names into Indonesian-sounding ones, in order to "speed up assimilation" (Suryadinata, 1978).

Indonesian citizens of Chinese descent were not allowed to attend Chinese-medium schools after 1957. The remaining Chinese-medium schools, which catered to the needs of Chinese students who were not Indonesian citizens (i.e., the WNA), were closed in 1966. All Chinese were urged to enter Indonesian-medium schools, either private or public. After the closure of Chinese schools, it was argued that the dichotomy between *totok* and *peranakan* broke down as many younger generation *peranakan* were "Indonesianized" while their *totok* counterparts were "*peranakan*ized" (Suryadinata, 1978). However, some wealthy Chinese families who wished their children to retain their Chineseness sent them abroad to study in Singapore, Malaysia, Taiwan or even China.

The above discussion shows that the New Order adopted a policy toward the Chinese similar to the divide-and-rule policy introduced by the Dutch colonial regime. Essentially, it was a paradoxical policy of privileging the Chinese business communities in an effort to expand the nation's economy, and concomitantly marginalizing the Chinese minority to near pariah status in all social and cultural spheres. Heryanto argues that in the history of Indonesia, never before had the Chinese business elite enjoyed such prosperity, but ironically, never before had they been so deprived of civil rights (1999). This strategy aimed "to keep the Chinese dependent, politically powerless, and easily controllable" (Mackie, 1991, p. 92). Since the Chinese were marked out from the *pribumi* by their assumed wealth, their jobs and their lifestyles, it was fairly easy to arouse anti-Chinese feelings based on either resentment or jealousy of the supposed economic status of the Chinese as a whole.

3.3 *The May 1998 anti-Chinese violence*

> "We were increasingly aware that we were easy targets at times of political turmoil. My friends who had always thought of themselves as Indonesian suddenly faced the fact they were actually regarded as Chinese, and as such deserved to be alienated. They had to seriously rethink what this meant and to reorientate themselves" (Zhou Fuyuan, Chinese Indonesian architect, 2003, p. 454).

In the 1990s, after the Cold War and the decline of Communism, there was reportedly a softening in the government's anti-Chinese stance and a reduced anti-Chinese sentiment in Indonesian society. The visit by Chinese Prime Minister Li Peng to Indonesia in 1990 was seen as a positive sign of change in the status of the ethnic Chinese minority in Indonesia. This positive development was, however, short lived. Anti-Chinese riots once again broke out in May 1998 when the nation was in the midst of its economic crisis. The devastating effects of the financial crisis brought anti-Chinese sentiment to the surface. The Chinese were taken as scapegoats and held responsible for the national crisis, which was partly the result of massive corruption and the state's mismanagement of the economy. The riots, triggered by the killing of four student protesters at Trisakti University, turned into a violent anti-Chinese pogrom. Properties owned by the ethnic Chinese were destroyed; many Chinese were attacked; and Chinese women were raped. Many middle- and upper-class Chinese families panicked and fled the country to seek refuge in safer places overseas. The result was a capital flight of up to an estimated USD165 billion, which cost the Indonesian economy dearly and hampered its recovery from the crisis (Chua, 2008). This behavior attracted much criticism from the *pribumi* community, who denounced the Chinese for being unpatriotic and called their nationalism into question (van Dijk, 2001).

One might pose the question: How were the ethnic Chinese identified and targeted, if there were palpable signs that they had been assimilated? It was indeed clear that the New Order's assimilationist policy had failed to solve the "Chinese Problem" and integrate the Chinese into Indonesian society. Suharto's divide-and-rule policy reproduced Chineseness as a conceptual category ready to be manipulated in times of political crisis. It has been argued that the riots were systematically instigated by the state to divert the masses' anger away from Suharto and his cronies and toward the Chinese. The Joint Fact-Finding Team (TGPF) established that much of the violence was instigated by provocateurs who incited the local masses, leading the crowds to run amok and start looting and rioting. Heryanto contends that the riots were not provoked by spontaneous racism and that the media propagated the economic-gap theory during the riots, escalating racist attacks on the Chinese (1999). However, others argued that the rioters would not have attacked the Chinese had there been no anti-Chinese sentiment to manipulate in the first place.

The ethnic dichotomy of *pribumi* and non-*pribumi* constructed by the New Order was forcefully reproduced during the May riots. It was used to distinguish who should or should not be targeted, exemplified in the following quote:

> "Because Chinese property was specifically targeted, people tried to protect their shops and houses by putting up signs that the owner was a *pribumi*, a Betawi (original inhabitant of Jakarta), a Muslim, a haji, and so on. Citations from the Koran and texts like Alumni Trisakti, Supporter of Reformation, *maaf milik pribumi* ("owned by a *pribumi*") could also be seen on walls and on banners" (van Dijk, 2001, p. 189).

In this way, the *pribumi* "self" [poor, original inhabitant, loyal citizen, Muslim] were eager to differentiate themselves from the non-*pribumi* "Other" [rich, foreign, disloyal, non-Muslim], so that they could be spared from attack. This shows that after 32 years of the New Order's social engineering, the artificial "us" and "them" binary had been internalized by Indonesian society. Although inter-group differences had been repressed during Suharto's era under the prohibition of any discussion related to ethnicity, religion, race or inter-class differences, they remain very important in both everyday life and legal identification.

4. The Wind of Change: The Resurgence of Chineseness in Post-Suharto Indonesia

> "The traumatic events seemed to be a wake-up call: many [Chinese] people, normally fearful of getting involved in politics, realized that if we do not take the risk and get involved, then politics would simply crush us" (Zhou, 2003, p. 454).

The collapse of the New Order regime marked the return of political freedom to Indonesia, including the emergence of civil society, as Indonesia underwent a process of democratization and *Reformasi* (reforms). The lifting of the 32-year-old restrictions on political participation and civil activism allowed a myriad of political parties, action groups and non-governmental organizations (NGOs) to spring up. Many ethnic Chinese utilized this political liberalization to establish organizations to fight for the abolition of discriminatory laws, defend their rights and promote solidarity between ethnic groups in Indonesia. Many post-Suharto Chinese organizations deploy the discourses of Indonesian nationalism to show that they are genuine Indonesians. This desire for authentication is particularly significant for the Chinese as they have been historically constructed as non-*asli* (non-indigenous) outsiders.

To affirm their ethnicity as an integral part of the nation and challenge the restrictive boundaries of indigeneity, Chinese organizations lobbied for the amendment of a clause in the 1945 Constitution which stated that, the "Indonesian president [should be] *asli* Indonesian." Some Chinese have argued that nationality should be defined in terms of citizen or non-citizen status rather than that of indigenous or non-indigenous categorization. Others contested the narrow definition of indigeneity and contended that anyone who was born in Indonesia should be considered "*asli*", including the Chinese. This debate shows not only that the ethnic Chinese have actively protested against the concept of nationhood based on indigeneity, but also that they have made a conscious effort to shed their "alien" image. The House of Representatives finally passed a Citizenship Bill in 2006, which, amongst other things, in effect abolished the distinction between "*asli*" and "non-*asli*." Although "*asli* Indonesian" still exists as a concept, it has been redefined to include all citizens who have never assumed foreign citizenship of their own free will. This new Law also allows the Chinese to hold several key government posts, including the presidency, from which they were formerly excluded.

The May 1998 anti-Chinese violence brought to the surface the highly problematic position of the ethnic Chinese in relation to the Indonesian nation. One consequence of the riots has been the resurgence of Chinese press, culture, religion and language. For the first time in several decades,

Chinese identity became more visible. In May 1999, President Habibie issued a presidential instruction to allow the teaching of the Chinese language and scrapped a regulation requiring ethnic Chinese to produce certificates of citizenship when registering for school or making official applications. Then in February 2001 President Abdurrahman Wahid lifted the 1978 official ban on the display of Chinese characters and the importation of Chinese publications. Following these decrees, Chinese-language education experienced a boom in Indonesia. Among young ethnic Chinese as well as *pribumi*, learning Mandarin has become a popular pursuit, triggering a proliferation of after-school and after-work Mandarin courses. Nevertheless, this "resurgence" of Chineseness in Indonesia needs to be read in the wider context of the recent economic rise of China and the ramifications of this for the Southeast Asian region. In fact, the national dignity regained by China in recent decades has led to greater respect for the Chinese in Southeast Asia. A new interest in Mandarin and Chinese culture is also common among Chinese and non-Chinese in other parts of Southeast Asia.

Under Wahid's administration, ethnic Chinese were given greater freedom to assert their cultural and religious identity. President Wahid issued a decree in 2000 to annul Suharto's discriminatory regulation that repressed any manifestation of Chinese beliefs, customs and traditions. In issuing the decree, Wahid assured the ethnic Chinese of their right to observe their cultural practices in the same way that other ethnic groups have enjoyed theirs. Following the amendment of the official cultural policy, the ethnic Chinese, for the first time in over three decades, could finally enjoy the freedom to celebrate Imlek (Chinese New Year) publicly without any restrictions. In January 2001, Wahid went a step further, declaring Imlek an optional holiday. In February 2002, Megawati declared that Imlek would be a national holiday, beginning in the year 2003 (Hoon, 2009). This edict is a landmark decision and a further restoration of the cultural rights of the ethnic Chinese.

In the economic sphere, the riots of May 1998 triggered an exodus of ethnic Chinese and generated a capital flight. In its aftermath, President Habibie was faced with the insurmountable task of stabilizing the ailing economy. The post-Suharto regime needed Chinese capitalists to help

Indonesia to recover from the economic crisis (Chua, 2008). In order to reassure the ethnic Chinese concerning their safety in Indonesia, to stem further flight of their capital and to persuade Chinese Indonesians business people to repatriate the capital they had transferred overseas, Habibie promised to carry out legislative reform to eliminate racial discrimination. He issued a decree in September 1998 to end the official usage of the discriminatory labels *"pribumi"* and *"non-pribumi."* This was seen as a declaration that indigeneity and alienness were no longer tenable distinctions. The pronouncement of the edict was followed by a series of law reforms to abolish various kinds of discrimination.

The Asian financial crisis and the collapse of the Suharto regime had severe impact on some large conglomerates owned and controlled by the ethnic Chinese. For instance, the Indonesian government and foreign investors took over the private banking sector, which had largely been controlled by ethnic Chinese conglomerates before the crisis (Thee, 2006). In spite of this, the ethnic Chinese are still dominating a significant part of Indonesian private economy, especially small and medium enterprises. Chua (1998) maintains that some Chinese tycoons have benefitted from the processes of democratization, decentralization and deregulation in the Reformasi period. These Chinese-owned business conglomerates have not only survived the crisis and recouped their losses, but have also worked out new strategies to navigate the new economic and political terrain. This again shows the adaptability and resilience of the ethnic Chinese minority.

Nevertheless, the political events of May 1998 changed the future of the Chinese Indonesians forever. Not only were their cultural and citizenship rights restored, for the first time in three decades, but the Chinese were now given the opportunity to explore beyond the economic field. The dynamic post-Suharto political scene, dominated by the growth of democracy and civil society, has given rise to a healthy Chinese politics. The ongoing political trauma suffered by many Chinese Indonesians notwithstanding, the unprecedented establishment of Chinese political parties and NGOs has enabled them to become more fully integrated into all facets of political life in Indonesia. Through these organizations, the historical stereotype of the ethnic Chinese as "apolitical" and as "economic animals" has been challenged and debunked. It is hoped that the new liberal and inclusive political space can empower the ethnic Chinese to reinvent their identity as being beyond that indicated by the disenfranchising stereotype of the "market-dominant minority."

References

Aguilar Jr, FV (2001). Citizenship, inheritance, and the indigenizing of "Orang Chinese" in Indonesia. *Positions*, 9(3), 501–533.

Chua, A (2004). *World on Fire: How Exporting Free Market Democracy Breeds Ethnic Hatred and Global Instability*. New York, NY: Anchor Books.

Chua, C (2008). *Chinese Big Business in Indonesia: The State of Capital*. London and New York: Routledge.

Coppel, CA (1983). *Indonesian Chinese in Crisis*. Kuala Lumpur: Oxford University Press.

Coppel, CA (2002). *Studying Ethnic Chinese in Indonesia*. Singapore: Society of Asian Studies.

Diao, AL and M Tan (2004). Chinese business in Southeast Asia. In *Indonesia*, ET Gomez and H-HM Hsiao (eds.). London and New York, NY: Routledge Curzon.

Kwee, TH (1969). *The Origins of the Modern Chinese Movement in Indonesia*, trans. by LE Williams. Translation Series, Modern Indonesia Project, Cornell University, USA.

Gilman, SL (1985). *Difference and Pathology: Stereotypes of Sexuality, Race, and Madness*. Ithaca, NY: Cornell University Press.

Gosling, PLA (1983). Changing Chinese identities in Southeast Asia: An introductory review. In *The Chinese in Southeast Asia: Identity, Culture and Politics* (Vol. 2), LAP Gosling and YC Linda Lim (eds.), pp. 1–14. Singapore: Maruzen Asia.

Heryanto, A (1998). Ethnic identities and erasure: Chinese Indonesians in public culture. In *Southeast Asian Identities*, JS Kahn (ed.), pp. 95–114. Singapore: Institute of Southeast Asian Studies.

Heryanto, A (1999). Rape, race and reporting. In *Reformasi: Crisis and Change in Indonesia*, A Budiman, B Hatley and D Kingsbury (eds.), pp. 299–334. Clayton: Monash Asia Institute, Monash University.

Hoon, C-Y (2006). Assimilation, multiculturalism, hybridity: The dilemmas of ethnic Chinese in post-Suharto Indonesia. *Asian Ethnicity*, 7(2), 149–166.

Hoon, C-Y (2008). *Chinese Identity in Post-Suharto Indonesia: Culture, Politics and Media*. Brighton and Portland: Sussex Academic Press.

Hoon, C-Y (2009). More than a cultural celebration: The politics of Chinese new year in post-Suharto Indonesia. *Chinese Southern Diaspora Studies*, 3, 90–105.

Koning, J (2007). Chineseness and Chinese Indonesian business practices: A generational and discursive enquiry. *East Asia*, 24, 129–152.

Lim, L and P Gosling (1997). Strengths and weaknesses of minority status for Southeast Asian Chinese at a time of economic growth and liberalization. In *Essential Outsiders: Chinese and Jews in the Modern Transformation of Southeast Asia and Central Europe*, D Chirot and A Reid (eds.), pp. 285–317. Seattle and London: University of Washington Press.

Mackie, JAC (1991). Towkays and tycoons: The Chinese in Indonesian economic life in the 1920s and the 1980s. In *Symposium: Indonesia: The Role of the Indonesian Chinese in Shaping Modern Indonesian Life* (Symposium at Cornell University), Southeast Asia Program Publications at Cornell University (ed.), pp. 83–96. Ithaca, NY.

Phoa, LG (1992). Chinese economy activity in Netherlands India: Selected translations from the Dutch. In *The Changing Economic Position of the Chinese in Netherlands India*, MR Fernando and D Bulbeck (eds.), pp. 5–18. Singapore: Institute of Southeast Asian Studies.

Somers, M (1965). *Peranakan Chinese Politics in Indonesia*. PhD Dissertation, Cornell University.

Suryadinata, L (1978). *Pribumi Indonesians, the Chinese Minority and China: A Study of Perceptions and Politics*. Singapore: Heinemann Educational Books.

Suryadinata, L (1988). Changing identities of the Southeast Asian Chinese since World War II. In *Chinese Economic Elites in Indonesia: A Preliminary Study*, J Cushman and G Wang (eds.), pp. 261–288. Hong Kong: Hong Kong University Press.

Tan, MG (1995). Southeast Asian Chinese: The socio-cultural dimension. In *The Ethnic Chinese in Indonesia: Issues and Implications*, L Suryadinta (ed.), pp. 13–27. Singapore: Times Academic Press.

Toer, PA (1998). *Hoakiau di Indonesia*. Jakarta: Penerbit Garba Budaya.

van Dijk, K (2001). *A Country in Despair: Indonesia Between 1997 and 2000*. Leiden: KITLV Press.

Wanandi, J (2012). *Shades of Grey: A Political Memoir of Modern Indonesia 1965–1998*. Jakarta: Equinox Publishing.

Wang, G (1981). *Community and Nation: Essays on Southeast Asia and the Chinese*. Selected by A Reid. ASAA Southeast Asian Publications Series

No. 6, Heinemann Educational Books (Asia) Ltd, and George Allen and Unwin Australia, Sydney.

Wu, DYH (1997). Facing the challenge of multiple cultural identities. In *Emerging Pluralism in Asia and the Pacific*, DYH Wu, H McQueen and Y Yamamoto (eds.), pp. 141–148. Hong Kong: Hong Kong Institute of Asia-Pacific Studies, Chinese University of Hong Kong.

Zhou, F (2003). Where do we belong. *Asian Ethnicity*, 4(3), 453–459.

Part 2

The Management of Business Networks and Change

Chapter 6

Trading Networks of Chinese Entrepreneurs in Singapore

Thomas Menkhoff and Chalmer E Labig

1. Introduction

The formation and extensive use of regional and global networks based on kinship, clanship, territorial, and ethnic solidarities for business purposes have often been cited as reasons for the success for business purposes have often been cited as reasons for the success of Chinese merchants in Southeast Asia (Landa, 1983; Lim, 1983; Goldberg, 1985; Yoshihara, 1988, pp. 53, 67). These networks, based on blood or locality ties, are also commonly found among Chinese business communities in other parts of Asia and beyond (Lim and Teoh, 1986). Writers have variously described such networks as family-centered personal networks, kin, or other ethnically defined networks, supra-family marriage networks, and close-knit communal tie-ups and connections (Greenhalgh, 1984; Landa, 1983; Mahathir, 1970). The terms network and networking[1] have a certain analytical merit. They

---

This is a reprint of an article originally published in 1996 in *SOJOURN — Journal of Social Issues in Southeast Asia*, 11(1), 130–154. The authors gratefully acknowledge the permission of the publisher, the Institute of Southeast Asian Studies, to reprint the essay in this edition.

[1] Tong (1989, p. 9) has summarized Chinese business networking strategies such as networking in the form of ownership links, economic links of mutual cooperation, links formed through the sharing of common directors, or marital links. Business networking often extends beyond national boundaries, as indicated by the large number of Chinese import/export companies and family firms which have become transnational (Lim and Teo, 1986, pp. 336–365).

are convenient labels for describing abstract complex business strategies and choices the nature of which are often difficult to verify empirically. In spite of their cultural importance, the conceptual clarification of the notion of network relations is lacking in the literature on Overseas Chinese entre-preneurship.[2] The result is a tendency to imbue Overseas Chinese business communities with a conventional image of their all-powerful economic positions in the societies in which they find themselves. Indeed, specula-tions about Chinese networks, often without the support of empirical evi-dence, have helped to perpetuate prejudices about the social exclusiveness of ethnic Chinese in Southeast Asia.

This study is based on a survey of 23 small family-based trading firms in Singapore dealing in Chinese foodstuffs, dried seafood products, tim-ber, rubber religious paraphernalia, and other items. The purpose of this chapter is to illustrate and analyze the structural features of international trading networks of these entrepreneurs (Menkhoff 1993). In the history of Southeast Asia, trading networks had been conduits for the exchange and transfer of goods and other resources over large areas in the region (Evers and Schiel, 1987, p. 468). Ng (1983), for example, singles out the 17th century Hokkien trading network extending from the coastal city of Amoy in southern China to the South Seas as an important part of these connec-tions. Yet little is known about contemporary Chinese trading networks, their structural organization and how they are affected by modernization.

The survey was conducted using semi-structured interviews with Chinese entreprencurs in Singapore, supplemented by secondary sources and field observations. Drawing on results of the survey, the study will focus on the social organization of these trading networks, particularly in relation to the entrepreneurs' connections with trading partners abroad. In addition, the paper identifies and examines significant actors who may facilitate the exchange of goods and information; these actors include personal friends, acquaintances in trade or clan associations, and relatives living abroad. The nodal points of the trading networks under investigation consist of

---

[2] No studies have come to our attention so far which link the often cited Chinese network-ing theses to the social network concepts of British social anthropology (for example, Radcliffe-Brown, 1940) or to the works of American network analysts who have tried to map interpersonal relations and to study social networks, using graph theory, computer models, and complex matrices (Wellman, 1988, pp. 21–30).

twenty-three Chinese businessmen in Singapore who have extensive economic linkages with overseas buyers and suppliers of the goods being traded.

The thesis that Chinese traders tend to do business with kinsmen serves as a starting point for discussing the *guanxi* (relationship) bases of their business transactions (Landa, 1983). The Chapter will first describe the export marketing strategies of the Chinese entrepreneurs interviewed. It will then examine the expanse of their trading networks and the influence of kinship connections on maintaining external trade relationships. Finally, the impact of modernization and social change on Chinese trading behavior will be analyzed. Two case-studies are presented to illustrate the social complexity of trading networks and to explore the hypothesis about the extent to which kinship obligations may restrict the making of the economic decision in a situation of rapidly changing market-places.

2. Guanxi and Overseas Chinese Trading Networks: A Typology

As in large-scale enterprises, small trading firms entering foreign markets encounter unique problems of cultural differences, diverse trading laws, and limited information. It is essential for these firms that their overseas agents, sales representatives, and trading partners are reliable, trustworthy, and co-operative (Menkhoff, 1992). To minimize risks, transaction costs, and uncertainties of external economic dealings, merchant exporters try to establish long-lasting social and business relationships with their trading partners. Burns (1985, pp. 1–44) refers to these relationships as forming "trusted networks" consisting of a set of individuals in whom a trader can have confidence and trust. The number and expanse of such trusted networks available to a businessman obviously depend on his position in the market system and in the society generally. As Burns goes on to argue:

> "A network will generate trust among its members when its interpersonal links will support the flow of reliable information and/or manipulation of sanctions reinforcing desired behavior or increasing the probability that disputes among members will be fairly settled" (1985, p. 32).

It is useful to transpose Burn's concept to the Chinese cultural context. A central notion for understanding Chinese trusted networks and networking strategies in business is that of *guanxi*, literally meaning social relationships or particularistic ties (Jacobs, 1979). These relationships or ties are an entrepreneur's connections with local of foreign businessmen, politicians, or friends who may guarantee support and provide access to favours, credit, or insider information. The cultivation of networks of useful personal relationships offers businessmen with commercial advantages over competitors, and such advantages are crucial not only in unstable and potentially hostile markets but also in familiar and relatively structured ones in which a person has operated for a long time (Eastman, 1988, p. 36). To have connections with people "who can be trusted and by whom one will be trusted" (Omohundro 1983, p. 68) is deemed an essential condition for business survival.

According to Jacobs (1979), in Chinese culture *guanxi* relationship depends upon two or more people having a commonality of shared identification. Such an identification may be ascriptive (native place or lineage) or it may rest upon shared experience. Jacob writes:

> "A person seeking allies will first turn to persons with whom he knows he has a *kuan-hsi* base... The existence or non-existence of a *kuan-hsi* base, therefore, determines the existence or non-existence of a *kuan-hsi*. However, a *kuan-hsi* may vary according to "closeness" or "distance" and this variation depends in turn upon a third variable, affect or *kan-ch'ing*" (p. 242).

The notion of *kang-ch'ing* (*ganqing*), on the other hand, refers to the affective or emotional component of a relationship (DeGlopper, 1978, p. 312; Lee, 1987, p. 61). *Ganqing*, or simply "sentiment," arises from social interactions as when people work together, belong to the same social club, or have attended the same school or university. Jacobs is particularly emphatic that such a sentiment differs from friendship in that it presumes a much more specific common interest, and conversely, much less warmth and more formality of contact. The closeness of *ganqing* can of course vary between different sets of relationships and may exhibit, within the same connection, different degrees of intensity over time (Jacobs, 1979, pp. 258, 261).

Writers often assume that Chinese family and kinship are the most common basis for building *guanxi* relationships because of the moral imperative that relatives should help and trust each other (Eastman, 1988, p. 36). But the fact is that, as Jacob (1979, p. 242) again points out, non-relatives and even foreigners can also be incorporated into one's identification system. *Guanxi* ties, however, are not the only criteria for establishing a business relationship. Exporters and importers, for example, may consider prices and quality of goods as well as the reliability of supplies before forming a more enduring relationship with any trader. Nonetheless it is clear that there is a significant social component in the development of all trading relations. Generally, from our study of Chinese traders in Singapore, the following types of business relationship with overseas buyers and suppliers can be listed.

2.1 *Consanguineal and affinal kinship ties*

The extensive use of *guanxi* based on consanguineal and affinal kinship ties is often regarded as a significant factor for explaining the economic success among the Overseas Chinese world-wide (Greenhalgh, 1984, p. 529). Chinese entrepreneurs in Singapore, whose companies have developed form small-scale businesses to large enterprises, have sometimes relied on family members to organize their business interests abroad. An illustrative example is the Hong Leong Group founded by Kwek Hong Png. According to the *Business Times*, in the Hong Leong Group

> The Malaysian cousins, led by nephew Quek Leng Chan, have always stressed their independence from the Singapore family. Nevertheless, Leng Chan is known to defer all major decisions to Hong Png, who still retains important posts in some of the Malaysian companies. (*Business Times*, September 19, 1989, p. 14)

However, such an example should not be over-generalized. Descendants of the business founder may shun the traditional enterprise started by their forefather and prefer to take up modern and more prestigious professional jobs (Menkhoff, 1993, pp. 73–88). While kinsmen may provide the most reliable and trustworthy support, difficulties such as that taking place in the "brittle relationships between adult brothers" do occur (Jacobs, 1979, p. 246). In a similar note, De Glopper has observed that cooperation between brothers in business is not a rule:

> "If they do, it is said to be because their personal relations are good, their *kan-ch'ing* is good… Some brothers have good kan-ch'ing and a lot of interaction (*lai-wang*), and others do not… In the long run, and in crisis, one can depend on one's brothers. But no one wants to be dependent on his brothers, and an able-bodied man should not expect his brothers or kinsmen to make sacrifices for his sake" (De Glopper, 1978, p. 312).

So doing business with close kinsmen carries certain social costs. Indeed Chinese traders are reported to have avoided commercial dealings with kinsmen because such transactions may run the risk of loosing autonomy, delayed payments, bad debts, or incurring problems in negotiating fair prices (Diamond, 1969; Silin, 1972, p. 351; Omohundro, 1983, p. 68; Wong, 1988a, pp. 135–137).

2.2 *Fictive kinship ties*

Our investigation of the Teochew-dominated sharks' fins trade in Singapore shows that kinship can also be created by transforming long-standing business friends into "uncles" in accordance with Chinese kinship system (Menkhoff, 1992, 1994). This form of fictive kinship goes some way in enlarging business connections and in ensuring that trading partners behave within the rules of kinship. If the mutual obligation in the relationship is strong, such fictive kinship ties may allow for a degree of social control and certainty of behavior. Generally close social dealings over time, writes a Chinese sociologist:

> "Tend to stress Chinese kinship relations, causing not only their perpetuation but also the expansion of their influence into relationships where no kinship ties actually exist. Many kinds of social dyads such as teacher-student, master-apprentice, employet-employee… are often patterned after kinship relations and are used to seek or establish authority in all interpersonal relations. In daily life people do not hesitate to use the pseudo-kinship terms for addressing a stranger and influencing him" (Hsieh, 1987, p. 204).

Another from of fictive kinship is created by the exchange of vows of blood brotherhood and through the system of god-parents (Jordan, 1985). Relationship is affirmed by the performance of rituals in a temple or ancestral hall. Under certain circumstances sworn-brother *guanxi* may become a basis for building a business network, as Omohundro has observed:

> "Loans, credit, supplies and emergency aid commonly flow along this line. Bloodbrothers may seek further to betroth their children or invite one another into a godparent relationship. They may join in a partnership, market each other's merchandise or accept each other's sons as apprentices" (Omohundro, 1983, pp. 69–70).

Finally *guanxi* can also be formed by appealing to the real or imaginary lineage connections among people with the same surname. Early Chinese migrants to Southeast Asia often formed surname associations, joining persons of a common surname in order to provide each other mutual assistance in a foreign environment. As Tan writes:

> "Clan associations are voluntary associations formed on the basis of consanguinity or blood ties. In overseas Chinese communities, this is often judged on the criterion of all those having common surnames. It is a well-known fact among Chinese that common surnames do not necessarily mean common ancestry. However, for an overseas Chinese a common surname is enough ground for him to claim kinship ties and to address even total strangers as if they are his kinsmen" (1986, p. 107).

Our study of the Hokkien association "Chin Kang Huay Kuan" in contemporary Singapore and Malaysia suggests that men — and often women — use association branches in Ipoh, Melaka, or Pulau Pinang in Malaysia as bases for establishing contacts or intermediaries to other Chinese voluntary associations in the country. The committee members of these associations are often influential local businessmen who can establish linkages between a Hokkien network in Singapore and those in Malaysia.

In the context of rapid changes associated with urbanization and modernization, surname ties have lost their former significance in South-east Asia. Many Chinese in Indonesia, for example, have adopted indigenous names barely resembling the original Chinese ones. In Singapore, it is reported that very few Chinese associations are organized around a lineage where members trace their descent from a common male ancestor (Hsieh, 1978, p. 205).

2.3 *Friendship ties*

Friendship is another possible basis for building *guanxi* relationships. Friendship here refers to personal ties developed through co-residence, schooling, work, and other forms of common social experience among people. Friendship ties, and the associated feeling of trust generated by shared experience and mutual knowledge, have less of the structural quality of relationship based on kinship, for example. The mutual affection tends to come about by having entered a relationship freely, by choice rather than by kin obligation or demand of status (Hart, 1988, p. 185). Friendship may be "used" for economic purpose, but it can also develop from social interactions with people with whom one has a long history of economic dealings.

The importance of schoolmate *guanxi* can be traced back to Chinese history (Jacobs, 1979, p. 247). In the past, candidates who passed the imperial examinations together often developed a special regard for each other. A contemporary equivalent of schoolmate *guanxi* is perhaps the so-called old boys' network among university graduates, a network which offers a means of recruiting people into business relations.

People who come to know each other during work sometimes share an identification with their work-place. A relationship established between clerks in a shop, for example, can play a potential role in forming business relations if they later become independent businessmen. It goes without saying that such a relationship may facilitate business contacts and transactions and serve as an incentive to form partnership.

One particular type of friendship can be singled out. The so-called locality ties are formed by people who claim a common place of origin in China. Locality in this sense was an important source of solidarity among the Chinese in nineteenth-century Singapore. Such solidarity, Freedman points out: "could be created or strengthened overseas... between men originating from the same area... in China" (1976, p. 36). However, as Jacobs (1979, p. 244) emphasizes, the concept of locality or native place also trends to be flexible and varies from situation to situation. The place of origin can range from a village to a city or a province in China. In Singapore, locality associations are formed based on five levels of administrative unit: province (*sheng*), prefecture (*fu*), district (*hsien*), borough (*chu*), and village (*hsiang*) or town (*ch'en*), cutting across people speaking several dialects (Hsieh, 1978, p. 206). Locality-based *guanxi* relationship is articulated among Overseas Chinese business organizations in preferential recruitment of employees from the same native place in China (Tong, 1989, p. 8). Loyalty of people from the same place of origin is often given as one of the reasons for such practice, but the situation is probably more complex than that (Evers, 1987).

Generally, it can be suggested that social connections with others from the same native place in China can facilitate the building of business relationships and investment flows between Singapore and China In the current situation those who help to set up joint ventures or identify new suppliers in China may function as intermediaries between government agencies or state firms in China and ethnic Chinese businessman in Southeast Asia. Outside China, locality *guanxi* ties can also be used to form trading networks among businessmen in Asian countries where Chinese communities are found, especially Singapore, Hong Kong, Malaysia, and Indonesia (Wong, 1988a, pp. 109–131).

2.4 *Outsiders*

The final category of *guanxi* relationships refers to ties formed with outsiders, that is, people not related by kinship and common place of origin. In theory, compared with other forms of social ties, the degree of closeness with and obligations toward outsiders are considered weakest and socially least sustainable. However, in the increasingly complex global or regional economic transactions, important business links can no longer draw from kinship or locality ties alone. Many owners of family firms now incorporate foreign partners into their trading network. In principle, establishing business ties with outsiders can proceed this way:

> "Should he [that is, a businessmen] desire to ally with another person, he may approach him directly or through an intermediary and attempt to

discover a *kuan-hsi* base on which to develop a closer *kuan-hsi*. If they discover a common *kuan-hsi* base, then the alliance may develop; if they cannot discover such a base, they may need to rely on intermediaries" (Jacobs, 1979, p. 242).

3. Survey Results

The firms investigated for this study had their most important markets in East and Southeast Asia. They imported from Indonesia, Hong Kong, Malaysia, China, and to a lesser extent the US, Thailand, India, Australia, and Italy. Some also acquired their supplies from the Philippines, Brunei, Japan, Taiwan, Mauritius, the Middle East, Switzerland, Canada, and Mexico. The major export markets for the firms were in South America, Malaysia, Hong Kong, Japan, Indonesia, and Australia, as well as the US and Europe. Clearly, the firms maintained world-wide commercial links of different degrees of intensity and economic importance, though Southeast Asia remained their strongest foothold. Most of the firms were aggressively entering new markets wherever feasible. At the time of the survey in 1988–1989, Mauritius and Thailand were highlighted as potential future markets especially for timber and wood products. The smallness of the market in Singapore, difficulties in getting raw materials, and the tariff walls imposed by many Southeast Asian economies, were given-as main incentives for the pursuit of new markets. Even a small marine foodstuffs merchant who imported dried seafood products from Indonesia emphasized that he intended to process his products outside Singapore where labour and transport costs are lower.

Among the 23 firms surveyed, "selling directly to customers" is most frequently quoted as the method of export (see Table 1). About 60 percent of the firms reported that they served their customers this way without commissioning agents. The firms who relied on local import/export agents perceived them as costly intermediaries. Importers usually had their own regular customers, local wholesalers, and foreign buyers and suppliers in Southeast Asia and beyond. Only two firms maintained overseas sub-branches which served as suppliers, buyers, or transit points for imports and exports.

Table 1. Methods of exporting cited

Sell direct to customers	1
Agents overseas	2
Through trading houses overseas	2
Through local import/export agents	2
Through subsidiary companies overseas	3
Through related traders overseas	3

1 = very frequently cited.
2 = frequently cited.
3 = seldom cited.
Source: Interviews, 1988–1989.

Table 2. Preferences for export marketing transactions

Face-to-face meetings and direct negotiations	1
Trust	1
Letters of credit	2
Contracts	3
Agents	3

Note: As for Table 1.

As indicated by Table 2, most entrepreneurs pointed to the importance of face-to-face meetings and direct negotiation with their partners in export-marketing transactions. The reason for this practice is that more immediate social interactions arguably nurture mutual trust. Nearly all merchant exporters reported that they usually insisted on payments via letters of credit, though there are occasional exceptions (Menkhoff, 1993, pp. 131–147).

4. Kinship and Business Network

Turning to Table 3, it reports our findings regarding the origin of the *guanxi* relationships of the 23 Singaporean Chinese entrepreneurs in our survey. Business partners of the firms surveyed are classified according to the four categories in our typology: kinsmen, fictive, or ritualistic kin,

Table 3. Trading partners of Singaporean Chinese traders

Kinsmen	
Consanguineal	3
Affinal	3
Fictive or ritualistic kins	
Long-standing family friends	1
Those with same surname	3
Sworn or godbrothers	3
Friends	
Personal friends	2
Those from same village, town, or province in China	3
Schoolmates	2
Former co-workers	3
Outsiders	
Non-Chinese (Europeans, Indians, Japanese, etc.)	1
Members of other Chinese dialect groups	1

Note: As for Table 1.

friends, and outsiders. Survey findings suggest that there is a strong tendency among Singaporean Chinese merchants to transact with "outsiders" and "friends" rather than with "kinsmen" or "fictive or ritualistic kins."

The majority of the respondents reportedly dealt with non-Chinese business partners (mainly Europeans, Japanese, and Indians) and with members of other Chinese dialect groups. Preferences for trading with members of one's own dialect group and kinsmen were not apparent. While only four trading firms relied on overseas kinsmen (brothers and fathers who lived in Hong Kong, Sibu, Surabaya, and Guangzhou) as regular business partners, overseas family members or distant kinsmen were of some importance for the businesses sampled. Several respondents stressed that one's kinsmen such as children studying abroad might be asked to gather market information rather than to involve in more direct economic dealings.

While long-standing family friends frequently assisted in various ways, respondents reported that they did not make much use of fictive and ritualistic kin relationship. Sworn-brothers seemed to be more important in information gathering, and in seeking occasional help when extra hands were needed. Instead, most traders described their business partners as coming from "friends of one's parents" or "business friends." Generally speaking, "business friends" are non-Chinese like Europeans and Japanese as well as those outside one's own dialect group.

Social ties based on locality or place of origin in China and common surname were seldom cited as bases for forming trading relations. Locality ties might be more important during the initial stage of a business life-cycle, as a source of capital and for connections with potential business partners. Consistent with the observation of Hong Kong enterprises, kinship often forms a weak framework for business transactions outside the immediate family. Wong (1988b, p. 136) writes:

"There is little evidence that a dualistic business ethic is prevalent or that honesty and trust are found only within the kin group while sharp practices reign without... The inter-firm economic order... is secured largely on non-kin solidarities... forging business alliances through a conscious marriage strategy is hardly practical with the decline of the custom of arranged marriages and the inability of Chinese family heads to disinherit their children for disobedience... the intensity of kinship reciprocity tends to limit economic options. Therefore, it invoked sparingly only when it suits one's ends."

The relative importance of the type of *guanxi* relationship can be illustrated by examining the following two cases from the survey among Chinese business firms in Singapore.

5. Singaporean Chinese Trading Networks Observed

Case One: Suzukawa Pte Ltd and the Japan Connection: Suzukawa Pte Ltd was established in 1980 as one of several local branches of the parent company Ng Chee Ltd, founded by a native from Fukien province in China (Jamann, 1994). The parent company and its branches are still owned by the Ng family. Their main businesses are marketing of food stuffs, though Ng Chee Ltd is a distributor of motor spare parts. According

to Mr Ng Chin Kang, fifty-two, managing director of Suzukawa Pte Ltd
and eldest son of the now-retired founder, the branch was established
because the parent company had "more or less reached the saturation
point in the spare parts business."

Mr Ng and his four brothers had previously worked together in the
company run by his father; but according to Ng, "[having five siblings
working in the same firm] became a burden to Ng Chee Ltd, so we
decided to diversify." Suzukawa, which had an annual turnover of about
S\$4.8 million for 1986 (Singapore Registry of Companies and Businesses),
currently concentrates on importing canned and manufactured foodstuffs.
The company is the sole distributor of Japanese products ranging from
confectioneries to beverages and dry foodstuffs. Some of the items it deals
in are salt, cooking oil, rice, sugar, soya bean sauce, and dried mushrooms,
as well as frozen food. Suzukawa also imports chocolate from Switzerland,
spaghetti and pasta from Italy, and rice from America. It exports these
products to neighbouring countries such as Indonesia and Malaysia,
where customers are supermarkets, hotels, and restaurants.

Neither the retired chairman of Ng Chee Ltd nor his sons had any previous experience in the food trade. Mr Ng, who holds a Master of Business
Administration (MBA) degree from a Japanese university, runs the company together with his younger brother who has studied in England. Their
earlier attempts to market Chinese foodstuffs were hindered by strong local
competitors located along Hong Kong Street in Singapore, a traditional
business quarters for firms dealing with China via Hong Kong-based middlemen (Menkhoff, 1993, pp. 181–195). Mr Ng entered the Japanese foodstuff business almost by accident. According to him,

> "We met a friend of ours who was in the food business and he recom-
> mended some items to us. So we started, first in a very small way, and
> later we expanded."

When asked whether the company is still connected with this friend,
Mr Ng pointed out that this friend is a Japanese businessman who was
one of their partners in the beginning but whose interest was later bought
out by the family. The Japanese partner was introduced to the Ng family
by a go-between who was himself a Japanese performing the significant

role of an "interconnecting cable," to borrow the metaphor of Yang (1989, p. 41).

This intermediary was Mr Ng's classmate whom he met during his studies in Japan. The friendship and social ties Mr Ng previously formed in Japan were of strategic importance for dealing in Japanese imports which have proved profitable. As Mr Ng explained:

> "We started very small. Initially we tendered only a few confectionery products, then we took over some items. We got some agencies from some new companies. We were looking for new sources, new products. I went to Japan very often in the initial stage. We failed with a lot of items and we succeeded with some."

The majority of Suzukawa's current suppliers are located in Tokyo and Osaka. These contacts were cultivated and revitalized by personal visits in the early years, but such visits are less frequent now. According to Mr Ng:

> "In the beginning we had to contact them by telex. We had to look for suppliers. Through suppliers you get new suppliers and then you go there. Before we go, we normally send a telex saying that we are coming over. When we arrive there we call them and try to see them."

Formerly, Mr Ng visited Japan four or five times a year. His good command of Japanese has been crucial in consolidating the relationship with the Japanese. Once the relationship is established, Mr Ng travels less frequently to Japan.

Suzukawa's trading relations with supplies in Europe were initiated by Mr Ng's brother. He attributes his brother's studies in the United Kingdom as one reason why the company now handles several European products:

> "He knows the other side better. He was actually studying engineering. He had not so much to do with food business. Both of us learned through experience and practical work. We failed in a lot of things but we more or less got through [the difficult times] somehow."

Even now, the contacts Mr Ng's brother enjoys in Europe continue to help the firm in establishing new and useful business relations with suppliers there.

Suzukawa's trading network shows an interesting pattern. In addition to fluency in the relevant language, communications by personal visits, telephone, and fax also help to build up a transacting framework. Friendship and schoolmate relations have shown to be crucial in this regard. More specifically, schoolmate *guanxi* between Mr Ng and his Japanese associate facilitated the commercial operations of Suzukawa and his relationship with other Japanese counterparts. The intermediary who was a mutual acquaintance of Mr Ng and his partner guaranteed what Yang (1989, p. 41) has termed the "transformation of identities" through activating mutual obligation between the two. Suzukawa's business success demonstrates that foreigners can be transformed into reliable trading partners. Finally, the trading network of Suzukawa is outgrowing its sole reliance on personalistic relations. Other sources of supply of cash and goods have to be sought.

On the whole, Mr Ng's recruitment of trading partners appears to contradict with Landa's (1983, p. 97) thesis about kinship as being the most favoured foundation for building commerce ties. It is superfluous in this case to speculate whether Mr Ng would prefer to deal with Chinese traders, kinsmen, or fellow villagers. In a pragmatic quest for business opportunities, Mr Ng made Japanese business contacts and learned about the Japanese way of doing business. He reported that his Japanese friends still advise him in his dealings with Japanese firms. Consequently we can infer from this case that Chinese trading networks are not invariably confined to among fellow Chinese but cutting across ethnic borders to form links with schoolmates and friends among the non-Chinese.

Case Two: Pipa Limited and the China connection: Pipa Limited was established in 1939 by the grandfather of the current managing partners. The founder of the firm was described by those interviewed as a Teochew sailor from the city of Swatow in Guangdong province who had traveled many years between China and Southeast Asia. In the 1940s an important market for temple embroideries, religious paraphernalia, and Chinese opera fittings existed in Singapore, and the grandfather began business by importing these goods from China and Hong Kong. Presently, the firm continues to import these ceremonial products and musical instruments from the two countries as well as Japan. Annual turnover for the year 1988 was estimated at S$300,000 with a profit somewhere between S$60,000 and S$80,000 after tax.

Pipa Limited has no branches and its trading partners are those who have been acquainted with the owners for many years. Its customers are buyers who represent local Chinese temples, schools, clan associations, community centers, and department stores in Singapore. The firm also exports to Brunei, Malaysia, Indonesia and Australia. Regular and long-standing customers in Singapore get credit for 30 to 60 days. As indicated by Figure 1, individual customers are identifiably "by-passers," "friends," and "other people" while 10 percent of the retail customers are tourists.

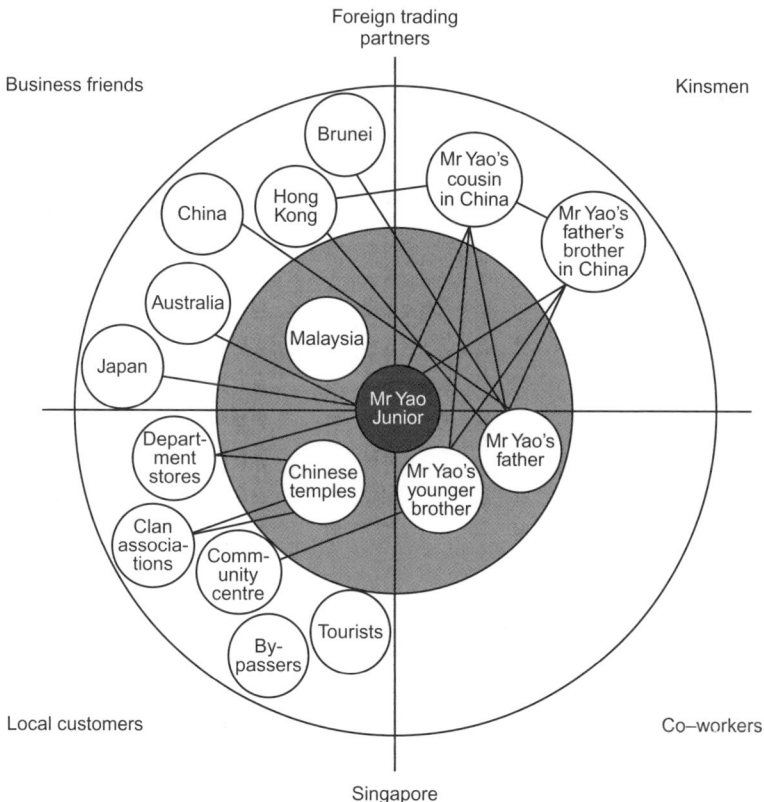

Figure 1.   Extract of Mr Yao's personal trading network

Source: Interviews, 1988–1989.

The figure depicts the total network of Pipa Limited from the perspective of Mr Yao, Jr, one of the managing directors. The figure shows the personal and business ties extending from him to overseas buyers who are often business friends and kinsmen. Local ties stretch to customers in Singapore, and to his co-workers and his brother and father. The figure distinguishes between active intimate ties and active non-intimate ties to illustrate the relative intensity of the types of relationship.

Pipa Limited has formed trading relationship with the suppliers from China in a number of ways. Until the 1980s, the company established links with officials of state-owned manufacturing firms who came to Singapore as part of trade missions. These missions were organized by the Singapore Chinese Chamber of Commerce of which Pipa Limited has been a long-standing member. Before 1978, Pipa dealt with state firms in Beijing and Shanghai. However, the quality of the goods supplied by these firms were not consistent, and there were disruptions in supply. Especially during the Cultural Revolution of 1968, the state firms were unable to supply *pipa* — a string plucking musical instrument — decorated with dragon heads. At the time the ornamentation was considered as symbolic of imperial power, and thus politically forbidden. Consequently, from the 1970s Pipa Limited began importing the instrument with the figure from Hong Kong to supplement the irregular supply from the mainland. In 1978 when the Chinese reform policy led to a flowering of the private sector, it was decided to purchase *pipa* from private firms in China. Two relatives — Senior Yao's brother-in-law and Junior Yao's cousin — acted as go-between for the Chinese producers and Pipa Limited.

Relationships with long-standing customers like representatives of temples or clan associations were initiated by the founder and later his son who is the father of the two managing directors presently running the firm. The grandfather had joined a surname association and a Taoist temple association of which he was a committee member. Although there was no direct link between membership in these organizations and Pipa Limited overall marketing connections, his involvement in the management committee probably helped to bring customers. Though Mr Yao, one of the current managers, maintains business connections with Hong Kong suppliers, he continues to import some of his products from China. That trading with China was assisted by his relatives there probably signifies the importance of kinship ties. Yet it was emphasized during interviews that this kinship *guanxi* was founded on material interests rather than on any *ganqing* (emotional) considerations based on primordial ties by blood.

6. Conclusion

Foreign trade often implies multiple barriers for small businesses which have limited knowledge about foreign markets and factors such as currency fluctuations. Given the uncertainties and associated transaction costs, traders aspire to deal with trustworthy trading partners and establish long-standing personal relationships (*guanxi*). The trading network provides businessmen with important resources such as capital, goods, information, and even access to other networks. In addition, social relationships in such a network give business transactions a certain degree of predictability. Trust is the social cement that holds business networks together (Menkhoff, 1992, 1993, pp. 89–131; Granovetter, 1985). In this context, it is important to point out that Chinese exporters in Singapore tend to operate with *guanxi* relationships built on a number of kin and non-kin principles. Business relationships are maintained not only with kinsmen, but also with those who are reliable, co-operative, and willing to share information. Face-to-face negotiations, personal visits, hosting of lunches, and communications via phone calls, and telefax are typical of the ways commercial ties are reproduced.

At the same time, the majority of the firms surveyed maintain long-standing relationships with "foreign" business associates in the United States, Europe, Latin America, and Asia. Our survey findings appear to support Yoshihara's (1988) argument that Chinese networks, based on kinship, clanship, territorial, and ethnic principles have disintegrated since the years after World War II. Together with the expansion of the market economy and increasing economic integration in Southeast Asia, Chinese trading networks in Singapore now extend across ethnic and national boundaries. The present generation of traders are able to transcend ethnic boundaries through Western education and the use of English. Mandarin language education promoted by the Singaporean government also tends to reduce barriers previously existing between different dialect groups.

The importance of Japanese, American, and European business partners both within Singapore and abroad testifies to the common wisdom that "You can't stick to your own kind if you are engaged in international business." It is a statement that underlines the pragmatic rationale of Chinese merchants in Singapore.

In view of these changes, many of the generalizations about Chinese networking strategies need to be re-examined. The often mentioned global network of Chinese businessmen interconnected by kinship solidarity has yet to be proved empirically. In our very modest survey, which does not pretend to be statistically significant, network of kinsmen and close acquaintances in providing capital and business contacts is relevant to no more than four of the 23 trading firms.

In any case, access to a commercial network cannot guarantee business success and the rate of failure among Chinese firms is reportedly high. Business failures, however, are seldom reported in contemporary studies on Chinese entrepreneurs. The result is the tendency to overestimate the utility potential of business network among ethnic Chinese in Southeast Asia. The narrative of "from rags to riches stories" is often told by the popular press to confirm the continuing success of Chinese commercial empires in East Asia. But networking is in fact practiced everywhere in all societies. Singaporean Chinese traders who intend to go regional or global know that they must learn to network with the locals, too.

In view of the hitherto inadequate empirical and conceptual exploration of Singaporean Chinese business networks, future studies should be devoted to examine particular aspects of such networks. The operations of power and credit relations among traders and their clients are just some of the crucial issues that have to be analysed. Furthermore, changes in Chinese trading networks in Southeast Asia over the last decade present an important focus for further research. Government policies and laws, global economic integration, improved transportation, modern communication, and fluctuating market conditions have all made a crucial impact on traditional and contemporary trading relations and systems (Evers, 1988, p. 99). Modern communications certainly affect how trading relations are now initiated. For example, the Singapore Government has created Singapore Network Services Pte Ltd (*Straits*

Times, October 17, 1989; December 4, 1989, p. 39), jointly owned by the Trade Development Board, Telecom, Port of Singapore Authority, and the Civil Aviation Authority of Singapore. Under the label TradeNet, this company is in charge of operating and managing the so-called "TradeNet System" designed to facilitate computer-to-computer transfer of trade documents: The objective is to speed up cargo clearance, and thereby improve the productivity and efficiency of Singapore's trading companies. Linked to other global network, TradeNet users are able to communicate with airlines, freight forwarders, and exporters and importers all over the world.

Traditional family-based small firms will take time before they can utilize these costly and sophisticated services. In principle, "there is no reason why the marketing of sharks' fins should not be facilitated by computers," as one respondent in our study has stated. The successful introduction of telefax machines, which were installed in nearly all firms surveyed, underlines the rationality of these supposedly "conservative" entrepreneurs (Wu and Wu, 1980). There is no reason why electronic data exchanges will not effectively complement personal relations and face-to-face contacts.

Another point to be made concerns the stability of cross-border trading networks. Political change often leads to disruption of traditional trade links. The decline of communism and the political and economic reform in China since 1978 were external forces to which Singaporean trading networks have had to adjust. In the context of these changes, it is uncertain if traditional Chinese cultural values will continue to underpin business connections, and to what degree modernization of cultural values will affect business networks (Harrel, 1985; Wu, 1973; Wong, 1993, p. 21).

References

Burns, JJ (1978). The management of risk, social factors in the development of exchange relations among the Kubber traders in North Sumatra. Doctoral dissertation, Yale University.

De Glopper, DR (1978). Doing business in Lukang. In *Studies in Chinese Society*, AP Wolf (ed.). Stanford, CA: Stanford University Press.

Diamond, N (1969). *K'un Shen: A Taiwanese Village*. New York, NY: Holt, Reinhart, Winston.

Eastman, LE (1988). *Family, Field, and Ancestors: Constancy and Change in China's Social and Economic History*. New York, NY: Oxford University Press.

Evers, H-D (1987). Chettiar moneylenders in Southeast Asia. *Marchands et bommes d'Affairs Asiatiques*, 199–219.

Evers, H-D (1988). Traditional trading networks of Southeast Asia. *Archipel*, 35, 89–100.

Evers, H-D and T Schiel (1987). Exchange, trade, and state: A theoretical outline. *Review*, 10(3), 459–470.

Freedman, M (1976). Immigrants and associations: Chinese in nineteenth-century Singapore. In *Immigrants and Associations*, LA Fallers (ed.). The Hague: Mouton.

Goldberg, MA (1985). *The Chinese Connection: Getting Plugged in to the Pacific Rim Real Estate, Trade and Capital Markets*. Vancouver: University of British Columbia Press.

Granovetter, M (1985). Economic action and social structure: The problem of embeddedness. *American Journal of Sociology*, 91, 481–510.

Greenhalgh, S (1985). Networks and their nodes: Urban society on Taiwan. *China Quarterly*, 99, 529–552.

Harrel, S (1985). Why do the Chinese work so hard? Reflections on an entrepreneurial ethnic. *Modern China*, 11(2), 203–226.

Hart, K (1988). Kinship connect and trust: The economic organization of migrants in an African city slum. In *Trust: Making and Breaking of Cooperative Relations*, D Gambetta (ed.). New York, NY: Basil Blackwell.

Hsieh, J (1978). The Chinese community in Singapore: The internal structure and its basic constituents. In *Studies in ASEAN Sociology: Urban Society and Social Change*, PSJ Chan and H-D evers (eds.). Singapore: Chopmen Enterprises.

Jacobs, JB (1979). A Preliminary model of particularistic ties in Chinese political alliances: *Kan-ch'ing* and *Kuan-hsi* in a rural Taiwanese township. *China Quarterly*, 78, 237–273.

Jamann, W (1994). *Business Practices and Organizational Dynamics of Chinese Family-Based Trading Firms*. Saarbruecken/Fort Lauderdale: Verlag Breitenbach.

Jordan, DK (1985). Sworn brothers: A study in Chinese ritual kinship. In *The Chinese Family and Its Ritual Behaviour*, HJ Chang and Y-C Chuang (eds.). Taipei: Academica Sinica, Institute of Ethnology.

Landa, J (1983). The political economy of the ethnically homogeneous Chinese middlemen group in Southeast Asia: Ethnicity and entrepreneurship in a plural society. In *The Chinese in Southeast Asia,* LYC Lim and LAP Gosling (eds.). Singapore: Maruzen.

Lee, SK (1987). A Chinese conception of "management": An interpretative approach. Doctoral dissertation, School of Management, National University of Singapore.

Lim, LYC (1983). Chinese economic activity in Southeast Asia: An introductory review. In *The Chinese in Southeast Asia,* LYC Lim and LAP Gosling (eds.). Singapore: Maruzen.

Lim, MH and TK Fong (1986). Singapore's corporations go transnational. *Journal of Southeast Asian Studies* 17 (2), 336–365.

Mohamad, MB (1970). *The Malay Dilemma.* Kuala Lumpur: Times Books International.

Menkhoff, T (1992). Chinese non-contractual business relations and social structure: The Singapore case. *Internationales Asienforum*, 23(1/2) 261–288.

Menkhoff, T (1993). *Trade Routes, Trust and Trading Networks: Chinese Small Enterprises in Singapore.* Saarbruecken/Fort Lauderdale: Verlag Breitenbach.

Menkhoff, T (1994). Trade routes, trust and tactics: Chinese traders in Singapore. In *The Moral Economy of Trade: Ethnicity and Developing Markets*, H-D Evers and H Schrader (eds.). London: Routledge.

Ng, C-K (1983). *Trade and Society: The Amoy Network on the China Coast 1683–1735.* Singapore: Singapore University Press.

Omohundro, JT (1983). Social networks and business success for the Philippine Chinese. In *The Chinese in Southeast Asia*, LYC Lim and LAP Gosling (eds.). Singapore: Maruzen.

Radcliffe-Brown, AR (1940). On social structure. *Journal of the Royal Anthropological Society of Great Britain and Ireland,* 70, 1–12.

Silin, RH (1972). Marketing and credit in a Hong Kong wholsesale market. In *Economic Organization in Chinese Society,* WE Willmott (ed.). Stanford, CA: Stanford University Press.

Tan, TTW (1986). *Your Chinese Roots.* Singapore: Times Books International.

Tong, CK (1989). The internal structure of Chinese firms in Singapore. Paper read at the Conference on Business Groups and Economic Development in East Asia, Hong Kong.

Wellman, B (1988). Structural analysis: From method and meraphor to theory and substance. In *Social Structures: A Network Approach,* B Wellman and SD Berkowitz (eds.). Cambridge, UK: Cambridge University Press.

Wong, S-L (1988a). *Emigrant Entrepreneurs*: *Shanghai Industrialists in Hong Kong*. Hong Kong: Oxford University Press.

Wong, S-L (1988b). The applicability of Asian family values to other sociocultural settings. In *In Search of an East Asian Development Model*, PL Berger and M Hsiao (eds.). Oxford, UK: Transaction Books.

Wong, S-L (1993). Business networks, cultural values and the state in Hong Kong and Singapore. Paper read at the Conference on Chinese Business Houses in Southeast Asia since 1870, London.

Wu, T-Y (1973). Chinese traditional values and modernization. *Southeast Asian Journal of Social Sciences*, 1, 113–22.

Wu, Y-L and Wu C-H (1980). *Economic Development in Southeast Asia*: *The Chinese Dimension*. Stanford, CA: Hoover Institution.

Yang, M-H (1989). The gift economy of China. *Comparative Studies in Society and History*, 31(1), 25–54.

Kunio Y, (1988). *The Rise of Capitalism in South-East Asia*. Singapore: Oxford University Press.

Straits Times (1989). SNS and SITA join forces in global EDI approach, p. viii.

Straits Times (1989). Trade net joins global electronic network, p. 39.

Chapter 7

Improving Small Firm Performance Through Collaborative Change Management and Outside Learning: Trends in Singapore

Thomas Menkhoff and Chay Yue Wah

1. Introduction: Small Enterprises between Continuity and Change

Locally-owned small and medium-sized enterprises (SMEs) form the backbone of Singapore's economy.[1] They comprise 92 percent of the city-state's total establishments, employing 51 percent of the workforce and generating 34 percent of total value added. The recession in 1985–1986, the Asian crisis 1997–1998 and the global economic turmoil in 2008–2009 have underlined the resilience and challenges of Singapore's SME sector in terms of employment generation or the imperatives of rapid environmental change. As Singapore progresses from her post-colonial

This is a reprint of an article originally published in 2011 in the *International Journal of Asian Business and Information Management*, 2(1), 1–24. The editors gratefully acknowledge the permission by IGI Global to reprint the essay in this edition.

[1] There is no homogeneous concept or definition of SMEs. As a consequence, SMEs can be defined in different ways depending on the country's development stage, policy issues, and administrative processes. While the number of employees remains a common criterion, other denominators like sales volume, invested capital and total assets differ from country to country. At the time of the survey, Singapore's Standards, Productivity and Innovation Board (SPRING, Singapore) defined local SMEs as having: (a) at least 30 percent local equity; (b) fixed productive assets (defined as net book value of factory building, machinery and equipment) not exceeding $15 million; and (c) an employment size of not exceeding 200 workers for non-manufacturing companies (http://www.spring. gov.sg/portal/products/assist/edf/letas.html).

dependence on Multinational Companies (MNCs) for technological transfer and financial capital to a knowledge-based economy that places emphasis on entrepreneurial culture, R&D, know why, intellectual assets and knowledge management capabilities (Menkhoff, Evers and Chay eds., 2010), the government recognises the important role of SMEs in increasing the economy's competitiveness in the global market as well as the strength and stabilizing role of this "indigenous" sector that "... is more permanent and durable than a foreign one" (Lee and Low, 1990, p. 23). Despite various SME success stories and the dynamism of the small firm sector as a whole, Singapore's policymakers have put in place various schemes to help local SMEs to master the transition to a knowledge-based economy. This requires the modernization of "traditional" structures and mindsets as well as the willingness to learn from outside sources which explains why the topic of this chapter, namely organizational change leadership, is so important in Singapore's business and society.

Examples of major environmental changes impacting upon SMEs include the on-going process of economic globalization, intensified competition or continuous IT innovations such as e-commerce. All this has focused management's attention on managing discontinuities in organizations' lives. As management scholars have argued, these external forces of change require not only "adaptive," "flexible" organizations and "new" management approaches but also competent leaders and managers able to adapt to changing times and to manage organizational change (Beckhard, 1969; Beckhard and Harris, 1987; Tushman *et al.*, 1997; Schaefer and Thomsen, 1998; Bjerke, 1998; Menkhoff and Gerke eds., 2002). In view of turbulent markets, the need for SME owners to make strategic responses toward the changing environment is crucial for sustaining success and survival (Pfeffer and Salancik, 1978; Hannan and Freeman, 1984; EIU and Andersen Consulting, 2000; Pfeffer, 2005; Chew and Chew, 2008).

Organizational change refers to both planned and unplanned transformations of an organization's structure, technology and/or human resources (Leavitt, 1965). Planned organizational change entails activities that are intentional and purposive in nature and designed to fulfill some organizational goals. It emphasizes managerial *choice* (Child, 1972, 1997) in contrast to unplanned change, which implies shifts in organizational activities due to forces that are external in nature and beyond the organization's control. In the literature on organizational change, planned change is often used synonymous with organizational development (OD) while unplanned change is discussed in the context of adaptation (Dyer, 1985; Kirkpatrick, 1985). Planned organizational change interventions are typically designed and sequenced by an internal or external change/OD agent, following a detailed diagnosis of an organization's shortcomings and needs. One of the core competencies of change agents is change leadership which is defined as a systematic process of aligning the organization's people and culture with changes in business strategy, organizational structure, systems and processes resulting in ownership and commitment to change, sustained and measurable improvement and improved capability to manage future change (Burke and Litwin, 1984; Hussey, 1995).

There is a dearth of empirical studies on change leadership and organizational change among SMEs in Singapore, most of which are owned and managed by ethnic Chinese. The few available studies (Chua, 2001; Menkhoff, Kay and Loh, 2002; Das, 2008) suggest that the response of many family-owned SMEs to the new wave of economic and technological forces is insufficient. Systemic management of change targets[2] such as strategy, people or technology represent challenges for SME owners. Studies of SMEs in Singapore conducted by Chua (2001) and Das (2008) showed that a relatively large proportion of these firms pay insufficient attention to IT skills upgrading, innovation as a source of competitiveness, product customization, customer satisfaction and e-commerce operations. Based on these indicators, we might argue that many SMEs in Singapore are not yet ready for the new economy. Predictors and key ingredients of entrepreneurial "new economy compliance," however, remain unclear.

---

[2] According to Leavitt (1965, p. 1145), change targets such as structure, technology, people and tasks are highly interdependent whereby "change in any one usually results in compensatory (or retaliatory) change in others." The task variable refers to the goal of organizations in producing goods and services, "including the large numbers of different but operationally meaningful sub-tasks that may exist in complex organizations" (Leavitt, 1965, p. 1144); actors (people) refer to individuals who, in return for a variety of inducements, make contributions to the organization; technology refers to the setting and techniques whereby work is performed; and finally, structure refers to the systems of communication, authority and work-flow that exist among participants of the organization.

The present study was carried out to explore the change propensity of the local Chinese business community *vis-à-vis* the rapidly changing business environment. The following research questions guided our inquiry: (i) What kinds of change management styles are prevalent in Singaporean SMEs? (ii) Are they mostly collaborative-consultative or directive-coercive? (iii) What kind of change approach is used and appropriate given the various change management scenarios local SME owner-managers may encounter in their firms in terms of urgency of change and resistance to change (which could be high or low) in the context of incremental and transformative change? (iv) Does the fit between styles and contexts lead to effectiveness in terms of outcomes?

2. Conceptualization and Propositions

Managing change processes in an enterprise is a challenge for many owner-managers. Key elements that influence the nature and outcomes of change processes include the adopted change management style, his/her personality, the particular scenario of change in terms of urgency of change and resistance levels, the extent of change as well as macro variables. While it is easy to argue that "effective change leadership" represents an essential precondition for the positive outcome of change measures, it is difficult to measure it. Perhaps, due to the methodological and access problems of doing research on change patterns in Chinese firms, there are hardly any empirical studies on corporate change in these firms.

Are the change management approaches adopted by Singapore's SME owner-managers "Western-centric," i.e., less autocratic and more participative (Quinn Mills, 2005), or "Asian-centric" with an emphasis on personalism and control (Tong and Yong, 2002; Mackie, 2003)? Studies of Chinese firms in Asia suggest that a large number of Singapore's owner managers of SMEs practice an *autocratic* style of management characterized by concern for production (rather than people), telling and directive leadership behaviors and a dearth of transformational leadership (Menkhoff, 1993; Tong and Yong, 2002, pp. 223–225; Tsui-Auch, 2003). Autocratic managers are often seen as less receptive to change compared to those who are more participative in their management style. According to the Western entrepreneurship literature, entrepreneurs who adopt a "one-man rule" (i.e., combining the role of both chairman and CEO) tend to dominate rather than to lead, practice a non-participatory board, have an unbalanced top team and lack of management depth and ultimately, respond badly to change. "One-man show" owners (Smith and Miner, 1983) tend to be autocratic in style, unilateral in decision making and short-term orientated and may not adapt well to change. Whether change initiatives implemented by managers who practice a more participatory management style are more likely to achieve positive outcomes in form of employee buy-in and overcoming resistance to change or even improved firm performance than those implemented by autocratic managers remains to be seen (Schaefer and Thomson, 1998; Pfeffer, 2005; Quinn Mills, 2005).

Theoretical-empirical studies on Chinese change management patterns in modern business and their outcomes hardly exist. Early studies such as those by Hofstede (1980), Redding and Wong (1986) and Redding (1993, 1996) suggest that the strong overlapping of ownership and management in Chinese businesses typically facilitates paternalistic leadership and authority styles. This may imply that the owner-managers of Chinese SMEs in Singapore are more likely to use a directive-coercive (authoritative) style of change leadership. In the present study autocratic change leadership approaches are defined as (i) *directive* styles based on the use of authority as well as (ii) *coercive* styles whereby the top decision-maker forces or imposes change on the organization (Mackie, 2003, p. 20). It is argued here that these "directive-coercive" modes prevail amongst the sampled owner-managers while "collaborative-consultative modes" such as *collaborative styles* on the basis of strong employee involvement or *consultative styles* with limited staff involvement are rather atypical in the sampled firms (Buchanan and Huczynski, 1997, pp. 464–467).

While it would be tempting to postulate that autocratic change management approaches are typical for *all* ethnic Chinese business leaders in Southeast Asia, the empirical reality and cultural complexity of doing business in this part of the world may suggest otherwise. Indeed, Silin's description of Chinese leadership styles as "didactic" (1976), Mackie's account of "five great Chinese empire builders" (2003) or the different success stories and managerial approaches of Li Ka Shing of Hutchison

Whampoa–Cheung Kong (with his two Western-trained sons) in Hong Kong, third generation family business Li and Fung or Stan Shih of Acer indicate that there is a great diversity amongst ethnic Chinese business leaders with regard to organizational change. Empirical studies on change (e.g., Kanter, 2000) suggest that the respective change leadership approaches are contingent upon both demographics and situational forces such as age or education, the urgency of change, the degree of resistance to change and/or the dynamics of the environment in which the firms operate. There are different routes to achieving change such as compliance or commitment both of which incur certain costs, but at different stages. Business environments and situations do differ from industry to industry and might necessitate either more participatory or more coercive change leadership approaches to implement sustainable changes according to circumstances.

As the (blended) change management approaches adopted by owner-managers vary according to mental models, internal challenges or external pressures, contingent and situational leadership theories in the tradition of Fiedler, Tannenbaum and Schmidt or House as summarized by Lussier and Achua (2004, pp. 138–163) are more appropriate conceptually to serve as heuristics in understanding the change management approaches used by ethnic Chinese owner-managers of Singaporean SMEs. Due to the wide variety of potential frameworks and difficulties to operationalize and to measure change management competencies objectively, this study adopted a pragmatic approach, utilizing two matrices developed by Dunphy and Stace (1990) and summarized by Buchanan and Huczynski (1997, pp. 464–467) as heuristics to gain more insights into the contingent change leadership behavior of local SME owners with regard to both incremental and fundamental change (Levy, 1986). The essence of their situational change leadership model is illustrated in Figures 1 and 2.

Dunphy and Stace distinguish between four different categories of *change leadership style*: (i) widespread employee involvement in key decisions affecting their and the organization's future (*collaborative style*); (ii) limited involvement in setting goals relevant to employees' areas of responsibility (*consultative style*); (iii) use of managerial authority in reaching decisions about change and the future, and about how change will proceed (*directive style*); and (iv) senior management forcing or imposing change on the organization (*coercive style*).

Scale of Change

	Fine	Incremental	Modular	Corporate
	Tuning	Adjustment	Transformation	Transformation

Style of Change

Collaborative	*Type 1*	*Type 2*
Consultative	Participative Evolution	Charismatic Transformation
Directive	*Type 3*	*Type 4*
Coercive	Forced Evolution	Dictatorial Transformation

Figure 1.   Change leadership styles to incremental and transformative change
Source: Buchanan and Huczynski (1997, p. 465).

The *scale of change* is defined in terms of four main categories: (i) improving and refining methods, policies and procedures, typically at the level of the division or department (*fine tuning*); (ii) distinct modifications to strategies, structures and management processes, but not radical enough to be described as strategic (*incremental adjustment*); (iii) radical realignment or restructuring of parts of the organization (such as departments and divisions) but not the whole (*modular transformation*); and (iv) revolutionary changes throughout the organization, to structures, systems and procedures, to mission and core values, and to the distribution of power (*corporate transformation*).

The matrix shown in Figure 2 suggests that there are *four ideal change strategies* depending on the particular *change management scenario*: participative evolution, charismatic transformation, forced evolution and dictatorial transformation (Buchanan and Huczynski, 1997, p. 465). There are four different change management scenarios: (i) low urgency of change and low resistance to change, i.e., the organization needs minor adjustment to meet environmental conditions, time is available, and key interest groups *favor* change; (ii) low urgency and high resistance,

<u>**Incremental Change Strategies**</u>

Modes

Participative Evolution

Collaborative-
Consultative Modes

Use when the organization needs *minor adjustment* to meet environmental conditions, where time is available, and where *key interest groups favor change.*

Forced Evolution

Directive-Coercive
Mode

Use when the minor adjustments are required, where time is available, but where *key interest groups oppose change.*

<u>**Transformational Change Strategies**</u>

Charismatic Transformation

Collaborative-
Consultative Modes

Use when the organization needs *major adjustment* to meet environmental conditions, where there is little time available, and where there is *support for radical change.*

Dictatorial Transformation

Directive-Coercive
Modes

Use when *major adjustments* are necessary, where there is no time for participation, where there is *no internal support* for strategic change, but where this is necessary for survival.

Figure 2. Dunphy and Stace's contingency approach to change implementation
Source: Buchanan and Huczynski (1997, p. 466).

i.e., minor adjustments are required, time is available, and key interest groups oppose change; (iii) high urgency and low resistance, i.e., the organization needs major adjustment to meet environmental conditions, there is little time available, and there is support for radical change; and (iv) high urgency and high resistance, i.e., major adjustments are necessary, there is no time for participation, and there is no internal support for strategic change although change is necessary for survival.

The contingent change leadership approach suggests that *incremental, collaborative-consultative modes* are not always appropriate, especially where there is a high urgency of change combined with high resistance towards change. In such situations, transformative, directive-coercive modes might be more efficient ways of implementing necessary changes quickly.

While in reality, a blend of different organizational change approaches might be used to tackle different situations and challenges, the change leadership concept of Dunphy and Stace represents a helpful device to explore the contingent change leadership behaviour of Singaporean SME owners.

In line with the cultural logic of Chinese management and leadership behavior as studied by scholars such as Hofstede (1980), Redding and Wong (1986), Redding (1993, 1996), Tsui-Auch (2003) or Quinn Mills (2005), we arrived at the following two propositions about the particular change leadership approach used by our respondents with regard to two particular change scenarios:

Proposition 1: When the Chinese owner-managers of SMEs in Singapore implement incremental change under conditions of low urgency of change and low resistance to change, the most frequent change leadership approach used can be characterized as directive-coercive.

Proposition 2: When the Chinese owner-managers of SMEs in Singapore implement transformative change under conditions of high urgency of change and high resistance, the most frequent change leadership approach used can be characterized as directive-coercive.

As our specific interest is to explore how SME owner-managers respond under contrasting business situations, we focus here only on the "low urgency and low resistance" versus "high urgency and high resistance" scenarios. The implications of the other two possible scenarios ("low urgency and high resistance" versus "high urgency and low resistance") will have to be examined in another study.

3. Methods and Sample

Information concerning participant and organizational characteristics for the present study was collected by means of survey questionnaires. The English version of the questionnaire was translated into Mandarin and back-translated into English to insure accuracy and consistency in the translation process. The questionnaire was pre-tested on a group of small business owners and subject matter experts to ensure that all the questions were adequately formulated and understood.

The target survey group was drawn from corporate members of the Singapore Chinese Chamber of Commerce and Industry (SCCCI), which has a total membership of about 3,000. Survey questionnaires in both English and Mandarin were sent to 1,000 SCCCI members randomly selected from the membership list. 101 completed questionnaires were returned with a response rate of 10.1 percent. The final sample comprised small and medium-sized firms (defined as firms with less than 200 employees) operating in different sectors that included manufacturing (28.7 percent), trading (23.8 percent), professional services (20.8 percent), retailers (8.9 percent) and others.

All respondents were ethnic Chinese as most members of Singapore's Chinese Chamber of Commerce and Industry are Chinese. Males represented 84.2 percent while female respondents comprised 15.8 percent. The majority of the survey participants (63.4 percent) turned out to be English-educated Chinese while the rest (35.6 percent) were Chinese-educated. Almost half of the sampled owner-managers had a tertiary education (47.5 percent), followed by 24.8 percent with a secondary school/vocational institute education and 22.8 percent who had studied enrolled at junior colleges. The number of uneducated owner-managers of small businesses, i.e., those with primary education only, was negligible (4 percent). Engineering (35.7 percent) and business management (35.7 percent) topped the list of educational specializations. About 12 percent of the sampled owner-managers had an educational background in arts and social sciences while about 7.2 percent of the respondents reported an educational specialization in science. On average, respondents had spent 13.3 years in their respective organizations and 10.5 years in their current position. The oldest firm of the sample, run by a tea merchant, was founded in the 1930s. 5.9 percent of the businesses were established in the period 1950–1959. 7.9 percent of the firms started their operations between 1960 and 1969. Most of the firms surveyed had been established in the 1990s (45.5 percent). 22.8 percent of all SMEs were found to be established between 1980 and 1984. The majority (48.5 percent) had been established by the respondents who — in 59.6 percent of those cases — turned out to be the present owners. About 18.8 percent of the surveyed establishments were founded by the respondents' fathers, followed by other relatives (5 percent). Of all enterprises surveyed, about 80 percent were incorporated companies (i.e., these firms have their own legal identity) while the other 20 percent were unincorporated. 14.9 percent were of the sole proprietorship type of operation (such firms are run by one owner who is solely responsible for the business). Partnerships represented 5 percent of the sampled firms. The majority of the SMEs in the survey were private limited companies (77.2 percent).

4. Results

4.1 *Business characteristics and profile of owner-managers*

The typical firm surveyed was a 100 percent locally-owned, private limited company established by the respondent, who owns a substantial proportion of the business without any involvement of external parties, such as institutional and/or equity investors. The average respondent turned out to be a middle-aged (42.4 years), English-educated, male Chinese Singaporean with tertiary education and a specialization in engineering or management. He has been in his current position for 10.5 years, with an average organizational tenure and total working experience of 13.3 years and 20.8 years respectively.

Most respondents perceived themselves as "opportunistic entrepreneurs" (46.5 percent) who are achievement-oriented, effective in terms of adaptation and business planning as well as willing to take risks (Smith, 1967; Carland, Boulton and Carland, 1984; Bracker, Keats and Pearson,

1988). "Craftsman entrepreneurs" typified in the entrepreneurship literature as relatively non-adaptive and more risk-adverse persons aiming for a comfortable living rather than the highest possible level of performance (Filley and Aldag, 1978) made up 36.6 percent of the sample. About 17 percent of the respondents could not be categorized. Most owner-managers (52.5 percent) classified themselves as risk-takers while 36.6 percent appeared to be more risk-averse (i.e., not willing to take risks); 10.9 percent were neutral. With regard to the degree of change propensity, 76.2 percent of the sampled owner-managers turned out to be receptive to change while 13.9 Percent were not; about 10 percent were neutral.

4.2 *Initiation of change and change targets*

The survey suggests that the sampled Singaporean SME owners implement organizational change measures on a routine basis. Changing the firm's strategic direction and technology, IT-related changes, and changes related to people and their task behaviors were the most frequently adopted measures (see Figure 3).

In terms of technology-related changes, internet and e-commerce, purchase of new tools and equipment, and office automation and implementation of online procedures were classified as the three most important, major and critical change areas. Significant people-related changes included the provision of employees with more company-related information, more consultation, and more staff participation in decision-making processes.

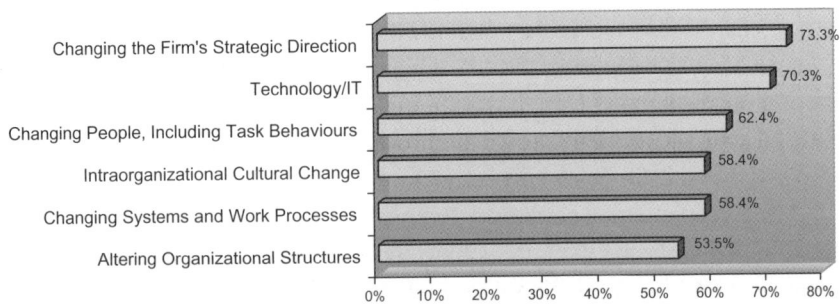

Figure 3.   Most frequently adopted change measure

Nature of Change Measure

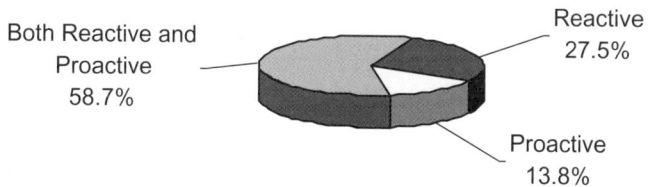

Figure 4.   Nature of organizational change measures

Planning of Organisational Change

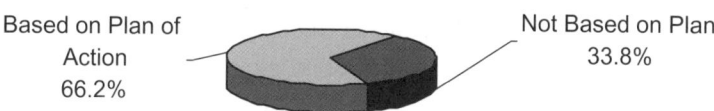

Figure 5.   Planning of organizational change measure yes/no

4.3 *Nature of organizational change measures*

Figures 4 and 5 present summaries of the planning of organizational change. Most respondents interpreted the nature of organizational change measures, which had been initiated in their firms during the post-Asian crisis years, as both reactive and proactive (58.8 percent); 27.5 percent assessed the changes as reactive in nature.

Only 13.8 percent of all respondents had proactively implemented organizational change measures in anticipation of future difficulties, threats and opportunities. The majority (66.3 percent) claimed that the adopted change measures were based on a detailed plan of action.

4.4 *Scale of organizational change measures*

As Figure 6 shows, more than two thirds of the respondents had implemented *incremental* change strategies (75.3 percent). Those who characterized the scale of change which had occurred in their firms, e.g., changes

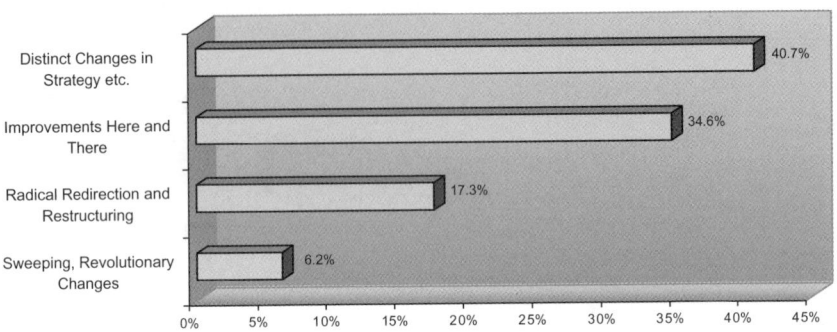

Figure 6. Scale of organizational changes initiated by respondents

with regard to strategies, structures and/or management processes, during the post-Asian crisis years as *distinct* (*incremental adjustment*) made up 40.7 percent while those who had refined methods and procedures (*fine tuning*) comprised 34.6 percent.

Those who had implemented *transformative* change strategies throughout their firms made up less than a third of the survey participants (23.5 percent). About 6 percent of these respondents characterized the changes as revolutionary (*corporate transformation*) while 17 percent categorized the scale of change as radical realignment and restructuring or what we have categorized as *modular transformation* (see Figure 1).

5. What Kinds of Change Leadership Modes Are Prevalent in Singaporean SMEs?

Our data contradict popular notions of ethnic Chinese owner-managers of small businesses as being typically autocratic change leaders. Two-thirds of the sampled owner-managers (70.3 percent) used *collaborative-consultative* change leadership modes *vis-à-vis* 29.7 percent of the respondents who relied on *directive-coercive* change leadership styles (see Figure 7). Altogether, 37 percent of the respondents ensured widespread employee participation in key decisions (*collaborative style*) compared to about 33 percent whose approach entailed limited involvement of subordinates (*consultative style*).

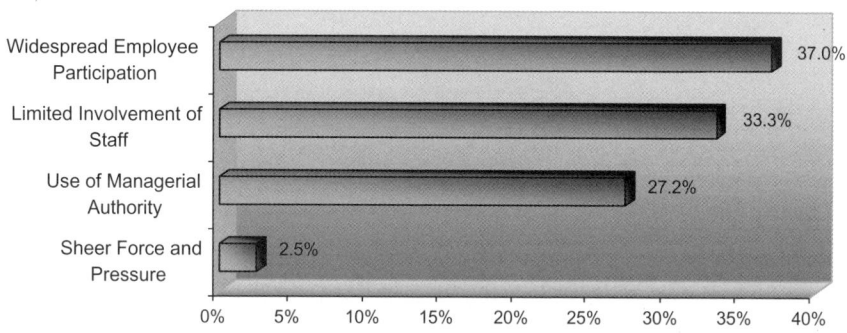

Figure 7. Change leadership style

The results of the chi-square procedure, $\chi^2 = 13.44$, $df = 3$, $p \leq 0.001$, show significant differences in the change management style used by our sample of owner-managers. Therefore, we can conclude that owner-managers of Chinese SMEs in Singapore are not likely to use directive-coercive change leadership styles as argued by the literature on Chinese business.

Of those who had used a more authoritarian approach, 27.2 percent reported that they use managerial authority to enforce change (*directive style*) while a small minority (2.5 percent) stated that they use force and pressure (*coercive style*) as shown in Figure 7. The data suggest that the respective change leadership styles are contingent upon situational forces such as the urgency of change, the degree of resistance to change and/or the dynamics of the environment in which the firms operate.

All firms encountered resistance to change, particularly amongst non-executive employees but also amongst middle managers and top managers. Slightly more than half of the survey participants felt that they had been successful in tackling this problem (57.5 percent) while 41.3 percent interpreted themselves as somewhat successful. A small proportion (1.3 percent) felt that they were not successful in overcoming resistance amongst staff. Cost factors, fear, bad habits and mindset problems, inability of old staff to catch up with new developments, insufficient knowledge about new technologies, managerial perception differences and poor communication were cited as main barriers to change.

Scenario of Change

High Urgency and
High Resistance
27.5%

Low Urgency and
Low Resistance
20.0%

High Urgency and
Low Resistance
46.3%

Low Urgency and
High Resistance
6.3%

Figure 8.   Change management scenario

In terms of change management scenarios, most of the respondents characterized the situation they had faced in their firms during past crises as one of *high urgency of change and low resistance toward change* (46 percent). As discussed earlier, such a scenario may require a "charismatic transformation" as an appropriate change strategy according to the literature. This was followed by *high urgency of change and high resistance toward change* (27.5 percent) — a situation which may legitimize what has been termed "dictatorial transformation" according to theory — and *low urgency of change and low resistance toward change* (20 percent). As stated earlier, the latter scenario can be described as "participative evolution." About 6 percent of the respondents classified the change management scenario they had faced during the past few years as one of *low urgency of change and high resistance towards change*, justifying "forced evolution" as change management strategy (Buchanan and Huczynski, 1997, pp. 465–466).

5.1 *Change strategies and leadership approaches to incremental and transformative change*

Do the Singaporean owner-managers of small businesses use "appropriate" (Buchanan and Huczynski, 1997, p. 465) change leadership approaches? According to Dunphy and Stace's contingency approach to change implementation, *incremental change strategies* carried out in collaborative-consultative modes are appropriate when the organization needs *minor adjustment* to meet environmental conditions,

INCREMENTAL CHANGE STRATEGIES

MODE	*Participative Evolution*
Collaborative-Consultative	"Low Urgency of Change / Low Resistance to Change"

	Forced Evolution
Directive-Coercive	"Low Urgency of Change / High Resistance to Change"

Figure 9. Appropriate change leadership styles for incremental change

where time is available, and where *key interest groups favor change* (= low urgency of change/low resistance to change). In case *key interest groups oppose this type of incremental change* (= low urgency of change/ high resistance to change), *directive-coercive modes* might be more suitable (see Figure 9).

Where *major and rapid adjustments* (revolutionary change) are necessary to meet environmental conditions, and where there is support for this type of strategic change (high urgency of change/low resistance to change), *transformative change,* e.g., based on managerial charisma approaches, can be effective. Transformative approaches carried out in directive and coercive ways might be suitable when there is no time for participation and no internal support for planned major adjustments, but where strategic change is necessary for survival (see Figure 10).

As illustrated in Figures 6–8, the majority of respondents characterized the change management scenario they had faced as one of high urgency and low resistance (46.3 percent) and had used predominantly incremental change strategies (75.3 percent) as well as collaborative-consultative change leadership modes (70.3 percent) to deal with it. This approach is labeled as "participative evolution" in line with the concept by Dunphy and Stace (Buchanan and Huczynski, 1997, p. 466). The most appropriate change implementation approach for a situation of high urgency of change and low resistance is "charismatic transformation"

TRANSFORMATIVE CHANGE STRATEGIES	
MODE	*Charismatic Transformation*
Collaborative-Consultative	"High Urgency of Change / Low Resistance to Change"
	Dictatorial Transformation
Directive-Coercive	"High Urgency of Change / High Resistance to Change"

Figure 10.   Appropriate change leadership styles for transformative change

according to Buchanan and Huczynski, 1997, p. 466). Did our respondents act in tune with theory or not?

Figure 11 shows the frequency/percentage of respondents who used a specific change leadership style for particular change scenarios. The data is interesting as the collaborative consultative style *dominates* all four change scenarios (low-low, low-high, high-low, high-high) in contradiction to theory and propositions.

Of those 46 percent of respondents who had characterized the situation they had faced in their firms since mid-1997 as one of *high urgency of change and low resistance towards change* (see Figure 9), the majority (81.1 percent) used *appropriate* change leadership styles, namely collaborative-consultative modes.

Most of those who had encountered a scenario of *high urgency of change and high resistance toward change* (27.5 percent) also used collaborative-consultative styles (68.2 percent) — contrary to the model by Dunphy and Stace which recommend directive-coercive modes to deal with issues such as resistance and urgent change requirements and the initial propositions. The results of the chi-square test ($\chi^2 = 18.78$, $df = 3$, $p \leq 0.001$) showed a significant difference between change leadership styles under conditions of high urgency and high resistance. In contrast to Proposition 2, the most consistent management change approach was not the *directive-coercive* mode but a *collaborative-consultative* approach.

	LEADERSHIP STYLE	
	Collaborative-Consultative	Directive-Coercive
CHANGE SCENARIOS		
Low Urgency of Δ and Low Resistance to Δ	**56.3%**	43.7%
Low Urgency of Δ and High Resistance to Δ	**60.0%**	40.0%
High Urgency of Δ and Low Resistance to Δ	**81.1%**	18.9%
High Urgency of Δ and High Resistance to Δ	**68.2%**	31.8%

Figure 11. Scenarios of change and adopted change leadership modes

Of those 20 percent of the sampled businesses whose owner-managers were confronted with a scenario of *low urgency of change and low resistance toward change*, more than 50 percent used appropriate (collaborative-consultative) leadership modes. The results of the chi-square test ($\chi^2 = 13.44$, $df = 3$, $p \leq 0.001$) showed a significant difference between change leadership styles under conditions of low urgency and low resistance. In contrast to proposition 1, the most consistent management change approach was not the *directive-coercive* mode but a *collaborative-consultative* approach.

A small group of respondents (6 percent) classified the change management scenario they had been confronted with during the past few years as one of *low urgency of change and high resistance toward change*. Their predominant change management style was also collaborative-consultative in nature rather than directive-coercive as prescribed by theory.

To sum up, the collaborative-consultative style has about twice as many respondents endorsing/using it compared to the directive-coercive. How can such findings be explained? One possible reason is that our sampled ethnic Chinese owner-managers of SMEs, contrary to popular belief, use the collaborative consultative approach because they are more consensus-seeking than the previous generation (Ng, 2002). Also, in the present work generation, directive-coercive leadership approaches may not be the "best" way to effect change; these are business people and they know what is most likely to be accepted by employees. However, the downside to this is that some may argue that in high urgency situations, decisions have to be made quickly, so will a collaborative consultative approach hinder or slow down decision-making processes? As the focus of this essay is *change management* and not decision-making, the authors are unable to provide a data-based answer to that question at this point in time.

6. Outcomes and Benefits of Change Measure(s)

More than half of all survey participants characterized the outcome of organizational change measures as successful (55.6 percent) and claimed that they had measured the effects of implemented organizational change measures (75.3 percent). Improved job performance (60.5 percent) and retained business (60.5 percent), higher sales volume (59.2 percent) and

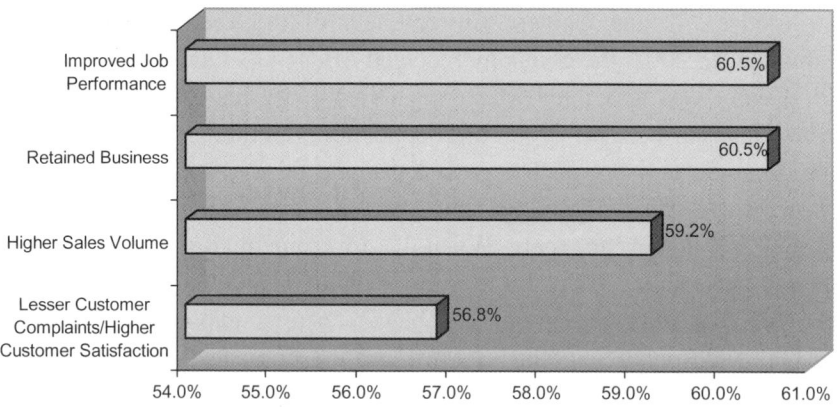

Figure 12.   Scale of benefits obtained by change measure

fewer customer complaints/higher customer satisfaction were cited as the three most important benefits of change initiatives (see Figure 12). Adverse administrative effects, increase in staff turnover and disruption of production were cited as the three most important negative consequences of implemented change measures.

7. Case Study: Change Management and Outside Learning at Qian Hu Corporation Ltd

One firm which has successfully managed change is Qian Hu Corp., Singapore's leading breeder and exporter of tropical fish, under the leadership of Dr Kenny Yap, Executive Chairman and Managing Director. Under his strategic stewardship, Qian Hu has grown tremendously. The company was publicly listed in 2000 and moved to Singapore's mainboard in 2002. Qian Hu has embarked on a very successful journey to business excellence by starting with a Strategic Business Planning exercise in 1997 and progressing to other upgrading projects such as Corporate Restructuring in 1998 and the National Cost of Quality Programme in 1999. In recognition of his entrepreneurial spirit and contributions to the society, Kenny was conferred the Singapore Youth Award in 1998. He was also one of the finalists for the Rotary-ASME Entrepreneur of the Year Award 2000 and is known as the "ornamental fish tycoon" in the industry. In 2001, Kenny became one of the 50 Stars of Asia (Business Week). In 2002, he was awarded the Young Chinese Entrepreneur of the Year title by Yazhou Zhoukan. In 2004, the company received SPRING's Quality Award.

Kenny was appointed Managing Director by his family in 1994 to head Qian Hu because of his high education, continuous enthusiasm for the ornamental fish industry, great ideas and business savvy. His family started out in chicken farming in the late 70s before establishing a pig farm in the early 80s in Singapore. When the government closed down most of the pig farms in the 1980s for reasons of public health, the family filled its concrete pig pens with water and began farming guppies. Heavy rains caused widespread flooding in 1989 and the company's entire stock of guppies was wiped out, resulting in a huge loss. Taking over the struggling family business, Kenny decided to embark upon a few changes. He believes that there are strong emotional issues in family-owned SMEs to contend with. Therefore, he ensured that his siblings understand that the company has to be run separately from the individual family member. His first challenge was to institute structural changes within the firm. To strike a balance, he instituted rules such as "no in-laws should interfere with family business" and that he is the only person accountable for the welfare of his immediate four siblings and two cousins who are involved in the business. He made it clear to his family that if they want to hire their own relatives, they will be responsible for their performance and welfare. In this capacity, Kenny has defined the roles and responsibilities of each member quite clearly, thus, striking a balance between family and company.

7.1 *Technological changes and external learning*

Kenny invested more than $6 million in 1995 to establish its farm infrastructure and purchase stock. He built a 4.2-hectare, high-tech farm to maximize the use of land and to optimize productivity. The company integrated its breeding, farming, import and export activities. Its high tech farming methods include a temperature controlled packing house, computerized system of trading records and a laboratory for fish examination and water analysis. The company's R&D division designed the world's first automated packaging machine for ornamental fish. It spent more than $200,000 to develop two auto-packing systems. Traditionally, nine people would work for nine hours to pack 300 boxes of fish. The new automated system, which packs fish into plastic bags before they are put in cartons for transport, is manned by just three workers who need four hours to pack 500 boxes of fish. The bulk-packing machine is likely to further cut the need for manpower.

Much of the technology comes from Qian Hu's own research and development efforts as well as its work with external consultants and specialists. The company collaborates with Temasek Life Science Laboratory in researching the breeding behaviors of Dragon fish. The firm was also able to cut costs for water and manpower by designing a filter system that helps to keep the fish "happy" with less water and fewer workers. It has also made great strides in the area of fish medicine. Their own system of medication has enabled their fish to be healthier and more likely to survive the trip to local fish retailers. Qian Hu's willingness to learn and to invest in new technologies has kept it ahead of the game: "The only way you can survive is by improving productivity, upgrading skills and equipping your employees with knowledge," Kenny pointed out.

7.2 *Embracing e-commerce and knowledge management*

Kenny is permanently looking for new ways to improve the business: "You have to be ready to change the culture of your industry by introducing new things," he argued during one occasion. Qian Hu has also ventured into the world of e-commerce and knowledge management. Kenny is hoping to capitalize the web revolution for its ornamental fish business to business (B2B) division because most of its customers in Asia and Europe are retailers rather than retail customers. He created an interactive portal site for customers, initiated the development of a corporate best practice archive which can be accessed via e-mail and SMS, propagated knowledge sharing amongst the various subsidiaries and pioneered the implementation of speech recognition technology enabling shareholders to obtain the firm's latest stock value from the SGX (Singapore Exchange) website in real-time via the phone.

7.3 *SME assistance schemes*

In terms of government assistance schemes for SMEs, Kenny feels that many SMEs do not take up the offer because of three reasons: (i) there are too many schemes and some overlaps; (ii) the application process takes too much time and many SME owners are not sufficiently educated to understand the schemes' requirements and (iii) many SME owners are not familiar with the schemes. However, Kenny himself did take part in one of the schemes offered by Singapore's Economic Development Board (EDB) which granted Qian Hu funds under the board's Innovation Development Scheme to invest into the development of his auto packing systems.

Kenny believes that successful entrepreneurship stems from a combination of values such as "the need to be your own boss" as well as a passion for learning and education. He attributes much of his business acumen to his education in the West, which has taught him management skills. He believes that successful entrepreneurs should start at a young age because the opportunity costs are lower and the fact that younger people tend to take more risks. The case supports the hypothesis that business leaders are often the main driving forces for change in organizations and that age and educational qualification are major predictors of successful knowledge management and learning capabilities in combination with other factors. Kenny's tertiary education in economics exposed him to different perspectives and viewpoints, which made him more cosmopolitan and reflective. It also equipped him with sound cognitive abilities and skills. Furthermore, he used effective leadership approaches such as open and skillful communication, persuasion, and consensus formation in combination with suitable reward incentives to propel change into the right direction.

8. Challenges ahead: Knowledge Leadership and Openness to Outside Sources of Learning

Business leaders who manage to leverage on outside sources of learning whether in form of scientific advice to support product development efforts or IP-related know how to create value through franchising contribute to organizational effectiveness and firm performance. While the effects of leadership and strategic learning on firm performance are relatively well documented in large firms, little is known about the effects of leadership on the openness of knowledge-intensive SMEs to outside sources of learning in the context of knowledge management. What is the relationship between the SME leader as knowledge leader, openness of the firm to outside sources of learning and firm performance?

Creating value through knowledge management *vis-à-vis* the political knowledge economy goals of the Singapore government represents a great opportunity for SME owner-managers (Menkhoff, 2010). Available studies indicate the effects of state-driven institutional isomorphism on strategic learning and technology upgrading by local SMEs in Singapore (Tsui-Auch, 2003; Chew, 2010), e.g., in the context of the so-called Get-up Scheme/Growing Enterprises with Technology Upgrade launched by SPRING. But doubts remain with regard to the sustainability and breadth of such measures due to the institutional characteristics of these small family-based firms such as low trust in outsiders and ignorance towards formal SME promotion agencies (Menkhoff, 1993; Ng, 2002; Menkhoff, Chay and Loh, 2004; Chew and Chew, 2008).

8.1 *Knowledge leadership as driver of knowledge combination*

We argue that strategic knowledge leadership is essential to create value-added knowledge outcomes, for example, through knowledge combination processes (Nonaka, 1994; Nonaka *et al.*, 2001; Ribière and Sitar, 2003; Chay *et al.*, 2007; Irick, 2007; Holcomb *et al.*, 2009). This includes the ability to strategize knowledge management frameworks and to use relevant knowledge management tools and technologies which have been identified in the knowledge management literature as key drivers of knowledge creation processes (Hosmer, 1995; Hansen, 1999; Helmstaedter, 2003; Ipe, 2003). Nonaka (1995) has conceptualized knowledge combination as one of four knowledge creation modi. Explicit (or tacit) knowledge can be shared during meetings, via document exchange, e-mails or through training and development measures. Knowledge leadership tools can be relatively simple ones such as story telling or hi-tech tools such as electronic sharing platforms, extra nets and so forth. The formation of temporary network alliances represent other suitable tools to achieve knowledge combination which can then lead to significant knowledge outcomes. The point we want to highlight here is that the use of relevant knowledge tools has to be initiated by the SME leader as knowledge leader so as to get the knowledge creation process started (Menkhoff *et al.*, 2008). If organizational leaders are unaware of the importance and power of knowledge tools, knowledge creation opportunities will be foregone. In view of the importance of knowledge tools as drivers of knowledge combination processes and one of the key factors for achieving knowledge outcomes, we hypothesize the following:

Proposition 3: *The role of the SME leader as knowledge leader will have a positive effect on the ability to effectively manage the knowledge combination process by utilizing outside sources of learning.*

Knowledge combination enables the cross-fertilization of ideas which often lead to product and/or service innovations as exemplified in Wirtz *et al.*, (2008). Other well-documented cases include communities of practice (COP) initiatives set-up by the World Bank or Singapore's Workforce Development Agency (WDA) to develop innovative development interventions by combining the respective competencies of various experts (Fulmer, 2001). Wenger and Snyder (2000) define communities of practice as groups of people who share a concern or a passion for something they do and learn how to do it better as they interact regularly. COPs have been implemented in business, organizational design, government, education, professional associations, development projects, and civic life. Members form powerful social networks that enable them to learn with and from each other. COPs flourish in collaborative organizational cultures characterized by care and trust (Hansen, 1999; Von Krogh, 2003; Ribière and Tuggle, 2005; Chay *et al.*, (2007). As Burt (2004) has stressed, organizations with management and collaboration networks that bridge structural holes in their markets seem to learn faster and be more creative.

8.2 Personality traits and leadership style influence the creation of knowledge outcomes

Studies by Nonaka and Takeuchi (1995) or Voelpel and Han (2005) suggest that knowledge creation is a key antecedent of knowledge outcomes and organizational effectiveness. Organizations can reap many benefits from proactively initiating knowledge creation processes based on knowledge sharing (both horizontally across departments, functions or business units and vertically up the organizational hierarchy) such as improved productivity and skills, enhanced customer relations, new product and/or service development, flexibility in production and innovation or improved organizational memory. Relevant here are broad issues of strategy and how the organization defines its business and uses both its internal and external knowledge assets to reinforce its core competencies. Without a clear business case and strategic imperatives, relevant knowledge outcomes will not be achieved. Other important variables include the personality and leadership style of SME owner-managers. As argued by Chay *et al.* (2007), openness to outside learning requires both openness as a personality trait and a participative leadership style. In view of this, we argue:

Proposition 4: The impact of the SME leader's role as knowledge leader on knowledge outcomes will be moderated by (1) his/her openness as personality trait and (2) his/her knowledge leadership style.

9. Knowledge Combination qua Utilization of Outside Sources of Learning Drive Firm Performance

Examples of innovative products and services successfully developed through knowledge combination such as Osim's iGallop, Apple's iPod or SIA's newly installed flat beds in the airline's brand new A380 fleet suggest that the act of combining knowledge resources in an innovative manner can be a profitable undertaking. While the empirical literature about the potential impact of this type of learning on firm performance in small firms is still evolving, we argue that knowledge combination via the utilization of outside sources of learning pays in terms of ROA (return on assets) and ROE (return on equity) as indicated by the following examples of Singaporean SMEs.

Example 1: Tropical pest management company Origin Exterminators teamed up with an internet business solutions provider to implement a web-based Enterprise Resource Planning (ERP) solution to integrate information between major functions such as human resources, operations and sales. It also leverages on the latest pest management science and techniques.

Example 2: Finger food company Old Chang Kee collaborated with SPRING Singapore and the Intellectual Property Office of Singapore (IPOS) to develop a strategy to create, own, protect and exploit their signature curry puff-related intellectual property (IP) rights. Part of that is a value-added franchise program which allows the franchise rights owner to sell the Old Chang Kee's distinctive and exclusive products.

Example 3: Tropical fish exporter Qian Hu is also successfully engaged in both open and networked innovation (e.g., qua collaboration with reputable life sciences labs to scale up some of its main products) in support of its internationalization strategies in Asia, the EC and beyond.

Thus, we hypothesize the following:

Proposition 5: Knowledge combination via the utilization of outside sources of learning will be positively associated with firm performance.

The extent to which local SME owner-managers can be characterized as knowledge leaders who are open to outside sources of learning and how this affects knowledge outcomes at firm level needs to be examined in a future study with a wider empirical basis.

10. Discussion and Conclusion

This study attempted to examine change leadership approaches in SMEs owned and managed by ethnic Chinese in Singapore. Contrary to the sometimes negative image of small businesses as being backward, risk-averse and static, survey data on the respondents' demographics suggest that the sampled small businessmen and women are flexible, adaptable individuals who — as a result of their personality traits — are open to the initiation of change and willing to take risks. This proposition is supported by data on the firms' change management practices. First of all, there is evidence that the majority of the sampled owner-managers of small businesses in Singapore do indeed initiate organizational change measures in their firms on a routine basis — contrary to widespread assumptions about their backwardness and insufficient responsiveness to external changes. While it was expected that technology changes would outnumber structural and other changes implemented by the owners of Singaporean SMEs, key change targets in order of importance comprised the firm's strategy, technology/IT, people, including their task behaviors, cultural change, systems and work processes as well as organizational structures.

As far as the nature of change is concerned, most of the changes implemented by the sampled owner-managers were interpreted as both *reactive* (unplanned) and *proactive* (anticipatory) in nature. In 27.5 percent of all cases, interviewees characterized the nature of change as *reactive*, i.e., shifts in organizational activities were conducted to adapt to forces that were external in nature and beyond the organization's control. The number of SME owner-managers who had implemented *proactive* and intentional measures, purposive in nature and designed to fulfill certain organizational goals, was — with 13.8 percent — larger than expected. About two-third of all respondents claimed that the adopted change measures were based on a plan of action. With regard to the scale of change, change measures implemented in local SMEs turned out (as expected) to be mainly *continuous* and *incremental* in nature (first-order change), consisting of minor improvements and adjustments that do not change the system's core, and that occur as the system naturally grows and develops (75.3 percent). The number of local SMEs who had implemented *transformative* change approaches (fundamental, radical, second-order change), involving many different levels of the organization, technology, structure and/or culture in terms of a paradigm shift, was comparatively small (23.5 percent), yet but larger than expected.

Another surprise was the trends detected in the analysis of the change leadership data. Contrary to the proposition that directive-coercive modes of change leadership styles would dominate amongst Singaporean SME owner-managers, a very large number of respondents used collaborative-consultative leadership modes (70.3 percent). The fact that we found reversed trends with regard to all three propositions is perhaps an indicator for the "convergence" of Asian and Western leadership styles as argued by Quinn Mills (2005) or simply the result of generational shifts and educational advancements of Singaporean SME owner-managers as well as their followers who operate in an environment which puts a premium on skills upgrading and lifelong learning (Tsui-Auch, 2003; Menkhoff, Chay and Loh, 2004).

Change leadership approaches to *incremental change*: while it was expected that the most frequent change management scenario local SME owners faced in the context of incremental change would be characterized by/perceived as one of low urgency and low resistance, it was, in fact, one of high urgency and low resistance. The most frequent change leadership approach used by local SME owners to implement incremental change was collaborative-consultative (participative evolution) rather than directive-coercive (forced evolution), contrary to our initial proposition. Whether the change initiatives implemented by business leaders who practice a more participatory and persuasive change leadership style are likely to bear positive outcomes in form of improved firm performance remains to be seen. With regard to change *leadership approaches to transformative change*, about a quarter of the respondents (23.5 percent) turned out to be transformational change leaders.

While it had been expected that the most frequent change management scenario local SME owners faced in the context of transformative change would be characterized by/perceived as one of high urgency and low resistance, resistance turned out to be an issue. This, however, was not tackled by using directive-coercive (dictatorial transformation) leadership styles. Again collaborative-coercive methods prevailed, suggesting that change initiatives implemented by managers who practice a more participatory change leadership style are perhaps more likely to bear positive outcomes in form of obtaining greater buy-in and perhaps improved firm performance.

The findings reported here have to be interpreted within its limitations. The first limitation is the sample size which is relatively low. This may limit the generalizability of the results. However, obtaining higher response rates in SME surveys in a small city-state such as Singapore (where survey fatigue is real due to the large number of students and researchers) is a real challenge. The second limitation is its reliance on self-reported data which may be subject to respondents' cognitive biases and distortions. The third limitation is the potential size effect which would make it possible that the predominance of the collaborative-consultative approach as reported above was due to not having to deal with large numbers of organizational members, since there were simply not that many employees to deal with in the first place. The fourth limitation is that so many of the owner-managers were English-educated. This may have influenced how they organized and managed their firms.

While possible limitations of the study such as sample bias and lack of representativeness have to be taken into account, it seems that Singapore SMEs are more sophisticated and professional when it comes to organizational change practices than had been anticipated. An important intervening variable in this context is probably the supportive role of Singapore's state as illustrated by Singapore's first SME Master Plan that operated from 1989 onwards and the subsequent launch of the second SME master plan (SME 21) in 2000. These policy and upgrading programme initiatives played a significant role in developing an entrepreneurship infrastructure (Tan, Tan and Young, 2000; Tsui-Auch and Lee, 2003), and it is very likely that the respondents are well aware of the benefits of change management and leadership. Therefore, future research will have to consider other facets in which government incentives have addressed human capital development gaps and areas of organizational change.

Business leaders who manage to leverage on outside sources of learning whether in form of scientific advice to support product development efforts or IP-related know how to create value through franchising contribute to organizational effectiveness and firm performance. While the effects of leadership and strategic learning on firm performance are relatively well documented in large firms, little is known about the effects of leadership on the openness of knowledge-intensive small and medium-sized enterprises (SMEs) to outside sources of learning in the context of knowledge management. Hence there is a need to examine the relationship between the SME leader as knowledge leader, openness of the firm to outside sources of learning and firm performance along the hypotheses outlined above in a future follow-up survey.

The cultural specifics of Chinese change leadership approaches have yet to be revealed by systematic empirical studies. A promising approach would be to contrast the various approaches, styles and values of Chinese-educated and English-educated Chinese change leaders in the tradition of Bond's "Culture Connection" works in various "Chinese societies" (Bond, 1991) and to merge it with "Western" contingency leadership theories so as to do justice to the complexity of the subject matter and Asia's vast internal differentiations in an era of rapid cultural change. As our data indicate, Asia's new technology leaders such as *Osim's* Ron Sim or *Qian Hu's* Kenny Yap are skillful in leading change and arguably not too different from non-Chinese owner-managers of companies with an entrepreneurial culture (Kanter, 2000). Despite all the differences, there are many common points management practitioners tend to overlook such as the need to respond to a younger, lifestyle-oriented crowd of customers and to initiate respective changes in terms of design, branding or supply chain management.

References

Beckhard, R (1969). *Organizational Development: Strategies and Models.* Reading, MA: Addison-Wesley.

Beckhard, R and RT Harris (1987). *Organizational Transitions — Managing Complex Change*, 2nd Edition. Reading, MA: Addison-Wesley.

Bennis, W (1969). *Organizational Development: Its Nature, Origins and Prospects.* Reading, MA: Addison-Wesley.

Bjerke, B (1998). Entrepreneurship and SMEs in the Singaporean context. In *Competitiveness of the Singapore Economy: A Strategic Perspective*, MH Toh and KY Tan (eds.), pp. 249–293. Singapore: Singapore University Press.

Bond, MH (1991). *Beyond the Chinese Face: Insights from Psychology.* Hong Kong: Oxford University Press.

Bracker, J, B Keats and J Pearson (1988). Planning and financial performance among small firms in a growth industry. *Strategic Management Journal*, 9(6), 591–603.

Buchanan, D and A Huczynski (1997). *Organizational Behavior — An Introductory Text.* London, UK: Prentice Hall.

Burke, W and GH Litwin (1994). Dignostic models for organizational development. In *Diagnosis for Organizational Change*, A Howard and Associates (eds.). London and New York: Guilford Press.

Burt, R (2004). Structural holes and good ideas. *American Journal of Sociology*, 110(2), 349–399.

Carland, JW, F Hoy, WR Boulton and JAC Carland (1984). Differentiating entrepreneurs from small business owners: A conceptualization. *Academy of Management Review*, 9(2), 354–359.

Chay, YW, T Menkhoff, B Loh and H-D Evers (2007). Social capital and knowledge sharing in knowledge-based organisations: An empirical study. *International Journal of Knowledge Management*, 3(1), 29–48.

Chew, R and S-B Chew (2008). A study of SMEs in Singapore. *Journal of Enterprising Communities: People and Places in the Global Economy*, 2(4), 332–347.

Chew, R (2010). Developments of SMEs in Singapore's services and wholesale and retail sectors: Issues and prospects. *International Journal of Business and Globalisation*, 4(3), 279–298.

Child, J (1972). Organizational structure, environment, and performance: The role of strategic choice. *Sociology*, 6, 1–22.

Child, J (1997). Strategic choice in the analysis of action, structure, organizations and environment: Retrospect and prospect. *Organization Studies*, 18(1), 43–76.

Chua, SE (2001). *The New Economy and Chinese Enterprises in Singapore*. Unpublished Manuscript. Faculty of Business Administration, National University of Singapore.

Das, SS (2008). Innovation in high-technology SMEs: Insights from Singapore. *International Journal of Innovation and Technology Management*, (5)4, 475–494.

Dunphy, DC and DA Stace (1990). *Under New Management: Australian Organizations in Transition*. Sydney: McGraw-Hill.

Dyer, WG (1985). The cycle of cultural evolution in Organizations. In *Gaining Control of the Corporate Culture*, R Kilmann, MJ Saxton and R Serpa (eds.), pp. 200–229. San Francisco/London: Jossey Bass.

EIU (Economist Intelligence Unit) and Andersen Consulting (2000). *Beyond the Bamboo Network: Successful Strategies for Change in Asia*. Hong Kong: Economist Intelligence Unit.

Filley, AC and RJ Aldag (1978). Characteristics and measurement of an organizational typology. *Academy of Management Journal*, 21(4), 578–591.

Greenberg, J and RA Baron, (1997). *Behavior in Organizations: Understanding and Managing the Human Side of Work,* 7th Edition. Upper Saddle River, NJ: Prentice Hall.

Hannan, M and J Freeman (1984). Structural inertia and organizational change. *American Sociological Review*, 49, 149–164.

Hansen, MT (1999). The search-transfer problem: The role of weak ties in sharing knowledge across organizational sub-units. *Administrative Science Quarterly*, 44(1), 82–111.

Helmstadter, E (2003). The institutional economics of knowledge sharing: Basic issues. In *The Economics of Knowledge Sharing: A New Institutional Approach*, E Helmstadter (ed.), pp. 11–38. Cheltenham and Northampton, MA: Edward Elgar.

Holcomb, TR, RD Ireland, RM Holmes and MA Hitt (2009). Architecture of entrepreneurial learning: Exploring the link among heuristics, knowledge, and action. *Entrepreneurship, Theory and Practice*, 33(1), 167–192.

Howard, R (1991). *Can Small Businesses Help Countries Compete? Entrepreneurship: Creativity at Work*. Boston, MA: Harvard Business School Press.

Hussey, DE (1995). *How to Manage Organisational Change*. London, UK: Kogan Page.

Kanter, RM (2000). The enduring skills of change leaders. *Ivey Business Journal*, 64(5), 31–36.

Ipe, M (2003) Knowledge sharing in organizations: A conceptual framework. *Human Resource Development Review*, 2(4), 337–359.

Irick, M (2007). Managing tacit knowledge in organizations. *Journal of Knowledge Management Practice*, 8(3).

Kirkpatrick, D (1985). *How to Manage Change Effectively*. San Francisco/ London: Jossey Bass.

Leavitt, HJ (1965). Applied organizational change in industry: Structural, technical and human approach. In *Handbook of Organizations*, JG March (ed.), pp. 1144–1170. Chicago: Rand McNally and Company.

Levy, A (1986). Second-order change planned change: Definition and conceptualization. *Organizational Dynamics*, 16(1), 4–20.

Low, L (ed.) (1999). *Singapore, Towards a Developed Status*. New York, NY: Oxford University Press.

Lussier, RN and CF Achua (2004). *Leadership: Theory. Application. Skill development* 2nd Edition. South-Western College Publishing, Thomson Learning.

Mackie, J (2003). Five SEA Chinese empire-builders: Commonalities and differences. In *Chinese Migrants Abroad*, MW Charney, BSA Yeoh and Tong, CK (eds.), pp. 2–21. Singapore: Singapore University Press and World Scientific.

Menkhoff, T (1993). *Trade Routes, Trust and Trading Networks — Chinese Small Enterprises in Singapore*. Saarbruecken, Fort Lauderdale: Breitenbach Publishers.

Menkhoff, T and S Gerke (2002). *Chinese Entrepreneurship and Asian Business Networks*. London, UK: Routledge Curzon.

Menkhoff, T, L Kay and B Loh (2002). Worlds apart? Reflections on the relationship between small entrepreneurs and external change advocates in Singapore. *Journal of Asian Business*, 18(1), 37–65.

Menkhoff, T, YW Chay and B Loh (2004). Notes from an "intelligent island": Towards strategic knowledge management in Singapore's small business sector. *International Quarterly for Asian Studies*, 35(1–2), 85–99.

Menkhoff, T, U Badibanga and YW Chay (2007). Managing change in Asian business — A comparison between Chinese-educated and English-educated Chinese entrepreneurs in Singapore. *Copenhagen Journal of Asian Studies*, 25, 50–73.

Menkhoff, T, H-D Evers and YW Chay (eds.) (2010). *Governing and Managing Knowledge in Asia*. New Jersey: World Scientific.

Menkhoff, T, YW Chay, H-D Evers and B Loh (2008). Leadership in knowledge sharing: Creating value through collaboration. *Journal of Asian Business*, 22, 265–281.

Ng, BK (2002). The changing role of ethnic Chinese SMEs in economic restructuring in Singapore. In *The Chinese in Singapore and Malaysia: A Dialogue between Tradition and Modernity*, L Suryadinata (ed.), pp. 255–275. Singapore: Times Books.

Nonaka, I (1994). A dynamic theory of organizational knowledge creation. *Organizational Science*, 5(1), 14–37.

Nonaka, I, N Konno and R Toyama (2001). Emergence of Ba: A conceptual framework for the continuous and self-transcending process of knowledge creation. In *Knowledge Emergence: Social, Technical, and Evolutionary Dimensions of Knowledge Creation*, I Nonaka and T Nishiguchi (eds.), pp. 13–29. New York, NY: Oxford University Press.

Nonaka, I and H Takeuchi (1995). *The Knowledge Creating Company: How Japanese Companies Create the Dynamics of Innovation*. New York, NY: Oxford University Press.

Pfeffer, J and GR Salancik (1978). *The External Control of Organizations: A Resource Dependency Perspective*. New York, NY: Harper and Row.

Pfeffer, J (2005). Changing mental models. In *The Future of HR: 50 Thought Leaders call for Change*, M Losey, S Meisinger and D Ulrich (eds.), pp. 163–171. New York, NY: John Wiley.

Quinn Mills, D (2005). Asian and American leadership styles: How are they unique? *Harvard Business School Working Knowledge* (June).

Redding, SG (1993). *The Spirit of Chinese Capitalism*. Berlin: de Gruyter.

Redding, SG (1996). Societal transformation and the contribution of authority relations and cooperation norms in overseas Chinese business. In *Confucian traditions in East Asian modernity*, WM Tu (ed.), pp. 310–327. Cambridge, MA: Harvard University Press.

Redding, SG and G Wong (1986). The psychology of Chinese organisational behavior. In *The Psychology of Chinese People*, MH Bond (ed.), pp. 267–295. Hong Kong: Oxford University Press.

Ribière, V and AS Sitar (2003). The critical role of leadership in nurturing a knowledge supporting culture. *Journal of Knowledge Management Research and Practice*, 1(1), July.

Ribière, V and FD Tuggle (2005). The role of organizational trust in knowledge management tools and technology use and success. *International Journal of Knowledge Management*, 1(1).

Schaefer, RH and HA Thomson (1998). Successful change programs begin with results. In *Harvard Business Review on Change*, pp. 189–213. Boston, MA: Harvard Business School Publishing.

Silin, RH (1976). *Leadership and Values: The Organisation of Large-Scale Taiwanese Enterprises*. Cambridge, MA: Harvard University Press.

Simon, H (1996). *Hidden Champions: Lessons From 500 of the World's Best Unknown Companies*. Boston, MA: Harvard Business School Press.

Smith, N (1967). *The Entrepreneur and His Firm: The Eelationship between Type of Man and Type of Company*. East Lansing, Mich: Michigan State University.

Smith, N and J Miner (1983). Type of entrepreneur, type of firm and managerial motivation: Implications for organizational life cycle theory. *Strategic Management Journal*, 4, 325–340.

SPRING Singapore (2006). Official website of Singapore's Standards, Productivity and Innovation Board. Available at http://www.spring.gov.sg/portal/main.html.

Stace, DA (1996). Transitions and transformations: Four case studies in business-focused change. In *Cases in human resource and change management*, J Storey (ed.), pp. 43–72. Oxford, UK: Blackwell Business.

Stanworth, J and J Curran (1986). Growth and the small firm. In *The Survival of the Small Firm*, J Curran, J Stanworth and D Watkins (eds.), pp. 77–99. Gower: Aldershot.

Tan, TM, WL Tan and JE Young (2000). Entrepreneurial infrastructure in Singapore: Developing a model and mapping participation. *Journal of Entrepreneurship*, 9(1), 1–25.

Thornhill, S (2006). Knowledge, innovation and firm performance in high- and low-technology regimes. *Journal of Business Venturing*, 21(5), 687–703.

Today (2006). BenQ mobile set for all-out assault. January 24, p. 28.

Toffler, A (1991). *Power Shift*. London, UK: Bantan Books.

Tong, CK and PK Yong (2002). Personalism and aternalism in Chinese business. In *Chinese Entrepreneurship and Asian Business Networks,* T Menkhoff and S Gerke (eds.). London and New York: Routledge Curzon.

Tsui-Auch, LS (2003). Learning strategies of small and medium-sized Chinese family firms — A comparative study of two suppliers in Singapore. *Management Learning*, 34(2), 201–220.

Tsui-Auch, LS and Y-J Lee (2003). The state matters: Management models of Singaporean Chinese and Korean business groups. *Organization Studies*, 24(4), 507–534.

Tushman, ML, WH Newman and E Romanelli (1997). Convergence and upheaval: Managing the unsteady pace of organizational evolution. In *Managing Strategic Innovation and Change — A Collection of Readings*, ML Tushman and P Anderson (eds.), pp. 583–594. New York, NY: Oxford University Press.

Voelpel, S and Z Han (2005). Managing knowledge sharing in China: The case of Siemens ShareNet. *Journal of Knowledge Management,* 9(3), 51–63.

Von Krogh, G (1998). Care in knowledge creation. *California Management Review*, 40(3), 133–154.

Von Krogh, G, K Ichijo and I Nonaka (2000). *Enabling Knowledge Creation — How to Unlock the Mystery of Tacit Knowledge and Release the Power of Innovation*. New York, NY: Oxford University Press.

Von Krogh, G, I Nonaka and T Nishiguchi (2000). *Knowledge Creation — A Source of Value*. London, UK: McMillan Press.

Wenger, E and W Snyder (2000). Communities of practice: The organizational frontier. *Harvard Business Review*, 139–145.

Wirtz, J, L Heracleous and T Menkhoff (2008). Value creation through strategic knowledge management: The case of Singapore Airlines. *Journal of Asian Business*, 23(1), 249–263.

Chapter 8

Ethnic Chinese Family-Controlled Firms in Singapore: Continuity and Change in Corporate Governance

Lai Si Tsui-Auch and Dawn Chow Yi Lin

"Not based in any one country or continent, [the Chinese] common-wealth is primarily a network of entrepreneurial relationships. From restaurants to real estate to plastic-sandal makers to semiconductor manufacturing — from a staff of five or six family members to a plant floor of thousands — the Chinese commonwealth consists of many individual enterprises that nonetheless share a common culture."

John Kao (1993, p. 24).

1. Introduction

The ethnic Chinese business has been recognized as a global economic force. Kao (1993) asserts that Chinese businesses located *outside* the People's Republic constitute the world's "other" economic power, with overseas Chinese in their closely-knit networks of family and clan running enterprises across national borders. Overseas Chinese dominate the Asian economies, including, but not limited to, the Southeast Asian Economies of Singapore, Taiwan and Hong Kong (Brocklehurst, 2005). After the British and Dutch colonial powers withdrew from the Southeast Asian region, ethnic Chinese firms gained immeasurable traction in the domestic and intraregional trade of Malaysia, Indonesia, Singapore, the Philippines, and Thailand. Importantly, ethnic Chinese capital comprises the largest block of overseas investment in the People's Republic of China (PRC) which indicates a reverse investment inflow from emigrant investors. Clearly, the ethnic Chinese business and governance model is here to stay.

Whilst some light has been shed on the ethnic Chinese family business management model and its features (see Redding, 1990; Silin, 1976; Wong, 1985), very few studies have sought to identify the temporality and periodicity of changes in the governance model of ethnic Chinese family-controlled firms. This chapter, therefore, provides an overview of how ethnic Chinese businesses have adapted to undertake corporate governance reforms whilst adhering to certain core values and norms. By doing so, it is hoped that the current discourse on the management structure of ethnic Chinese businesses would shift from stasis to a more dynamic, nuanced conceptualization.

The context of Singapore was chosen for particular purpose. The fact that the majority of the population of Singapore is constituted by ethnic Chinese, and that the majority of the ethnic Chinese enterprises is family-controlled makes Singapore a highly relevant case for studying ethnic Chinese family-controlled firms' corporate governance change. At the same time, the openness of Singapore's economy and its state agencies' role in mediating pressures for corporate governance reforms provides us with a particularly interesting case on how ethnic Chinese firms exercise strategic choice in response to institutional change shaped largely by the global capital market and the developmental state.

The chapter is divided into four sections. The first section considers Singapore's institutional environment, and global and local pressures for change versus continuity in ethnic Chinese family firms' corporate governance structures. The embeddedness of family-controlled firms and government-linked corporations within the local institutional environment is discussed *vis-à-vis* the state's promotion of the contending global capital market logic. The second section deals with pertinent features of the ethnic Chinese family business, and provides an overview of the ownership structure and control of prominent family firms in Singapore. The third section presents an analysis of continuity versus change in corporate governance, with the professionalization of management, maintenance of family control, and an increase in outsider representation but with a primary focus on independent directors' resource provision role being the key themes. In the last section, the OCBC, the largest family-controlled firm in Singapore, is used as an illustrative case. The chapter ends with a brief conclusion which summarizes the analysis.

2. The Institutional Environment of Singapore

As Flood (2007) observes, globalization has fundamentally accelerated and altered the nature of business transactions. The relentless search for lower labor costs and cheaper raw materials has led to a proliferation of international transactions. Increasingly, countries have been vying for a share of the global investment pie to increase their economic growth. Singapore is no exception, especially given its extreme openness to international investments and trade.

With the advent of Singapore's independence, the government adopted a "two-legged" policy that relied on multinational corporations for foreign capital and government-linked corporations to spearhead industrialization attempts (Rodan, 1989). By adopting a foreign-capital centric development strategy, the state had to enforce "legal-rationalism and modernization" (Tsui, 2004, p. 701), as exemplified by changes in its regulations on companies. In line with the Anglo-American model, the state imposed mandatory requirements on auditing so as to increase overall financial transparency (Tan *et al.*, 1999). As such, the Asian financial crisis of 1997 merely gave added impetus to the initiative to restructure the Singapore economy to increase its competitiveness in international financial markets (Tsui, 2004). Unlike many regional family-controlled firms that sought outside equity from Western institutional investors for the recapitalization of their troubled firms after the 1997 Asian economic crisis (*The Economist*, 2000), and were thus compelled to adopt international accounting standards and other regulatory reforms, Singaporean firms' habit of emulating Anglo-American best practices had its roots long before the crisis.

The Singapore government's position on the need to adopt Anglo-American best practice can be effectively summed up in this statement issued by Prime Minister Lee Hsien Loong at the launch of the Council on Corporate Disclosure and Governance (CCDG) (August 16, 2002):

"To position Singapore as a key business and financial centre, there is a need to give investors the confidence that companies registered in Singapore present true and fair financial statements that are in accordance with internationally accepted accounting standards. The recent developments in other jurisdictions have also highlighted the importance of having good corporate governance and disclosure practices, especially among companies that raise capital from the public."

Additionally, since one marker of a country's international competitiveness is its emphasis on corporate governance, the state tried to improve corporate governance regimes, specifically by trying to persuade local family-controlled firms to appoint professional managers and independent directors to their boards. This sentiment is reflected in comments by Lee Kuan Yew (Singapore's Prime Minister from 1965 to 1990):

> "The old family business in Singapore is one of the problems in Singapore. . . business is kept in the family. And the idea of sinking money into an anonymous corporation run by professionals over whom they have no direct personal control is foreign to them. . . So we have to accelerate this process" (Kwang *et al.*, 1998, p. 187).

The foregoing analysis seems to signal that Singapore's corporate governance system has exhibited convergence toward international corporate governance standards. Indeed, such an argument would provide evidence for low context perspectives such as agency theory, which typically tone down national distinctiveness and emphasize universal rationales (Child, 2000). In these perspectives, given the impetus of economic and cultural globalization, it is postulated that convergence in governance structures and systems is an eventuality. However, Singapore's reality is far more complex than this. Whilst the state encouraged companies to adopt a global capital market logic, the local market is in fact dominated by government-linked corporations and large family-controlled firms which are embedded in the local institutional environment.

High-context perspectives such as institutional theory (Dimaggio and Powell, 1983) examine how national distinctiveness in culture and institution accounts for differences in governance structures and systems. Among family-controlled firms in Singapore, there is a hard-to-erase feeling that a firm ultimately belongs to the founder and his or her family (Redding, 1990). Government-linked corporations are similarly embedded in the relational norms of trusting insiders. For instance, their tradition of appointing civil servants as board chairs and CEOs is similar to the Japanese practice of *amakudari* (descent from heaven) whereby senior civil servants, upon their retirement, often take up the post of board directors in large firms in order to maintain state influence and business connections (Low, 2001).

There is thus some resistance amongst key local actors to embrace the global capital market logic with its associated practices of incorporating independent directors as a majority in company boards.

In order to better understand the temporality and periodicity of changes in the corporate governance structures of Singapore's Chinese family businesses, the next section presents the key features of a typical Chinese family business, the profiles of prominent family-controlled business groups, the key corporations within these groups and their ownership and control patterns.

2.1 *Singaporean family-controlled business: Profiles, ownership and control*

Definitions of the family business are generally thought to be multicriteria, i.e., they could include (i) the fact that the family dominates the management echelons of the firm; (ii) the shared, inimitable resources accrued to family involvement; and (iii) the overarching stretch goals or objectives meant for transgenerational pursuance (Chrisman, Chua and Litz, 2003; Habbershon *et al.*, 2003). Whilst definitions of the family business are many and varied, they share in common that most presume significant family ownership and control. This definition resonates with the archetypal ethnic Chinese family business, in which decision-making tends to be centralized in the founder, successor, or in a core that comprises of family members and friends (Hamilton, 1997). Recruitment of outsiders to top management echelons is often carried out through personal recommendation, friendship ties or prior acquaintance of current employees (Brocklehurst, 2005). Apart from these characteristics, cost and financial controls are stringently adhered to within such firms (Brocklehurst, 2005); job flexibility is defacto, and few procedures covering conditions of employment are writ in stone (Tam, 1990). Overall, such businesses exhibit strong ties and cooperation within the family in-group and networks, but compete intensely against other business groups and networks.

While Singapore's ethnic Chinese family businesses may not entirely fit into this ideal-type, research has shown that ethnic Chinese enterprises within a business group exhibit strong ties and cooperation within the group. The 10 largest (based on the total assets of the group) family-controlled business groups are controlled by just four families, and some groups are controlled by other groups under the same family, as illustrated by the chain of control among *United Overseas Bank (UOB)*, *United Overseas Land Limited (UOL)*, *United Industrial Corporation (UIC)* and *Singapore Land* under the *Wee family* (see Figure 1).

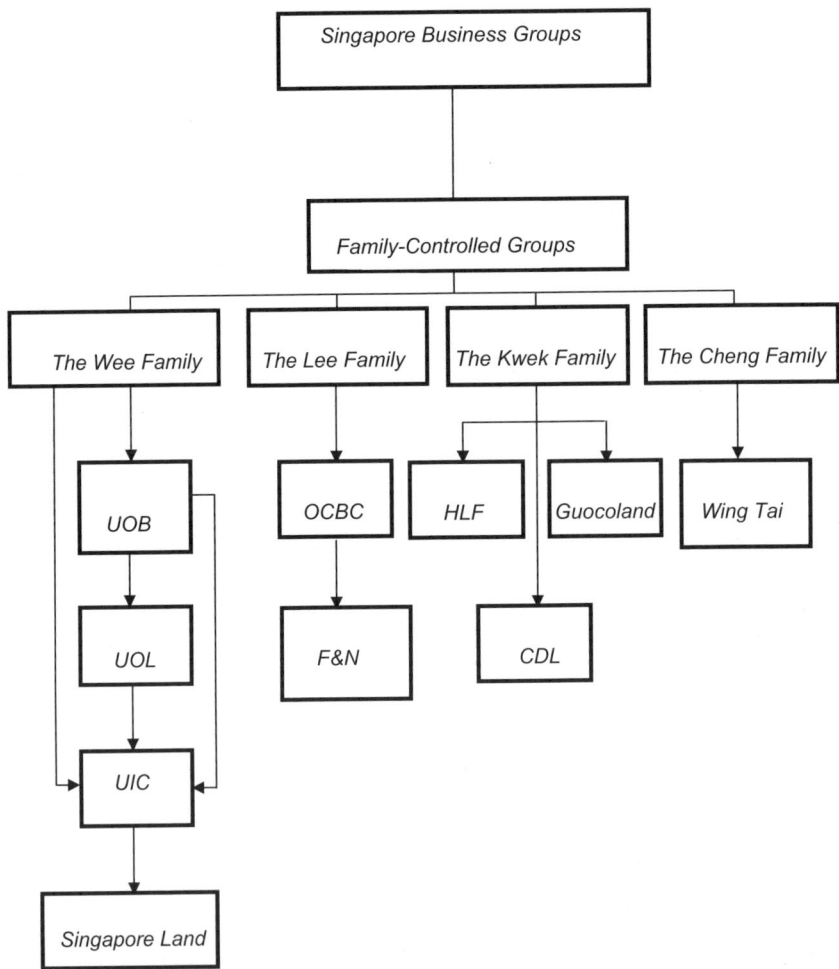

Figure 1.   Family-controlled business groups in Singapore (2006)
Source: Modified from Tsui-Auch (2010)

Each group consists of autonomous firms that are linked to a core company; both the core company and its independent firms often pursue unrelated diversification and exhibit a web-structure rather than a unitary organization (Hamilton, 1997). The ethnic Chinese family firms diversify substantially in order to maximize revenue and reduce risks, especially given the fact that they have to compete intensely against their rival business groups including the GLCs, which also operate in similar spheres except for the food and beverage sector. The interlocking ownership, management ties and the founder's authority typically pervade the entire group and its subsidiaries through tight control over decisions on finance, investment, and appointment of top managers. Through cross-ownership and a number of fiscal and managerial methods such as relational contracting, the founding families are typically able to control and coordinate the strategies of firms within their business groups (Hamilton and Biggart, 1988).

The unwieldy holding structure of large family-controlled business groups can be explained in terms of cultural, historical as well as practical factors (Tsui and Yoshikawa, 2010). Culturally, the Chinese family system is based on patrilineage and equal inheritance amongst sons (Hamilton and Biggart, 1988). Upon the demise of the founding patriarch, the family business might be split and the sons are left to develop their own business lines, and subsequently the family firm becomes highly diversified. Historically, family-controlled business groups emerged from smaller, private companies which were established by immigrants and operated by their family members across generations. The Overseas Chinese Banking Corporation (OCBC) was incorporated in 1932 as a result of a merger between three local Hokkien family banks. Given that historically these local banks often engaged in unrelated diversification and thus developed tremendously dissimilar business lines, grouping them together under a single holding company would be impractical for management purpose. Family ownership remains significant in these companies. Separately, in a study of all family firms listed on the Singapore Stock Exchange (Dieleman, Wiwattanakantang and Jungwook, 2011), the authors found that, on average, families owned at least a 33 percent stake in their company. Notably, some families owned even more than 33 percent — the highest observation in the researchers' data set was an 85 percent stake.

3. Continuity and Change in Corporate Governance Structures

This section discusses continuity and change in the corporate governance structures of ethnic Chinese family-controlled businesses in Singapore, the firms' uneasy relationship with the professionalization of management and the persistence of family control, as well as firms' corporate governance change. Right after the Asian financial crisis in 1997, the Singapore government introduced a slew of regulations which aimed at enhancing firm legitimacy in the eyes of global investors. The measures included the Code of Corporate Governance (first introduced in 2001 and revised in 2005), the Singapore Exchange's (SGX) Listing Manual, the Company's Act, the Securities and Futures Act, the Banking Act and the Accounting Standards Act. The Monetary Authority of Singapore (MAS) and Singapore Exchange (SGX) were designated the regulatory bodies responsible for corporate governance monitoring; the former for firms within the financial sector and the latter for listed companies. The Code of Corporate Governance adopted a "comply or disclose" approach (KPMG Audit Committee Institute 2010) and offered recommendations relating to best practices. Banks, on the other hand, were subjected to the Banking Act. At the same time, in a bid to make Singapore a global financial hub, in 1999 the MAS announced a five-year plan to liberalize the banking sector by removing regulatory barriers against foreign banks to provide a level playing field with the local banks. By the end of 2001, the consolidation of the banking sector was largely complete (Bowers *et al.*, 2003) and only the three local banks (including two family-controlled banks, OCBC and UOB) remained.

However, in spite of the seeming internationalization of Singapore's banking sector and pegging of corporate governance reforms to international norms, Singapore's state of corporate governance still fell short of international standards (Chow, 2005). Essentially, given that the state's GLCs and many ethnic Chinese family firms were embedded in a local institutional environment, the state had to walk the tight-rope in coming up with a locally tailored solution that, at the same time, accommodated the global capital market logic.

Fundamentally, the major point of contention with international codes of governance lay in the definition of effective board appointment. Independent directors are a critical governance mechanism to protect shareholders' interests (Hu, 2003). The UK Combined Code and the Higgs report state that independent directors are essential for protecting minority shareholders and the recommendation is that at least 50 percent of the board members, excluding the board chair, should be independent (Combined Code, 2003 and Higgs, 2003, as cited in Hu, 2003). There are thus very stringent requirements placed on the definition of independence, as well as the composition of the board. Finally, there is also the need to separate CEO and chairman positions because conflict of interest may occur when the management role is not distinct from the monitoring role (Jensen, 1993). However, during the state's lengthy consultation process with the corporate sector, many firms were manifestly concerned about these seemingly stratospheric expectations. They were concerned about the impact of appointing so many independent directors to their board as they believed that too many voices would be stultifying. They argued that there would be negative impact on efficiency, and that only insiders, with their close personal connections, would be able to facilitate collaboration and enhance firm performance.

Therefore, to reconcile this with the need to accommodate the global market logic, regulatory authorities recommended that independent directors make up at least one-third of the board, which is lower than that stipulated in the regulations in major Anglo-American markets[1]. In addition, Singapore's criteria for independence are arguably more lenient than US, UK or Australian interpretations. These modifications enabled domestic firms to have a limited degree of outsider representation on the board and thus more autonomy. Although updated banking regulations effective from 2012 now stipulate that financial institutions need to have a majority of independent directors in their boards, and that at least one-third of directors should be free from relationships with the company or its related companies[2], in practice, requirements are not so stringent. Indeed, the

---

[1] http://www.mas.gov.sg/en/Regulations-and-Financial-Stability/Regulatory-and-Supervisory-Framework/Corporate-Governance/Corporate-Governance-of-Listed-Companies/~/media/resource/fin_development/corporate_governance/CG%20Code%202005%20Code.ashx

[2] http://www.mas.gov.sg/Regulations-and-Financial-Stability/Regulatory-and-Supervisory-Framework/Corporate-Governance/Corporate-Governance-of-Listed-Companies/~/media/resource/fin_development/corporate_governance/CGCRevisedCodeofCorporate Governance3May2012.ashx

MAS acknowledged that there is space for a more flexible interpretation of the rules. Accordingly, Banking Regulations, similar to governance codes, permit the nominating committee of a bank to exercise the residual power to determine whether a director who falls short of meeting the definition of independence is still independent (MAS, 2005).

Therefore, despite Singapore's being the highest ranked Asian nation for corporate governance (Gill *et al.*, 2010), the Dieleman, Wiwattanakantang and Jungwook (2011) study found that 44 percent of family firms listed on the SGX failed to comply with the code of governance in that both board chair and CEO were the same person. It is likely that these firms' benefited from the state's comply or disclose approach, which is encapsulated in the following MAS[3] quote:

> "Compliance with the Code is not mandatory but listed companies are required under the Singapore Exchange Listing Rules to disclose their corporate governance practices and give explanations for deviations from the Code in their annual reports."

It is clear that, with regard to financial institutions, while regulations and codes on corporate governance generally reflect the global capital market logic, the few provisos (especially those concerning independence) included by the MAS appear to allow banks to keep local practices in their boardrooms. There is a tendency for family-controlled firms to deviate from the recommendations stipulated in the Code of Corporate Governance instead of complying. For example, if their independent directors do not meet the strict definition of independence, companies simply justify these appointments in their company's corporate governance reports. This tendency has led to what KMPG has called a dominance of "form" over "substance" (KPMG Audit Committee Institute, 2010), in terms of companies meeting the bare minimum of corporate governance requirements.

The state regulators also pressured companies to "professionalize" management, in the form of recruiting talents from outside the family. For

---

[3] http://www.mas.gov.sg/Regulations-and-Financial-Stability/Regulatory-and-Supervisory-Framework/Corporate-Governance/Corporate-Governance-of-Listed-Companies/Code-of-Corporate-Governance.aspx.

instance, with the aim of injecting professionalism into the management structure, local banks had to establish "nominating committees" for the appointment of senior management positions, and appointments were subject to the approval of the MAS. To a certain extent, listed firms did comply with standards so as to achieve legitimacy in the eyes of authorities and investors. For example, to meet mandatory requirements on reporting and auditing, the firms recruited managers with the relevant professional training; however, top management positions were still occupied by family members (Tsui-Auch and Lee, 2003). As Chan and Chiang (1994) observe, when their children were still too young to join the family businesses, the founding patriarchs often relied on long-serving managers. At the same time, these founders insisted that family control would enhance firm performance, citing reasons such as continuity and the unique capability of the current stable of management. UOB, for example, through its strong adherence to family control, showed its belief that family influence was good for the firm. For instance, although the second generation successor, Wee Cho Yaw, relinquished the CEO position to his son in 2007 and the board chair in 2012, he has been serving as a board director, and holding a title of "chairman emeritus," being an adviser to the board (Ng, 2012). Overall, although family-controlled firms had to have a modicum of professionalization given that they increasingly depended on foreign institutional investors, they tried to retain control in terms of equity ownership, occupying board positions and/or delegating these to chosen others.

Table 1 shows that, in comparison to 1997, family ownership, as of 2006, fell in six main firms of the 10 family-controlled business groups but increased in four others. In addition, only four out of nine companies increased outsider representation on the board, while the other four lowered such representation and one remained unchanged (Table 2). Finally, two companies did not appoint any outside director to their boards and no firm had a majority of such directors. In addition, few of the most senior posts were relinquished to managers recruited from the external labour market (see Table 3), though some long-term associates were co-opted.

Therefore, the upshot of all this is that there are signs that family-controlled business groups increased professionalization of management by

Table 1. Equity holding in the family-controlled firms by the largest block shareholder

Core companies	1997 (percent)	2006 (percent)
UOB	31.65	21.82
UOL	40.02	28.31
UIC	26.85	26.91
SG Land	56.47	72.42
OCBC	40.47	19.29
F&N	25.64	22.06
CDL	48.44	48.62
HLF	54.65	47.04
GuocoLand	57.49	72.78
Wing Tai	42.20	39.69

Source: Modified from Tsui-Auch and Yoshikawa (2010)

Table 2. Percentage of outside directors on the boards of the core companies of the largest family-controlled firms

Core companies	1997 (percent)	2006 (percent)
UOB	22	30
UOL	0	0
UIC	25	NA
SG Land	14	7
OCBC	11	21
F&N	25	40
CDL	18	0
HLF	8	40
GuocoLand	50	29
Wing Tai	33	18

NA: due to a lack of information on the majority of directors (5 out of 9 directors are unknown).
Source: Modified from Tsui-Auch and Yoshikawa (2010)

employing professional managers for certain senior management positions. Business groups that sought outside equity from institutional investors tended to increase their professionalization attempts. Nevertheless, they were unwilling to relinquish family control.

Table 3. Relationships of Board Chair/President, CEOs/ Managing Directors to the controlling families of the largest family-controlled firms

Core companies	Chairman		CEO/MD	
	1997	2006	1997	2006
UOB	F	F	F	F
UOL	F	F	L	L
UIC	F	F	L	L
SG Land	F	F	L	L
OCBC	F	L	F	E
F&N	L	L	NA	E
CDL	F	F	F	F
HLF	F	F	F	F
GuocoLand	L	L	F	F
Wing Tai	F	F	F	F

F: family members

E: recruited from external labour market

L: long-time associate

NA: Implies insufficient data to determine the backgrounds of the personnel.

Source: Modified from Tsui-Auch and Yoshikawa (2010)

4. The Case of OCBC

The OCBC group appeared to be more proactive in terms of official compliance with the state-led corporate governance reforms, arguably professionalizing management to a greater extent than other local firms. However, it will be shown that this was due largely to the fact that there was a lack of availability of willing and able family members to succeed the business.

The bank was amalgamated as a limited company in 1932 based on a merger of three local Hokkien family-controlled banks. The new entity was meant to counteract the legacy problems of traditional Chinese banks- for example, bad debts due to loose credit extended to relatives and friends, insufficient exposure to modern banking practices, inadequate checks and balances in management structure, and limited English-speaking and well-educated employees to handle the needs of modern clients. Lee Kong Chian, who was the largest shareholder with 20 percent of the shares, took the post of Chairman from 1938–1965. Other Chinese families held the rest of the equity.

The OCBC group expanded to encompass a number of key businesses in the areas of banking and insurance, stockbroking and property. The Group is now the second largest banking group in Singapore by total assets, and as of 2011, had assets of above 228 billion SGD[4]. As is typical of other Chinese family business groups, the OCBC group has a complex network of crossholdings and interlocking directorates, which enhance communication, resource allocation and liaison amongst interdependent firms within the network (Zang, 2000).

Although the group's investment portfolio has changed with its divestment of the Robinson Co and Asia Pacific Breweries since 2006, the holding structure of the group, as well as its complex interlocks are still intact (Tsui-Auch and Yoshikawa, 2010).

The Lee family's involvement constituted a large part of OCBC's succession history, which is summarized in Table 4. From 1966 to 1995, the position of Chairman was handed over to trusted insiders. Yet, even the Chairman, Tan Chin Tuan, was subject to the scrutiny of the Lee family (Lim 1979). Although Lee Seng Wee, Lee Kong Chian's son, took a relatively non-interventionist approach on operational management, he frequently consulted his elder brother, Seng Gee (who held no formal position in the OCBC but presided over the family's private business, Lee Rubber) on strategic managerial decisions (Tsui, 2004).

However, in the wake of the Asian currency crisis, the OCBC was one of the three largest Chinese family-controlled banking groups which could no longer resist governmental pressure to change its corporate governance structure, and acceded to calls for self-renewal by retiring altogether 10 long-serving elderly board directors (*Sunday Times*, 2000).

Therefore, it was palpably obvious that professionalization of the bank's top and senior levels of management was only able to proceed, though slowly, after those elderly board directors had retired. Since 2000, the bank has hired over 110 senior managers from overseas, including its

---

[4]Taken from http://www.ocbc.com/group/investors/historical-financial-highlights.html and the main OCBC website.

Table 4.   OCBC's succession history

1932	Formed after a merger of 3 local Hokkien banks
1932–1938	Lee Kong Chian is the largest shareholder and the vice chairman, with approx 20 percent shares in the company.
1938–1965	Lee Kong Chian is the chairman.
1942–1972	Tan Chin Tuan is Managing Director of the Company.
1966–1983	Tan Chin Tuan is Chairman.
1966:	Lee Seng Wee, son of Lee Kong Chian, is elected to the board of directors.
1995	Lee Seng Wee becomes Chairman.
1998	Alex Au, former Hong Kong banker, becomes CEO.
2002	Alex Au resigns and David Conner takes over as CEO.
2003	Dr Cheong Choong Kong succeeds Lee Seng Wee as Chairman.
2012	After a 10 year period as CEO, David Conner retires and is named non-executive director of OCBC. Samuel N Tsien is appointed as Chief Executive Officer on April 15, 2012.

first foreign CEO, Alex Au (Far Eastern Economic Review, 2001). Nevertheless, Lee Seng Wee remained the largest shareholder and maintained significant influence over the running of the bank. In 2002, when Alex Au hastily resigned, industry analysts attributed it to his inadequate support from the board of directors (Tsui-Auch, 2004). Although the OCBC separated the roles of CEO and Board Chair earlier than the UOB, making it seem as if OCBC had made more progress in corporate governance, this action was probably forced by circumstance, since by that time the Lee family did not have any descendants who were keen on and able to run the bank (Tsui-Auch, 2004).

Similar to its rivals, the OCBC also benefited from the "comply or disclose" approach advocated by the MAS. This enabled it to meet its corporate governance obligations. For example, like the UOB, the OCBC had increased outsider represnetation on board. However, some of these outside, independent directors had business relationships with the bank, which could, potentially, lead to a conflict of interest. However, the Nominating Committee was given overriding power to decide upon the suitability of the candidates for appointment, and there is a focus on directors' advisory and counseling role over their monitoring function.

5. Conclusion

In this chapter, we sought to present the temporality and periodicity of changes in the Chinese family business management structure. The analysis is divided into the pre-1997 and post 1997 periods. The Asian Currency crisis of 1997 gave the Singapore government a legitimate reason for demanding corporate governance reforms. Nevertheless, it appears that ethnic Chinese family firms did not adhere entirely to the Whitehall diktat of international corporate governance norms, but adopted a slightly more lenient stance towards the interpretation of independence. We illustrated the mediating role of state agencies in enabling incremental corporate governance changes among family-controlled firms (particularly banks). The responses of organizations are thus a function not only of the degree of "institutional contradiction" (Friedland and Alford, 1991, p. 256, in Greenwood *et al.*, 2010), but also of the enforcement mechanisms in place. Concurrently, this chapter also provides some evidence to validate Child's (2000) framework for cross-national research which specifies the role of institutions (such as the various bureaucratic-administrative agencies) in bridging global and local forces.

When Chinese family firms increased outsider representation on their boards, they tended to emphasize independent directors' resource provision role rather than their monitoring role. This is in line with the conceptualization of directors as critical resources for the competitive advantage of firms. Perhaps surprisingly, in spite of this skewed emphasis, family firms outperformed non-family firms, garnering a 5 percent return on assets as opposed to 3 percent for non-family firms (Dieleman, Wiwattanakantang and Jungwook, 2011; Tan, 2012). According to Tan (2012), this finding is "consistent with other studies on family firm performance in developed countries." It appears that relational ties and insider-control may reduce transaction costs, and this seems to outweigh efficiency savings gained from information transparency. It is also likely that the stability and continuity engendered by such ties led to the implementation of long-term, rather than short-term investment models, which explains the firms' superior performance (Dieleman, Wiwattanakantang and Jungwook, 2011; Tan, 2012). At the same time, "patient capital" also plays a role, in that "people put their own money so they work very hard for their firms" (Tan 2012). This is consistent with Wee Ee Cheong's (UOB's current CEO) argument that family members have a "long-term commitment in the business" (Straits Times, 2001, p. S21).

However, the downside of having long-staying family members on the board is that there would be succession issues, and the business might not be sustainable in the long run without external talents or informational transparency. In fact, family firms in general scored poorly on the Governance and Transparency Index (GTI), and only three were represented in GTI's top 20 (Dieleman, Wiwattanakantang and Jungwook, 2011; Tan, 2012). Complementing family resource by employing external talent is an option, but firms will increasingly need greater information transparency to increase their competitive advantage and foster all-round stakeholdership. Therefore, in order to foster sustainable growth, the challenge lies in how family-controlled firms can adequately reform their corporate governance structures for greater transparency. This chapter suggests that, in newly industrialized economies like Singapore, the process is an evolutionary one.

References

Bowers, T and G Gibb (2003). *Banking in Asia — Acquiring a Profit Mindset.* Singapore: John Wiley and Sons.

Brocklehurst, M (2005). Chinese family business. In *Blackwell Encyclopedic Dictionary of Strategic Management*, DF Channon (ed.), pp. 1–36. London, UK: Blackwell Publisher.

Chan, K and C Chiang (1994). *Stepping out: The Making of Chinese Entrepreneurs.* Singapore: Prentice Hall.

Child, J (2000). Theorizing about organization cross-nationally. *Advances in International Comparative Management*, 13, 27–75.

Chow, M (2005). Singapore's new code of corporate governance. Available at http://www.asialaw.com/Article/1971612/Search/Results/Singapores-New-Code-of-Corporate-Governance.html?Keywords=Corporate+governance.

Chrisman, JJ, HJ Chua and R Litz (2003). A unified systems perspective of family firm performance: An extension and integration. *Journal of Business Venturing*, 18(4), 462–472.

Dieleman, M, Y Wiwattanakantang and S Jungwook (2011). *Drawing a Portrait of Family Firm Governance in Singapore: A Study of SGX-Listed Family*

Firms. Study in collaboration with the National University of Singapore and the Family Business Network Asia. Singapore.

DiMaggio, PJ and WW Powell (1983). The iron cage revisited: Institutional isomorphism and collective rationality in organizational fields. *American Sociological Review*, 48, 147–160.

Flood, J (2007). Lawyers as sanctifiers: The role of elite law firms in international business transactions. *Indiana Journal of Global Legal Studies*, 14(1), 35–66.

Gill, A, J Allen and S Powell (2010). CG Watch 2010. *Corporate Governance in Asia*. CLSA Pacific Markets and Asian Corporate Governance Association.

Greenwood, R, AM Diaz and JC Lorente (2010). The multiplicity of institutional logics and the heterogeneity of organizational responses. *Organization Science*, 21, 521–539.

Habbershon, TG, ML Williams and IC MacMillan (2003). A unified system perspective of family firm performance. *Journal of Business Venturing*, 18, 451–465.

Hamilton, GG (1997). Organization and market processes in Taiwan's capitalist economy. In *The Economic Organization of East Asian Capitalism*, M Orrú, NW Biggart and GG Hamilton (eds.), pp. 237–296. Thousand Oaks, CA: Sage Publications.

Hamilton, GG and NW Biggart (1988). Market, culture, and authority: A comparative analysis of management and organization in the Far East. *American Journal of Sociology*, 94, S52–S94.

Hu, HW (2003). Independent directors: A new chapter of the development of corporate governance in China. Paper presented at the 15th Annual Conference of the Association for Chinese Economics Studies Australia (ACESA), Melbourne, October 2–3.

Jensen, M (1993). The modern industrial revolution, exit and the failure of internal control systems. *Journal of Finance*, 48, 831–880.

Kao, J (1993). The worldwide web of Chinese business. *Harvard Business Review*, March–April, 24–36.

KPMG Audit Committee Institute (2010). Scaling greater heights in corporate governance. Avaliable at http://www.kpmg.com/SG/en/IssuesAndInsights/ACI-publications/Documents/ScalingGreaterHeightsCorporateGovernance.pdf.

Kwang, HF, W Fernandez and S Tan (1998). *Lee Kuan Yew: The Man and His Ideas*. Singapore: Singapore Press Holdings and Times Editions.

Lee, HS (2002). Speech at the Launch of the Council of Corporate Disclosure and Governance (CCDG). Available at http://was.nl.sg/wayback/20060525-133457/http://www.ccdg.gov.sg/index.html.

Lim, QP (1979). Exploring the intricacies of Tan Chin Tuan's OCBC. *Euromoney*, July, 96–98.

Low, L (2001). The political economy of Chinese banking in Singapore. Research Paper Series #2001-015, Faculty of Business Administration, National University of Singapore.

MAS Code of Corporate Governance (2012). Available at http://www.mas.gov.sg/ Regulations-and-Financial-Stability/Regulatory-and-Supervisory-Framework/ Corporate-Governance/Corporate-Governance-of-Listed-Companies/Code-of-Corporate-Governance.aspx.

MAS Corporate Governance Code (2012). Available at http://www.mas.gov.sg/ Regulations-and-Financial-Stability/Regulatory-and-Supervisory-Framework/ Corporate-Governance/Corporate-Governance-of-Listed-Companies/~/media/ resource/fin_development/corporate_governance/CGCRevisedCodeof CorporateGovernance3May2012.ashx.

MAS Corporate Governance Code (2005). Available at http://www.mas.gov.sg/en/ Regulations-and-Financial-Stability/Regulatory-and-Supervisory-Framework/ Corporate-Governance/Corporate-Governance-of-Listed-Companies/~/ media/resource/fin_development/corporate_governance/CG%20Code%20 2005%20Code.ashx.

Ng, M (2012). UOB is in my blood, says, Wee Cho Yaw. *Straits Times*, August 8, p. A8.

OCBC Group Financial Results (2012). Available at http://www.ocbc.com/group/ investors/historical-financial-highlights.html.

Redding, SG (1990). *The Spirit of Chinese Capitalism*. Berlin: De Gruyter.

Rodan, G (1989). *The Political Economy of Singapore's Industrialization: National State and International Capital*. Basingstoke: Macmillan.

Silin, RH (1976). *Leadership and Values: The Organization of Large-Scale Taiwanese Enterprises*. Cambridge, MA: Harvard University, East Asian Research Center.

Straits Times (2001). UOB not looking at merger with local banks. February 28, p. S21.

Sunday Times (2000). Younger stalwarts at helm of 3 banks. April 16, p. 2.

Tam, S (1990). Centrifugal versus centripetal growth processes: Contrasting ideal types for conceptualizing the development patterns of Chinese and Japanese firms. In *Capitalism in Contrasting Cultures*, SR Clegg and SG Redding (eds.). New York, NY: de Gruyter.

Tan, J (2012). Family firms "need to have better governance." *The Business Times*, March 21.

Tan, TM, KS Leong and YH Pang (1999). Business education in Singapore: The past, the present and the future. *Review of Pacific Basin Financial Markets and Policies*, 2(4), 527–554.

The Economist (2000). Asian capitalism: The end of tycoons. April 29, pp. 75–78.

Tsui-Auch, LS (2004). The professionally managed family-ruled enterprise: Ethnic Chinese business in Singapore. *Journal of Management Studies*, 41, 693–723.

Tsui-Auch, LS and D Chow (2013). Ethnic Chinese family business. In *Encyclopedia of Management*, 3rd Edition, J McGee and T Sammut-Bonnici (eds.). New York, NY: Wiley.

Tsui-Auch, LS and T Yoshikawa (2010). Business groups in Singapore. In *The Oxford Handbook of Business Groups*, A Colpan, T Hikino and J Lincoln (eds.), pp. 267–293. Oxford, UK: Oxford University Press.

Tsui-Auch, LS and Y-J Lee (2003). The state matters: Management models of Singaporean Chinese and Korean business groups. *Organization Studies*, 24, 507–534.

Wong, SL (1985). The Chinese family firm: A model. *British Journal of Sociology*, 36(1), 58–72.

Zang, X (2000). Intercorporate ties in Singapore. *International Sociology*, 15(1), 87–105.

Chapter 9

Building a Successful Brand: The Story of Eu Yan Sang

Jessica Chong, Willem Smit, Thomas Menkhoff
and Christopher Clayman (with Richard Eu)

1. Introduction

Founded in 1879, Eu Yan Sang (EYS) has grown from a simple herbal medicine shop to the leading innovator in Traditional Chinese Medicine (TCM). With over 1,000 herbs and 900 proprietary products in manufacture, as well as 1,700 employees, the family business EYS now under 4th-generation leadership has made a name for itself in Asia and is a pioneer in the movement of TCM products abroad. Since 1989, Group CEO Richard Eu has led EYS on a path to new growth opportunities through modernisation, creating value through both branding and innovation. As "guardians of the knowledge" credibly endorsed by long-term owner-family commitment, EYS has successfully repositioned itself as a relevant wellness brand for new and modern consumer segments by translating TCM know-how into modern products, as well as to market those products in a state-of-the-art way preparing the brand for global expansion. Such a position will likely enable EYS to grow its wholesale and retail business further despite ongoing challenges.

2. Overview of Eu Yan Sang

EYS's impressive consistent growth over the last two decades made it into a leading consumer healthcare group in Traditional Chinese Medicine (TCM) (see Figure 1 for an overview of the company's growth). Its product range

This chapter is based on a presentation given by Eu Yan Sang International Ltd Group CEO Richard Eu at the Singapore Management University (SMU) on November 6, 2012.

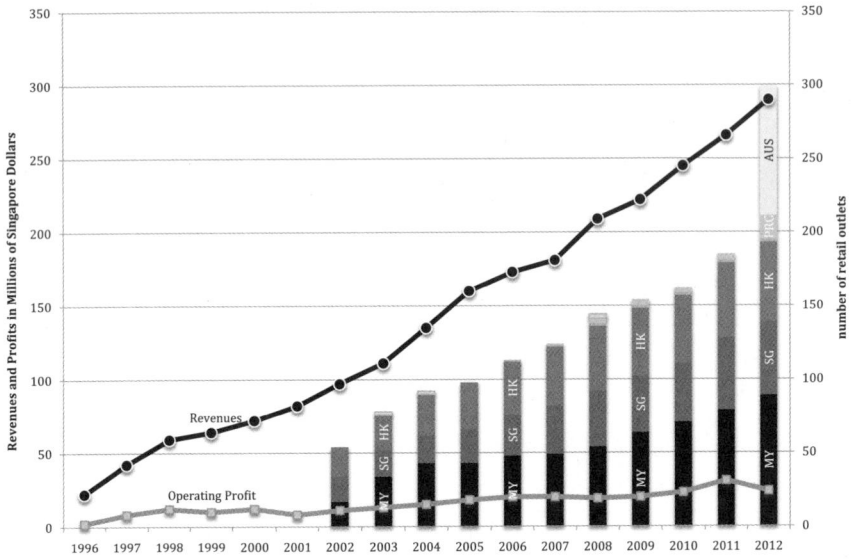

Figure 1.   Company growth Eu Yan Sang (1996–2012)
Source: Company annual reports 2000–2012

includes over 1,000 herbs and 900 proprietary products, including loose herbs, Chinese Proprietary Medicine, whole foods, health foods and beverages, nutritional supplements, and personal care products. Its multinational presence encompasses 1,700 employees engaged in four core business activities: manufacturing, retail, export and distribution, and clinic services.

Manufacturing: EYS has two factories: one in Hong Kong and one in Malaysia. Both have adopted Good Manufacturing Process (GMP) best practices.

Retail: As of September 30, 2012, there were 217 EYS stores in Singapore, Malaysia, Hong Kong, Macau, and China. In Australia, EYS owns 88 stores under the brand name Healthy Life.

Export and Distribution: EYS has wholesale operations to special retailers, exporting to Australia, the US, New Zealand, and Indonesia. In addition, EYS's Healthy Life national distribution centre in Australia provides food, supplements, complementary medicines, and personal care products to health food stores in addition to its own network.

Clinic Services: As of September 30, 2012, EYS operated 22 TCM clinics in Singapore, three TCM clinics in Malaysia, and two integrated medical centres in Hong Kong.

The EYS brand portfolio now consists of its corporate brand, Eu Yan Sang International Ltd.; retail brands Eu Yan Sang and Healthy Life; product brands Eu Yan Sang, Honey Market, ProNature, Zing, Healthy Life, HL, Natural Alternative; and Eu Yan Sang clinics.

EYS has been particularly resilient during dire global financial straits, having experienced steady growth in revenue since its listing and flourishing in spite of the Asian financial crisis, the dot-com bubble, SARS, the global financial crisis, and so forth. In fact, between FY02 and FY12, its compound annual growth rate (CAGR) was 12.3 percent.

A crucial part of EYS's success is its family business identity as a "guardian of knowledge," leveraging on its expertise in TCM and modernising it for contemporary consumers, as well as consumers in new markets. How did an arguably traditional company such as EYS manage to reposition itself as a wellness brand and transform itself into a modern, scientifically validated enterprise while celebrating its family roots in tradition?

2.1 *History and tradition*

> In Guangdong, there is a crane from this kingdom
> It bears in its chest a sense of righteousness
> It builds its family through the righteous path
> For its steadfastness, it will be rewarded with success.

「有國鶴廣東，經義在其中，傳家守正道，立志可成功」

The above poem has been passed down from the elder Eu He Song and through the Eu family for generations. The twenty characters in the poem not only provided characters for the names of descendants within the family, but also inspired Eu Kong (1853–1890) — the eldest son of Eu He Song — to open the first Yan Sang medicine shop in 1879.

As a young entrepreneur in Gopeng, Perak, Eu Kong ventured into tin mining. He was distressed that many miners turned to opium to help with various ailments. Upon seeing the negative effects that opium had on his employees, Eu began selling traditional Chinese medicinal herbs as a healthy alternative. Naming the shop "Yan Sang," which is Cantonese for "Caring for Mankind," Eu grew a small but appreciable customer base for his expertise in herbal medicine.

Eu Kong's son, Eu Tong Sen (1877–1941) continued the family's legacy and started remittance services to help his workers to send money back to their hometowns. By Eu Tong Sen's death, the family business included interests in tin, finance, property, remittances, rubber, banking, and insurance.

After Eu Tong Sen's death, the family business was distributed among his thirteen sons. The family was unable to come to a consensus about what to do with the business legacy, and most family interests were liquidated or sold by the 1980s. Only one business entity remained from Eu Tong Sen's business portfolio: the Yan Sang medicine shops.

3. The Modernization of Eu Yan Sang

In 1989, after William Eu's retirement as Executive Director of Eu Yan Sang Holdings, his nephew Richard Eu — now the fourth generation of the Eu family in the business — joined the company as General Manager.

At that point, EYS owned five outlets in Malaysia and one in Singapore. Without their own manufacturing facilities, EYS's product range did not extend far beyond raw herbs and traditional herbal pills. Sales were less than S$10 million. The EYS business in Hong Kong was run separately by other Eu family members. It comprised two stores and a factory.

It was the fourth generation of leadership that transformed EYS from a small family business (Lian and We, 2004; Chung, 2006) into a modern company experiencing rapid growth. By 1997, EYS had consolidated under one holding company and expanded to 16 outlets in Malaysia, five in Singapore, and eight in Hong Kong. EYS owned manufacturing facilities in Hong Kong and Malaysia. The product range had expanded beyond raw herbs and traditional herbal pills to include pre-packed soups, herbal teas, lozenges, vitamins, Western medicines, and more. Sales topped S$42 million.

3.1 *Twin-pronged approach toward revitalizing Eu Yan Sang: branding and science*

How was the fourth generation of the Eu family able to revitalize their company so quickly and effectively?

The story of EYS's growth to present day is one of modernization through a twin-pronged approach to value creation: *branding backed by science*.

Beginning in 1993, Richard Eu and other executives began the groundwork to redefine and reposition the real business of EYS. Following a typical strategic brand management process, the first step that was taken was to truly understand the EYS as a brand and what it means to its current customers and prospects (see Figure 2). "We had to really determine who we were, who our customers were, and how to differentiate from the competition," says Eu. Traditionally, the company had dealt in loose herbs and herbal pills. According to Eu, the customer base at that time consisted mainly of middle-aged women who were familiar with the process of preparing the herbs. The management recognised that in order for the company to grow, they needed to expand their customer base, and attract new customers less educated in the field of TCM.

In doing so, EYS underwent extensive consumer research to define their true customer base. They performed a SWOT analysis, set goals, determined their vision, and sought out the factors that are the points-of-difference and points-of-parity in consumer minds. They concluded that, in order for EYS to grow, it needed to build brand equity beyond the customer groups it was serving — a name that people could trust. Significantly, EYS was ready to take on the challenge of proving TCM's purpose and feasibility of use in a modern world accustomed to pharmaceutical drugs. Executives determined that they must also use design principles to create value and enhance competitiveness. They needed to innovate and expand from the simple loose herbs sold at their locations. This required a change in workforce mindsets and attitudes, as well as an expansion of distribution channels and markets. Finally, in order to expand the capability for expansion of product range, EYS needed to quickly upgrade their manufacturing facilities.

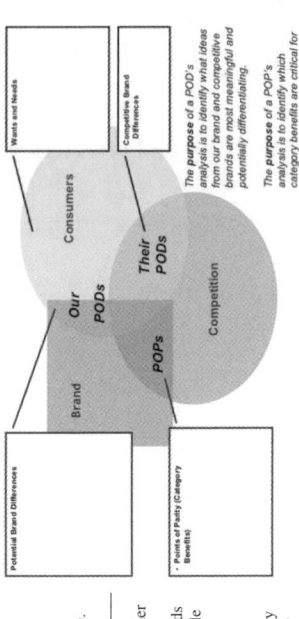

Four Key Strategic Brand Management Processes*	Two Brand Positioning Guidelines

Understanding Brand: Identify and establish brand positioning and values

- **Brand positioning;**
- Brand resonance;
- Brand value chain

Crafting Brand: Plan and implement Brand Management Programs

- Choosing brand elements,
- Integrating brand into marketing activities
- Leveraging secondary associations

Measuring Brand: Measure and Interpret Brand Performance

- Brand measurement system,
- Brand audits

Managing Brand: Grow and Sustain Brand Equity

- Defining the brand architecture
- Building brand portfolio,
- Introducing brand extensions

1. Defining and Communicating the Competitive Frame of Reference

Starting point in defining the competitive frame of reference for a brand positioning is to determine category membership: with which products/services does the brand compete with?

2. Choosing and establishing PODs and POPs

A brand must offer a compelling and credible reason for choosing it over the other options. Clearly communicated point-of-differences and points-of-parity are essential.

Point-of-Difference Associations (POD)

PODs are attributes or benefits that consumers strongly associate with a brand, positively evaluate, and believe that they could not find to the same extent with a competitive brand.

Point-of-Parity Associations (POP)

POPs are associations customer have that are not necessarily unique to the brand but may in fact be shared with other brands. They can be necessary (but not necessarily sufficient) conditions for brand choice.

Brand Positioning

As a result of following the guidelines, the brand owner should be able to clearly explain how the brand will create a sustainable competitive advantage in the minds of prospects and customers, using the following simple phrase.

"For [Target Segment/s], [Brand] is the only/best [competitive frame of reference] that [statement of key benefit or guiding value/PODs] because/by [reason to believe/key credibility point]."

Figure 2.   Key strategic brand management processes and brand positioning guidelines

*Source: Keller (2012).

3.2 *Guardians of knowledge: The Eu Yan Sang brand*

Under the new leadership, EYS underwent a dramatic brand repositioning in the 1990s. At the time, TCM was languishing as a newer consumer generation embraced Western medicine. Poor perception of TCM among non-users, lack of standardization, and difficulty of use restricted TCM acceptance amongst non-Chinese and younger Chinese were some of the issues. EYS saw this as an opportunity to stand out by leading the way for modernization of TCM and integrating it with Western medical practice. It set out to reposition itself by first redefining and broadening the competitive frame of reference in the minds of consumers: from a narrow frame of TCM, EYS made itself more relevant to more people by positioning itself in the wellness category – its new vision was becoming a trusted leader of TCM offering the best of integrative health care for a good life and long health.

Significantly, EYS's main differentiation comes from its position as a "guardian of the knowledge." In drawing from over one hundred years of traditional knowledge, EYS can expertly translate old TCM processes into modern products, and market those products in a way that is relevant to modern consumers.

EYS's foundations as a family-centered company are crucial to the brand strategy according to Mr Richard Eu:

> "My belief is that if the family still owns a significant stake in the business, they should never completely leave it in the hands of professionals. I think you need a guardian of the corporate values. A lot of things have gone wrong in a corporate world because of a lack of values. So family businesses have the opportunity to be the guardian of certain values. You have to do business in an ethical way. It helps if there is a family member who understands this, and who is there [to continue these values]."

EYS's stated values also include compassion and righteousness — a commitment to wellness for its customers. This means an inclusive, integrative, and natural approach to health care. For EYS, it's important to take a natural approach because, as Richard Eu says: "It's where we came from." It's also important that EYS takes a preventative approach to stop people from falling sick, which help people save money in terms of health care costs.

Indeed, ensuring wellness for customers, whether in terms of health or finances, is central to EYS's ethos. The family commitment lasting for more than 130 years is employed to provide consumers with a credible *Reason to Believe* (RTB), testifying the authenticity of the brand's purpose.

During the past few years, EYS's leaders have encouraged progressive change. While paying homage to its origins as a traditional family business, EYS simultaneously works to make its processes modern and scientifically validated.

4. Six Key Areas of Modernization

To make the repositioning of the brand resonate with the current and newly targeted customer segments, EYS's carefully managed consumers' perceptions of desirability and deliverability of the Wellness positioning by modernizing across six key areas:

4.1 *Product and marketing innovation*

As, the product itself is the primarily influence of what consumers experience with the brand, EYS's repositioning began with expanding and adapting its product offerings. Initially, EYS's shops primarily sold loose herbs to be taken home and boiled in particular combinations. Younger consumers proved inconvenienced when asked to boil herbs for hours before taking medicine. In addition, they had little knowledge of the proper combinations for their formulas. Therefore, the company went about introducing convenient ways to consume Chinese medicine by changing formulations and packaging. Instead of selling only loose herbs, they formulated soup packs, granules, sachets, tea bags, and eventually also capsules and ready-to-drink formulas.

As an example, ginseng, one of EYS's flagship herbs, was originally sold as a loose herb. Customers would slice up the ginseng, then steep it or double boil it. To simplify matters, EYS introduced the concept of putting ginseng into a tea bag, which could be sold at supermarkets for customers seeking the benefits of ginseng, but with added convenience. The ginseng was also put into capsules for customers who did not want to drink the tea.

Another example is the innovation of Bak Foong pills, which transformed its packaging over the course of fifty years. Called Xiao Yao Wan in Chinese, the best-selling women's wellness product was traditionally made by grinding herbs mixed together and rolled into a ball with honey. In the 1950s, Bak Foong were made into tiny pills. Nowadays, they are sold in form of capsules. As the Bak Foong brand aimed for younger, working women, the packaging had to be changed in order to make it attractive for this new customer segment.

But perhaps EYS's greatest innovation in product branding and marketing was its hamper sales. In Chinese culture, it is widely considered to be bad luck to buy medicine during Chinese New Year. Therefore, it's no surprise that Chinese New Year has traditionally been an annual slow period for TCM sales. EYS recognized this as an opportunity to rebrand their medicines not as medicines, but as "gifts of health" in time for Chinese New Year. They packaged their products in gift-wrapped hampers, rebranded their medicine as health and wellness, and targeted gift givers during the holiday season. In effect, they created a new "gifts of health" category of TCM products. Now for many it is customary to buy a wellness hamper for relatives during Chinese New Year, and hamper sales have become one of the biggest revenue-generating businesses for the company.

4.2 Retail expansion and modernization

To communicate and reinforce consumer's perception of product innovations, EYS remodeled its most important customer touch point: their shops. As Richard Eu remembers:

> "In [the 1980's], TCM shops were pretty foreboding places. They were dark. The herbs were in bins in some cases. In our case, we didn't have anything on display; we had a high counter and people would come up and ask the salesman very nicely if they could buy ginseng. The interaction with the customer was not very close... [in fact, it was rather] daunting."

As part of the brand upgrade, EYS moved away from dark medical shops to bright and modern retail environments. Instead of locating their shops in residential areas, EYS adapted to the changing model of retail and placed shops in shopping centers. Their TCM retails now catered to affluent, working consumers in city centres. Stores were adaptable to stand alone or fit into a shopping mall. In addition, Mr Eu, whose background in luxury retail exposed him to prestigious brands like Piaget, Cartier, etc., also understood that customers were willing to pay a premium to shop in luxurious spaces. Thus, the shop spaces were modernized to reflect this.

When Richard Eu first began the retail expansion of EYS, his goal was to turn EYS into a monolithic brand. For inspiration, he looked to *The Body Shop*, whose retail shops carry only The Body Shop brand of products. Part of EYS's strategy for differentiating itself from the competition was to adopt a similar private-brand strategy as The Body Shop. While other medical houses at the time sold many different brands or did not have their own in-house brands, the EYS shops would only carry EYS products. However, as EYS evolved and expanded into different categories of wellness products, the management recognized that the stores had to begin carrying other brands. As Richard Eu acknowledges: "One brand was not enough as we expanded into different categories."

4.3 *Expanding distribution channels and market*

With the new range of pre-packed herbal medicines, soup packs, and other herbal preparations, *EYS* began distributing their products through supermarkets by the end of 1991. The first retail counter outside of an *EYS*-owned store was set up in Yaohan Parkway in 1992. By 1998, *EYS* was distributing through higher-end drugstores such as *Watson's* and *Mannings* in Hong Kong. It is interesting to note that *Guardian* and *Watson's* in Singapore did not sell many TCM products then. However, in Hong Kong such TCM products are available on the shelves at convenience stores. This is because Hong Kong customers are already accustomed to buying TCM products in stores such as *Watson's* and *Mannings*. It also expanded distribution into hospitals and clinics in Singapore, Malaysia, and Hong Kong. By acquiring the *Australian Healthy Life Group Pty Ltd* in February 2012, *EYS* has extended its reach into the Australian market with over 80 stores. As Richard Eu pointed out:

> "Health food stores in the Western market cater to customers who are primarily Westerners. So [Asian companies] won't understand Western consumer behavior. What we're trying to do there is to find a way of introducing our TCM herbs into that market. We can't just take our existing product and sell it as it is. You might change the form, change the packaging and communication. There is a unique approach, one that a lot of people cannot copy: the East–West approach. We will combine elements of both Western and Chinese herbal in a way that validates the use. So we actually have to put some research behind it. What we mean by "guardians of the knowledge" is our knowledge about herbs, whether it's Western herbs or Chinese herbs or Indian herbs. We need to know how it works and how they can be combined together, and what works together. And this is the research we have to do. So we will be launching the first range of fusion products in Australia towards the first quarter 2013, that's the target. It will be a Western brand. But it has the 'Powered by Eu Yan Sang' on the packaging."

4.4 *Upgrading manufacturing capability and processes*

A brand repositioning can only be successful when consumers are convinced of the deliverability of the new value proposition. The company's competences had to be adjusted accordingly. Prior to 1997, all pills and powder products were manufactured in Hong Kong facilities. Herb preparations were processed manually at a corresponding warehouse. As Richard Eu recalls: "They chopped the herbs, they dried the herbs, grinded it, rolled it in 10 baskets, until it became bar. That's how it was done, all by hand."

With the advent of GMP (Good Manufacturing Process, a WHO classification for pharmaceutical products) regulations, *EYS* set up a new GMP factory in Cheras (Malaysia) to expand capacity for herb preparation and Chinese proprietary medicine manufacture. The factory received ISO 9001:22000 certification. When the business consolidated in 1997, *EYS* expanded the Hong Kong facilities' production capacity. By 2002, the company established the first fully GMP-certified TCM facility in Hong

Kong, which received ISO 9001:2008 certification. A new factory opened in Yuen Long, Hong Kong in 2006. These GMP-certified facilities include automated manufacturing processes and improved warehousing systems. As Mr Eu explained: "We employ fewer people in manufacturing today, maybe 20 times the value compared to the old days."

4.5 *Greater control of supply chain*

The supply chain depends on four steps of production: good herbal production, good laboratory practices, good manufacturing practices, and good distribution practices. In taking greater control of the supply chain at all steps, *EYS* ensures good quality raw material with full traceability and food safety; accurate laboratory results with chemical and genomic profiling; assured quality during the manufacturing process; and traceability in transportation of finished goods. Hence, *EYS* sees quality and safety control through all parts of the chain by tracking the products from growing through to the manufacturing, distribution, and sales.

Given the recent scandals involving food and medicine safety in China, Mr Eu wants to "make sure that every step along the way we know exactly what we're doing and where the herbs come from. We are using our knowledge and leveraging it into products." This lends the brand added legitimacy and consumer confidence.

4.6 *Intellectual property and marketing intelligence-driven product development*

Mr Eu acknowledges that while a lot of research has been conducted regarding Chinese herbs, he is adamant that *EYS* will not be the kind of company that will take that single magical compound in the herb and synthesize it into a pharmaceutical drug. However, he concedes: "If you stay and just do classical formulations you'll forever be a TCM company." Being a straightforward TCM company might not be an issue in, for example, China, where there will continue to be a big market for TCM. However, as *EYS* looks to expand globally, it needs to differentiate itself and validate its products with science and research partnerships with universities.

EYS recently collaborated with the world's largest food company — *Nestle* — to add TCM herbs to selected products including herbal soups. *EYS* is also creating anti-aging products, which, according to Mr Eu, are a "very Western concept." The plan is to use Chinese herbs to create a unique, differentiated, science-validated product to offer to consumers.

In another recent joint venture, *EYS* has been collaborating with a Singapore-based company, *Cell Research*, to blend traditional product with stem cells to treat acute wounds and burns. The blended product has been trailed in Vietnam with patients who had been suffering from deep wounds, which refused to heal for years; however, when the blended product was applied, their wounds started to heal within a matter of weeks.

5. The Outcome of Eu Yan Sang's Repositioning

Refreshing the brand to keep it relevant to new customers has been paying off for *EYS* in terms of a consistently high growth rate. The increase in sales from 97 million SGD to 290 millions SGD equals a CAGR of almost 12 percent. Primarily driven by organic growth, this can be attributed to EYS's strategy of having made it a priority to share knowledge of TCM with non Chinese-speaking consumers so that these new segments can better understand how it works and its benefits. By doing so, *EYS* has successfully attracted many new customers. At the moment, *EYS* runs a customer loyalty program with a membership of about half a million people, 100,000 of whom reside in Singapore. To keep the CRM up to date, customers have to pay to stay opted in. This is *EYS's* way of ensuring that its members are current and willing to engage with the company, and it helps them track the demographics of their customers. At the moment, 30–40 percent of *EYS's* customers are in their mid-20s to late 30s — a far cry from the demographic makeup of its customer base in the 90s.

EYS will continue to communicate the wellness benefits of TCM and how it works by using various media to achieve this, including product packaging, ads, websites, Facebook, and wellness magazines.

6. Future Challenges

According to an SRI International 2010 report, the wellness industry cluster represents a market of nearly $2 trillion globally. This includes conventional, medically oriented approaches (reactive) as well as integrated, wellness-oriented approaches (proactive). This bodes well for *EYS* as it is directly in line with *EYS's* strategic direction, and EYS is positioning itself to be a strong player in the global wellness market.

To accomplish this, *EYS* is set to follow a dual-growth strategy. First, it will continue its organic growth path by expanding its retail network, and creating new product lines. For example, food supplements are a growing market for *EYS* consumers. Also, as Mr Eu has stressed: "Food is becoming a big part of our business so it's not just herbs for medicine, it's also herbs for food. Natural wellness, I think, is a huge category and potential for us." *EYS* will continue to attract new target audiences, and stay relevant to the present and future marketplace, and focusing on innovation. In fact, the need for innovation has led to the establishment of a separate innovation division in the *EYS* head office.

A second growth strategy is through acquisitions. Its recent acquisition of *HealthyLife* in Australia is a first step. Taking over existing retail operations gives the firm a ready testing ground for *EYS's* product range to be included in the assortment. Additionally, it must be noted that *EYS* is uniquely positioned to enter Western markets because of its roots in Singapore. As Mr Eu explained: "Being a Singapore-based company, I think that people will buy into the messaging because they understand Singapore to be a crossroads of East–West."

To be sure, there are numerous challenges facing the TCM industry more broadly. The regulatory environment can be difficult to navigate; applications are long and arduous, and there are severe restrictions on packaging descriptions. It's also very difficult to regulate the kind of healthcare that *EYS* hopes to provide. Richard Eu has stated that his dream is "personalized medicine," wherein the patient is given a formulation tailored to suit his or her body type and other factors that may affect his or her condition. Crucial to TCM is the idea of customised treatment, which is difficult to regulate.

Companies must also contend with the lack of standardization of policies across countries. For example, a product that has been successfully registered in Country A may have to be modified to use a slightly different formula in Country B, because Country B does not allow the use of some of the herbs as in the Country A formula.

The industry is also experiencing a shortage of trained expertise, and it is difficult to recruit experienced practitioners. To address this, *EYS* established Singapore's first TCM scholarship, providing financial assistance to students enrolled in the Double Degree Programme in Biomedical Sciences and TCM at Nanyang Technological University (NTU). Students in the programme spend three years at NTU studying biosciences, and then spend two years at the Beijing University of Chinese Medicine, to learn TCM advanced principles and clinical training. Once they have graduated, the physicians go through *EYS'* internal residency programs and stay on to become practitioners in *EYS* clinics.

Unlike the Western pharmaceutical industry, TCM suffers from a shortage of funding for new products and innovations. The TCM industry must also grapple with poor perception and misconception by non-users, which *EYS* tries to address through the media and education. But Mr Eu is optimistic about the future of TCM: "When I started work people were saying 'why do you want to go into a sunset industry, traditional medicine is dying, pharmaceutical drugs are going to replace everything and you know you don't have much of a future.'"

7. Conclusion

Now that *EYS's* 20-years evolution to a wellness brand is completed, the brand is well positioned to take advantage of the growing natural wellness market. Ultimately, the story of *EYS* is proof that traditional medicine is not a sunset industry. In fact, with the brand repositioning done correctly, there is a lot of common ground between TCM and modern healthcare methods. The *EYS* story shows that the repositioning of an already successful brand has to be conducted with utmost caution, because changing the brand's identity too abruptly and radically may alienate existing customers. It is essential to strike a careful balance between innovating and attracting new customers, and keeping existing loyal brand users satisfied.

EYS undertook this repositioning journey by thoughtfully going through the key strategic brand management processes of understanding, crafting, measuring and managing the brand. First of all, the firm recognized the fact that staying in the category of TCM would not make it easy to convert new people into that category. It realized that the rising opportunity of young consumers' growing needs to stay well and make a conscious effort to follow a healthy lifestyle could only be addressed by broadening the brand's frame of reference. The second step was to define and reinforce the brand's points-of-difference by modernizing the product range and retail outlets.

Yet, the modernization of the front-office operations was performed with much respect for the existing loyal customers. For instance, *EYS* consciously maintained the old traditional herbs and leafs in the shops, prominently displayed in the display counter.

Furthermore, the sustainable reason-to-believe for the renewed positioning that no other competitor is able to copy is that the brand has been owned and managed by the same family from the start in 1879. All of this helps to explain why the EYS brand positioning was successfully changed to what brand positioning guidelines would describe as: "For every person young and old who finds it important to live a healthy life style, EYS is the only wellness brand that is truly serious about fusing the rich history of TCM with the demands of today's modern life, because our dedication as 'guardians of knowledge' is authentic and has been passed on from generation to generation in our family business."

References

Businessweek entry on Eu Yan Sang. Available at http://investing.businessweek.com/research/stocks/snapshot/snapshot.asp?ticker=EYSAN:SP

Chung, S (2006). The transformation of an overseas Chinese family — Three generations of the Eu Tong Sen family, 1822–1941. *Modern Asian Studies*, 39(3), 599–630.

Eu Yan Sang Corporate Site. Available at http://www.euyansang.com/

Eu Yan Sang Annual Reports. Available at http://www.euyansang.com/index.php/investors/financials/annual-reports

Eu Yan Sang on Facebook. Available at https://www.facebook.com/euyansang

Keller, KL (2012). *Strategic Brand Management*, 4th Edition. Singapore: Pearson.

Lian, KF and KK We (2004). Chinese enterprise in colonial Malaya. *Journal of Southeast Asian Studies*, 35(3), 415–432.

Singapore Infopedia entry on Richard Eu. Available at http://infopedia.nl.sg/articles/SIP_1151_2009-02-10.html

SRI Presents Comprehensive Study of the Global Wellness Industry at the 2010 Global Spa Summit in Istanbul, Turkey. Available at http://csted.sri.com/content/sri-presents-comprehensive-study-global-wellness-industry-2010-global-spa-summit-istanbul-tu

Chapter 10

Generational Change in Chinese Indonesian SMEs?

Juliette Koning

1. Introduction

The rise of the Southeast Asian tiger economies in the 1980s and the role of ethnic Chinese businesses therein have created an intriguing debate about the "success" of ethnic Chinese business and management practices. As stipulated by Dahles (2007) traditionally, scholars have argued that ethnic Chinese businesses in Southeast Asia function well and are successful because of shared Confucian values, preference for intra-ethnic networks, and the importance of personal relationships, sometimes taken together under the expression "Chinese capitalism." As a result, ethnic Chinese communities are often assumed to be quite separate societal groups both in terms of business conduct as well as in terms of identity. Such claims have become quite dominant in academic writing as well as in the popular press (Redding, 1990; Weidenbaum and Hughes, 1996; Chan, 2000). These more *culturalist* approaches have been criticized by more *critical* perspectives for being a-temporal and a-contextual (Ooi and Koning, 2007) or for being focused too much on socio-cultural questions and less on entrepreneurship and business matters (Gomez and Hsiao, 2004; Menkhoff and Gerke, 2004).

In this chapter, I will argue that there are two issues that are quite remarkable if we look at these debates. First of all, in all these debates we rarely "hear" the voice of those concerned, in other words how do ethnic Chinese entrepreneurs themselves describe their business conduct, what do they consider to be "best practices"? And secondly, the fact that in many of the Southeast Asian countries there is a second or third

231

generation now active in business. Can we assume that they do as the first generation did in terms of business and management, the generation on which many of the conclusions about successful ethnic Chinese business acumen are based?

In order to address these two "missing links," this chapter will explore perceptions of both "older" and "younger" generation ethnic Chinese entrepreneurs in Indonesia with regard to their business conduct and what they consider to be important features therein. The few studies that have been conducted among second or third generation ethnic entrepreneurs in, for instance, Europe (Masurel and Nijkamp, 2004; Rusinovic, 2006), suggest differences in terms of start-up motives, sector choice and/or embeddedness in intra- and inter-ethnic networks. Based on research among ethnic Chinese entrepreneurs in the small and medium sector, this chapter will look more closely at such developments in Indonesia. The point of departure is that people in different generations possibly experience and understand their world and context differently based on different frames of reference. With the flow of time, circumstances change. If we look at younger generations of ethnic Chinese in Southeast Asia it can be argued that they have been given the opportunity to get a better education than their parents and that they have grown up under rather different circumstances, such as processes of nation state building and nationalism. Possibly, younger generations form a contrast with their parents and grandparents, in terms of worldviews and available opportunities (Gomez, 2007; Koning, 2007; Koning and Susanto, 2008). Older ethnic Chinese entrepreneurs as recent arrivals might have tapped into their Chinese social network to do business but the younger generation might have other choices; what changes, then if any, have come about in "the Chinese" way of doing business?

The remainder of this chapter provides first the necessary context for understanding entrepreneurship as I take a discursive-contextual approach (Van Gelderen and Masurel, 2011). Hence I will briefly address the debate on ethnic Chinese entrepreneurship in Southeast Asia as well as the position of the ethnic Chinese in Indonesia. This is followed by a description of the research context (city of Yogyakarta) as well as the research approach (ethnographic). The empirical data give voice to older and younger generation entrepreneurs and their views about "doing business."

The chapter ends with several conclusions on the issue under investigation: generational change in ethnic Chinese SMEs in Indonesia.

2. Ethnic Chinese Business Conduct: What Is Being Discussed?

A recurring theme in the study of the ethnic Chinese in Southeast Asia is their past and present ability to thrive in business and accumulate wealth.[1] Since the 1980s scholars have been trying to understand the success of East and Southeast Asian economies. Among others, the ethnic Chinese attitude of working-hard, personal network arrangements and respect for authority were deemed causes of this regional success. However, characteristics assumed to boost prosperity were also brought forward as the cause for economic hardship, especially so after the 1997 economic crisis that started in Thailand and spread throughout Southeast Asia. Personalism was interpreted as nepotism and initially advantageous networks were labelled exclusive. The 1997 crisis had some profound impacts on some Chinese communities in the region who were often put to blame, leading to violence in Indonesia.

As briefly outlined in the introduction, two perspectives dominate the debate on ethnic Chinese business acumen. The culturalist perspective on the Chinese way of doing business argues that the Chinese traditionally attach much value to intra-ethnic ties, recognizable in the practice of family business in the first place. The use of family labour allows Chinese patriarchs to maintain a high level of trust and keep costs low, thereby creating competitive advantage over those who prefer separating family and business life. The ethnic Chinese are said to operate within *guanxi*, or personal, networks, which create valuable ties among ethnic Chinese entrepreneurs in society. These *guanxi* ties allow access to capital and social resources (Hefner, 1998, pp. 10–13) and make "that a person can capitalize on reciprocal obligation and trust implicit in strong social ties to facilitate the exchange of favours and informal influences outside the domain of the original social ties" (Ly-yun and Tam, 2004, p. 24). Next to these social mechanisms, ethnic Chinese in general are argued to possess

---

[1]For a more detailed overview of this debate see Koning and Verver (2013).

advantageous cultural characteristics such as diligence, an emphasis on education and moral obligations, entrepreneurial skill and loyalty. These supposed values, referred to as "Confucian values," which can be traced back to mainland China, are used to explain ethnic Chinese enterprise development. Taken together, the culturalist perspective can be defined as "the view that culture is seen as the definite traits of a community and that these traits are enduring and stable, which largely defines social behaviour at the individual and social level" (Ooi and Koning, 2007, p. 108). In short, a rather essentialist view of culture.

Many scholars display a more historical, critical and nuanced perspective. Gomez and Benton (2004, p. 17) argue, "the development of Chinese enterprise cannot be understood as a function of Chinese culture, for cultural practices and identity are not the foundations on which enterprises are built or the reason they thrive." Not less critical, Ooi (2007, p. 120) points out that by "packaging" Chinese culture, culturalists have created "a shopping list of traits" that is reductionist and simplistic, and that they have "created their own imagined Chinese communities" (2007, p. 120). Entrepreneurial and organizational imperatives inform business conduct more than supposed cultural incentives (Ly-yun and Tam, 2004, p. 28).

Historically, the Chinese in Southeast Asia were often put in middleman positions in between the European elite and the indigenous workers. As a result, when independence was claimed after the Second World War, the Chinese were in many countries treated as outsiders in the nationalistic discourses of that time. Politically excluded and in a hostile environment, it is argued that the Chinese had to establish themselves without much outside support. They were able to create solidarity within their ethnic group by means of horizontal ties, thereby developing themselves economically without dependence on the state or other ethnic groups in society (Bardsley, 2003, p. 34). Therefore, rather than explaining Chinese networks by referring to Confucian values it can be argued that "the formation of closely knitted Chinese business networks decades ago emerged out of problems faced by migrants in terms of securing start-up capital, hiring labor and seeking partners" (Ooi, 2007, p. 122). This can also mean that when these problems fade away, which might be the case for many second and third generation Chinese, generational attitudes also change. As a general trend in Southeast Asia, Gomez and

Benton (2004, p. 17) content that "migrant's descendants tend to view their identity, and especially their ethnic identity, differently from their migrant forebears." Whether this is also visible in management and organizational styles, is the topic under investigation in this chapter. First, I briefly address the concept of generations.

3. Generational Change

By understanding a generation as individuals who share a "common location in the social and historical process," in which the latter potentially provides them with overlapping experiences, beliefs, and views, it follows that with each new age group there is the potential for new attitudes and new modes of thought (Mannheim, 1952, p. 291). This argument is helpful in a context in which the generations are confronted by quite different experiences, for instance migration trajectories, state building processes and/or democracy. Mannheim (1952) observed that especially in rapid changing societies new attitudes and new generation styles develop. "The quicker the tempo of social and cultural change is, then, the greater are the chances that particular generation location groups will react to changed situations by producing their own entelechy" (*Ibid.*, p. 310). This happens not only because people from different time intervals live together but because they have different social and historical experiences and backgrounds to which they relate.

An interpretation of the generation concept in merely age cohort terms is limiting in that it "presumes that generational identities are constant and unchanging" (Edmunds and Turner, 2005, p. 561). Mannheim already acknowledged that reactions to specific events would differ according to geographic or cultural location (Pilcher, 1994).

There are two interesting lines of research stemming from Mannheim's classic work. First of all, a more sociological line of investigation that explores generational cultures, collective memory and experience and consciousness. In such research "the specific date of a cohort may be less important than the general historical setting of generations" (Edmunds and Turner, 2002, p. 6). And secondly, recent research in entrepreneurship studies that uses generational encounters to understand processes of identity formation and identification in business and management (Down and Reveley, 2004). Generational encounters, as direct interactions between members of the generations, creates a juxtaposing of "the young" versus "the old" (*Ibid.*, p. 237).

For the research focus in this chapter, the concept of generations is used in the sense that age cohort, context (cultural location and historical setting), and collective memory combined create specific frames of reference that play a role in the narratives of older and younger ethnic Chinese entrepreneurs in Indonesia. In order to do justice to the importance of such historical and cultural context, in the next section I will briefly address the position of the ethnic Chinese in Indonesia.

4. The Indonesian Research Setting: The City of Yogyakarta

In the Indonesian case being ethnic Chinese, or Chinese Indonesian, has for long been a contested identity; an ethnic identity that was *not allowed* between 1965 and 1998 when the New Order regime of former president Suharto ruled the country. His Assimilation Programme (*Program Pembauran*) was an attempt to construct a national identity by "identifying significant others" (Hoon, 2006, p. 151), the significant other being the Chinese. Obviously, this impacted on issues of ethnic identity and self-identification among the ethnic Chinese groups. The systematic othering of the ethnic Chinese in the New Order period did take on a meaning and life of itself with an anti-Chinese rhetoric expressed in many violent attacks. In discussions on such Chineseness in the Indonesian case, it is clear that the state (bureaucracy and instruments of government) has been one of the most important "variables which has contributed to the 'separateness' of the Chinese in Indonesia, particularly in Java" (Suryadinata, 1993, p. 77).

A brief overview of such state mingling shows that Presidential Instructions and Decrees in 1967 limited the scope of Chinese traditions to the family worship house and required Indonesian ethnic Chinese to change their Chinese names into Indonesian ones in order that "such citizens shall be assimilated as to avoid any racial exclusiveness and discrimination" (Winarta, 2004, p. 72). In 1966, the use of Chinese language and characters in newspapers and shops was prohibited and a much contested law was installed earlier regarding citizenship, stating that Indonesian ethnic Chinese needed to have evidence of the change of their Chinese names into Indonesian names, and a letter to prove their Indonesian citizenship (*Ibid.*).

It took until the late 1990s before several restrictive laws on Chineseness were lifted. After the fall of Suharto (1998) a few amendments have been made, such as approval for the formation of Chinese political parties, the abolishment the law on the manifestation of Chinese cultural and religious expression and a national holiday for Chinese New Year.

In the most recent history, the year 1998 stands out. Although it is the year President Suharto was forced to step down (May 21) and as such marked the end of the New Order regime that had severely restricted Chineseness, one week earlier (May 13–14, 1998) many Chinese Indonesians were killed, raped and lost their houses and shops during violent mass riots. These riots resulted from a lingering economic crisis during which basic consumption goods, such as fuel and energy, became extremely expensive. People took to the streets to protest and somewhere these protests changed into massive attacks on people of Chinese decent. These attacks on ethnic Chinese groups follow a pattern in history in which people of Chinese decent have become the scapegoats in times of national upheaval. A common stereotype, leading to such outbursts, is the idea that all ethnic Chinese are "rich" and have befriended political power holders to create wealth.

Turning to their economic position, for the Indonesian case it is important to point out that the ethnic Chinese were historically not allowed to occupy civil servant positions or to own land. In the New Order period the ethnic Chinese "were prohibited from participating fully in political, civic and military affairs" (Freedman, 2000, p. 3) and hence mostly ended up in entrepreneurial and business occupations, the private sector of the economy where the majority in fact are small shop keepers and traders. Only some ethnic Chinese, the so-called *cukong* — a Hokkien term to refer to ethnic Chinese businessmen who cooperate with the power elite — were chosen as business partners by the Suharto regime and received favors not accessible to others. This very small group of *cukong* became synonymous of "the ethnic Chinese" in general and especially the display of their exorbitant wealth caused much of the "hatred" directed against the ethnic Chinese as an ethnic group.

The ethnic Chinese population in Yogyakarta in the year 2000 was approximately 3.5 percent of the total population (Data Monograph Yogyakarta, 2001). The largest age group of ethnic Chinese now living in Yogyakarta are those who were born in Yogyakarta between the 1950s and 1960s (Suryadinata *et al.*, 2003, p. 92), often the first generation born in Indonesia from a parent who migrated from China. The rest of the ethnic Chinese population consists of those who came from other parts of Indonesia in the 1970s. The ethnic Chinese in Yogyakarta have various backgrounds, with respect to cultural orientation, sub-ethnic groups (speech group), occupation, economic activities, religion, and education.

The economic presence of Chinese Indonesians in Yogyakarta is quite visible in the small and medium sized businesses, and there are particular businesses in which Chinese Indonesians are dominant, such as the car and motorcycle business, gold shops, building materials, textile, and electronics. While the majority of Yogyakarta Chinese are in business sectors, there are also quite a few professionals such as doctors, lawyers, accountants, managers, lecturers, beauticians, and architects.

Two groups of ethnic Chinese entrepreneurs were included in the research on which this chapter is based; an older generation of Chinese Indonesians (born in the 1930s–1950s) who often witnessed the severe curtailing of their Chineseness with the coming to power of the New Order regime in the mid-1960s (such as the banning of Chinese language and the closing down of Chinese schools), and a younger group born under the assimilation policy of the New Order (1960s–1970s).

Ethnographic fieldwork took place in 2004 and 2007. The timeframe is quite relevant. Part of the interviews took place in the autumn of 2004, during the election of Susilo Bambang Yudhoyono as President, and room for ethnic Chinese expression was only just starting to open up. In 2007, the situation had further improved.

Semi-structured interviews were conducted with 11 older and 11 younger ethnic Chinese entrepreneurs in the form of life and business histories. Three major themes were addressed with all of them: the role and meaning of being ethnic identity, business conduct, and the role of networks.

They all have a business that can be labelled small (less than 10 employees) or medium (between 10–100 employees) sized, for which start-up capital was most often derived from family resources (parents). In some cases, the business is a continuation of a family business, in other cases the parents either sold their business or provided capital, or they continued their business with the child setting up a related or different business. The older generation owner-managers of the medium sized firms are nearly all involved in side-businesses as well (in several cases export related); this was seldom the case among the small entrepreneurs and the younger ones. The majority of the small and medium enterprises in this study are in retail and services, with some manufacturing companies, examples of businesses include: printing and publishing, car repairs, sanitary sales, car and motorcycle spare parts, drugstore, cement trade etc.

The interviewees were approached based on their ethnic Chinese identification and their belonging to different generations and being owner-manager of a small or medium sized enterprise. As such the sampling was within and across cases, a method that "puts flesh on the bones of general constructs and their relationships" (Miles and Huberman, 1994, p. 27). At the same time the sampling was purposeful with the aim to have information-rich cases. Fitting the interpretive approach here taken, the point of departure is more concerned with "description of persons, places and events... the cornerstone of qualitative research" than with an attempt to generalize across time and space (Janesick, 1998, p. 50).

The interviews have been transcribed and systematically and repeatedly rearranged and analyzed by identifying major themes. The thematic analysis focused on expressions of "Chineseness" in relation to organizational and business practice and meanings of working life. The following section presents the discursive expression of both generations in terms of "doing business" in Indonesia as ethnic Chinese.

5. The Old and Young on Doing Business in Indonesia

This section presents reactions of the older and younger generation ethnic Chinese entrepreneurs on what they consider to be their business practices and style.[2]

---

[2]A more elaborate discussion can be found in Koning (2007).

5.1 *The older generation on trust, personal relationships, and reputation*

The business practices considered central to "the Chinese way of doing business" among older generation entrepreneurs are the use of personal networks, trust, and trustworthiness. Trustworthiness, often in combination with credit-worthiness, appeared in all the interviews.

"I think tribe is important for the Chinese. Trust is very important, but how do we build trust? It starts with tribe, this leads to a familiarity that shapes a bond and sympathy and this opens the road to do business together. Trust networks are the basis. If the trust network is strong everything is possible" (small tile factory owner interviewed in 2004).

"I mostly work with Chinese; trust is very important among the Chinese. We work on recommendation. Before a deal, first information is sought via other Chinese on the reputation and most importantly on the credibility of the other" (small automobile and motorcycle shop owner interviewed in 2004).

"Trust has been very important in setting up my own business. Access to capital is much easier through my trust relationships" (sanitary sales shop owner interviewed in 2004).

"The trust relationship is based on the fact that we know each other but we have to have a good relationship. If I want to approach someone I do not know yet and who does not know me, this has to go via a close friend of this person. Otherwise it is not possible. This will bring the two together. The community knows who can be trusted and who not" (small drugstore owner interviewed in 2004).

5.2 *The older generation on doing business with "local" entrepreneurs*

These personal networks are not only a basis for access to capital and goods; often the use of these networks is seen as synonymous with trust and trustworthiness and inherently different from *local* ways of doing business.

"In general Chinese seek other Chinese for businesses. The chance that I start a business with a local is very small. This is because their sense of business is very different. If Chinese people make a profit they save it in order to open a new store or to invest again, buy new equipment but also for educational purposes" (small computer sales and repair shop owner interviewed in 2004).

"Most of my business relations are with other Chinese because the locals have different feelings of responsibility. For a Chinese it is important that if he does not live up to his financial promises he will loose his name. Responsibility is very important. If this is jeopardized the relationship ends" (small printing business owner interviewed in 2004).

"In business, personal networks are most important, and these are most often also the Chinese personal networks. The family network is stronger among the Chinese than among the local population" (medium printing and publishing business owner interviewed in 2004).

5.3 *The older generation on the younger generation*

Although this generation mentions the importance of such trust and credit networks, they also frequently make remarks about the younger generation who does not exhibit these values and practices any longer.

"The younger Chinese are not really trustworthy. They have not been to Chinese schools and thus are difficult to trust. The later generations who went to Indonesian schools did get the same lessons. One of the most important moral lessons according to me is: don't ever forget the people that have helped you. This is very strong among the Chinese with that background. Such morals are disappearing especially among the younger Chinese" (interior design store owner interviewed in 2004).

"Next to personal networks and trust, helping each other is prominent among the Chinese of my generation. This is breaking down among the generation after me. My parents only had a small business, just enough to keep the family going. So I had no start-up capital. Based on the culture that the Chinese always help each other I was able to organize a savings group and start a business of my own" (small drugstore owner interviewed in 2004).

5.4 *Inspired by migration history*

Hence, good relationships, trust- and creditworthiness, responsibility and good name, and helping each other are mentioned as important business values and ways in which access to capital and partners was established. The stories are filled with qualifications that make 'the Chinese way of doing business' the best way. This is often linked to a history of migration:

> "Our forefathers migrated from China with nothing; only their shirts. They were courageous and had spirit. They went everywhere. They started to change what was around them. Also with trade one can create richness. But thinking ahead is very important; I have the feeling the local groups do not think about tomorrow as we do, I don't know why" (small drugstore owner interviewed in 2004).

> "The Chinese are very dynamic, they are never satisfied with the way things are. They always want more. You can either judge this as positive or negative. It is the same to me. This is the way it is. We are not satisfied with a *status quo*. Already my parents told me this. This is because the Chinese people here are migrants, people who wanted to change things, people who were brave enough to take many risks, to leave behind everything without knowing if they would be successful. That is the background" (small computer sales and repair shop owner interviewed in 2004).

The picture that emerges from the above is one in which the older generation juxtaposes itself against the local population but also against the younger generation ethnic Chinese. The older generation feels the younger generation is influenced by the Indonesian surroundings and culture in which they grew up in which there was no room for anything "Chinese." They stress certain Chinese business practices and styles such as building trust, the role of reputation via word of mouth, personal networks and the role of the family and some of this is strongly related to the migration history. They also feel such practices are becoming less among the younger generation because the latter have grown up in an Indonesia where these values are not deep-seated; and there is a strong stereotyping of a Chinese way of doing business versus local ways of doing business, in which the former is seen as the more successful way. Even though several nuances are made, such as the pragmatism and the profit focus which might jeopardize certain acclaimed values, the discursive practices employed express a strong belief in the business practices of the older generation ethnic Chinese entrepreneurs, as they have been constitutive in setting up a business in the small and medium sized sector and in running it. In the next section I shall elaborate on this older versus younger generation discourse.

5.5 *And the younger generation?*

The generational differences as expressed by the older generation of Chinese Indonesian entrepreneurs represent an interesting phenomenon that is worth further exploration. Their narratives reflect on the differences between their business conduct and morals and those of the younger generation. There is disappointment and a feeling of loss in their voices, especially the loss of Chinese business practices, values and customs. Is this merely an older generation expressing that things were much better in the past (which is often seen as a common generational phenomenon)? How about the younger generation? Do they fit the discourse of the older entrepreneurs?

All of the younger entrepreneurs argued that "Chinese traditions" are no longer important for them. In most cases expressions of what they refer to as Chinese traditions are restricted to Chinese New Year and eating Chinese food. In their daily life they state that they feel Indonesian:

> "If I had lived in China I would have loved China. But I was born in Indonesia, so I am Indonesian. If people ask me where I am from I always reply that I am Indonesian, not that I am Chinese" (small car repair shop owner interviewed in 2004).
>
> "We, the younger generation are more influenced by the local culture and therefore maybe less Chinese. I think we can say that Chinese family values are more and more disappearing with each new generation" (small marketing firm owner interviewed in 2004).
>
> "There are no real Chinese traditions that we still follow; it is not strong anymore. At most during Chinese New Year we great each other in Chinese and the younger children go to the older relatives to offer good wishes. But that is all. We are in fact Indonesians; there is already an Indonesian flavor to our culture" (small contracting business owner interviewed in 2004).

Interestingly enough, however, in business matters being Chinese is seen as important. According to the younger generation, when it comes to doing business Chineseness does make a difference. In this regard their discourse resembles very much the discourse of the older generation:

"Chinese people have a better eye for business; Chinese are more focused on how to make the business into a success compared to the Javanese." (small car repair business owner interviewed in 2004).

"In fact for me, being Chinese equals hard work and being in business" (small multilevel marketing firm owner interviewed in 2004).

"When in business it is not okay to relax. The Chinese never do, a real entrepreneur is ready to take risks and not to sit back and feel comfortable. It took several years before I understood that certain business practices of my mother are quite important. I learned that in business the Chinese way of always being involved in relationships is very important; one never knows when these come in handy" (small sanitary sales shop owner interviewed in 2007).

"I just trust the Chinese more in doing business, many Chinese are entrepreneurs, and they are keen businessmen" (small household supply distributor interviewed in 2004).

"In business, working with Chinese is just the better option because they have more business talent. At the same time there is mutual understanding, that's a nice way to do business" (small mobile phone repair shopkeeper interviewed in 2004).

5.6 *Education changes everything?*

A prominent issue in the stories of both generations is the influence of the changing educational background and the related ideas on how to run a business.

"Doing business is not something you can inherit easily. The children don't understand why the father was successful. By the time they take over, it becomes problematic. Some, however, do a better job. One of the problems is that the children get their diplomas abroad, MBA's from other countries. There they learn how to become professional. However, management and professionalism is only a tool, it is not yet a successful business. How to run a successful business cannot be studied abroad. So according to me the fact that the children do not focus on the business practices as conducted by their father, prevents them from understanding the success. In fact they might be smarter but business is not just a science" (small computer sales and repair shop owner; older generation entrepreneur interviewed in 2007).

"When I was asked to join the family business, I did so. However, it was not really a success. This was because my mother, who in fact still runs the business, felt she became useless because I started to work with computers while she did the bookkeeping still by hand. With my MBA from America I came in with new ideas and technology which she did not want. She also disliked the choices I made in management and in recruiting personnel; she could not understand why I was only sitting behind a desk in the back office all the time instead of being at the counter in the store to oversee the business" (small sanitary sales shop; younger generation entrepreneur interviewed in 2007).

6. Meaning-making

The voices above are those of ethnic Chinese entrepreneurs active in small and medium sized enterprises in Indonesia. They narrate about their business conduct and ponder about possible generational shifts. What stands out is that *both* the younger and the older generation entrepreneurs emphasize the importance of "being Chinese" in terms of business mentality and practice. "Being Chinese" seems to fuse ethnic identities and business or entrepreneurial identities. What the discursive practices have in common is that the ethnic Chinese entrepreneurs consider themselves to be more entrepreneurial compared to non-Chinese entrepreneurs. The ethnic Chinese are focused on the success of the business; they will invest their profits in new business opportunities, rely on hard work and are risk oriented. Both generations also seem to share a preference for doing business or for partnering up with "Chinese"; whereas the older generations mainly speak in terms of trust, trustworthiness, helping each other and reputation, we can see that the younger generation is focused more on business talent and being a keen business person which can be expressions of educational differences. But in both cases, the trustworthy and more talented partner is ethnic Chinese or Chinese Indonesian.

Notwithstanding this overlap in thinking that the ethnic Chinese are more entrepreneurial and business minded, the older generation is disappointed that the younger generation no longer makes use of the business practices, values and styles they consider important and "Chinese," such as Chinese personal networks, Chinese trust relationships and helping each other (as in other Chinese) without direct benefits. For most of the older entrepreneurs, these Chinese values are closely related to having been educated in Chinese schools. With the arrival of the New Order and the banning of Chineseness from public life these values have been lost in their eyes. Comments made by the older generation point into the direction of the different (non-Chinese) cultural influences in which this younger generation grew up. However, they also feel that their own aspirations to have their children educated abroad are part of this change, as this teaches their children many different and new ways of running a business.

The discursive and contextual focus shows that the older generation wants to reinstall the content of Chineseness from the times before it was erased and silenced by state policies in the 1960s. Their discourse returns explicitly to those times and relates how both Chinese manners and business practices were put to a halt under a regime in which they could no longer employ (at least in the open) their cultural values and norms. As a result, their children who have grown-up under the assimilation politics have lost this rich heritage. Obviously, at home these Chinese norms and values were still part and parcel of family life; but they were certainly not part of the public spheres in which their children acted out in daily life. The younger generation seems to reflect this partly in their expressions that Chinese "traditions" are disappearing and no longer very relevant for them, but much less so in their business practices. The way in which the younger generations set up their businesses reveals that relationships, networking and trust still matter. Most partnerships are with other ethnic Chinese, often referred to as friends they know from school or their church. Thus, the voices of the younger generation offer a more mixed message: they state to be and feel Indonesian, but in business matters they juxtapose themselves with Indonesians (Javanese in this case).

7. Concluding Remarks

In this chapter I have opted for a discursive-contextual approach in exploring generational change in small business conduct among ethnic Chinese entrepreneurs in Indonesia because this informs us not only about the business practices but also about the ideological, socio-cultural, and political bearings that lie underneath them. These dimensions cannot be ignored if we discuss business practices in Indonesia, particularly because of the "contested" position of ethnic Chinese citizens in Indonesia's history (Freedman, 2000; Hoon, 2006).

To a large extent the voices of older and younger generations are expressions of the different historical, political, and cultural contexts in which the generations grew up (Pilcher, 1993; Edmunds and Turner, 2005). For instance migration for the older generation versus nationalism and nation state building for the younger generation; Chinese schools for the older generations and New Order and foreign education for the younger generation; Chinese cultural contexts versus more Indonesian or in this case Javanese cultural settings for the younger generations. By understanding entrepreneurship as closely intertwined with the context in which it occurs, it is argued that such contextual settings subsequently have bearings on how the entrepreneurs perceive of their business conduct (Van Gelderen and Masurel, 2011). Some shifts have been noted, however, the more revealing outcome is that both generations seem to have internalized quite specific views on the entrepreneurial qualities of their community. These discursive expressions concern an inward looking perspective (on the self as entrepreneur) and do not narrate about interactions with customers or buyers.

From the contextual approach adopted in this chapter, the interpretation of why both the older and younger generations ethnic entrepreneurs active in small and medium sized companies express the value of personal networks that are intra-ethnically based is quite possibly related to the fact that under the circumstances of an oppressive system, such as the assimilation policy and the manipulation of ethnic identities by nation policies, staying within one's own community is a "safe" and "proven" way. Maybe the migration history and coping with a intimidating environment is still a very prominent collective memory (Bradsley, 2003; Ooi, 2007). This contextual interpretation is, however, only one possible interpretation. It might be interesting to explore more social psychological interpretations in future research studies.

Looking back at the on-going debate on how to explain the predominance of ethnic Chinese business conduct in the Southeast Asian region, it can be concluded that the business practices as such show an interesting mixture of "cultural values" and "best practices business-wise"; in fact a merging of the cultural and critical perspectives. The discursive, contextual and generational approach thus provides us with a more nuanced understanding of 'ethnic Chinese' business acumen in an Indonesian setting.

References

Bardsley, A (2003). The politics of "seeing Chinese" and the evolution of a Chinese idiom of business. In *Ethnic Business: Chinese Capitalism in Southeast Asia*, KS Jomo and BC Folk (eds.), pp. 26–51. London, UK: Routledge.

Chan, K-B (ed.) (2000). *Chinese Business Networks: State, Economy and Culture*. Singapore: Prentice Hall and Copenhagen Nordic Institute of Asian Studies.

Dahles, H (2007). On (mis-)conceptions of culture as a vehicle of business success: Singapore Chinese investment strategies after failing in China. *East Asia: An International Quarterly*, 24(2), 173–193.

Down, S and J Reveley (2004). Generational encounters and the social formation of entrepreneurial identity: "Young guns" and "old farts". *Organization*, 11(2), 233–250.

Edmunds, J and B Turner (2005). Global generations: Social change in the twentieth century. *British Journal of Sociology*, 56(4), 559–577.

Freedman, A (2000). *Political Participation and Ethnic Minorities. Chinese Overseas in Malaysia, Indonesia and the United States*. London, UK: Routledge.

Gomez, ET (2007). Family firms, transnationalism and generational change: Chinese enterprise in Britain and Malaysia. *East Asia: An International Quarterly*, 24(2), 153–172.

Gomez, ET and H-HM Hsiao (2004). Introduction: Chinese business research in Southeast Asia. In *Chinese Business in Southeast Asia: Contesting Cultural Explanations, Researching Entrepreneurship*, ET Gomez and H-HM Hsiao (eds.), pp. 1–37. Richmond: Curzon Press.

Gomez, ET and G Benton (2004). Introduction: De-essentializing capitalism: Chinese enterprise, transnationalism, and identity. In *Chinese Enterprise, Transnationalism, and Identity*, ET Gomez and H-HM Hsiao (eds.), pp. 1–19. London and New York: Routledge Curzon.

Hefner, R (1998). Introduction: Society and morality in the new Asian capitalisms. In *Market Cultures: Society and Morality in the New Asian Capitalisms*, R Hefner (ed.), pp. 1–36. Boulder: Westview Press.

Hoon, C-Y (2006). Assimilation, multiculturalism, hybridity: The dilemmas of the ethnic Chinese in post-Suharto Indonesia. *Asian Ethnicity*, 7(2), 149–166.

Janesick, V (1998). The dance of qualitative research design: Metaphor, methodolatry, and meaning. In *Strategies of Qualitative Inquiry*, N Denzin and Y Lincoln (eds.). London, UK: Sage Publications.

Koning, J (2007). Chineseness and Chinese Indonesian business practices: A generational and discursive enquiry. *East Asia: An International Quarterly*, 24(2), 129–152.

Koning, J and A Susanto (2008). Chinese Indonesians and "the rise of China": From business opportunities to questions of identity. In *China in the World: Contemporary Issues and Perspectives*, EK-K Yeoh and JH-L Loh (eds.), pp. 161–184. Kuala Lumpur: Institute of China Studies, University of Malaya Press.

Koning, J and M Verver (2013). Historicizing the "ethnic" in ethnic entrepreneurship: The case of the ethnic Chinese in Bangkok. *Entrepreneurship & Regional Development: An International Journal*.

Ly-yun, C and T Tam (2004). The making of Chinese business culture: Culture versus organizational imperatives. In *Chinese Enterprise, Transnationalism, and Identity*, ET Gomez and H-HM Hsiao (eds.), pp. 23–38. London and New York: Routledge Curzon.

Mannheim, K (1952). The problem of generations. In *Karl Mannheim. Essays on the Sociology of Knowledge*, P Kecskemeti (ed.). London, UK: Routledge and Kegan Paul.

Masurel, E and P Nijkamp (2004). Differences between first-generation and second-generation ethnic start-ups. *Environment and Planning C: Government and Policy*, 22, 721–737.

Menkhoff, T and S Gerke (eds.) (2004). *Chinese Entrepreneurship and Asian Business Networks*. London, UK: Routledge Curzon.

Miles, MB and AM Huberman (1994). *Qualitative Data Analysis: An Expanded Sourcebook,* 2nd Edition. London, UK: Sage Publications.

Ooi, C-S (2007). Un-packing packaged cultures: Chineseness in international business. *East Asia: An International Quarterly*, 24(2), 111–128.

Ooi, C-S and J Koning (2007). Introduction: The business of identity. *East Asia: An International Quarterly*, 24(2), 107–110.

Pilcher, J (1994). Mannheim's sociology of generations: An undervalued legacy. *The British Journal of Sociology*, 45(3), 481–495.

Redding, G (1990). *The Spirit of Chinese Capitalism*. Berlin and New York, UK: Walter de Gruyter.

Rusinovic, K (2006). *Dynamic Entrepreneurship. First and Second-Generation Immigrant Entrepreneurs in Dutch Cities*. Amsterdam: Amsterdam University Press.

Suryadinata, L (1993). The state and the Chinese minority in Indonesia, In *Chinese Adaptation and Diversity. Essays on Society and Literature in Indonesia, Malaysia & Singapore,* L Suryadinata (ed.). Singapore: Singapore University Press.

Suryadinata, L EN Arifin and A Ananta (2003). *Indonesia's Population. Ethnicity and Religion in a Changing Political Landscape*. Singapore: Institute of Southeast Asian Studies.

Van Gelderen, M and E Masurel (eds.) (2011). *Entrepreneurship in Context*. London, UK: Routledge.

Weidenbaum, M and S Hughes (1996). *The Bamboo Network: How Expatriate Chinese Entrepreneurs Are Creating a New Economic Superpower in Asia*. New York, NY: Free Press.

Winarta, F (2004). Racial discrimination in the Indonesian legal system: Ethnic Chinese and nation-building. In *Ethnic Relations and Nation-Building in Southeast Asia. The Case of the Ethnic Chinese*, L Suryadinata (ed.), pp. 66–81. Singapore: ISEAS Publications.

Chapter 11

The Salim Group: The Art of Strategic Flexibility

Marleen Dieleman

1. Introduction

After successfully surviving the Asian crisis, Anthony Salim, CEO and president of the Salim Group, now has time to focus on the future development of the Group for the next decades. Before the Asian crisis, the future seemed bright for Indonesia's largest family conglomerate. It consisted of hundreds of separate companies, in a variety of countries, grew rapidly and had an annual turnover of over US$20 billion by 1995.

By late 1997, however, the outlook for the group changed completely. Having been a close friend of the Suharto family, the Salim Group went out of favour during the Asian crisis. Their Bank Central Asia (BCA), the largest commercial bank in Indonesia, along with many other Indonesian banks, had to be rescued and recapitalised by the government. Anthony Salim suddenly had to raise some US$5 billion to repay the government. To the surprise of many he cooperated and handed over 107 companies to pay off his debts. By openly submitting his assets to the Indonesian Bank Restructuring Agency (IBRA), Anthony Salim was the first and only obligor who, at that time, seriously tried to repay his company's debt to the monetary authorities of Indonesia.

Now, a few years later, the worst problems are dealt with and Anthony Salim has time to re-consider the strategy of what was once one of the largest Asian conglomerates. He sees the main business opportunities in

This is a reprint of an article originally published in *Asian Case Research Journal*, 10(1), 1–25 (2006). The editors gratefully acknowledge the permission to reprint the article in this edition.

mediating on the axis between Australia, ASEAN and China — where he believes business will be lucrative.

Rather than being a product-based company focussing on core business — like many big western multinationals — he has a radically different corporate strategy. He insists on remaining flexible in order to capture whatever opportunities may arise, regardless of the products or services. But as Anthony Salim stated: "whether this is the right strategy for the group is the one-million dollar question."

2. History of the Salim Group

2.1 *The beginning*

In 1938, Liem Sioe Liong, second son of a rice farmer, arrived in Indonesia from Fujian province in South China with little more than the clothes on his back. He joined some relatives in Java who were active in a peanut oil business. After a while, he changed his name to Soedono Salim[1] and set up his own trading business, mainly in basic commodities like cloves and coffee through his companies P.T. Waringin and P.T. Mega. He also supplied goods to the Indonesian army during and after the struggle for independence from Dutch colonial rule. It was during those times that he became acquainted with a young army officer by the name of Suharto.

2.2 *Early expansion and diversification*

After the independence of Indonesia, during the Sukarno era, the business environment became very politically oriented and closed. Despite this, even in those early times, Liem was successful and started to diversify and become active in processed goods as well as trading, following his belief that "all businesses are good." Some textile factories started operating as well as a soap factory; and what was to become the group's main bank, the BCA bank, was established in 1957. As Anthony Salim, the son of

---

[1]The Javanese meaning of this is the following: soe = good; dono = capital; sa = three (referring to three brothers) and Lim stands for Liem.

Liem Sioe Liong explains: "the group evolved not by design, but by necessity. Whatever opportunity was good, we just grabbed."

In 1966, when President Suharto came to power, the business context changed and a new economic policy emerged in which industries opened up for private investment. Liem, who benefited from his earlier contacts with Suharto, started to see this new business environment as an opportunity. Using a combination of business skills and political contacts, he acquired several export licenses and held import monopolies on cloves, an ingredient for the popular Indonesian *kretek* cigarettes. These trading businesses in basic commodities gave Liem large and steady annual revenue.

2.3 *Industrialization*

From 1970 onward, when many Asian governments promoted import substitution industrialisation, Liem used these revenues to diversify into various industrial activities. Apart from textiles and finance, the group set up activities in flour milling around 1971–1972, cement in 1974 and automotive industries in 1975.

In all these industries favorable conditions were created by the government in order to promote the industrialization of Indonesia. Activities in other industries such as real estate, construction and plantations were started as well. Many of the Salim companies were market leaders or held monopolies.

During that time, the family also benefited from its regional ethnic Chinese networks around Asia. The Bangkok Bank in Thailand, for example, was helpful in funding some of the liquidity requirements.

2.4 *Designing the portfolio*

It was probably around 1972 that a crossover occurred in the strategy of the Salim Group. Rather than being driven completely by opportunity, the group began selecting its business opportunities. It also started to introduce professional management in addition to family management and attempted to decrease the dependency on government contracts. It began to become more market based in its outlook and strategy. It also gained access to international business networks, including the international capital market by listing its companies in Hong Kong, Jakarta, Singapore and elsewhere.

Having outgrown its home markets, from 1975 onward, the family business expanded internationally to Hong Kong, the Philippines, Singapore and The Netherlands. Around 35 percent of the assets are presently outside Indonesia and 65 percent within.

Along with the change in economic policy from import substitution industrialization to export-led growth in the 1980s, the *Salim Group* started to organize its businesses along the value chain. In food, for example, they attempted to control the whole chain from the Indonesian basic natural resources, the processing and transport up until the product reached the consumer through their retail chains. The result was a powerful and diversified conglomerate, an organization structure that was typical for many ethnic Chinese family firms in Asia, but also for family firms in other countries like Mexico and Brazil.

2.5 *Rapid growth in the 1990s*

In 1993, Liem Sioe Liong passed on the leadership of the family business to one of his sons: Anthony Salim — although he himself remained active in the group on various boards of directors or as a commissioner. Anthony Salim, who started his career in 1971 after graduating from a London technical college, continued the path toward appointing professional managers to run the ever expanding empire. The family business was slowly transferred to the second generation.

In the 1990s, Anthony Salim remembers, "it was as if every business you touched turned into gold." This booming era for many Southeast Asian countries induced the rise of conglomerates — many of them run by former Chinese immigrants. Especially in Indonesia, where many of the largest businesses saw a rapid increase in wealth, a large proportion of the main conglomerates were owned by the Indonesian Chinese, a minority that made up only around 3.5 percent of the population.

By 1995, the Salim Group had become a giant and was estimated to generate around 5 percent of Indonesian GDP. It was probably the largest conglomerate, not only in Indonesia, but in Southeast Asia generating a turnover of more than US$20 billion and employing hundreds of thousands of people (see Annex 1 which gives an overview of the *Salim Group* prior to the crisis).

When the Salim Group, by then closely connected with the presidential family, tried to move its noodle company out of Indonesia under the umbrella of a Singapore-based affiliate, many suspected that the group had inside information on upcoming political changes, and there were rumours and speculations of capital flight and possible fall of President Suharto.

3. The Salim Group in Crisis

3.1 *The Asian crisis*

The economic boom of the 1990s would end in July 1997. During the period when capital poured into Southeast Asia, many businesses, among them the Salim Group, had started to borrow heavily from foreign banks, who offered substantially lower interest rates than local banks. The result was a general rise in the debt-to-equity ratio of many Asian companies, and an increase in dollar denominated loans. This made the corporate sector vulnerable to currency fluctuations.

When the Thai currency came under increasing pressure, the Indonesian government initially assured local con-glomerates that the Indonesian currency would not be devalued. This proved to be unsustainable. The rupiah started a rapid decline in late 1997 and 1998, causing a ballooning corporate debt since companies had most of their loans denominated in dollars whereas assets and income were measured in rupiah. Since financial institutions were generally not properly monitored, banks were suddenly stuck with increasing amounts of non performing loans. Many conglomerates also used their banks for inter-group lending, something officially not allowed but a common practice in Indonesia.[2]

Because of related lending and the widespread use of pyramid ownership structures nobody really knew what condition the large conglomerates were in. At the same time these conglomerates controlled large chunks of the Indonesian economy.

---

[2]The legal limit for this was a maximum of 20 percent but this was violated by most banks owned by Indonesian conglomerates.

4. The Fall of Suharto

This general analysis of the corporate sector also applied to the Salim Group. Being widely known by the public as "cronies" of President Suharto, the group's debt problems only became worse during the period up to the fall of Suharto on May 21, 1998.

The Suharto family had a considerable stake in their BCA bank, and all kinds of rumours spread in Indonesia. This resulted in a bank run on BCA by worried customers. For weeks, people were lining up to withdraw their money. Having initially tried to rescue the bank, on May 20, 1998 the Salim family gave up and handed over the bank to the government for recapitalization.[3]

Public anger was mostly directed at the Suharto family and his so-called "cronies," mostly Chinese businesses, among which the Salim Group was considered the largest. Indonesia witnessed yet another period of violence against the Chinese minority and the family house of the Salims in Jakarta was set on fire. Within this hostile environment, the top management of the group withdrew to Singapore for a few weeks to monitor how things were evolving from a political perspective.

4.1 *Facing reality*

In a profoundly different political situation, the newly appointed government, together with the IMF, started to draft the new rules of the game. They came up with plans on how to deal with the financial, monetary and corporate sector. In the last category, the Salim Group was by far the largest debtor, owing some US$5 billion in total. The government established the Indonesian Bank Restructuring Agency (IBRA) which was tasked with recovering these debts, either in cash or in assets. Assets that IBRA received were subsequently sold on to investors or the general public.

According to Anthony Salim, "Our approach is: ok, we open up. We don't believe that negotiation will be hide and seek. This is our wealth; now let's negotiate how this is going to solve the problem." The government and the Salim Group both appointed investment banks, and in a relatively short time the group signed an agreement and handed over

---

[3]Newspapers reported that the BCA Bank was placed under government supervision on May 28, 1998 (*Associated Press*, May 28, 1998).

107 companies to the government, the assets at that time in 1998 being valued at the total obligations of US$5 billion (see Annex 3 for an overview of Salim assets and shares transferred to the government).

In a political country like Indonesia, known for its widespread corruption, this process caused political turmoil. Rumours kept on circulating, and governments, ministers and chairmen of IBRA changed frequently. Public criticism focused on the question of why the government made an arrangement with the Salim Group to allow them to manage the 107 transferred assets, and on whether several corporate debtors were trying to buy back assets that were now cheaply sold by IBRA.

When the last Salim assets were sold by IBRA in 2003 the government obtained a total of around US$2 billion, a recovery rate of around 40 percent. Many in the general public complained since they felt that the remaining balance had to be covered by the Indonesian public. Nevertheless, Salim is generally believed to be the most cooperative debtor from whom most debts were recovered. As one IBRA employee put it: "It was such an emotional period. Anthony Salim got us through by just focusing on the problem." Anthony Salim admits that the group has learnt a few very hard lessons. But the issue is: "Simply face reality. Confront the problems. Never give up."

5. Ownership and Organization Structure of the Salim Group

5.1 *Confederation under private holding*

The Salim Group is a loosely connected confederation of companies that does not operate under one legal basis. It is linked through investments, sometimes direct, sometimes indirect through a range of holding companies and proxies (see, for example, the ownership structure of First Pacific Company in Annex 4). Whether or not a company belongs to the Salim Group is often a matter of inside information or rumours, as the group only publishes results of its publicly listed companies, not of the private operating units or private holding companies. Anthony Salim comments that "a private holding is much more flexible, but it does not mean that we have no checks and balances. We operate with very stringent rules." The holding company has the following units: legal affairs and taxation; internal audit and financial analysis; treasury; and human resource management.

5.2 *Controlling shareholders*

The family-controlled Salim holding is chaired by Liem, whereas the day-to-day decisions are made by president and CEO Anthony Salim, assisted by his top management, including executive director Benny Santoso and many other executives. Some investments are done by the so-called "group of Liem investors" which include the Liem family (Liem Sioe Liong and his son Anthony Salim); the Djuhar family (Sutanto Djuhar[4] and his son Tedy Djuhar); and two Indonesians, Ibrahim Rishad and Sudwikadmono, the latter being a cousin of Suharto. An example of a "Liem Investor" company is First Pacific Company (the ownership structure and composition of the board of directors of First Pacific Company is displayed in Annex 4 & 5).

The general pattern is that the Salim family tends to have the majority of shares in the main operating companies, which are ultimately controlled by a privately held holding company. In addition to those companies jointly owned by the Liem Investors, such as First Pacific Company and Indocement, the Salim family also has other companies on its own, such as Indomobil and the group's palm oil plantations.

The family actively controls the operating companies. The board of executive directors of a Salim operating company generally is composed of professionals. But Anthony Salim may hold a position on the supervisory board or as a (non)executive director, along with Benny Santoso (see, for example, the composition of the board of First Pacific Company in 2003 in Annex 5). Apart from official board meetings, informal meetings with the managing directors and Anthony Salim may take place if major decisions need to be made.

5.3 *Group size and structure*

The total group consists of hundreds of separate legal entities in a variety of industries and directly employs more than 100,000 people scattered around the Pacific region. The main contributors to the profits of the Salim

---

[4] An old friend of Liem whom he met in Java; also originally from Fujian.

Group are the listed companies in which the group has a stake. The listed companies in which the Salim family is involved include:

Company	Industries	Main countries
Indofood	Noodles	Indonesia
First Pacific Company**	Telecom, Property, Trading, Food	Philippines, Indonesia, Hong Kong
PLDT	Telecom	Philippines
Indomobil*	Automotive	Indonesia
Indocement*	Cement	Indonesia
Indosiar*	Media	Indonesia
BCA*	Banking	Indonesia
UIC	Chemicals	Indonesia
Futuris	Agro-business, various	Australia
QAF	Food	Singapore & other countries
Cosco Development	Property	China

*Shareholding of the Salim family substantially reduced after the Asian crisis.
**This company owns a substantial stake in Indofood (since 1999) and PLDT.

The non-listed companies include companies in the following sectors:

- Property (residential areas, industrial estates and resorts mainly in Indonesia).
- Plantations (palm oil plantations in Indonesia).
- Telecommunications (satellite TV and other media in Indonesia).
- Food (large pig farms in Bulan, close to Singapore, noodle factories in China and the Middle East, wheat production and trading in Australia).
- Insurance (several branches throughout Southeast Asia).

New business ventures often start out as a private company. Once developed, they may become listed on the stock exchange, or may be acquired by an already listed affiliated company. The Salim Group is managed as a portfolio of investments. Each OPU (operating unit) has to be able to stand on its own feet. Nevertheless, there is a certain amount of cross-fertilisation between the group's OPUs in terms of financial transactions.

6. Management Practices of the Salim Group

6.1 *Corporate identity: Portfolio*

Anthony Salim does not see himself as a cement expert or a noodle producer. "See, we always think that we have no technology, no products. What we are good at is being close to the customer. We have the capacity to package from opportunity to reality and get the necessary management to organize it. This is our expertise."

The group is not really strong in technology. Whatever technology is necessary they would buy from a partner, like, for example, from *Suzuki* in the automotive business. According to Anthony Salim, the synergy between the seemingly different types of businesses of retail (Indomarco) noodles (Indofood) and a TV station (Indosiar) is more in understanding consumer trends. "If you are able to understand the shelf, where people are buying; the product produced by Indofood; and TV, then you can understand the behavior of the people that are going to buy. Synergy for us means that we understand how people are creating new products."

The Salim Group is always open to new opportunities. They are regularly approached by possible partners in various projects and businesses, which is mostly the reason why the group starts in a new industry. Take, for example, the large plantations, which were initially developed in a partnership with another Indonesian group. Later the Salim plantations, initially privately owned, were sold to publicly listed company Indofood. In joint ventures, the Salim Group attempts to learn to manage that type of business, enabling them to find more opportunities in that industry on their own. According to Benny Santoso, "Opportunities arise every day. So, sometimes we have to make quick decisions in order to grab the opportunity."

6.2 *Management style*

Anthony Salim is a very hard worker, informally dressed in an Indonesian style batik shirt. He generally comes in around 10 am and works until after midnight to run his family empire. Why? His motto is: "The worst competitor is Salim. If you can compete with yourself all the time you're advancing and you'll be able to survive. Strength is given; weakness is something you have to improve."

He calls the group's culture informal and open. When talking about management style, Anthony Salim's explains "the basic philosophy is still the same. I don't think we change. Still family oriented, still more informal than formal. When you talk about measurement we are very strict." The strict internal measurement is facilitated by a large number of internal auditors employed by the group and tasked with monitoring the performance of the different businesses in detail. Anthony Salim is also known as someone with an in-depth knowledge of his various businesses. "I always believe that people who do not control details will not able to perform well. This is my basic belief. I certainly don't believe that if you are only talking generalisations you are able to generate ideas or meet the standards that you want."

He spends around 80 percent of his time in Indonesia, the other 20 percent travelling. His attention is divided between making new contacts and business relations and monitoring OPUs. Although there is no need to visit them in the field, being controlled by his professional managers, Anthony Salim spends considerable amounts of time to review very detailed information on each OPU. Aside from that he reads very widely, "I spend a lot of time reading materials not related to business, to understand where the world is going. Because by understanding what is outside your scope you will be able to do much better."

His previous involvement with the IMF and World Bank as well as his recent involvement in some advisory boards of large European companies like the German insurance giant Allianz and the Dutch bank Rabobank also enable him to monitor and learn from best practices of multinational corporations.

6.3 *Management information systems*

When the group grew so rapidly, an advanced management information and control system became crucial for being able to ensure accountability of the OPUs. Through his financial reporting system he is able to closely monitor the performance of all his companies in a detailed manner.

Anthony Salim explains that "We are using week-basis. If you are talking months, then you get your report on the 15th of next month, you do your corrections, and you can only do this every 3 months. If we use the weekly basis, you can make at least 48 corrections."

Although investments in this system are continuous, the group always looks at the yield. If it is necessary for an OPU to invest in a high-tech solution for generating management information, the group will certainly invest, but only depending on the necessity and the yield of the investment. Apart from internal rigorous control systems, most of the group's contributors to profit are listed companies, exposing them to the external control mechanisms of the market and (minority) shareholders.

6.4 *Human resources management*

Within Indonesia, the Salim Group is seen as one of the better run conglomerates, a forerunner in new corporate practices. People stay with the group for a very long time. During the Asian crisis, none of its top management left the company. In terms of human resources management the company gives excellent incentives to its management. Angky Camaro, former top-manager of Indomobil, commented: "I was working with Mercedes at that time. They just hijacked me and paid me a much higher salary than the multinationals would pay."

Yet, Anthony Salim believes this is an area where they can improve, basically finding the right managers has so far been an ad-hoc hiring process, they mostly rise to the top after many years with the company.

People describe the professional managers of the Salim Group as "characters on their own," strong personalities that may rebel against Anthony Salim and argue to prove their case. Despite the presence of strong personalities, it is Anthony Salim who is the final decision-maker when it comes to new acquisitions, strategic decisions or even implementing detailed corrections based on the weekly reports.

6.5 *Corporate communications*

The group manages to almost shield itself off from journalists and media completely. Despite the internal goal of transparency, the outside world is ignorant about the size and performance of the group as a whole. Even relative insiders such as board members of the OPUs do not know exactly what the Salim Group as a whole is up to. There is no public relations department, the last brochure dates from 1995, and the group follows the old Chinese motto of never to draw attention in a negative manner.

As Benny Santoso explains: "We don't give interviews to reporters, normally. In the past, because of our relationship with President Suharto, people are always skeptical. No matter what we say — it is always controversial. That's why Anthony's policy is to have a really low profile. Even if people accuse us we keep quiet." The group may have strict internal management information systems, but towards the outside world communication is restricted and low-profile.

7. Future Strategy

7.1 *Fire-fighting*

The crisis years were probably one of the most difficult periods in Anthony Salim's life, since much of his attention was devoted to solving his debt problems with both international banks and with the Indonesian government. At the moment he has more time for reflection and he is reviewing his OPUs in-depth one by one. As several businesses were lost during the crisis, the largest Salim Group companies are now First Pacific (which in turn owns large stakes in Indofood and PLDT) as well as a few smaller listed companies (such as QAF and UIC) and the remaining non-listed companies that were not handed over to the government. Having been distracted by the "fire-fighting" in his own backyard for too long, he is also looking at new opportunities to bring the group on track for the coming decades — until the next generation takes over.

7.2 *The axis of prosperity*

Instead of implementing far-reaching programmes of cost control; or returning to its core business and achieving economies of scale — strategies common to Western multinationals — the Salim Group follows an entirely different path.

The strategy for the future has already been designed, albeit in an abstract sense. One of the elements of the new strategy is a new geographical orientation, with less dependence on Indonesia and more focus on other regional economies, particularly China and Australia. Within the Asian region, Anthony Salim sees the WTO increasingly as a basic platform for business. He plans to focus his attention on the axis between Australia–ASEAN–China, where he believes a large number of business opportunities will arise. While explaining his strategy Anthony Salim uses various metaphors. He explains that he wants to link production sources in Australia to consumer markets in China and ASEAN: "It is like creating a toll-road with many stations."

Another element of the strategy relates to the composition of the portfolio. Previously the Salim Group was involved in a very large number of smaller businesses. Anthony Salim wants to focus much more on those industries he knows best — food, telecom, property, media. But he is not planning to limit the group to just one or two core businesses. Instead, his view is to capitalise on what he believes to be a key competence of the group: flexibility. On this axis of prosperity therefore, the Salim Group does not want to be a product based company: they will use their expertise and capital to mediate in any lucrative business in the region, be it in agribusiness, telecom or other activities. "The big multinationals may be strong in China, but they are still product-based. If you don't change, one day you wake up and you are under the sand, like the Greeks." Anthony Salim sees the new strategy of the Salim Group as a continuous transformation: "We have to transform ourselves to manage our resources. To transform our assets. It does not mean money, you see, it is whether we have the contacts. We believe we can operate in different markets."

Despite the impressive size of the group, Anthony Salim positions himself as a small player compared to some multinational giants such as Unilever and GE. "Big whales swim in the deep sea, in the salt water, but we are talking fresh water here." In order not to be eaten by the "big whales" his strategy is to maintain a majority stake in crucial group companies. Therefore the implementation of his future strategy will be limited by capital availability. According to Anthony Salim: "if you want to play music, you either have a full orchestra, a big band or a small chamber music trio. We start small, we don't need a nine-lane toll-road immediately."

7.3 *Strategy implementation*

In view of his goal to balance the portfolio more between Indonesia and other regional economies, Anthony Salim already initiated various activities in China, including a listed company in the property sector. Yet "we don't consider ourselves successful in China. We have mixed feelings because China is something new. But we have quite a good starting point." The group experienced some of the difficulties of the Chinese market when they tried to put Indonesian management in China. Anthony Salim explains: "it does not work. We need Chinese people in China. But with Indonesian values, Indonesian ways of doing things." Despite these difficulties the group CEO sees enormous potential in the Chinese market.

Australia is another area of attention for the group. The Salim Group recently acquired a pig farm in Australia, and a minority stake in a listed Australian conglomerate, Futuris, with wheat trading activities. It plans to bring the superior knowledge of Australian farming to less developed Asian economies. An example of this strategy is a recently started dairy farm in inner Mongolia.

The concentration on fewer businesses is also evident in the new investments done by the group after the crisis. The Asian crisis had already reduced the portfolio in terms of industries, since a number of firms were handed over to the government. New investments occur mainly in areas the group is familiar with, such as TV stations in Indonesia — one of the more recent investments. Most of the management attention goes to strengthening the existing food and telecom businesses, which entail a large share of the total revenue (see Annex 2 for turnover figures of key Salim Group companies).

7.4 *One-million-dollar question*

The main question running through Anthony Salim's mind is how he can ensure the future survival and growth of the Salim Group. Is his future strategy right? Has he repaired the weaknesses that surfaced in the crisis? What are the long term threats and opportunities, and how to prepare for them?

Annex 1. Salim Group overview before the Asian Crisis[5]

Division	Subdivisions	Approx. turnover 1995 (US$ million)
Agribusiness	Plantations	250
	Livestock	
	Floriculture	
Automotive & Shipping	Automotive	370*
	Shipping	
Banking and Financial Services (revenue)	Bank Central Asia (BCA)	11,000
	International Banking Insurance, leasing, money, securities brokerage	
Chemicals	Inorganic/ Petrobased Organic/ Oleochemicals Specialty Chemicals & others	1,000
Computers & Communications	Computers	Unknown
	Communications (TV)	
Construction Materials	Cement	1,100
	Galvanized Iron Sheets	
Food & Consumer Products	Processed Food	2,100
	Flour	
	Edible Oil	
	Consumer Products	
International	First Pacific Group (Hong Kong)	6,000
	KMP Group (Singapore)	
Multi-Industry	Textile	720
	Footwear	
	Packaging	
	Mosquito Coils	
	Pharmaceuticals	
	Steel	
Natural Resources	Coal	Unknown
	Granite	
	Oil and Gas	
	Forestry	

(Continued)

---

[5] *Source*: Salim Brochure, 1995–1996.

(*Continued*)

Division	Subdivisions	Approx. turnover 1995 (US$ million)
Property & Leisure Industry	Hotels	Unknown
	Resorts & Golf Courses	
	Real Estates	
	Commercial Buildings	
	Shopping Centers	
	Industrial Estates	
Trading & Distribution	Trading & Retailing	700
	Distribution	
Total revenue (approx.)		**20 billion US$**
Total # employees (approx.)		**200.000**

* vehicle sales only

** Bank Central Asia only

Annex 2: Turnover of listed Salim Group companies (1994–2003)[6]

	Indofood US$ mln	Indocement* US$ mln	First Pacific US$ mln	QAF US$ mln	Indomobil* US$ mln	Indosiar* US$ mln	UIC US$ mln
1994	622	1568	3804	206	1049	0	131
1995	930	1753	5249	231	1335	0	141
1996	1207	1824	7025	265	1361	53	157
1997	1715	540	8308	224	1557	65	156
1998	882	159	2894	243	172	15	125
1999	1470	254	1671	276	253	40	160
2000	1508	291	2299	284	598	71	167
2001	1408	332	1851	326	137	82	181
2002	1842	442	1892	477	194	110	172
2003	2115	491	2161	476	320	119	251

*Salim Group shareholding substantially reduced after the Asian Crisis.
NB: not corrected for cross-ownership or pyramid structures. Excludes BCA Bank (nationalized in 1998) as well as Futuris and Cosco (in which the *Salim Group* has been involved only recently).

---

[6] *Source*: Figures are calculated from annual reports of all mentioned companies and converted into USD using annual average historic rates posted by Asian Development Bank.

Annex 3: Salim Group & Asian Crisis[7]

Submitting assets to the Indonesian Bank Restructuring Agency

Holdiko Perkasa ("Holdiko") is a company established in relation to the settlement between the Salim Group and the Indonesian Bank Restructuring Agency ("IBRA") with regard to the liquidity credits provided to PT. Bank Central Asia ("BCA") and BCA loans to affiliated companies which exceeded the Legal Lending Limit. As part of the Settlement Agreement with IBRA, the Salim Group transferred shares and assets in 107 companies to Holdiko (...). The industries/sectors coverage of the companies under Holdiko are as follows:

Industries/sectors	Number of companies
Palm Plantation	24
Oils & Fats	3
Sugar	4
Coal & Granite	5
Plywood	4
Communication	1
Textile & Garment	3
Chlor Alkaly	4
Oleochemicals	9
Food & Consumer Product	10
Trading	3
Multi Industry	6
Property	25
Publicly listed	6

[7] *Source*: Holdiko Perkasa report (1999).

Holdiko's industry/sector coverage in percent based on the value of each company:

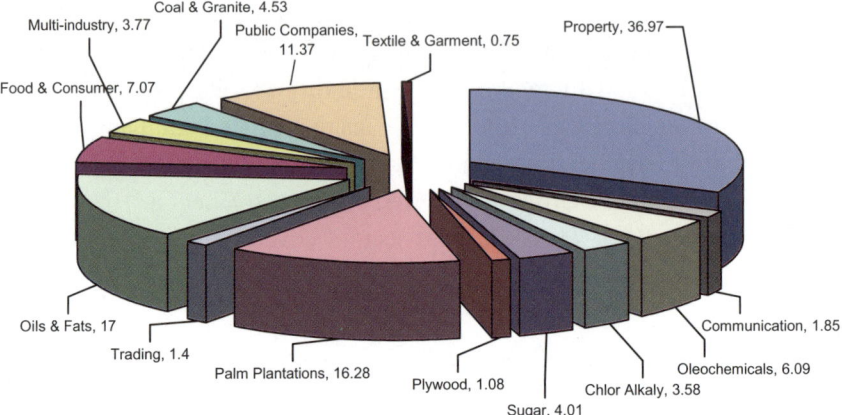

Annex 4: First Pacific Company: An example of ownership of the "Liem Investors"[8]

First pacific company: Interests of directors in the company and its associated corporations in 2003

(A) First Pacific; long position in shares

Name	Approx. percentage of issued share capital	
Sutanto Djuhar	30 percent interest	
Tedy Djuhar	10 percent interest	
Ibrahim Risjad	10 percent interest	
Anthoni Salim[9]	10 percent interest all via First Pacific Investments Limited[(i)]	24.80
Anthoni Salim	33.3 percent interest via First Pacific Investments (BVI) Limited[(ii)]	19.72
Manual Pangilinan		0.19
Edward A Torrorici		0.41

(i) Soedono Salim, the former Chairman, and Sudwikatmono, a former non-executive Director, respectively own 30.0 percent and 10.0 percent interests in First Pacific Investments Limited
(ii) Soedono Salim, the former Chairman, ownes a 33.3 percent interest in First Pacific Investments (BVI) Limited.

(B) Associated corporations; long positions in shares

* Manuel V Pangilinan owned 15,048,064 common shares(P) in Metro Pacific Corporation (MPC), 42,002 common shares(P) in Philippine Long Distance Telephone Company (PLDT) and 360 preferred shares(P) in PLDT as beneficial owner and a further 15,417 common shares in PLDT as nominee for another person, as well as 300,000 common shares(P) in Pilipino Telephone Corporation (PTC).
* Edward A Tortorici owned 2,450,000 ordinary shares(P) in P.T. Indofood Sukses Makmur Tbk (Indofood), 3,051,348 common

---

[8] *Source*: First Pacific Company, Annual Report (2003).
[9] The First Pacific annual report spells "Anthoni Salim" whereas in most other documents and on his business card the name is spelled "Anthony Salim." Since the annex quotes the First Pacific annual report the original spelling is retained.

shares(P) in MPC, 96,874 common shares(P) in PLDT and 5,000,000 common shares(P) in PTC.

- Sutanto Djuhar owned 15,520,335 ordinary shares(C) in Indofood.
- Tedy Djuhar owned 15,520,335 ordinary shares(C) in Indofood.
- Ibrahim Risjad owned 6,406,180 ordinary shares(P) in Indofood.
- Anthoni Salim owned 632,370 ordinary shares(C) in Indofood.
- Albert F Del Rosario owned 63,525 common shares(P) in PLDT, 1,560 preferred shares(P) in PLDT, 21,822,680 preferred shares(P) in Prime Media Holdings, Inc (PMH) as beneficial owner and a further 32,231,970 preferred shares in PMH as nominee for another person, 4 common shares(P) in PMH, 100 common shares(P) in Negros Navigation Company, Inc, 4,922 common shares(P) in Costa de Madera Corporation, 19,999 common shares(P) in FPD Savills Consultancy Philippines, Inc as beneficial owner and one common share in FPD Savills Consultancy Philippines, Inc as beneficiary of certain trusts, 4,999 common shares(P) in FPD Savills Philippines, Inc as beneficial owner and one common share(P) in FPD Savills Philippines, Inc as beneficiary of certain trusts, 15,000 common shares(P) in Metro Pacific Land Holdings Inc, and 80,000 common shares(P) in Metro Strategic Infrastructure Holdings, Inc.

(P) = Personal interest, (C) = Corporate interest

Annex 5: First Pacific Company: An Example of Control through Board of Directors

Composition of the board of First Pacific (June 2003)[10]

Manuel V Pangilinan, CEO and Managing Director [11]

Age 56, born in the Philippines. He served as First Pacific's Managing Director after founding the company in 1981, and was appointed Executive Chairman in February 1999. Mr Pangilinan also serves as President and CEO of PLDT; Chairman of Smart Communications, Inc; President Commissioner of Indofood; Chairman, President and CEO of Metro Pacific; Chairman of Landco Pacific Inc; and as a Director of Escotel and of Negros Navigation Inc.

Anthony Salim, Non-executive Chairman

Age 53, born in Indonesia. Mr Salim is the son of Soedono Salim and is President and CEO of the Salim Group. Mr. Salim is Commissioner of Indofood; Board Member of Futuris Corporation Limited; Member of the Advisory Board for ALLIANZ Group; and has served as a Director of First Pacific since 1981.

Albert F Del Rosario, Independent Non-executive Director

Mr Del Rosario is currently Philippine Ambassador to the United States and also serves as Non-executive Director of Philippine Long Distance Telephone Company ("PLDT").

Robert Charles Nicholson, independent Non-executive Director

Mr Nicholson is currently a special advisor to the Board of Directors of PCCW Limited and prior to that, was a senior partner of the Richards Butler law firm in Hong Kong.

Benny Santoso, Non-executive Director

---

[10] *Source*: First Pacific Company, Annual Report (2003).

[11] The information provided here is a summary of the rather long description given in the First Pacific Company annual report.

Mr Santoso currently serves as Director or Commissioner of various Salim Group companies. He is an advisor to the Board of PLDT.

Tedy Djuhar, Non-executive Director

Age 51, born in Indonesia. Mr Djuhar is Vice President Director of PT Indocement Tunggal Prakarsa Tbk, Director of Pacific Industries and Development Ltd, and a number of other Indonesian companies. He is the son of Sutanto Djuhar. Mr Djuhar joined First Pacific's Board in 1981.

Edward KY Chen, CBE, JP, Non-executive Director

Age *57,* born in Hong Kong and educated at the University of Hong Kong and Oxford University. Professor Chen serves as President of Lingnan University; Director of Asia Satellite Telecommunications and Eaton Vance Management Funds; and Non-executive Director of Wharf Holdings Limited. Formerly, he served as Chairman of Hong Kong's Consumer Council; as Executive Councilor of the Hong Kong Government; and as Legislative Councilor. He joined First Pacific's Board in 1993.

Ibrahim Risjad, Non-executive Director

Age 68, born in Indonesia. Mr Risjad serves as a Commissioner of PT Indocement Tunggal Prakarsa Tbk and as Vice President of the Board of Commissioners of Indofood. He joined First Pacific's Board in 1981.

Sutanto Djuhar, Non-executive Director

Age 74, born in Indonesia. Mr Djuhar has founded numerous Indonesian companies involved primarily in real estate development. He is a Commissioner of PT Kartika Chandra and serves as Director of PT Bogasari Flour Mills and Pacific Industries and Development Ltd. Mr Djuhar, who is the father of Tedy Djuhar, joined First Pacific's Board in 1981.

David WC Tang, Obe, Non-executive Director

Age 48, born in Hong Kong. Mr Tang is the founder of the Shanghai Tang stores and the China Clubs in Hong Kong, Beijing and Singapore, as well as the Pacific Cigar Company Ltd. He holds Hong Kong directorships on the Boards of Lai Sun Development Ltd and Free Duty Ltd; London directorships include the Boards of Asprey Ltd and Garrard Ltd; and the International Advisory Board of The Savoy Group of London. Mr Tang joined First Pacific's Board in 1989.

Edward A Tortorici, Executive Director

Age 63, born in the United States. Mr Tortorici received a BS from New York University and an MS from Fairfield University. He EA Edwards Associates, an international management and consulting firm with offices worldwide. Mr Tortorici joined First Pacific as an Executive Director in 1987, becoming responsible for organization and strategic planning. Mr Tortorici also serves as Director of Indofood, Metro Pacific, Bonifacio Land Corporation, Fort Bonifacio Development Corporation and ACeS.

Soedono Salim, Honorary Chairman and Advisor to the Board

Age 86, born in China. Mr Salim served as *First Pacific's* Chairman from 1981 until February 1999, when he assumed his current titles. He serves as Chairman of the Salim Group, and is Commissioner or Director of numerous other Indonesian companies.

Sudwikatmono, Advisor to the Board

Age 68, born in Indonesia. Mr Sudwikatmono served as Director of First Pacific from 1981 until February 1999, when he assumed his current title. He is Director of PT Bogasari Flour Mills, Vice President Commissioner of PT Indocement Tunggal Prakarsa Tbk and holds Board positions with a number of other Indonesian companies.

Part 3

Leadership, Knowledge and Learning in Chinese Business

Chapter 12

In Search of Asian Conceptions
of Leadership with a Focus on Mindfulness

Chay Yue Wah, Charles Chow, Hans-Dieter Evers,
Lee Cher Leng, Thomas Menkhoff, Jochen Reb,
Jayarani Tan and Elfarina Zaid

1. Introduction

Given the instability and volatility in current global markets, highly capable leadership in both public and private sectors is a key requirement to leverage on growth opportunities and to steer emerging Asia to greater heights. While there is still a large number of Western MNCs whose CEOs are reluctant to empower local (Asian) managers as corporate leaders, an increasing number of firms located in Asia are implementing strategic leadership development (LD) programs to ensure a sustainable talent pipeline and to combat the stigma of "accidental leadership transition." This term was coined by leadership experts Bruce Avolio and Peter Ong in one of their Asian Leader Studies (Avolio and Ong, 2008). Their research suggests that there are many Asian managers who became CEOs because they did well in their current positions and, as a result, increasingly were offered leadership roles. Others were members of the inner circle of family businesses which enabled them to occupy new leadership positions. Unlike a formalized LD program integrated into a strategic talent management framework (Day *et al.*, 2009), accidental leadership transition is incremental in nature. To tackle the shortage of effective leaders, emerging Asia needs to adopt best (strategic) LD initiatives. This is easier said than done.

2. In Search of Asian Leadership

While substantial research has been conducted to identify required competencies and attributes of effective leaders in Asia such as visionary thinking, courage or resilience, there is still widespread confusion when it comes to defining what is uniquely "Asian" in Asian leadership (Sinha, 1984; Xin and Tsui, 1996; Dorfman *et al.*, 1997; Jung and Avolio, 1999; Fu and Yukl, 2000; Javidan, 2006; Menkhoff *et al.*, 2008; Palrecha *et al.*, 2012). When asked about this, executives sometimes construct a simple dichotomy between the "assertive Western" and the "risk-averse Asian" corporate leader (Mills, 2005). Are such notions facts or fiction? Asian leadership traits arguably include humility and collectivism. Humility refers to the quality of being modest, reverential and politely submissive, which is in stark contrast to being arrogant, rude or self-abasing. Collectivism implies that group goals have priority over individual goals and that group cohesion is seen as something positive. In everyday corporate life which is increasingly diverse and complex, such traits can sometimes be in conflict with competing value systems imported through foreign talents from the US, Europe or other parts of Asia. So, what is the challenge when it comes to developing global leaders with an Asian focus?

One prominent study which has helped to shed light on such issues is the "Global Leadership and Organizational Behavior Effectiveness" study (in short, GLOBE) conceived by Robert J House from the Wharton School of Business, University of Pennsylvania (House *et al.* eds., 2004; Chhokar *et al.* eds., 2007). The GLOBE team surveyed over 17,000 middle managers from 951 organizations in the food processing, financial services, and telecommunications services industries in 62 societies across the globe to establish what is so unique when it comes to Asian leadership.

Building on Geert Hofstede's classic studies of how values in the workplace are influenced by culture, GLOBE empirically established nine cultural dimensions to capture the similarities and/or differences in norms, values, beliefs — and practices — among societies aimed at examining leader effectiveness across cultures. Examples of these cultural dimensions include *institutional collectivism* (the degree to which organizational and societal institutional practices encourage and reward collective distribution of resources/collective action), *assertiveness* (the degree to which individuals are assertive, confrontational, and aggressive in their relationships with others) and *performance orientation* (the degree to which a collective encourages and rewards group members for performance improvement and excellence). This allowed them to analyze the responses of thousands of middle managers around the globe to 112 leader characteristics, such as *modest, decisive, autonomous, and trustworthy,* based on the following definition of leadership: "An outstanding leader is a person in an organization or industry who is exceptionally skilled at motivating, influencing, or enabling you, others, or groups to contribute to the success of the organization or task." Among altogether 21 (7-point) leadership scales (ranked from the "most universally desirable" to "the least universally desirable), a couple of universally desirable key leadership competencies and attributes were identified such as integrity (6.07), inspirational (6.07), visionary (6.02), performance-oriented (6.02), team-integrator (5.88), decisive (5.80), administratively competent (5.76), diplomatic (5.49), collaborative team orientation (5.46), self-sacrificial (5.0), and modesty (4.98).

GLOBE also empirically established six typical leader styles: (i) team-oriented; (ii) self and group-protective (with an emphasis on "face-saving" behaviors and security of the individual); (iii) autonomous independent (implying an individualistic, self-centric approach to leadership); (iv) humane (emphasis on compassion and generosity); (v) performance-oriented (stress on high standards, decisiveness, innovation and inspiring vision); and (vi) participative (with regard to decision-making, delegation and equality).

The *team-oriented style* with its emphasis on pride, loyalty, collaboration, and team cohesiveness turned out to be the most preferred leader style in the so-called "Confucian cluster," comprising Singapore, Hong Kong, Taiwan, China, South Korea, and Japan. The study also helped to answer the question: What contributes to a person being seen as an outstanding leader? The answer: trustworthy, just, honest, foresight, plans ahead, encouraging, positive, dynamic, motive arouser, confidence builder, motivational, decisive, excellence-oriented, dependable, intelligent, effective bargainer, win-win problem solver, administratively skilled, communicative, informed, coordinator and team builder (a note of caution should be added here as the study measures opinions and values rather than actual leadership behavior).

2.1 *Toward mindfulness in spirit and practice*

The ongoing discussion about Asian leadership suggests that there is an urgent need for aspiring Asian corporate leaders to develop a broader range of skills in line with the rapidly changing and increasingly diverse, complex and globalizing business environment. A promising resource base for discussions about effective leadership in Asia and the type of skills required is arguably *mindfulness*, which can be defined as a sort of enlightened state of being in which greed, hatred and delusion have been overcome, and are absent from the mind (Brown and Ryan, 2003; Bishop *et al.*, 2004; Boyatzis and McKee, 2005; Carrol, 2007). In the context of everyday leadership behavior, this might imply the necessity of staying aware of one's responsibilities, for example, by paying close attention to the concerns and needs of one's followers. Coupled with clear comprehension of what is taking place now and here, i.e., *present moment-awareness*, mindful leadership represents a powerful force for "real" leaders to transform other people's fears and anxieties into hope which some consider as the the hallmark of good leadership. The power of mindful leadership becomes more obvious if we contrast it with less-mindful (or "mindless") leadership (Levinthal and Rerup, 2006; Weick and Sutcliffe, 2006). Symptoms may include not paying attention to or not having

Table 1.   Benefits of mindfulness

- Less stress and anxiety
- Better mood and increased well being
- Improved concentration and memory
- Accepting reality
- Being in control of one's thoughts
- Focused (present) attention
- Internal awareness
- External awareness
- Lack of absentmindedness
- More empathy, patience and kindness

awareness of the activities one is engaged in, including the internal states and processes (emotions) one is experiencing. Less mindful leaders often only pay partial attention to the people they come in contact with. As a result they might be perceived as disrespectful and incompetent.

Mindful leaders listen, show respect and are supportive. They are motivated by a larger purpose (than their ego) and willing to make decisions which are "right." Through their authentic values, beliefs, and behaviour, they can become role models for the development of associates and help to transform/develop them into leaders themselves.

We argue that mindfulness is of central importance in most if not all philosophies and religious doctrines. In the following we attempt to ascertain this argument by briefly discussing the role of mindfulness in Buddhism, Hinduism, Confucianism, Christianity and Islam as well as psychology before we draw conclusions with regard to the development of mindful leadership skills.

2.2 *A Buddhist perspective of mindfulness*

Mindfulness (*sati* in Pali and *smṛti* in Sanskrit) is a central concept in Buddhist teaching and philosophy. It is one of the prescriptions in the "Eightfold Path" toward enlightenment. From a Buddhist perspective being alert both in body and mind reduces agony and worries, and enables the precise and speedy accomplishment of tasks and duties. *Satipatthana vipassana*, a form of meditation, leads to Mindfulness, to being aware of one's own body, own feelings and state of mind as well as of the presence of objects and other persons and their behaviour. Seeing things as they really are and being devoid of illusion is an important aspect of mindfulness. Right Mindfulness (*sammá-sati*) in combination with two other items of the Buddhist Eightfold Path leading to the extinction of suffering *(atthangika-magga)*, namely Right Effort (*sammá-váyáma*), and Right Concentration (*sammá-samádhi*) enable a person to reduce suffering, be relaxed and focused on whatever he or she is doing. Right Effort, Right Mindfulness and Right Concentration guarantee success, but as Buddhist teachings abhor greed and the maximisation of material gains, the use of these concepts in the construction of management practice have their limit and could be seen as an aberration and perversion of the teaching of the Buddha, at least from the perspective of the Theravada school of Buddhism. From a Buddhist perspective, not just mindfulness, but the practice of RIGHT mindfulness is essential. A connection to Corporate Social Responsibility (CSR) may show a way out of this Buddhist dilemma, as classical Buddhism can be seen as rather solipsistic and underrating social responsibility.

Right mindfulness is also emphasized in Chinese Mahayana Buddhism and Japanese Zen. The latter combines mindfulness with concentration and target-oriented behavior as found in the so-called "art of archery" in Japan. Popular Buddhism in any case appears to provide cultural values, supporting mindful leadership behavior.

2.3 A Hindu perspective of mindfulness

Among the many Hindu scriptures, mindfulness can best be explained through the Bhagavad Gita (in Sanskrit literally "The Song of God"), an ancient holy text that forms part of the Hindu war epic Mahabharata. It explains individual righteousness for the orderly fulfillment of one's inherent nature. This wisdom is revealed in 700 verses (*shlokas* in Sanskrit) by the God of Growth (Vishnu) as avatar Lord Krishna in a dialogue with warrior Arjuna representing ordinary man.

As stated in Chapter 2, Verse 47: "Your right is to work only; but never to the fruits thereof. May you not be motivated by the fruits of actions; nor let your attachment be toward inaction."[1] "*Nishkama*" in Sanskrit means "without desire" and "*karma*" means "action." Hence, "*Nishkama karma*" is desireless action that is not blind execution but bold commitment to a purpose as illustrated in Figure 1.

When one acts without knowing, this could be a reflex (like blinking when an object is too near the eye) or a risk, especially under unsure or dangerous circumstances. However, when one acts knowingly, detachment becomes a mental act. It has to be supported by discrimination and discretion. Discrimination takes away the clutter and confusion. Then with discretion, one cultivates the right attitude by doing duties skillfully.

---

[1] Ranganathananda S (2010).

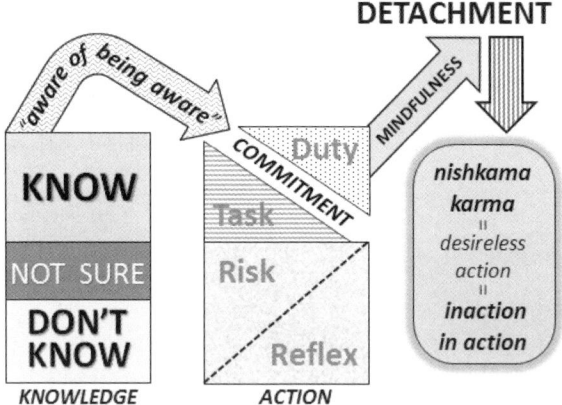

Figure 1. Components leading to mindfulness

Source: Adapted from the Bhagavad Gita, Chapter 2, Verse 47.

However, one would need to be *aware of being aware* in order to link individual capacity with capability.

When an action is performed in total self-awareness (knowing the doing — *inaction in action*), one has commitment. Then an ordinary task would blossom into a delightful duty. This requires the conscious conditioning of one's attitude with complete dedication and constant diligence to the present moment which in turn requires absolute discipline. In this state of "mindfulness," one would not only hear but also listen. One would see without prejudice, thus be attuned to the "here and now."

Figure 2 attempts to illustrate the implications of this ancient wisdom in the context of modern management that thrives in Zone 1. Basically, there are benchmarks (*should be*) to reward or punish organizational members based on performance in the *present*. While everyone is endowed with numerous capabilities and capacities (*can be*), these potentials can only be harnessed when the commitment to do (the *doing*) is elevated to a higher purpose as illustrated in Zone 2. An action comprises basically the doing, the delivery and the deliverables. When the *fullness of the moment* is merged with *meeting the moment*, then one becomes more mindful of the doing — i.e., one becomes more *attentive*, and in the delivery — actually more *accessible*, while with regard to the deliverables — always *appropriate*.

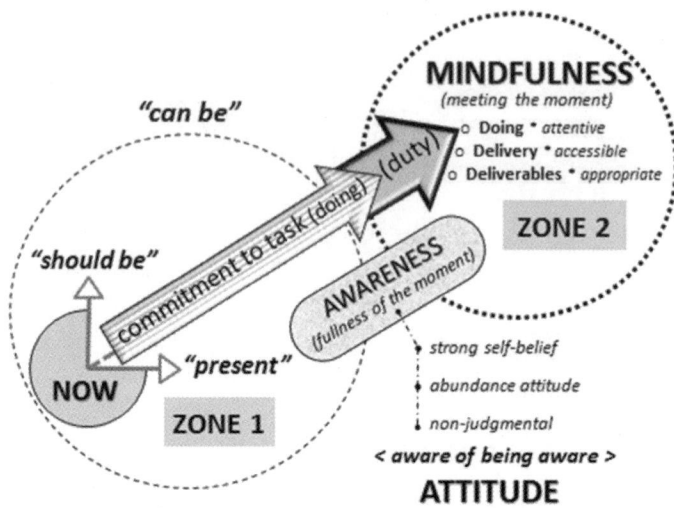

Figure 2.   When work becomes worship

Source: Adapted from the Bhagavad Gita, Chapter 2, Verses 33, 38, 40 and 41.

Such awareness (*aware of being aware*) is both a skill and a habit that are embedded in strong self-belief (trusting one's own rhythm), an abundance attitude and being non-judgmental about others. This awareness is like a switch that links the invisible with the visible, making the intangible tangible. It is like invisible electricity that moves a visible fan. The cooling which is intangible turns into tangible comfort like if one experiences no stickiness on the skin or perspiration. With this attitude of mindfulness, one would not only hear but also listen, not merely look but actually see, discriminating ordinary clutter and apparent confusion in order to allow individual discernment and proper discretion. In merging Zone 1 with Zone 2, a task blossoms into a duty, work becomes worship. In the context of management, a routine occupation becomes a joyful preoccupation driven by an attitude of aware of being aware.

2.4 *A Confucian perspective of mindfulness*

Unlike Buddhist or Hindu conceptions of mindfulness, a Confucian perspective of leadership mindfulness leans towards the informal practices in which the leader applies mindfulness in daily activities. In the *Analects of Confucius*, the concept of leadership is discussed using the character *zheng* 政 which means to govern or to administer (Confucius, 1983; Lee, 2001; Lee, 2008 and 2012).

According to Confucius, to "govern" (*zheng* 政) is to "correct" (*zheng* 正). The character "govern" consists of two radicals: the radical "correct" on the left and the character of "literacy" on the right. In other words, to "govern" is to correct using language. He emphasizes that the leader has to set an example of being correct himself in order to make others correct. If you set an example by being correct, who would dare to remain incorrect? (Analects [AL] 12:17; Lau, 114–115). If a man manages to make himself correct, what is there to taking office for him? If he cannot make himself correct, what business has he with making others correct? (AL 13:13; Lau, 124–125). The way to set an example is to "give of one's best" and to "work hard". The Master said: "Do not allow your efforts to slacken" (AL 13:1; Lau, 120–121).

The "self" in Confucianism is to be seen in the context of one's relationships with others (Lee, 2012; Tu, 1994). Personal ordering and socio-political harmony are mutually implicative in that the former can take place in the context of socio-political participation while the latter is justifiable as attendant upon the achievements of personal cultivation (Hall and Ames, 1987, p. 164). Therefore, besides setting a good example of being correct, the leader should also take care of the welfare of subordinates by making sure that their daily necessities are met, bringing them comfort (AL 14:42; Lau, 146–147), and ruling over them with dignity and kindness (AL 2:20) so as to win their trust and respect. With regard to government, the Master said: "Give them enough food, give them enough arms, and the common people will have trust in you..." (AL 12:7; Lau, 110–111). He stressed that things have to be in the right hierarchical order ("rectification of names") before any governing process can be successful and advocated the observance of the rites by leaders for successful governance.

Confucius likens the importance of "virtue" in government to the "Pole Star which commands the homage of the multitude of stars simply by remaining in its place" (AL 2:1; Lau 10–11). He states that *zhongyong* (中庸) which means "moderation," "appropriateness" or "perfection" is the supreme moral virtue (AL 6:29; Lau, 52–53). As such, the master should be cordial yet stern, awe-inspiring yet not fierce, respectful yet at ease (AL 7:38; Lau, 66–67) and stern in speech (AL 19:9).

Confucius views the ruler as a moral gentleman with virtues such as benevolence (AL 6:30; Lau, 54–55), wisdom, courage (AL 14:28; Lau, 140–141), and righteousness (AL 4:16). He views benevolence as "to love subordinates," and wisdom as "to know subordinates" (Lee, 2008). To him, these are essential qualities that the leader must possess in order to be a moral manager in collectivist society. Based on these virtues, the leader is to lead with the following mindfulness:

> "There are nine things the gentlemen turns his thought to: to seeing clearly when he uses his eyes, to hearing acutely when he uses his ears, to looking cordial when it comes to his countenance, to appearing respectful when it comes to his demeanour, to being conscientious when he speaks, to being reverent when he performs his duties, to seeking advice when he is in doubt, to considering the consequences when he is enraged, and to seeking what is right at the sight of gain" (AL 16:10; Lau, 164–167).

In summary, Confucius' perspective of mindfulness leadership requires the leader to lead by example, to care for the needs of the subordinates, stressing on the importance of hierarchical propriety with personal and social ethical behavior (Tu, 1994).

2.5 *Mindful leadership from a Christian perspective*

While to be mindful means a host of different things for different people in different contexts, religious perspectives also shape the principles and practice of mindfulness in the daily operations of a leader's life. A leader is influenced by his or her culture, values and faith to a large extent. From a Christian point of view mindfulness is not about distancing from the real world but being very involved in it. Involvement takes the form of putting one's beliefs into action. Faith without action is considered dead faith or no faith. As such, every leader is first and foremost expected to be mindful of the teachings and the word of God, that is, to fill his/her heart and mind with deeper truth as expounded by the trinity: God, the Father; Jesus Christ, the Son of God; and Holy Spirit. The leader is expected to honor and put into action by faith scriptural principles and truth in the daily demands of every sphere of life and this includes work life. A leader has to be always mindful in the sense of being aware of his/her purpose, destiny and call of his life here on earth. Mindfulness revolves around mercy, justice and love of Jesus Christ, which is to be demonstrated in whatever the leader plans and does. It also implies using authority responsibly with humility day after day without any separation between the sacred and the secular.

A Christian leader must be mindful in the sense of reckoning what his or her strengths, resources and limitations are since a leader is finite and God is infinite and almighty. Empowered to do God's work in any area of life is the vocation for which a leader is personally accountable. It is not merely being focused to achieve performance at the workplace but rather it is all about finishing right. In other words, it is never about getting targets for personal advancement but the process of how all manner of work is accomplished and for what purpose it was done, being mindful of outcomes. The element of motive, intentions and driving force must be centered on the will of God. Mindful leadership is thus a process of aligning the leader's body (his physiological aspects, including intelligence, energy, etc.), soul (his thoughts, feelings and talents put into action) and spirit (his belief and faith) to the very heart beat and mind of a gracious, loving and just God. A mindful leader would constantly be yielded and dependent on God's guidance in all that he or she does.

2.6 *Mindful leadership from an Islamic perspective*

Orthodox Christian *nepsis* (watchfulness), Buddhist mindfulness and Islamic *dhikr* (remembrance) are related concepts, as they stress personal qualities of leaders and their enhanced capacity for action. Mindfulness is, however, interpreted in different ways. In Islam, we can highlight the practice of fasting (abstinence) which is one of the five pillars of Islam. Fasting is a practice of consciousness and cleansing, humility, patience, improved willpower, discipline and character building as well as the acknowledgement of community and something bigger than oneself — notable leadership attributes. Islam encourages the study of remembrance *(dhikr)*, inner consciousness *(wejdan)*, knowledge *(ilm)* and disposition *(akhlaq)*. These principles and values were embodied by Prophet Mohammed *(peace be upon him)* and remind followers to be aware of leading their lives in awareness of God, self and others.

In Islam, the reverence of rigorous monotheism in Allah *(subhanahu wa ta'ala)* brings believers toward fulfilling the *remembrance of God* as indicated by the following quote taken from the Quran (Quran 13:28): "Verily in the remembrance of Allah do hearts find rest!" (Pickthall, 1938). In itself, the verse hints at mindfulness through "purification of self" *(tazkiah al-nafs)*, and Muslims seek to look within to find relationship between themselves and God. This practise is *tasawwuf*, which focuses on the spiritual development of a Muslim and relates to personality, empathy, kindness and inner peace, to be consciously practised daily. Sufism, a branch of Islam that stresses *tasawwuf*, is also known for its spiritual leaders.

3. Mindfulness and Focused Attention

From a psychological point of view, mindfulness has strong connotations of being focused and paying full attention. What happens when we focus, that is, pay attention to a speaker at a rally, listen up when the piano virtuoso begins her performance, concentrate on the start of an athletic 100 meter Olympic sprint final, or search for a face among a jostling, surging crowd coming out of the airport, or making an important decision when reviewing multiple management scenarios in our mind? Can we effectively manage a number of tasks (multi-tasking[2]) at the same time or does our attention, and hence performance, suffer when we are confronted with a myriad of competing problems that require solutions?

The evidence from cognitive science suggests that our ability to focus attention on specific complex tasks is limited; the more complex the

---

[2] Also termed divided attention in cognitive science.

sensory environment, the more novel or unfamiliar the stimuli or situation, the harder it is to concentrate on a particular task. Attention is either automatic (bottom-up, from environmental stimuli to the brain) or regulated (top-down, from the brain).

Why is this important? Clearly, our cognitive system selectively processes information as our senses are bombarded with stimuli all the time. We are often "distracted" at work and even in our leisure time and personal lives when having to focus our attention can bring significant benefits to our lives. Understanding attention helps us identify problems associated with multi-tasking such as attention-deficit/hyperactivity disorder (Hallowell, 2005). It allows us the opportunity to set up optimal learning environments where we can capitalize on realizing effective, desired outcomes when faced with decision making situations. Clearly, our cognitive system selectively processes information as our senses are bombarded with stimuli all the time. We are often "distracted" at work and even in our leisure time and personal lives when having to focus our attention can bring significant benefits to our lives.

How is this related to mindfulness? The cognitive model underlying mindfulness, one instance of which is meditation, is focused attention, in which the brain is directed at processing information and channels attentive effort towards that goal (Kahneman, 1973; Caudron, 2001; Wickens and McCarley, 2008). Mindfulness, as a philosophical and Buddhist precept, is concerned with the will and mind, channeling cognitive processes towards a single focal point. The two are yin and yang, complementing each other by way of explanation. We can, however, train our attention so that we direct more of our resources for information processing, as in multi-tasking. This is one of the applications arising from research in cognitive attention.

4. Achieving Leadership Effectiveness through Mindfulness

As Harvard Professor Bill George has pointed out:

> "The practice of mindful leadership gives you tools to measure and manage your life as you're living it. It teaches you to pay attention to the present moment, recognizing your feelings and emotions and keeping them under control, especially when faced with highly stressful

situations. When you are mindful, you're aware of your presence and the ways you impact other people. You're able to both observe and participate in each moment, while recognizing the implications of your actions for the longer term. And that prevents you from slipping into a life that pulls you away from your values" (George, 2012).

This expert opinion is echoed by empirical research studies conducted by Reb and Narayanan (2011) who have shown that mindfulness improves negotiation success. It also reduces stress and burnout. Besides that, it is related to both higher psychological well-being and job performance. The research by Reb *et al.* (2012) suggests that mindful employees do not only show greater well-being and performance but that a leader's mindfulness is also associated with higher well-being and performance of his/her subordinates. Further evidence is provided by Reb's 2012 evaluation of a Corporate Based Mindfulness Training Programme at Carlsberg which showed pre- to post-training improvement in self-rated mindfulness, perceptions of supervisor support, focused attention, emotional commitment and reduction in exhaustion (http://potentialproject.com/news/recent-news.html).

Full awareness of current activities (i.e., "not rushing," not "running on autopilot," etc.) or paying full attention to a follower's problems brought up during an unplanned conversation without being preoccupied with thoughts about the future, the next appointment or the past represent hall marks of mindful leaders (Dane, 2011). To master present moment-awareness, for example, during difficult performance appraisals or long town hall meetings between leaders and followers can be a challenge if fear, urgent demands or anger preoccupy the mind. Mindful leaders can make a big difference to people as the popularity of Singapore's former President, the late Mr Wee Kim Wee, suggests who, according to some observers, "wore his heart on his sleeve."

Mindful leadership is arguably the apex of authentic, transformational leadership with an emphasis on self reflection, transparency, openness, and ethical conduct as well as the soliciting of sufficient opinions and viewpoints prior to making important decisions. Any attempt to appreciate the power of mindful leadership and to acquire mindfulness as a competency must start with the willingness for personal stocktaking in terms of self awareness and openness towards frank feedback. A key question is: To what degree am I aware of my strengths, limitations, how others see me and how I impact others?

A key requirement is to make time available for respective in-depth reflections either individually or in peer circles of trust. For example, if a leader regularly puts off others by appearing to be unattentive or cold, it might be good to develop his or her emotional intelligence and mindfulness skills to become a better leader. To motivate and train executives to become more assertive, directive, persuasive or politely submissive if the situation warrants it are key requirements of leadership development programmes.

An individualized leadership development program with an emphasis on self-awareness and mindfulness training which draws upon a leader's crucial anchoring events or moments of truth, psychological strength self evaluation and personal challenges, moral perspective and development needs embedded in an organizational climate of care and concern with an engaging employee value proposition is instrumental in achieving positive leadership behaviors in emerging Asia. Meditation, yoga, in-depth introspective discussions, simple reflective techniques or exercises such as journaling or interdisciplinary group reflections about difficult leadership moments where each member identifies and evaluates personal coping strategies in the context of others and then jointly reflects about outcomes achieved (whether positive or negative) represent useful LD tools (Caudron, 2001). The mastery of mindful leadership will arguably enhance effectiveness at individual, team and organizational levels (Gehani, 2011; Schuyler, 2010; Hallowell, 2005) and ensure that more Asians successfully claim leadership roles in East and West.

4.1 *Leadership development through formal and informal mindfulness practice*

Both formal and informal mindfulness practices have been developed, and they can both be useful in supporting a leader's performance and development. Formal practices consist of activities such as mindfulness meditation, meditation on the breath, mindful yoga, or self-reflection. Informal practices consist of our efforts to apply mindfulness in our daily activities.

For example, mindfulness, or full, open engagement in the present moment, can be practiced when emailing, being in meetings, or having conversations with peers, subordinates, or superiors.

In a sense, informal practice of mindfulness is both a practice, in that it enhances one's ability to be mindful, and an application, as it uses mindfulness to change how we interact with the world. And it is this changed interaction with the world that arguably is both the ultimate goal of formal and informal practices. In other words, the idea that mindfulness is something that a leader would have to practice for 5, 15, or 45 minutes in the morning, before going to work, or in the evening, before retiring to bed, misses the crucial point that mindfulness is an approach to life that, ideally, is practiced moment-to-moment-to-moment.

Being mindfully, that is, fully and openly, engaged in the present moment is said to enable a more objective, realistic perception of oneself, one's environment, and one's relation to this environment (e.g., whether interacting with a certain person arouses feelings of happiness or anger, etc.). In this sense, being in a mindful state is characterized by authenticity in that one just "is," without immediately judging or commenting on one's experience in the moment. At the same time, however — and this is crucial for leader development — this more realistic and clearer awareness and understanding of oneself, the environment, and one's relation to it, helps the practitioner in recognizing what kind of aspects of oneself and the environment require to be changed in order to achieve one's goals.

Table 2.   How mindfulness can be achieved and trained

- Pausing in the midst of a hectic day
- Sitting silently and observing one's breath (and thoughts)
- Identifying one's concerns, fears, priorities, values, etc. once one's ego has "quieted"
- A quiet ego helps to cope with ego threat (less defensiveness)
- Managing difficult conversations with directness (and empathy)
- The stress-reducing effects of mindfulness training enhances the ability to learn in developmentally challenging situations

5. Conclusion

In this chapter, we attempted to make a case for appreciating both the practice and value of effective mindful leadership in Asian business and society. A key argument put forward is that executives can become better leaders through focused attention, better (internal and external) awareness and lack of absentmindedness (in other words: through mindfulness). We attempted to show that mindfulness is of central importance in most if not all Asian philosophies and religious doctrines. Whether it is wise to leverage on notions of mindfulness in Buddhism, Hinduism, Confucianism, Christianity and Islam in the ongoing search process of practical Asian leadership (development) paradigms needs to be further examined. What seems to be obvious is the potential of harnessing Asian versions of mindfulness concepts with regard to meaningful leadership development initiatives qua training and coaching. Regular mindfulness activities such as concentrated (reflective) breathing techniques, journaling or real sharing sessions with a focus on deciphering important lessons learnt during challenging leadership moments (e.g., with regard to mindful or less-mindful leadership behavior) can be very useful in developing one's mindfulness potential. We believe that the mastery of mindful leadership represents an effective strategy of enhancing personal effectiveness at individual, team and organisational levels. Besides that there is evidence that it helps to manage undesirable distractions, reduce stress and improve one's immune system. With all this, chances are that mindfulness is an important asset for talents in East and West interested in successfully performing leadership roles in business and society (a proposition which needs to be further tested in the Asian context with robust sampling frames).

References

Avolio, BJ and P Ong (2008). Accelerating the growth of the Asian leader. *Ethos*, 5, CGL Centre for Governance and Leadership. Available at http://www.cscollege.gov.sg/cgl/pub_ethos_8f1.htm.

Bishop, SR (2004). Mindfulness: A proposed operational definition. *Clinical Psychology: Science and Practice*, 11(3), 230–241.

Boyatzis, RE and A McKee (2005). *Resonant Leadership: Renewing Yourself and Connecting with Others through Mindfulness, Hope, and Compassion*. Boston, MA: Harvard Business School Press.

Brown, KW and RM Ryan (2003). The benefits of being present: Mindfulness and its role in psychological well-being. *Journal of Personality and Social Psychology*, 84(4), 822–848.

Carroll, M (2007). *The Mindful Leader: Ten Principles for Bringing out the Best in Ourselves and Others*. Boston, MA: Trumpeter.

Caudron, S (2001). Meditation and mindfulness at sounds true. *Workforce*, 80(6), 40–46.

Chhokar, JS (ed.) (2007). *Culture and Leadership Across the World: The GLOBE Book of In-Depth Studies of 25 Societies*. Mahwah, NJ: Lawrence Erlbaum.

Chinmayananda, S (2002). *The Holy Geeta*. Central Chinmaya Mission Trust, Mumbai, India.

Dane, E (2011). Paying attention to mindfulness and its effects on task performance in the workplace. *Journal of Management*, 37(4), 997–1018.

Day, D, M Harrison and S Halpin (2009). *An Integrative Approach to Leader Development*. New York, NY: Routledge.

Dorfman, PW, JP Howell, S Hibino, JK Lee, U Tate and A Bautista (1997). Leadership in Western and Asian countries: Commonalities and differences in effective leadership processes across cultures. *Leadership Quarterly*, 8(3), 233–274.

Fu, PP and G Yukl (2000). Perceived effectiveness of influence tactics in the United States and China. *Leadership Quarterly*, 11, 251–266.

Gehani, RR (2011). Individual creativity and the influence of mindful leaders on enterprise innovation. *Journal of technology Management and Innovation*, 6(3), 82–92.

George, B (2012). Mindfulness helps you become a better leader (HBR Blog Network), October 26, 2012. Available at http://blogs.hbr.org/hbsfaculty/2012/10/mindfulness-helps-you-become-a.html.

Hall, DL and RT Ames (1987). *Thinking Through Confucius*. Albany, NY: State University of New York Press.

Hallowell, EM (2005). Overloaded circuits: Why smart people underperform. *Harvard Business Review*, January, 2–9.

House, RJ, PW Hanges, M Javidan, P Dorfman, and V Gupta eds. (2004). *Culture, Leadership, and Organizations: The GLOBE Study of 62 Societies*. Thousand Oaks, CA: Sage Publications.

Javidan, M, P Dorfman, M Sully de Luque, and RJ House (2006). In the eye of beholder: Cross cultural lessons in leadership from project GLOBE. *Academy of Management Perspectives*, 20(1), 67–91.

Jung, D and B Avolio (1999). Effects of leadership style and followers' cultural orientation on performance in group and individual task conditions. *Academy of Management Journal*, 42, 208–218.

Kahneman, D (1973). *Attention and Effort*. Lipper Saddle River, NJ: Prentice-Hall.

Lau, CC (1983). *Confucius: The Analects*. Hong Kong: The Chinese University Press.

Lee, CL (2008). "Traditional" Chinese conceptions of knowledge (*zhi*,知): A "modern" interpretation with reference to business. *Journal of Asian Business*, 22/23(2–3), 25–32.

Lee, CL (2012). Self-presentation, face, first-person pronouns in the Analects. *Journal of Politeness Research*, 8(1), 75–92.

Lee, J-K (2001). Confucian thought affecting leadership and organizational culture of Korean higher education. *Radical Pedagogy*, 3(3). Available at http://radicalpedagogy.icaap.org/content/issue3_3/5-lee.html.

Levinthal, D and C Rerup (2006). Crossing an apparent chasm: Bridging mindful and less-mindful perspectives on organizational learning. *Organization Science*, 17(4), 502–513.

Menkhoff, T, YW Chay, H-D Evers, and B Loh (2008). Leadership in knowledge sharing: Creating value through collaboration. *Journal of Asian Business*, 22(2–3) and 23(1), 265–281.

Mills, DQ (2005). Asian and American leadership styles: How are they unique? *HBS Working Knowledge*, June 27. Available at http://hbswk.hbs.edu/item/4869.html.

Palrecha, R, WD Spangler and FJ Yammarino (2012). A comparative study of three leadership approaches in India. *The Leadership Quarterly*, 23(1), 146–162.

Ranganathananda, S (2010). *Universal Message of the Bhagavad Gita. An Exposition of the Gita in the Light of Modern Thought and Modern Needs*. Kolkata: Advaita Ashrama, 6th Impression, Vol. 1.

Reb, J and J Narayanan (2011). Mindfully eating raisins improves negotiation success: The effect of mindfulness on negotiation performance, June 26. IACM 24th Annual Conference Paper. Available at http://ssrn.com/abstract=1872908 or http://dx.doi.org/10.2139/ssrn.1872908.

Reb, J, J Narayanan and S Chaturvedi (2012). Leading mindfully: Two studies on the influence of supervisor trait mindfulness on employee well-being and performance. *Mindfulness*, September 4, 2012.

Schuyler, KG (2010). Increasing leadership integrity through mind training and embodied learning. *Consulting Psychology Journal: Practice and Research*, 62(1), 21–38.

Sinha, JBP (1984). A model of effective leadership styles in India. *International Studies of Management and Organization*, 14, 86–98.

Tu, WM (1994). Embodying the universe: A note on Confucian self-realization. In *Self as Person in Asian Theory and Practice*, RT Ames, W Dissanayake and TP Kasulis (eds.), pp. 177–186. Albany, NY: State University of New York Press.

Weick, KE and KM Sutcliffe (2006). Mindfulness and the quality of organizational attention. *Organization Science*, 17(4), 514–524.

Wickens, CD and J McCarley (2008). *Applied Attention Theory*. Boca-Raton, FL: Taylor and Francis.

Xin, KR and AS Tsui (1996). Different strokes for different folks? Influence tactics by Asian–American and Caucasian–American managers. *Leadership Quarterly*, 7(1), 109–132.

Chapter 13

Exploring Lee Kong Chian's Knowledge Leadership Style in Nam Aik Company

Dai Shiyan and Zhang Guocai

1. Introduction

In the era of knowledge-based economy, many organizations have come to realize the importance of knowledge management (KM) and have made active attempts to practice and adopt various KM strategies so as to survive the fast changing environment and maintain sustained growth. Past research reveals that effective KM enables organizations to lever their organizations' core competencies and to achieve competitive advantage. Effective leadership often leads to high performance coupled with job satisfaction, organizational commitment, and trust (Politis, 2001, p. 354). Likewise, in pursuit of KM, relevant research has found that the leadership of an organization plays a very crucial role as enabler (Menkhoff *et al.*, 2005). A great number of KM studies, especially in the area of management information system research, have attested to the crucial role of KM and the impact of senior leadership as KM champions on effective organizational performance (Lakshman, 2005; Armstrong and Sambamurthy, 1999).

Lee Kong Chian (1893–1967), a well-known ethnic Chinese entrepreneur and philanthropist throughout Southeast Asia, was the founder and

This is a reprint of an article originally published in 2008 in the *Journal of Asian Business*, 22–23(1–3), 283–293. The editors gratefully acknowledge the permission to reprint the essay in this edition.

leader of the Nam Aik Rubber Company.[1] In those days when Lee Kong Chian ran his Nam Aik Rubber Company, the term "knowledge management" had not come into existence; its first occurrence was reported in 1986 (Wilson, 2002). However, several of the management approaches and practices during the Lee Kong Chian's era can actually be categorized as antecedents of what we would describe as knowledge management activities today. Likewise, many of Lee Kong Chian's leading management practices and activities are also found to demonstrate features and/or antecedents of KM. This paper aims to explore and discuss Lee Kong Chian's knowledge leadership style and practices by drawing on the organizational practices of Nam Aik Rubber Company in its earlier days.

2. Lee Kong Chian and his Nam Aik Enterprise

Lee Kong Chian (henceforth referred to as LKC), a well-known Chinese entrepreneur and philanthropist, was the founder of the Nam Aik Rubber Company and the first Chancellor of the University of Singapore, predecessor institution of the current National University of Singapore (Zheng, 1997, p. 182). Born in 1893 in Nan'an of East China's Fujian province, he spent the first 10 years of his childhood in his home village, receiving some basic education in a private school. At the age of 10, he came to Singapore to join his father, a tailor. In Singapore, LKC was sent to an English school during week-days but continued to learn Chinese in a Chinese school every weekend. At the age of 15, he won a scholarship for an advanced education program back in China's Nanjing. Four years later, LKC returned to Singapore to work as a secondary school teacher in the

---

[1] In this study, we have investigated Lee Kong Chian's leadership style and practices as a founder and leader of Nam Aik Rubber Company. After Lee Kong Chian established his first rubber company using an official name as Nam Aik Rubber Company in 1928, the company enjoyed constantly growth with new branches and subsidiaries being set up one after another in subsequent years. The official name of the company was also altered in accordance with the important conditions such as the ownership structure and business activities, changing from Nam Aik Rubber Company to Lee Rubber Company Pte. Ltd., and later Lee Rubber Group. However, the authors wish to use the name of Nam Aik or Nam Aik Company wherever possible, to refer to the company throughout the different periods of time, simply for the sake of convenience and consistence.

daytime and served as a part-time translator for a Chinese press in the evenings. Concurrently, he continued to pursue his civil engineering degree through an American correspondence course.

While working in a Chinese department store, LKC was introduced to Tan Kah Kee (henceforth referred to as TKK), who was already an established trader and philanthropist. TKK was impressed with LKC's bilingual competence, diligence and potential. When TKK needed to expand his rubber trade business, he managed to persuade his friend, who was co-owner of the department store, to release LKC so that he could hire LKC in his rubber company to help with his business. Thus, LKC started work in TKK's company, which also marked LKC's first entry into the rubber business. LKC proved to be so competent and efficient that in 1920, as one informant noted, "Kah Kee quickly married his daughter to him because [he] was afraid Kong Chian would leave" (Tong and Yong, 2002, p. 219).

After about 11 years of working with his father-in-law, LKC initiated his first rubber venture with a friend by establishing a small rubber smoke house in Muar (near Malacca of West Malaysia) in 1927. He developed his business throughout the period of the Great Depression and later diversified into pineapple canning, sawmills, biscuits, timber, banking and real estate. With his unique acumen for leading and managing businesses, LKC succeeded in making his businesses gradually grow into a multi-million dollar business empire. He soon became one of the richest and best known entrepreneurs and philanthropists in Southeast Asia, gaining fame as the "King of Rubber" and "King of Pineapple."

One year after he started with a small smoke house with his friend, LKC again cooperated with his friends in founding Nam Aik Rubber Company in 1928. Three years later, the company was restructured and renamed the Lee Rubber Company Private Limited, which later became the Lee Rubber Group. Meanwhile, LKC also set up Lee Pineapple Company Private Limited jointly with other friends.

By 1941, Nam Aik had come to own a total of about 30,000 acres of rubber and pineapple plantations as well as subsidiary branches throughout Southeast Asia. In terms of employees, Nam Aik had some 2,000 clerks, executives and managers and 30,000 workers on its rubber plantations and factories, thus making Nam Aik the largest rubber manufacturer in Southeast Asia (Zheng, 1997). By the early 1950s, Nam Aik further grew to be the biggest rubber supplier in the industry.

LKC was, in his time, often regarded as a far-sighted and open-minded entrepreneur, attaching importance to the progress of science and technology and actively making use of new technology in his business operation and management. For example, in the early 1950s, Nam Aik was the first Chinese company in Singapore to use the computer when it was introduced in the region (Zheng, 1997, p. 232).

Meanwhile, LKC was actively involved in charity work, making generous donations to public welfare and educational programs. He allocated a considerable proportion of his stock in the Lee Rubber Group to establish the Lee Foundation in 1952 for the purpose of supporting and sponsoring educational and cultural undertakings and other social programs.

LKC donated land and money to benefit many educational institutions in Singapore. He also built several schools in his home town of Nan'an in China's Fujian province, where he spent his childhood and received his elementary education. In addition, he assisted his father-in-law TKK, founder of Xiamen University (now one of top 30 universities in China) in building and developing the university facilities and campus through his generous donations. The Lee Foundation has remained active supporting and funding various activities and undertakings for the benefit of society since LKC's passing in 1967.

3. Features of LKC's Leading and Managing Style and Practices

In the past decade or so, KM has developed into a wide range of fairly formal and systematic processes and activities along with rapid advances in information technology as well as the dramatic changes of our environment. Technologies for processing data and information are playing a role much greater than ever before in KM systems. However, evidence suggests that human factors remain crucial and indispensable in the KM process because of its unique role in acquiring, gathering, analyzing, sharing, creating and innovating information and knowledge. Effective KM requires the appropriate integration of technologies and human resource in an organization. Few people will doubt that human resource is the most critical of all resources needed for the successful operation and development of a company or organization. Other studies and observations also indicate that effective leadership in managing knowledge and organizations (Lakshman, 2005) mobilizes and motivates employees to perform at their best.

Looking back, it is clear that LKC, President of the Lee Rubber Group, formulated a wide range of innovative operational and managerial ideas and practices. The features of his leadership style and practices show a combination of Chinese traditional ideas of virtue and righteousness and Western modern management concepts, which according to Lakshman (2005) pertain in one way or another to the elements of KM. In our study, we attempt to identify, summarize and analyze specific features of LKC's leadership and management practices that are relevant to knowledge leadership. The major features include the following:

- Adhering to good business ethics, manifested in the four principles of *honesty, credibility, discipline, and prudence,* set by LKC as cardinal principles for the company and his employees;
- Attaching great importance to the value of communication, as evidenced by LKC's personal daily involvement in obtaining, processing and exchanging business and market information with managers of divisions/branches throughout different locations of Southeast Asia;
- Applying new technology for better information and communication;
- Recruiting the right people and providing the appropriate training;
- Caring for employees' benefits, providing good remuneration system;
- Adopting a modern organizational structure; and
- Contributing generously to education and society and promoting learning.

The features summarized above reflect various elements of KM and knowledge leadership. They constitute a solid and favorable social and technical foundation or environment for workers, in particular, management executives who demonstrated their commitment and loyalty to the organization's continuous growth and success throughout the years.

4. LKC's Knowledge Leadership Style

In a case study of Jack Welch's knowledge leadership of General Electric, Lakshman (2005, pp. 434–435) identified and investigated the following activities and practices as KM components: best practice transfer, job rotation, information technology, modifying the organizational structure, organizing meetings/conferences, participation in information sharing, implementing knowledge sharing, using teams and taskforces, training and development, external benchmarking, micro-level knowledge leadership.

Interestingly enough, what we summarized as features of LKC's leadership style and practices earlier show much similarity to the KM components identified by Lakshman (2005). In the next section, we analyze and discuss the relevant practices illustrating LKC's knowledge leadership style based on the features we identified and summarized earlier, making relevant comparisons, where possible, with Jack Welch's knowledge leadership practices as highlighted in Lakshman's study.

4.1 *Ethical principles as the code of Nam Aik company's business activities*

One important issue involved in KM may be the ethical dimension of knowledge application. Information and knowledge can be used in different ways, leading to different results. Specifically, knowledge might be used either to benefit the whole organization and/or relevant parties involved or benefit only a handful of people involved. LKC, as a leader of Nam Aik, often exhorted his staff to strictly abide by the four principles of *honesty, credibility, discipline, and prudence* in their daily business activities, as he believed they were the basic and vital principles for a company and a man alike to exist and develop in society. To LKC, it was crucial for a company to maintain virtues such as justice, honesty and frugality (Lim, 1999, p. 214). Under his leadership, Nam Aik was always highly honored by the public as a result of its sincere treatment of its staff, its honest dealings with the relevant stakeholders such as government organizations, financiers, banks, clients and consumers. For example, Nam Aik was never in arrears with its payment. The company prohibited its staff from conducting any deceptive acts in any transaction with clients and consumers. When the company received complaints from a client or consumer about product quality, or from a supplier about their goods underpaid in accordance with the contract, the company would promptly have the cases investigated. If the complaints were true and reasonable, the company would take immediate action to provide reasonable compensation and meanwhile mete out due punishment to the staff involved.

Consequently, the virtues highlighted in the four principles constituted a crucial part of Nam Aik's corporate value. In an organizational culture where honesty, credibility, discipline and prudence are emphasized and upheld, human application for knowledge management would certainly have a higher probability of being directed towards ethical, honest and trustworthy business operations.

4.2 *The importance of effective communication*

Effective communication is vital to the success of the KM process in an organization. Although there was no formal scientific concept of information management in the 1930s and 1940s, the value of information was nevertheless widely recognized in business practices. Being an entrepreneur who obviously received the most formal education among his other successful peers in his time (Lim, 1999, p. 205), LKC knew the importance of communication and business information. Consequently, he attached great importance to managing and maintaining effective flow of business information in his daily business transactions and decision making process. Early every morning, he would personally call up managers of different branches in Malaysia to enquire about business and market information, exchange information and opinions with them respectively, and then make business decisions based on the latest development of the market and the inputs of his subordinates (Lim, 1999, p. 209; Zheng, 1997, p. 80).

In addition to daily telephone contact, LKC would regularly make personal inspection tours to divisions and local offices, where he would meet and talk with managers and directors, gathering and exchanging information and opinions about the various divisions and/or branches throughout the Malaysia and Indonesia.

While making sufficient effort to maintain formal communication with his subordinate staff on a regular basis, LKC also paid much attention to engaging in informal communication with his senior managerial staff and local celebrities as well. For example, he would hold lunch meetings with senior managerial staff from divisions and local offices and with local celebrities from different walks of life every Wednesday. LKC would never miss opportunities to earnestly solicit views and opinions about the company's operation and development and about society as a whole. This kind of regular contact and exchange would help LKC develop close rapport with his staff and the community.

It is interesting to note that what LKC did, as described above, bears much similarity to Jack Welch's personal side of KM in Lakshman's study (2005). In discussing the evidence reflecting Welch's knowledge leadership, Lakshman (2005, p. 443) pointed out: "Every week, he made unexpected visits to plants and offices, hurriedly scheduled luncheons with managers several layers below him.... Welch was also known for writing personal notes to communicate with employees and managers at all levels in the organization."

4.3 *Adopting new technology for better information and communication*

It goes without saying that business communication and administration can benefit from the progress of science and technology in many ways and so can KM. One exemplary example that shows LKC's readiness to accept new technology for a better information and communication process comes from his support and adoption of computers in the operation of the company in 1952, when computers were first introduced in Asia. Nam Aik was the first Chinese company in Singapore to use the computer for business administration, which at that time appeared to be a technological "monster," taking up a large room and creating a hit with Chinese society (Zheng, 1997, p. 81; Li, 1998, p. 87). The computerization of its business enabled the company to take big strides forward, greatly improving the speed and efficiency of data and information management, providing conditions conducive to KM activities among its organizational members.

Again, shortly after telex technology was invented, LKC quickly adopted the new technology and installed a communication system in all its division offices, thus making the process and exchange of information and communication even more efficient (Li, 1998).

It is clear that the adoption of new technologies enhances communication and information exchange between the senior management and staff, and between the head office and all the divisions and branches in different locations. Moreover, the readiness of LKC to accept and adopt the new technologies also demonstrated his understanding of what drives information, knowledge and how best to harness technology for the success of his business.

4.4 *Recruiting the right people and providing appropriate training*

The quality of an organization's human resource plays a decisive factor contributing to the sustained competitiveness of an organization. LKC was mindful of this and he adhered to a personnel policy by selecting and hiring those with the appropriate knowledge, skills and abilities, and relevant qualifications. He treasured only those personnel with both strong ability and moral integrity.

In LKC's time, science and technology developed at a pace much more slowly than what we see today. University education was available only to a minority and hence university graduates were an elite group. Work in a rubber industry was usually arduous, the work environment grimy, an occupation university graduates would all but avoid unless they had no other options. Consequently, graduates, even if they were recruited into the industry, would often fail to commit themselves to their work and many resigned. This turnover problem was common at Nam Aik too, despite it offering attractive remuneration packages. Faced with such a situation, LKC did not blindly pursue university graduates. Instead, he chose to recruit the fresh graduates from secondary schools as he believed they possessed the necessary drive and ability to learn about the rubber business. He also believed they had the potential for further development within the company. As a result, it was relatively easier for the company to retain appropriate talent with staff from such an educational background (Lee, 1998, p. 74).

In the selection process, the company would give priority to recruiting secondary school graduates with better academic performance, that is, those who were academically ranked among the top 10 percent in their class. The rationale behind this selection policy was that such graduates were in a better position to learn and acquire the skills required in the work and constantly develop in their careers. The company held formal interviews with job applicants, and LKC would usually personally sit in during the interviews, especially for senior position recruitment. Moreover, each job applicant was usually required to provide recommendations from an incumbent employee, his school principal, a relative or friend. Through such referrals, LKC believed that the new recruit would be more likely to observe the company rules and avoid doing anything negative to tarnish the referee's reputation (Li, 1998, p. 72).

Naturally, the practices adopted by LKC would more likely help the company recruit the right people and also retain the better employees, thus maintaining a qualified and stable work force for the business, which would in turn promote the process of acquiring, sharing, developing and creating specialized skills, knowledge and know-how among organizational members. Herein lies the sharing and management of knowledge.

4.5 *Caring for employees' benefits and fair remuneration*

As the leader of a successful enterprise, LKC always paid attention to motivating his employees, fostering their sense of belongingness and loyalty to the company. LKC treated the company like a big family and, as head of the company, he took it as a personal obligation to look after every employee's welfare (Zheng, 1997, p. 75). Under his leadership, the Nam Aik Company adopted a wide range of unique and attractive remuneration policies and measures. Consequently, Nam Aik was able to maintain and grow a stable team of well motivated and dedicated managers, staff and workers throughout the long years.

One example of this welfare system for workers is that, under LKC's leadership, Nam Aik adopted a profit-sharing system, which linked the employees' salary directly with the company's productivity and annual performance. The company allocated 20 percent of its annual profits to reward staff and workers in the form of year-end bonuses. The employees' remuneration comprised two components, basic pay and bonus, the latter was variable depending on the company's actual performance.

> "Nam Aik was popular for giving out very generous bonuses to its employees, and it was said that employees from some units with very good profits could often receive a bonus equal to a sum of their three- or four-year's salary. It was reported that someone had even received a bonus amounting to three million dollars" (Zheng, 1997, p. 76).

Another significant example is that LKC practiced life-long employment in his company. An employee would not be fired unless he committed a very serious mistake or violated laws. When an employee made a minor error, the company would often take such measures as to criticize him or change his position in the hope of giving him a chance. The company would only fire an employee as a last measure since it did not want to see the employee and his family fall into financial difficulties as a result of his poor performance (Zheng, 1997, p. 75).

Apart from the life-long employment policy, another measure illustrating Nam Aik Company's human resource initiative was a scheme designed to let every staff member in Nam Aik eventually own a house. The company offered long-term interest-free loans to its staff who did not have their own houses. The amount of a housing loan could be equivalent to a total of about three-year's salary. With the generous allocation of the company's annual profits for its employees' year-end bonuses as described above, Nam Aik's housing loan was actually made affordable to employees in pursuit of their home ownership.

As early as 1947, the Nam Aik Company started to implement a program of insurance funds for its employees, a fund with a function similar to the Central Provident Fund (or CPF) initiated by the Singapore government in 1954. According to the program, five percent of an employee's monthly salary was deducted, together with another 10 percent offered by the company. The two components totaled 15 percent of the employee's salary and were credited into the employees' account every month. The employees would start to use the money in the fund as a retirement pension only after they retired (Li, 1995, p. 19).

Nam Aik Company's motivation programs for its employees included other incentive schemes such as free medical benefits, scholarships and study-aids for the employees' children, and building schools close to locations of remote rubber and pineapple plantations and farms.

As we can see, all these incentive and motivation programs adopted by LKC integrated the company's objectives with individual employees' needs, thus effectively motivating the employees to dedicate themselves to the continuous growth of the company, fostering their sense of belonging and loyalty to the organization. Today, the integration of organizational objectives with individuals' needs is widely advocated and adopted as a fundamental and effective principle of modern management practice among enterprises.

4.6 *Adopting a modern organizational structure*

From the time LKC set up his first rubber smoke house in Muar with his friend in 1927, his business had been continually expanding. However, LKC was always keen to adopt and practice new scientific technology and management principles to further grow his business empire. He was not only active in adopting new and advanced technology in an attempt to continually raise the efficiency and productivity standards of his business process and operation, but he was also keen to adopt a modern organizational structure for his company amid the changing environment. Obviously, LKC was fully aware that a modern organizational structure would better enable his business empire to operate and develop in an efficient way. For example, in 1931, LKC's Nam Aik underwent significant re-organization. LKC restructured Nam Aik Rubber into the Lee Rubber Company Private Limited with a larger number of stockholders (Lim, 1999, p. 200; Zheng, 1997, p. 225).

Amid Nam Aik's continual expansion of businesses along different product lines and in different countries in the region in subsequent years, LKC further turned the company into Lee Rubber Group toward the end of the 1940s.

As a Chinese entrepreneur, LKC was fully aware of a Chinese saying that wealth in a rich family could rarely be sustained for three generations, a phenomenon he personally witnessed during his life time; many Chinese family-owned enterprises seldom survived three generations resulting from family, social and business issues, for instance, the abuse of power, embezzlement of company funds by family members, nepotism, failure to differentiate between enterprise and family affairs, the struggle for control among the family members, and poor-management. As a well-educated and far-sighted entrepreneur, LKC was determined to take proactive measures to prevent his business empire from falling apart after his death. He adopted the Western principle of management for his Nam Aik Group by separating ownership from management right and formulating a series of rule-of-law methods and approaches for running the Nam Aik family-owned business empire. Specifically, he obtained the support of the stockholders on July 30, 1951 to issue 40,000 management shares. The purpose of it was to ensure the commanding power of the group was kept under the control of the board of directors and to ensure that Nam Aik Company always remained a Lee-family enterprise (Lim, 1999, p. 207). LKC also formulated specific rules prohibiting family members from utilizing company funds and stipulating how family members with director positions or non-director positions should obtain their remuneration and dividend at the end of each financial year. Such far-sighted measures initiated by LKC helped ensure the survival and success of Nam Aik enterprise. These measures have also helped Nam Aik remain a dynamic family-owned enterprise filled with vitality and cohesiveness ever since. Meanwhile, LKC's pioneering experimental practices of modern concepts and principles pertaining to company structure and management methods exhibited clear evidence of knowledge leadership for his business empire in his time.

4.7 *Contributing generously to education and society/promoting learning*

Despite his continual success in businesses and his increasingly responsibilities as a leader of the expanding businesses, LKC never ceased to be mindful of the welfare of the general public, nor did he neglect his responsibility for the progress of society. He believed deeply in the value of knowledge for the sustained development of his company and for society. LKC understood that knowledge is power, for society and for business alike. Therefore he continuously made enthusiastic and generous contributions to promote public education and social welfare.

The year 1952 witnessed a historic event, in which LKC donated a part of Nam Aik's assets to set up the Lee Foundation, a charitable foundation to fund and sponsor programs that promote education and other philanthropic work for the benefit of general public and society. In 1960 and 1965, the Lee Foundation was established in Malaysia and Hong Kong respectively (Zheng, 1997, p. 92).

In 1964, he donated all his personal stock shares in Nam Aik Company, which took up 48 per cent of the total stock shares in Nam Aik, to the Lee Foundation, thus making the charitable organization the largest stockholder of Nam Aik Company (Zheng, 1997, p. 92). Between 1952 and 1993, the Lee Foundation donated a total sum of 300 million Singapore Dollars to various education and other philanthropic causes, regardless of race, language, religion, nationality, geographical location. Of the total donation, it was estimated that 75 percent was given to various education causes like building schools and libraries in Singapore, Malaysia, and LKC's home village in China and some other research and academic projects (Zheng, 1997, p. 93).

Here we can see that LKC's enthusiasm for promoting social welfare, especially his pursuit of public learning and education, went further than many other successful entrepreneurs in that he was well aware of the power of knowledge not only for his employees but also for the general public. He was fully conscious that the development and prosperity of society was closely hinged to education of the general public and that acquisition and application of new knowledge and technology was directly based on the education of youths. In his inaugural speech as the first Chancellor of the University of Singapore, he cited Cicero, an eloquent debater from Ancient Roman, saying (Zheng, 1997, p. 184), "Nothing can be compared to our contribution to the nation when we work for the education of youths," which clearly indicates LKC's belief in knowledge power and his awareness of and emphasis on the importance of knowledge management in a context much larger than just an organization.

5. Conclusions

Our study explored the leadership and management practices of LKC as the founder of Nam Aik Company, the characteristics of which are related to or reflect the elements and/or components of KM in contemporary management. From this study, we see that LKC's leadership style, even in the days when the concept of KM had not formally emerged, included considerable features of knowledge leadership, as revealed in his thinking and management initiatives. The features of his unique leadership style include his emphasis on the upright principles for business operation and development for his company and his employees, his pursuit of new technologies and communication facilities, his efforts to treat his employees as valuable assets and motivate them. All these leadership features helped make the company a positive environment for employees. Among other things, it facilitated the process of information exchange, learning and sharing new knowledge in an efficient way, thus fostering employee royalty to the organization. The unique system of human resource management he developed resulted in a motivated and committed workforce.

Furthermore, LKC contributed hundreds of millions of dollars to educational institutions in Singapore and China, which clearly revealed his foresight and belief in the power of education. He was fully aware of the power of knowledge not only for his business empire but also for the whole of society. This is irrepressible evidence of LKC's knowledge leadership, which we cannot neglect today.

References

Armstrong, CP and V Sambamurthy (1999). Information technology assimilation in firms: The influence of senior leadership and IT structures. *Information Systems Research*, 10(4), 304–332.

Bai, QP (2004). Developing and thinking methodologies for tacit information. *Modern Information*, 8, 190–191.

Cabrera, A and EF Cabrera (2002). Knowledge sharing dilemmas. *Organization Studies*, 23(5), 687–710.

Hansen, MT, N Nohria and T Tierney (1997). What's your strategy for managing knowledge? *Harvard Business Review*, 77(2), 106–118.

Lakshman, C (2005). Top executive knowledge leadership: Managing knowledge to lead change at General Electric. *Journal of Change Management*, 5(4), 429–446.

Li, CF (1995). What I know about Mr Lee Kong Chian. *Proceedings of Monographs from Academic Forum on Lee Kong Chian* [in Chinese]. Beijing: China Overseas Chinese Publishing House.

Li, T (2003). Lee Kong Chian's methods of managing enterprises and Lao-tzu theory. *Journal of Yibin University*, 6(6), 21–23.

Li, Y (1998). *Biography of Lee Kong Chian* [in Chinese]. Hong Kong: Mingliu Publishing House.

Lim, HS (1999). Chapter 8: Lee Kong Chian's Business empire. *Chinese Society and Businessmen in Singapore* [in Chinese]. Singapore: Society of Asian Studies.

Menkhoff, T, YW Chay, H-D Evers, and B Loh (2005). Leadership in knowledge sharing: Creating value through collaboration. *Internal Research Paper Series, Singapore Management University*. Singapore: Singapore Management University.

Pan, SL and H Scarbrough (1999). Knowledge management in practice: An exploratory case study. *Technology Analysis and Strategic Management*, 11(3), 359–374.

Politis, JD (2001). The relationship of various leadership styles to knowledge management. *Leadership and Organization Development Journal*, 22(8), 354–364.

Tong, CK and PL Yong (2002). Personalism and paternalism in Chinese businesses. In *Chinese Entrepreneurship and Asian Business Networks*, T Menkhoff and S Gerke (eds.), pp. 217–231. London, UK: Routledge.

Wilson, TD (2002). The nonsense of "knowledge management." *Information Research*, 8(1).

Zheng, B (1997). *Biography of Lee Kong Chian* [in Chinese]. Beijing: China Overseas Publishing House.

Chapter 14

Organizational Learning Approaches of Small and Medium-Sized Enterprises: A Comparative Study of Chinese Firms in Singapore

Thomas Menkhoff

1. Introduction

Small and medium-sized enterprises (SMEs) form the backbone of most economies in East and West in terms of value added or employment generation (Lee and Li, 2008; Tong, 2008; Tsui-Auch, 2003; Ng, 2002; Rauch *et al.*, 2005; Howard, 1991). In the Republic of Singapore, local SMEs comprise more than 92 percent of the total establishments, employing 51 percent of the workforce and generating 40 percent of total value added. Given their small size and the increasing volatile business environment, SMEs are faced with numerous challenges and issues such as succession problems, technological upgrading demands, international market expansion and so forth. Creating new value through learning and skills upgrading in increasingly knowledge-centric business contexts is often regarded as a particularly difficult issue by many SME owner-managers due to urgent business demands or lack of specialized skills (Collins *et al.*, 2009; Menkhoff, 2010).

The Republic of Singapore (located at the tip of the Malaysian Peninsula) represents an interesting case study in this respect given its track record in developing an "intelligent island" and continuous human

The author gratefully acknowledges the support of the UOB–SMU Asian Enterprise Institute at the Singapore Management University (SMU) as well as the three entrepreneurs featured in this article in completing this research study which was funded by SMU (OR Ref No. 11-C207-SMU-005).

capital development appeals by policy-makers which are supported by strategic (and well funded) measures toward nation-wide learning at various levels from primary school education to science and technology (Tsui-Auch, 2003; Hornidge, 2007). Although the number of SMEs participating in official SME upgrading schemes rolled out by Singapore's Standards, Productivity and Innovation Board (SPRING) has steadily increased over time, there are still a large number of SME owner-managers who do not utilize such schemes due to skepticism about their value added or unwillingness to get involved in the necessary paperwork. As a consequence organizational learning benefits are foregone. According to the official SME definition adopted by SPRING Singapore, a SME must have at least 30 percent local equity to qualify for SME assistance schemes with annual sales turnover of not more than S$100 million and an employment size of not more than 200 workers for both non-manufacturing and manufacturing enterprises. An important question in this context is what characterizes those small firms and their owner-managers who proactively tackle strategic learning challenges and those who do not.

Margin annotations (handwritten): "Many SMEs don't take advantage of govt assistance"; "eligibility criteria"

1.1 *Purpose of study, context and methodology*

This chapter is part of a major exploratory study on the learning strategies of small-scale ethnic Chinese business organizations in Singapore (Menkhoff and Gerke eds., 2002; Armstrong and Foley, 2003; Tsui-Auch, 2003). Conceptually, the three case studies presented here are based on an evolving research model as summarized in Figure 1 which puts emphasis on the theory and practice of Asian family firms with their distinct organizational and managerial practices, particular CEO behaviors with regard to knowledge leadership and openness, firm attributes such as absorptive capacity, fair process and knowledge transfer aimed at examining the antecedents of the firms' organizational learning capability and its impact upon SME performance. The various components of the model have been described in greater depth in Menkhoff and Chay (2011, 2013). Figure 1 illustrates the evolving research model aimed at examining the antecedents of organizational learning capability and its impact on performance in Asian SMEs.

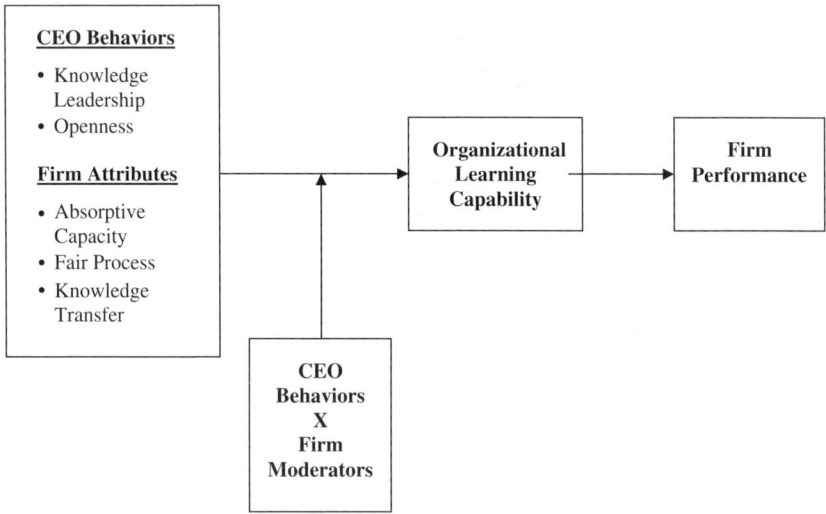

Figure 1. Antecedents of organizational learning capability and firm performance of Asian SMEs

The model components were developed and plausibilized based on both the relevant literatures and several exploratory interviews with SME owner-managers. Key research questions included:

- How do SME leaders view the importance of leveraging on learning and knowledge (whether in form of internally induced peer learning or IP-related know how to create value through franchising) with regard to enhanced organizational effectiveness and firm performance (Kogut and Zander, 1992; Nonaka, 1994; Crossan *et al.*, 1999; Neilson, 2001; Ribière and Sitar, 2003; Holcomb *et al.*, 2009)?
- What particular (leadership) behaviors are crucial in driving value-added knowledge management and creation processes in the organization as well as successful learning (Garvin, 1993; Grant, 1996; Guns, 1997; Menkhoff and Chay, 2013)?
- To what extent is the firms' learning orientation shaped by its culture and openness towards new possibilities derived internally or externally (Redding, 1993; Chay *et al.*, 2007; Wood and Hampson, 2005)?

- How do SME leaders view their firms' capacity to absorb new information, to assimilate it (e.g., via knowledge transfer) and to successfully integrate it into business models in order to sustain and further improve their competitive advantage (Argote and Ingram, 2000; Cohen and Levinthal, 1990; Fosfuri and Tribo, 2008)?
- What is the role of procedural justice (Brockner and Siegel, 1996; Colquitt 2001; Colquitt *et al.*, 2001) in enabling organizational members to make full use of new learning resources acquired internally or externally in these small firms?

The implications of the latter have not been systematically examined in the context of small-scale Chinese businesses whose leaders often differentiate strongly between a (privileged) inner core of (often related) top management team members and "others" who might perceive organizational dynamics from an "outsider" perspective with little hope to be involved in key decisions or ever climb up the corporate ladder due to the non-existence of a proper talent management system. In sum, we hope that the study findings will be instrumental in helping to foster the learning capacity of small-scale ethnic Chinese business organizations in Singapore and Asia.

Our methodological study approach is embedded in the tradition of interpretative case study and exploratory research (Eisenhardt, 1989; Stebbins, 2001) based on the analysis of relevant literature, discussions with small business owners and SME experts as well as observations during field excursions. Two in-depth case studies, Seafood Restaurant and Advertising X are presented here in greater detail in order to understand and showcase the wide variety of learning approaches adopted by local SMEs and to identify areas where further inputs are required so that these small firms can reach the next level of development. Both firms are then contrasted with a well known local firm, Qian Hu, which has successfully managed the transition from a SME to a public-listed corporation due to its capability to leverage on good management know how, learning and knowledge. The case studies were developed and analyzed with the help of qualitative methods in form of in-depth interviews, transcription, concept mapping and triangulation. We argue that the development of several evaluative arguments about the antecedents of organizational learning capability and its impact on performance in Asian SMEs will be useful for both future, quantitative and theory-driven SME research as well as practical interventions by SME promotion bodies.

2. Three Cases

2.1 *Firm A: When the second generation initiates change — Organizational learning management at Seafood Restaurant*

Singaporean Seafood Restaurant specializes in seafood dishes. It was established several decades ago and is registered as a private limited company. It currently has two outlets. The following section is based on in-depth interview data generated during a meeting with the firm's founder's daughter Siok San (not her real name) who belongs to the second generation in the business and is in charge of business operations matters.

Learning has to be a top-down approach

Asked what she thinks about the importance of learning in general, Siok San replied that learning is very important for the firm and that it has to be a *top down approach* driven by the leadership or the people in management who must also be willing to learn. She added that all this is not just about learning. It is also about the mindset as "people sometimes do not want to learn because they don't like change."

In the case of the family-owned Seafood Restaurant featured here, Siok San continues to play an important role as change maker, for example, by initiating alterations with regard to business processes. As she pointed out, her parents who ran the company alone before she and one of her siblings joined the management team a few years ago were quite open toward change, "except for the fact that in a lot of instances they either didn't know how to do it or didn't have access to the necessary resources to do it." There were other constraints like lack of time or "not having the right people to do it." As she opined, especially in

SMEs, it is critical to have the right people on board to help to change and learn:

> "The people that you might hire to come in to help you do not always understand the culture of the organization enough to help you do it effectively. So often they will come in for 3 months and then you say 'this is how you do it' and then it works great for the short term but the employees within the firm have problems sustaining it."

... but sometimes urgent work demands prevent that from happening

A big challenge in terms of learning sustainability in the restaurant business is that employees are very much involved in daily operations due to the nature of a restaurant. As Siok San pointed out, often there is simply not enough time to teach and learn properly due to busy schedules or the lack of teaching and communication skills.

The Founder's daughter as change maker and technological innovator

When Siok San joined the business, the first thing she did was to introduce a new point of sales system (in short: POS system) because it would make operations a lot more effective. POS systems allow SMEs to optimize business operations by keeping track of sales, inventory management, customer relationship management and so on. Some vendors offer customized POS systems for restaurants which comprise a restaurant POS PC and specialized POS software, enabling high-speed credit card transactions, inventory tracking, order supplies, management of employees etc. With her emotional intelligence and hands-on approach, she managed to convince most of the employees that the change was a positive and necessary one rather than a "nuisance": "Although you can send staff for training and they would probably learn a little bit from it, it's the hands on approach that makes the difference." As she explained, employees appreciate if someone is holding their hand for a while when it comes to technological changes because of initial fear of the new technology: "So you had to be there by their side and reassure them that it's okay. I think emotional support is very important."

As part of the change measure, every kitchen station has been equipped with a printer:

> "So, for example, you have your already fried dishes, already steamed fish or ready chopped seafood. They all have a different printer and when they get an order they will prepare for it. For the kitchen staff it wasn't too different from what they did previously when they had to write things down and then pass it to every department."

External learning by observation and proactive search

Asked how she managed to identify the "right" system, she explained that she met up with several vendors:

> "A Chinese restaurant operation is quite different from, say, a café or a Western restaurant, and certain features had to be customized. So, from talking to the vendor you can see how open they are, how flexible they are to adapt and accept certain requirements. Some vendors couldn't do it and so we just went with the one who was willing to help us customize."

In order to find the right vendor, she also searched online and took a look at the POS systems of other restaurants whenever she ate outside: "I would go to cafés and other Chinese restaurants and take a look at the hardware they were using."

Asked whether it was difficult to convince her parents to invest in this innovation, she replied:

> "No, it wasn't because they realized that they needed to change. They just didn't know how to, and they didn't know who to go to for information and how to go about thinking what to purchase. They don't have much knowledge about new technology so it's difficult for them to make that step. They also didn't want to make the wrong decision about picking a vendor that wasn't good and could not give them enough support. So, they rather just continued with what they were familiar with."

Utilization of SPRING schemes

In contrast to other Singaporean SMEs, Seafood Restaurant utilized SPRING schemes to get partial funding for the new POS system. This also helped to ease her parents' worries about the change "because they knew that there was a small cushion financially." Asked how she learned about the availability of external support, she said that through friends, taking part in external events and through her own initiative:

"I joined a company, an organization where there was no one really my age, and while I could learn through experience there was no one who was telling me what to do. So my parents gave me a lot of freedom to explore what I wanted to do... I had to get more information myself, and it's just learning from friends who advised that SPRING has schemes for SMEs and just meeting with people. So whenever there was a networking event, or an event about something that was vaguely relevant to what I did... I would call and turn up and get more information. At the beginning when I first joined the family business I wasn't in the office at all. I was out all the time. Until I had enough resources in terms of contacts or people I knew that I could speak to, then I started spending more time, you know, trying to get this done."

The limits of in-house training

As in many other small Chinese family firms, Seafood Restaurant's internal training approach is not fully formalized:

"I am really trying to do it, but it's definitely not formalized. We depend on the managers' daily roll calls (TM: roll call training) to inform or tell the staff about an event that might have happened before that was good or bad and that's how we are trying to learn from things that have happened. It's very difficult to organize formal trainings because the attention span of operational staff is quite short. May be it's the trainer or the manager but they don't respond so well. They don't like classroom type learning situations. They prefer short roll call trainings where they can quickly absorb information. We have tried formal training and getting external trainers to come in but most of the time they take it as just like a break time for them. They're not really taking in the information."

Career progression issues

Up to now, Seafood Restaurant has not yet implemented a fully fledged career progression system. The company is in the process of revamping its HR system

"… to address a few issues such as the lack of manpower in the industry. And so we don't have that yet but that's a good idea. I just don't know if we can implement it successfully because if you don't have enough resources to let the staff help with training or to attend courses, then you can't have such a structure in place. So there's a bit of a chicken and egg problem."

Like other Singaporean firms, Seafood Restaurant is struggling with the current labor crunch:

"In a way I can understand why the government is making this move but it's a bit of a shock to the system. They were quite open may be 5 years ago and then you know the market was flooded with foreign, unskilled labor and now they're just like pulling it all back without making sure that there are enough people in the workforce."

While there are numerous opportunities for leveraging on external training opportunities, she feels that many companies (while they would like to make use of them) simply do not have the time to let staff out:

"I think the other issue is that the courses they offer for the food industry in general are not practical enough… I am not sure what the right format should be but I know for sure that it shouldn't be a classroom environment. It could be something more interactive. For example, if it would be in the area of F&B, the training could be set up in a café where you can actually see things happening."

To find the right training approach is crucial for the restaurant sector due to the generally low educational background of service staff. Many of the employees of Seafood Restaurant do not even have O level education and some don't have a formal education at all.

Attracting talent

In terms of recruitment, the company utilizes several channels. To attract Singaporeans, community centers are utilized where they put up ads:

> "We pick a community center that is near an MRT station. When people show up we try to convince them to join. It usually seems to be quite successful because they turn up at the centres. But for the number of people who actually report to work and stay on for at least three days... it's just like drops off a cliff. That's the problem. I think for us the other challenge is that it's not a very pleasant environment to work in. You know its dirty work... like you are clearing tables or you are in the kitchen. It's not a nice cafe or fine dining restaurant. So that's the other reason why it's difficult to get people to work like that. So we're trying very hard to change the concept of the restaurant and just so that we can keep up with how things are changing in Singapore."

Culture of innovation and experimentation

Asked how she would describe the firm's culture of innovation and experimentation, Siok San said that they practice "a lot of it" but that the problem is with implementation:

> "We explore a lot of new dishes and we try new ways of doing things all the time. The biggest problem is that when you think of work we don't always successfully implement it. So, whether it's something as simple as a new addition on the menu or say a different way of doing things like the time card system, we don't do it because we have a significant amount of people who don't agree with it. When it comes to a new dish, there is not enough proper structure in place to ensure that the kitchen staff is trained to make that new dish or to promote it to customers. There is a bit of miscommunication sometimes."

Traditionally, her Dad has been the key driver of innovation:

> "So, in the past he would see something that was interesting or good and then replicate it in the restaurant quite quickly because it was smaller. It was just one restaurant, and he was in control of most things.

But now that the company is growing, there are more managers in place and the information flow is a bit different. I think we haven't quite adapted to the new structure of the company, so we're still trying to get there."

Main innovations include the dishes and how Seafood Restaurant runs certain business processes. The company used to accept deposits for reservations during Chinese New Year Eve which was initially done by fax or by asking customers to come down to make a partial payment: "As this was troublesome, we replaced it with a new online console which allows customers to pay by PayPal." Nevertheless, it is not all smooth sailing according to her perception because not everyone knows how to use the system "but we just try and deal with problems. So that was one thing that we did about two years ago. Online reservations are also becoming more common."

Asked whether she considers PayPal expensive for small entrepreneurs, Siok San denied: "There is a charge but it's not a lot more expensive than a regular credit card payment. It's quite easy and also with today's technology which is getting very affordable there's a lot of free software that you can use."

The company employs "about a hundred" employees and there is one HR administrative person. Besides Siok San, her sibling and one manager jointly "overlook" HR. HR works are facilitated by the use of a web-based software solution: "It's quite straight forward. We do it ourselves. It's not too time consuming, probably like 2 hours a month." Siok San is currently revamping the HR system:

> "In the past we had employment contracts. We are now trying to simplify that so that we can act quickly when someone does break a term or condition of the contract it. There is no point of having a whole list of rules and regulations that you cannot act upon."

She managed to find a HR consultant who is fine-tuning HR functions such as compensation and benefits:

> "We think that's most important for now. Also, in terms of trying to attract more Singaporeans, we have to look at the number of hours that they work, what they do when they come in. And also, how to

compensate them and what kind of benefits to give for our people who just want to work part time."

Work-life balance is seemingly a challenge in Singapore's small restaurants.

Procedural justice

Asked what she thinks about procedural justice, she replied that one related issue in a family firm is that family members who own the business must work very closely with the rest of the employees: "It's interesting… perhaps employees do feel that people who own the firm have more benefits than they do in terms of not just monetary rewards but everything else." Traditionally, procedural justice has been a challenge in Chinese family firms with their clear distinction between insiders and outsiders (Tsui-Auch, 2003). A recent case study in her MBA class kept her thinking about whether her own employees have a real stake in Seafood Restaurant:

> "It got me thinking because the one very obvious benefit in my family firm that we have over the employees is that, we get to eat at the restaurant. It's with my parents; it's with my sibling and me. We don't do it because we want to behave like customers… we do it because we want to taste the food. It's like a quality control type of process. But it's also very visible because then you have the employees serving you because it's a restaurant, right? And yeah, although we are quite happy to get our own food and drinks, they still do it."

In the subsequent minutes, both Siok San and myself pondered about the implications of this practice with regard to procedural justice and whether it is possible to devise an alternative, perhaps less hierarchical system in order to avoid any potentially wrong perceptions, e.g., by communicating clearly that this is actually quality control:

> "That's something quite noticeable for me right now I am trying to change it, and I think it's very easy for my sibling to stop doing it. But I am not sure whether my father will be able to stop doing it. Sometimes it is done out of convenience… but for the staff it looks like that you obviously have benefits…."

2.2 *Firm B: Staying innovative and committed to external learning — Organizational learning management at Advertising X*

Advertising X is an agency well-versed in marketing and advertising concepts. It is registered as a private limited company with a staff size of 30 employees. The following section is based on in-depth interview data generated during a meeting with the firm's co-founder Sian (not her real name).

Learning — A necessity to keep up with rapid technological change

Asked what she thinks about learning and its importance as far as her own business is concerned, Sian pointed out that she regards learning as "absolutely important and paramount" in a creative company:

> "There are a couple of reasons. First and foremost I think that in terms of the changing business landscape during the last 30 years technology has changed our life of how we get treated, how we actually work, how we actually live, how we actually play. If you can't keep up with that, there is absolutely no way that you could be able to stay relevant, and that really seeps through so many crevices within the organization."

She continued to stress the importance of learning with regard to the nature of her competitive business, namely advertising, marketing and communications, which requires originality, productivity, efficiency:

> "That in itself really pushes the forefront of learning. Originality really needs to be based on leading edge approaches, cutting edge channels and ways to do things as well. So that's the sort of business aspect. But even within the organization, I think that you're learning how to become more productive, how to become more efficient, how to become more competitive. You know, that's something that you live and breathe every single day. And it's not just something that the sales or the creative guys do. It has to be within the organization even from the finance perspective. My finance department has been fighting tooth and nail to retain the old model of doing things, sort of clocking in accounting and finance or billings as well as data."

As she explained, there is a new type of accounting software in the market, an integrated invoicing and accounting management software whose features help SMEs to simplify the way they quote, track and invoice jobs. It simultaneously tracks business transactions and reduces the time to send out quotes, invoices, etc. and to get paid. As the interview suggests, it has not been easy to implement such an innovative system at Sian's firm despite its apparent advantages: "Being able to access data anywhere, anytime as well as to be able to churn out an analysis with real time data will further change the ways of traditional finance and how they used to see things."

From an organizational standpoint, the company attempts to think creatively and to really push the forefront in terms of what organizational members are learning every day:

> "We do try to always break the box as far as we can and to adopt new techniques of doing the business that we do. I think it is very important that the support departments think likewise. We also need to push a little bit more in certain areas… we do try to negotiate and push with them."

External and internal sources of knowledge and learning

Advertising X uses several sources of external knowledge and learning such as global fora on marketing as well as communications, marketing portals, including blogs. An important source is Campaign Asia (http://www.campaignasia.com/), an e-newsletter on the ad and marketing industry, which reports on emerging media and other key trends, "So, for example, you've got Campaign Asia. You've got marketing interactive, but you've also got a whole stew of creative resources online which we chat into."

In Sian's industry, these sources are important knowledge providers of business relevant specialist knowledge and content. Specialized applications have also been deployed such as "GWT intelligence" (Google Web Toolkit) or "e27" in terms of content management. The latter features "startups, people and technologies that are changing Asia's web and mobile ecosystem." It is managed by Optimatic Pte Ltd, a community-centric media company (http://e27.sg/):

> "It's basically making sure that you run a fast company by using business portals, technology portals, marketing portals, advertising portals,

creativity portals. For us this is important because the nature of our business is adventurous. One day you are doing a HR campaign and next day you are doing a banking campaign. So you know, the knowledge base of the internet is extremely important for us."

The company subscribes to various online publications and blogs in order to pull in relevant information sources such as news articles.

"As an ad agency, being up to date on what is going on in the market place is important. Being inspired by cutting edge content and ideas is also important. Hence, we have an open sharing culture within the agency where people are constantly sharing content with everyone, whether it is a blog topic, or a YouTube video or an installation or a painting that inspires. In terms of content, to us, the worldwide web presents an immense library of resources and ideas that spurs our creativity."

Interns play another valuable role in this respect because they know how to conduct relevant online research.

About creativity

Creativity is seen as something of utmost importance in her business according to Sian, especially "if you want to stand out in the market":

"I think the danger also of external knowledge, especially in a business like ours, is the copy cat syndrome. So what happens quite often, given the fact that content is so readily available, is that copying becomes something like a very natural progression. I think that the key question really is whether you really want to be creative. If the answer is yes, you have to be original. That's where the external factors can only sort of help you in the consideration of your creative endeavor. Eventually, it should be more research based rather than based on an understanding of the market place, rather than sort of, you know, trying to, sort of, copy in that direction."

Sian herself was not trained as a creative person. As a matter of fact, she is more involved on the strategic business management side of the firm: "We have two key partners, myself as well as my partner who is literally the guy who does the creative work. I'm more on the strategic side of things where I look at the marketing as well as." Asked whether she thinks that creativity can be trained, she stressed:

> "I think it can be trained to a certain part, you know where you are honing somebody into the process approach of how you could unleash your creativity. But at the end of the day, I truly believe that it depends on the kind of person you are, whether you're more operational or whether you are more the 'out of the box type.'"

Procedure of justice

In terms of procedural justice as potential driver of learning sustainability, Sian argued that what really matters is the company culture and whether it empowers or stifles learning:

> "In empowering learning you also empower employees. I think at the core of it is really the company culture. This was very important to us when we started this firm. There were a couple of things. Number one was to build a very transparent, very honest and authentic culture where we try as far as possible to give clear directions to the team. We are very consistent in the way we communicate and we are also very consistent in the way we praise employees. We are results focused rather than process focused. I think that is something that is very clear in this organization."

With regard to the alignment of company culture and learning, Sian stressed that she understood from the beginning that to drive a performance culture requires a transparent performance management system with clear key performance indicators:

> "The interesting thing about the advertising industry is that KPIs aren't something that are well practiced in many advertising firms. Thanks to my experiences at IBM what we do here is based on very clear KPIs that every single staff member has on a yearly basis. We also follow up with staff and update each other quarterly. What then happens is that staff does not need to sort of grow in the dark in terms of what he or she needs to achieve in a given year. With that in mind I think that employees

understand that if they're not doing very well that they therefore either need to buck up or leave."

According to Sian, such transparency also ensures that employees do not gossip and work together as a team:

"Its really interesting. After two years in the making, we now have a culture that can self-select and that is generally the mark of a high performance culture. So that in itself really does harness a sort of strong team culture that then opens up the flood gates of learning and empowerment. One thing we were very clear about from the beginning is that every staff is empowered in the sense that they should not complain about certain processes that are not fixed, but to always come back with solutions for the processes that need to be fixed."

Her former IBM exposure arguably had a strong impact upon the performance culture of Advertising X:

"I have been with many organizations before. But I felt that implementing the IBM approach to appraisals as well as culture was probably a really good way to start off this sort of Advertising X culture."

Training and development challenges

In terms of the firm's training and development system, there are a couple of issues which prevent it from achieving talent management excellence at this point in time although Sian is a very strong advocate of people development:

"I think being a startup we don't really have the necessary funds to send people to expensive learning courses but what we did realize as a team is that there is actually a lot of the domain knowledge in each of us. There are many people in this organization that actually do have a lot of talents that they can then harness and actually teach other people. So, since the beginning of this year I have put together a short timeline, a sort of schedule that includes lunch learnings as well as weekend learnings. We try not to eat into people's weekends but for key milestones in terms of certain training modules, we do try to get the team back into our training. It's not just about hard skills, it's also about soft skills. It's about motivational skills."

Efforts continue to formalize this process:

> "There's a planned document which we email out to the staff, we update
> regularly. We probably aren't the most punctual in terms of the timelines
> but we get it done. So, I think I've seen about six trainings as well as
> luncheon workshops."

Recent learning contents included brief writing skills ("to delve into how
to write really, really well to inspire the creative guys to actually take it
on") and accounting skills.

Talent recruitment matters

Sian stressed that it is crucial to differentiate the business from others
because of the high competitive pressures in the industry which she considers to be

> "a really cut-throat business. The way that we've always differentiated
> ourselves as Advertising X is to be more value driven rather than cost
> driven to our clients. We're not cheap and we're not necessarily expen-
> sive. The kind of competition that we go against is really the big boys.
> It is a real uphill climb to find the right people. Once you have recruited
> them, what you need to do then is to train and train and train them."

In terms of attracting creative potential, she pointed out that talent can
be recruited from polytechnics and universities because they have programs on communications or marketing:

> "General degrees are fine but then when you want to go into things like
> art direction and design and designing, we do take a lot of people from
> the likes of, you know, Temasek Polytechnic with graphic design experi-
> ence, Lycel and the Academy of Fine Arts."

Due to the firm's reputation, the company has good contacts which
help to sustain the business. Sian opined that cold calls do not really
work:

> "We have been pretty blessed and I think contacts helped at the begin-
> ning. Word of mouth has been pretty good. I think we also rely a lot

on our network partners. They've sort of introduced us to different clients such as the media houses that we work with or vendors we collaborate with."

Innovation, experimentation and idea generation

In terms of innovation, experimentation and idea generation, it is not good enough to be creative in order to come up with new ideas according to Sian. In order to be successful, the business model itself has to be innovative and differentiated:

> "The reason why our unique model came about is that we saw a gap in the marketplace. Traditionally, the way agencies actually function has been pretty much sliced up whether you're above the line agency or you're an online agency or below the line agency, or events agency. The big boys try very hard to do integration but they also find it very hard to do because of bottom-line and profit concerns. So I think there was a good opportunity for us to come and really innovate from the perspective of making sure that integration actually happens at the helm of the business rather than chopping ourselves up into too many different departments. It is difficult to put us into a box. We are not in the advertising print ad box and we are not in the online box. It's one-stop and a lot of clients actually do tell us that we really sort of walk the walk and talk the talk."

Pushing the boundaries of innovation — Conquering fear and lack of imagination

As Sian pointed out, there is a need to push the boundaries a little bit more to enhance the firm's innovation capability:

> "I don't think that we're really there yet. Innovation means leading edge. How do we really stay at that forefront of the things that we do very well? That's something that we're still actually trying to hone."

Number one barrier toward that goal is fear:

> "Fear of change, fear of abandoning the safety net. I think that innovation really requires taking risks. It's about turning things on its head. We

really need to dream big and go far. I definitely think that fear and that safety net is definitely one huge barrier."

Asked whether she thinks that there is something uniquely fearful in Singapore, she agreed:

"Yes, definitely. I find it interesting that you mention fear in Singapore society. I think that fear is engrained in Singapore society. You have heard the word *kiasu* many times. It is really engrained in the whole culture of not wanting to sort of venture, adventure you know. I think definitely, fear is one."

Even amongst her employees she can observe that fear:

"Definitely. You know, I myself sometimes also experience that in me. Lack of imagination is another one, and I think that lack of imagination could possibly also be part of the Singapore culture which I'm sure you've read about many times. We do lack imagination quite a bit. I think that especially in Asian culture you know, we are probably a lot less innovative because we tend to take other people's ideas in but do it better. Yeah, so as we talk about this whole thing of having to push the cutting edge of things, I think that we probably struggle with a lot more than maybe a Western advertising agency would. Yeah, so I think basically, lack of imagination as well as fear would be the two key issues."

Leveraging on SPRING schemes

Unlike Case companies A and C, Advertising X has not yet made full use of government schemes to support SMEs although Sian is aware of the possibility to tap into SPRING's IT grants: "We haven't had such a huge initiative on IT. So we have not been able to use it as yet." As it turned out, the experience with SPRING's productivity and innovation schemes has been somewhat limited:

"I think unfortunately my experience with SPRING so far hasn't been too topnotch honestly. I think that besides the schemes and what is on SPRING's website you actually do need people who can properly explain the details to you. I tried to schedule something and that *SPRING* person actually met me. But at the end it seemed that the available grants were not pertinent to my requirements. I guess there was a little bit of a letdown. I think that that person was sort of just ticking the boxes. It felt like a wasted effort."

One local SME which she admires in terms of innovation is Hungry Go Where. According to her, they really had a vision and managed to finally realize that vision: "I think that not being paid for two years before they started, getting a little bit of salary, believing in that dream, that's very very commendable."

2.3 *Firm C: Qian Hu — Achieving learning organization status through systematic benchmarking and effective learning*

One local firm which has successfully managed organisational learning challenges is Qian Hu Corp., Singapore's leading breeder and exporter of tropical fish, led by Dr Kenny Yap, Executive Chairman and Managing Director. Keeping up with the changing times is essential if companies are to survive and excel in the new economy. In this aspect, Kenny Yap seemingly has all the right ingredients to thrive and excel in the new economy (see case study in Chapter 7).

The structural balance Kenny implemented in terms of systems of authority and workflows took about two to three years before it was finally accepted. Initially, Kenny experienced some structural inertia from his brothers. He feels that people are reluctant to change as change creates uncertainties. One of his brothers was against the more structural ways of doing things and was hoping that they could all go back to the "good old days" where everybody was doing everything together. His brother felt threatened when Kenny introduced formal titles and roles. Kenny had to convince his brother which he felt was a real challenge and difficult but something which "had to be done." Over the years, Kenny has learned that changing mindsets is only effective if the person can accept change. "If he can't, you either accept him the way he is or you ignore him if you can afford to do so," Kenny said during one of the interviews.

Continuous learning through best practices (Swee and Richards, 1997) and a strong performance management culture is one of the mantras of Qian Hu. The firm's organizational culture has evolved from one which is predominantly based on family values to one which encompasses more professional practices by instituting best employer practices. The company intensively studies best practices of other leading organizations such as Robinson (major department store in Singapore) or DBS (Development Bank of Singapore) and adapts the appropriate ones for value creation, entrepreneurship, organizational culture, and the training and development of its people. However, for effective change management and effective internal knowledge sharing, it is essential to retain some elements of the family culture. To monitor the prevailing culture, Qian Hu uses various diagnostic measures like employee opinion surveys (EOS), performance achievement, third party feedback, employee involvement and staff turnover feedback. Bridging initiatives include recreational activities, informal gatherings, training and transparency. Staff feedback is garnered through informal gatherings and a formal employee opinion survey.

3. Discussion

Case A (Seafood Restaurant) suggests that the firm's organizational learning management is driven to a large extent by the founder's daughter who

Kenny Jap (left) in the process of engaging senior managers through sharing

Table 1. Qian Hu's benchmarking and learning activities

Areas	Companies benchmark	Explanations
Customer		
Distribution	OSIM	Qian Hu is currently learning from OSIM's chain store strategy adapting strong points into its own chain store concept.
Customer Service	Robinson	Qian Hu has adopted customer service standards and practices and continues to reinforce through regular training of the retail staff.
Operation		
Export of Fish, including sales and quarantine	Sunbeam (leading fish exporter in Singapore)	Qian Hu learned much and adapted from export sales strategy and procedures in the past years.
Financial		
Corporate Governance	DBS, ST Engineering, Singtel	Qian Hu's adoption and creation of several good practices in these
Transparency	ST Engineering	2 areas had won several recognitions at the national level. Our consistent action towards these are reflected in the awards given.
People		
Training/Development	Attending information sharing, best practices seminars.	Qian Hu is adopting the People Developer framework, incorporating appropriate best practices from other companies.
Compensation Issues	Learning from other companies that have implemented better systems.	Implemented flexible bonus system tied in to sales/profit performance for our subsidiaries' management. Will be looking at other flexible wage issues like what had been done by Phillips Singapore.

Source: Qian Hu Corporation Limited 2004 Quality Award Winner Executive Summary.

continues to have a positive impact on the restaurant's performance as evidenced by the POS system she introduced. While she has a very open personality and great external networking talent (both are positive traits *vis-à-vis* the firm's ability to leverage on learning and knowledge), internal learning opportunities are not fully exploited yet due to the limited trainability of staff with their low educational attainment backgrounds, lack of training time and other difficulties such as operational demands and suitable training methods. As a consequence, it seems that the absorptive capacity of Seafood Restaurant is not yet fully developed and utilized. Routines and processes that allow organizations to analyze, process, interpret and understand data and information obtained externally and to transform such knowledge into a competitive advantage are arguably not sufficiently formalized despite the overall rather promising innovation and experimentation culture. A strong HR system embedded in a proper performance management system with a focus on business excellence could certainly mitigate these issues. While the operation manager (Siok San) has a clear understanding of the importance of ensuring procedural justice for enhancing the (external) learning capability of family-based Seafood Restaurant and its employee value proposition, more could be done to beef up the company's talent management system and to cope with new challenges such as the current labor crunch. To sum up, there is no doubt that Seafood Restaurant could further strengthen the potentially positive impact of its growing internal learning capability on its corporate performance.

In Case B (Advertising X), the firm's strategic knowledge leadership is quite successfully performed by the company's co-founder whose former experiences in a MNC has shaped Advertising X' KPI driven performance management system and culture. This ensures good synergy between its business model, internal business processes, externally sourced information and overall firm performance. The various sources of information utilised such as blogs and fora in conjunction with the outgoing personality of the co-founder seem to suggest that Advertising X is characterized by a rather open culture with enormeous networking capabilities. These are clearly great assets with regard the firm's ability to leverage on external learning resources and knowledge in general. Official (formal) learning opportunities provided by external parties such as SPRING, however, are largely foregone due to the perceived limited relevance of those grant schemes. Given the vast corporate MNC experiences of Sian, recruitment of tertiary educated talent from polytechnics and universities as well as the strategic utilization of social media, etc., we conclude that the absorptive capacity of Advertising X is steadily increasing. Routines and processes that allow organizations to analyze, process, interpret and understand data and information obtained externally and to transform such knowledge into a competitive advantage have been implemented and are perceived as strategically important given the need for constant innovation amidst heavy competition. As in Case A, the respondent in Case B (Sian) had no doubts about the importance of procedural justice for enhancing the (external) learning capability of the firm. She made it clear that the firm's merit-based performance culture is KPI driven. In other words, if performance is slacking, employees will feel the consequences. As summed up in Table 2, Advertising X is operating at a fairly high level of performance management sophistication. However, a further formalization of HR systems, including training and development, would be helpful in further strengthening the positive impact of its internal and internal learning capability on corporate performance.

Case C (Qian Hu) supports the hypothesis that business leaders are often the main driving forces for change in organizations and that age and educational qualification are major predictors of successful learning in combination with other factors. Kenny's tertiary education in economics exposed him to different perspectives and viewpoints, which made him more cosmopolitan and reflective. It also equipped him with sound cognitive abilities and skills. Furthermore, he used effective leadership approaches such as open and skillful communication, persuasion, and consensus formation in combination with suitable reward incentives to propel change into the right direction.

Kenny is the classic example of a change master cum knowledge leader who is able and skillful to leverage on outside sources of learning

Table 2. Mastery of organisational learning in firms A, B and C
(Scale from 1 = Needs Improvement to 5 = Very Good)

	Seafood Restaurant	*Advertising X*	*Qian Hu*
Knowledge Leadership	3	4	5
Openness	5	5	5
Absorptive Capacity	2	4	5
Procedural Justice	2	3	5
Organizational Learning Capability	3	4	5

and to sustain change even in the face of resistance and organizational inertia. His demographic traits in terms of age (low) and educational achievements (high) determine his high receptivity to change and willingness to take risks, which together with effective knowledge leadership, openness toward external expertise, the firm's capability to absorb, deploy and transfer relevant knowledge as well as intraorganizational process fairness are responsible for Qian Hu's overall good performance.

4. Conclusion

In this chapter, I utilized both theoretical and practical research strands of Asian (Chinese) family firms (with their unique organizational and managerial practices) as well as organizational behavior studies with reference to learning, knowledge management, leadership, absorptive capacity and procedural justice (fair process) to examine the learning management approaches adopted by three Singaporean family firms in the services sector. As the previous paragraphs have shown, the three firms continue to be enaged in leveraging on learning, knowledge, and innovation management and external consultancy services cum grant schemes provided by the Singapore state, albeit with different degrees of strength, depth and outcomes (see Table 2). The interpretative analysis shows both the difficulties and opportunities which arise for local SMEs out of the volatile business environment with its competitive cost pressures and structural weaknesses as well as the benefits which these firms can derive if they integrate their learning strategies professionally into their business models and performance management systems *vis-à-vis* best practices elsewhere. Besides highlighting the undervalued role and very significant contributions of female business managers in Chinese family firms, the study underlines the need to develop more customized grant schemes for local SMEs in various sub-sectors of the services sector in order to meet the specialized needs of these smaller establishments which continue to form the backbone of Singapore's economy.

References

Argote, L and P Ingram (2000). Knowledge transfer: A basis for competitive advantage in firms. *Organizational Behavior and Human Decision Processes*, 82(1), 150–169.

Armstrong, A and F Foley (2003). Foundations for a leaning organization. *The Learning Organization*, 10(2), 74–82.

Brockner, J and PA Siegel (1996). Understanding the interaction between procedural and distributive justice: The role of trust. In RM Kramer and TR Tyler (eds.), *Trust in Organizations*, pp. 90–413. Thousand Oaks, CA: Sage Publications.

Chay, YW, T Menkhoff, B Loh, and H-D Evers (2007). Social capital and knowledge sharing in knowledge-based organisations: An empirical study. *International Journal of Knowledge Management*, 3(1), 29–48.

Cohen, WM and DA Levinthal (1990). Absorptive capacity: A new perspective on learning and innovation. *Administrative Science Quarterly*, 35(1), 128–152.

Collins, JD, TR Holcomb, ST Certo, M Hitt, and RH Lester (2009). Learning by doing: Cross-border mergers and acquisitions. *Journal of Business Research*, 62, 1329–1334.

Colquitt, JA (2001). On the dimensionality of organizational justice: A construct validation of a measure. *Journal of Applied Psychology*, 86, 386–400.

Colquitt, JA, DE Conlon, WJ Wesson, CO Porter, and KY Ng (2001). Justice at the millennium: A meta-analytic review of 25 years of organizational justice research. *Journal of Applied Psychology*, 86, 425–445.

Crossan, MM, HW Lane, and RE White (1999). An organizational learning framework: From intuition to institution. *The Academy of Management Review*, 24(3), 522–537.

Dogson, M (1993). Organisational learning. *Organisational Science*, 48, 147–160.

Dutrenit, G (2000). *Learning and Knowledge Management in the Firm: From Knowledge Accumulation to Strategic Capabilities*. Cheltenham and Northampton, MA: Edward Elgar.

Earl, MJ and I Scott (1999). What is a chief knowledge officer? *Sloan Management Review*, 40(2), 29–38.

Easterby-Smith, M and L Araujo (1999). Organizational learning: Current debates and opportunities. In M Easterby-Smith, L Araujo and J Burgoyne (eds.), *Organisational Learning and the Learning Organisation: Developments in Theory and Practice*, pp. 1–21. London, UK: Sage Publications.

Eisenhardt, KM (1989). Building theories from case study research. *Academy of Management Review*, 14, 532–550.

Fosfuri, A and JA Tribo (2008). Exploring the antecedents of potential absorptive capacity and its impact on innovation performance. *International Journal of Management Science*, 36, 173–187.

Garvin, DA (1993). Building a learning organization. *Harvard Business Review*, 71(4), 78–91.

Grant, RM (1996). Towards a knowledge-based theory of the firm. *Strategic Management Journal*, 17, 109–122.

Guns, B (1997). The chief knowledge officer's role: Challenges and competencies. *Journal of Knowledge Management*, 1(4), 315–319.

Gosling, SD, PJ Rentfrow, and WB Swann Jr. (2003). A very brief measure of the big five personality domains. *Journal of Research in Personality*, 37, 504–528.

Haley, GT, UCV Haley, and CT Tan (2004). *The Tao of Chinese Business*. Hong Kong: Wiley.

Holcomb, TR, RD Ireland, RM Holmes, and MA Hitt (2009). Architecture of entrepreneurial learning: Exploring the link among heuristics, knowledge, and action. *Entrepreneurship, Theory and Practice*, 33(1), 167–192.

Hornidge, A-K (2007). *Knowledge Society — Vision and Social Construction of Reality in Germany and Singapore*. Germany. LIT Verlag: Muenster.

Howard, R (1991). *Can Small Businesses Help Countries Compete? Entrepreneurship: Creativity at Work*. Boston, MA: Harvard Business School Press.

Kogut, B and U Zander (1992). Knowledge of the firm, combination capabilities, and the replication of technology. *Organization Science*, 3, 383–397.

Lee, J and H Li (2008). *Wealth Doesn't Last 3 Generations: How Family Businesses Can Maintain Prosperity*. Singapore: World Scientific.

Menkhoff, T and S Gerke (eds.) (2002). *Chinese Entrepreneurship and Asian Business Networks*. London and New York: Routledge Curzon.

Menkhoff, T (2010). Creating value through knowledge management. *Business Times*, June 15, p. 24.

Menkhoff, T and YW Chay (2011). Improving small firm performance through collaborative change management and outside learning: Trends in Singapore. *International Journal of Asian Business and Information Management*, 2(1), 1–24.

Menkhoff, T and YW Chay (2013). Fostering the learning capacity of small-scale ethnic Chinese business organizations: An exploratory study. *International Journal of Asian Business and Information Management*, forthcoming.

Ng, BK (2002). The changing role of ethnic Chinese SMEs in economic restructuring in Singapore: From "two-legged" policy to "three-legged" strategy. In L Suryadinata (ed.), *Ethnic Chinese in Singapore and Malaysia: A Dialogue Between Tradition and Modernity*, pp. 255–275. Singapore: Times Academic Press.

Neilson, RE (2001). Knowledge management and the role of the CKO. In *Knowledge Management: The Catalyst for Electronic Government*, RC Barquin (eds.). Vienna: Management Concepts.

Nonaka, I (1994). A dynamic theory of organizational knowledge creation. *Organizational Science*, 5(1), 14–37.

Redding, SG (1990). *The Spirit of Chinese Capitalism*. Berlin: De Gryter.

Ribière, V and AS Sitar (2003). The critical role of leadership in nurturing a knowledge supporting culture. *Journal of Knowledge Management Research and Practice*, 1(1), July.

Scarbrough, H, M Bresnen, L Edelman, S Laurent, S Newell and J Swan (2004). The processes of project-based learning: An exploratory study. *Management Learning*, 35(4), 491–506.

Singapore Productivity and Standards Board (2000). *SME 21: Positioning SMEs for the 21ˢᵗ Century*. Singapore: SPSB.

Starbuck, WH (1992). Learning by knowledge intensive firms. *Journal of Management Studies*, 29, 713–740.

Stebbins, R (2001). *Exploratory Research in the Social Sciences*. Thousand Oaks, CA: Sage Publications.

Stenmark, D (2001). Leveraging tacit organizational knowledge. *Journal of Management Information Systems*, 17(3), 9–24.

Swee, GC and G Richards (1997). Benchmarking the learning capability of organizations. *European Management Journal*, 15(5), 575–583.

Tong, CK (2008). Rethinking Chinese business networks: Trust and distrust in Chinese business. *Journal of Asian Business*, 145–167.

Tsui-Auch, LS (2003). Learning strategies of small and medium-sized Chinese family firms: A comparative study of two suppliers in Singapore. *Management Learning*, 34, 201–220.

Wood, SA and SE Hampson (2005). Measuring the big five with single items using a bipolar response scale. *European Journal of Personality*, 19, 373–390.

Chapter 15

Understanding the Role of Cultural Orientations in Students' Predispositions toward Knowledge Transfer in Project Teams: Evidence from Singapore

Thomas Menkhoff, Chay Yue Wah
and Hans-Dieter Evers

1. Introduction

The last few years have seen a rapid increase in the literature on knowledge transfer which refers to the processes by which knowledge, expertise or skills transfer between people, i.e., in our context between student team members to contribute to the successful outcomes of student team projects (Nonaka, 1991; Argote *et al.*, 2000; Kogut and Zander, 1992; Zander and Kogut, 1995; Osterloh *et al.*, 2000; Szulanski, 2000; Goh, 2002; Reagans and McEvily, 2003; Agarwal *et al.*, 2004; Scarbrough *et al.*, 2004; Joshi and Sarker, 2006; Loh *et al.*, 2010). Knowledge comprises both an implicit and an explicit component (Polanyi, 1975). Through discourse, reflection and discovery, tacit knowledge (knowledge that is internalized but is not articulated or made public) can be transformed into an explicit form that can be shared in the form of data, scientific formulae, specifications and so on. The very processes by which such knowledge is transformed have been conceptualized as socialization, externalization, combination and internalization (Nonaka, 1994; Nonaka and Takeuchi, 1995). "Combining" different types of knowledge and/or expertise, for example, through intense brainstorming sessions or via student group projects, often leads to new and sometimes unexpected insights. Examples of innovations developed through knowledge combination are exemplary case analyses during university-led international case competitions or the Swatch watch where various groups of people provided inputs and ideas (Zaltman *et al.*, 1973; Rice *et al.*, 1980; Rogers, 1983). While there are potential challenges when it comes to the exchange of explicit and tacit knowledge relevant to team tasks, both theorists and practitioners agree that knowledge transfer adds value to the performance of individuals, teams and organizations (Starbuck, 1992; Shapiro *et al.*, 2002; Szulanski, 2003).

1.1 *Importance of knowledge transfer in singapore*

Knowledge transfer has a particular significance in the context of Singapore, a dynamic city-state located at the southern tip of the Malaysian Peninsular. The population of 5 million comprises 77 percent Chinese, 14 percent Malays, 8 percent Indians and 1 percent others. The Government of Singapore under the leadership of the People's Action Party (which led the country from Third World to First World status in a short 40 years) continues to transform Singapore into a fully fledged knowledge-based economy (Menkhoff, 2004; Hornidge, 2007). Singapore's state-led knowledge creation achievements are evidenced by its development success and the large number of patents registered. Many of these patents have been developed in collaboration with so-called "foreign talents." Like other globalized, culturally-diverse hot spots round the world (Sassen, 2001; Saxenian Lee *et al*, 2003), Singapore is heavily reliant on foreign knowledge due to its small size and the shortage of "local talents." Singapore's success would not have been achieved without both the state and multinational corporations as well as the effective transfer of knowledge from foreign experts and professionals to local learners (Tsui-Auch, 2003). The evolution of Singapore's precision engineering cluster which was built up with technical assistance from Britain, Germany and France or the current expansion of the life sciences sector represent examples.

While knowledge transfer has been acknowledged as an important concept with immense practical implications due to dozens of new knowledge management studies and journals, its implications in the educational sector have been relatively unexplored. This article examines knowledge transfer processes amongst student teams at the Singapore Management University

(SMU) which was founded in 2000 as part of Singapore's knowledge economy vision. In line with the country's so-called Global Schoolhouse Initiative fostered by the powerful Economic Development Board (EDB), the proportion of foreign students is gradually increasing and will represent about 15 percent by 2010. The knowledge transfer dynamics amongst teams of foreign/local students from different cultural backgrounds are hardly understood despite the fact that demand for higher education is booming in Asia and around the world. An earlier knowledge management survey within a multi-cultural Singaporean institution of higher learning revealed that knowledge sharing would help members to avoid costly mistakes, make innovation easier, save time by not "reinventing the wheel," and make more informed decisions with the inputs from colleagues. There was concern that knowledge hoarding may cause members to be excluded from information and that it would negatively affect their reputation as well as difficulties in creating new knowledge (Chay *et al.*, 2007; Loh *et al.*, 2010). Increased diversity of peers and co-workers can aggravate horizontal knowledge sharing due to different systems of knowing, behavioral patterns, cultural misunderstandings and conflicting societal-cultural values (Appel *et al.*, 1996; Berrel *et al.*, 2002; House *et al.* eds., 2004). As one student interviewed in the context of this study stressed:

> "What I enjoy most about working with foreign students is being able to expand one's network globally, as well as to have the opportunity to learn about other cultures and in some cases, have the opportunity to learn a new language. However, foreign students often also travel during term time, and as such, having them as project mates can sometimes be frustrating, as they miss meetings and/or deadlines due to their travelling. In conclusion, I would say that foreign students make excellent friends but not necessarily excellent group mates."

Cultural differences can reduce the salience of team identity, which in turn can lead to effort-withholding behaviors (Shapiro *et al.*, 2002). Territorial behavior and fierce competition can imply knowledge transfer difficulties (Brown and Menkhoff, 2008). The study by Shaheen and Sim (2009) suggests that academic institutions should review their instruction approaches to make the learning process less competitive and to tackle knowledge hoarding tendencies among students.

Our discussion about knowledge transfer presents an interesting opportunity to look at it from a cultural perspective comparing individualistic and collectivist contexts as well as examining potential antecedents. Studies by Triandis (1995), Triandis and Gelfand (1998), Chow *et al.* (1999), Retna (2001), Berrell, Gloet and Wright (2002) or Joshi and Sarker (2006) indicate that cultural patterns affect people's openness (or closeness) in transferring knowledge to others which can have positive or negative effects in terms of collaborative learning. Our study fills a gap in the literature about knowledge transfer in educational contexts and adds value by examining the following core research question: What are the effects of cultural proclivities of undergraduate business management students as well as other factors such as capability, credibility, cohesion, communication and the type of knowledge shared on knowledge transfer activities in a project-based Leadership and Team-Building (LTB) course?

By exploring the complex relationship between these factors and knowledge transfer which is derived from combining theories of knowledge transfer, teams and cross-cultural behavior, this study deepens our understanding of team member knowledge transfer processes in a diverse student population. It advances our theoretical and practical knowledge about potential knowledge transfer difficulties such as barriers of pedagogical peer learning in culturally diverse learning environments in higher management education. While an international, diverse student body is often celebrated in university brochures and ad campaigns, in reality "multi-monoculturalism" is sometimes practiced by students who stick together because of cultural similarities rather than blending in (*The Economist*, 2010, p. 41).

2. Theoretical Framework and Hypotheses

2.1 *The effects of cultural proclivities on knowledge transfer*

Triandis *et al.* (2001, p. 74) define national culture "as a shared pattern of categorizations, attitudes, beliefs, definitions, norms, values, and other elements of subjective culture." Cultures are never fixed entities, but change, interact with each other, integrate new aspects and diminish others. Cultures may create tendencies, dispositions, mental maps or support certain value patterns. But the behavior of individuals, like knowledge transfer, can never be explained by culture alone, though outcomes in groups may well tilt to one or another direction due to recognizable cultural patterns. We, therefore, accept with some hesitation for heuristic purposes the definition of culture as "a collective programming of the mind" (Berry, 2004).

Knowledge transfer is a potential challenge among individuals in culturally diverse teams because of several potential problems such as knowledge transfer barriers, for example, between individualists and collectivists (Triandis, 1988; Bhagat *et al.*, 2002; Shapiro *et al.*, 2002). Contrary to members from individualistic cultures, members of collectivistic cultures are likely to engage more actively in knowledge transfer with co-ethnics and in-group members due to the importance of group loyalty and moral obligations toward in-groups. As Chow *et al.* (1999) found out in their comparative study of the United States and China, the Chinese were less inclined than their Anglo–American counterparts to share information files with employees who were not considered as in-group members. Countries such as Singapore, China, Japan and Korea have been described as dominantly "collectivistic" by researchers (Schwartz, 1992; Schwartz and Bardi, 2001; Merritt, 2000; Tan and Chee, 2005). People in collectivistic cultures are arguably more willing to put the success of the group ahead of themselves. One perspective is that individuals from individualistic cultures will not favor knowledge transfer and that those from more collectivist cultures will look at knowledge transfer more positively.

2.2 *The individualism-collectivism cultural pattern*

Individualism-collectivism as characteristic cultural patterns (Bhawuk, 2004) influence but do not determine individual's behaviors, goals, values, attitudes, and norms. Individualists tend to be independent minded, regard themselves as separate entities unconnected to their immediate social environment, and they are often motivated by personal achievement and goals (Triandis and Gelfand, 1998). Collectivists on the other hand, see themselves as part of a larger inter-dependent unit. They are usually driven by norms, obligations and duties, and they may assign greater priorities to the group's objectives over the individual's preference (Triandis, 1996). In social interactions, the collectivist tends to emphasize more communal sharing whereas the individualist is mainly interested in an exchange relation (Mills and Clarks, 1982). Ingroup harmony, integrity and solidarity are the key attributes in collectivism and consequently this classification tends to be inward rather than outward focused (Triandis, 1990). In general terms the hallmarks of individualists on the other hand, include self-enhancement, competition and emotional detachment. Personal achievement is celebrated even if it is performed at the expense of interpersonal relations.

How does the construct influence knowledge transfer behaviors? The collective self-concept is closely intertwined with the circuit of people revolving around the person, and these include the network of relations and the immediate social context. Consequently, for the collectivist, we should expect to see changes in the pattern of communication as a function of their social environment and the interaction partner. For the individualist, the pattern of communication is independent from the type of relationship with the target and other social contextual attributes. There is greater attention assigned to the potential tangible benefits in interacting with the target, rather than to the subjective interpersonal connections.

In terms of knowledge transfer, the type of content transmitted and shared among collective members is likely to reveal more historical, tacit and less "codifiable" materials (Bhagat *et al.*, 2002, p. 212). This is in line with the construct's emphasis on developing intimate, interdependent and contextual based networks. In individualist cultures, the priority is getting the message across and making them understood. Under an exchange engagement, it is necessary that the intention and information between the communicating partners be transmitted and decoded without ambiguity. It is therefore expected that the type of knowledge transferred will involve more current, explicit and "codifiable" content.

2.3 *The vertical-horizontal cultural pattern*

This dimension demonstrates the degree of social inequality within a particular culture. This social dimension is thematically similar to the Hofstede's cultural typology on power distance (Hofstede, 2001), hierarchy and egalitarian commitment value systems (Schwartz, 2004, 2006) and individual-level differences on social dominance orientation (Pratto *et al.*, 1994; Sidanius and Pratto, 1999). In vertical societies, there is a strong endorsement for a hierarchical organizational arrangement that distinguishes individuals on the basis of power and status. Members from vertical cultures consider it desirable to "stick out"; there is an emphasis on the application of appropriate status differentiation and the reinforcement of social boundaries. In horizontal cultures, the social distance is significantly smaller between members from the low and high status groups. People in horizontal societies prefer not to stand out among the group and the demarcation of titles and status is not strictly adhered.

The vertical-horizontal dimension plays an important role in moderating cross-cultural knowledge transfer. The communication pattern and the amount of knowledge transfer vary according to the members' status group. In vertical cultures, superiors have greater access to the knowledge generated from external sources and they are empowered to regulate the process of knowledge transfer, including the diffusion of information and deciding who the recipient members are. Not surprisingly, communication in vertical cultures tends to flow from a top-down channel and there is relatively less knowledge exchange between members of different status groups.

In horizontal cultures, there is relatively more interaction among people from different group memberships. The communication process is bidirectional, from top to bottom, and bottom to top; and superiors do not have privilege or exclusive right to external knowledge.

When the vertical-horizontal dimension is superimposed on the individualism-collectivism construct, a sophisticated model comprising four quadrants of cultural patterns emerges: vertical-individualism (VI), vertical-collectivism (VC), horizontal-individualism (HI), and horizontal-collectivism (HC), as illustrated in Table 1 (Triandis 1995; Triandis and Gelfand, 1998; Bhagat *et al.*, 2002; Lee and Choi 2005; Hornik and Tupchiy, 2006).

In VC and HC, both cultural patterns advocate the need to maintain strong connection to their in-group membership. The two typologies however, differ on their organizational structure — VC stresses the need for a

Table 1. Interface of vertical-horizontal individualism-collectivism

	Vertical	Horizontal
Individualism	Vertical-Individualism (USA, UK)	Horizontal-Individualism (Australia, Denmark, Sweden)
Collectivism	Vertical-Collectivism (China, India, Egypt)	Horizontal-Collectivism (Israel, Japan)

Source: Triandis (1995); Triandis and Gelfand (1998)

clear distinction of roles and status but HC regard members as occupying similar positions. Regardless of hierarchy, contextual cues and the relational ties between partners provides the needed platform for cross border knowledge transfer with a common emphasis on the tacit, interdependent and contextualized exchanges.

At the other end of the continuum, both VI and HI cultural patterns share an individualistic view towards relationships and self-concepts. In this respect, the emphasis is on achieving the desired individual goals in the course of knowledge transfer whereas the type of organizational structure is considered secondary. Knowledge transfer is centered on the transmission of explicit, direct and codified information.

In the light of the discussions concerning the individualist-collectivist (VI, HI, VC and HC) attributes of team members transferring knowledge, we hypothesize the following:

H1:   The individualistic and collectivistic attributes, VI, HI, VC and HC, are associated with knowledge transfer among project team members.

An important precondition to benefit from knowledge transfer in terms of learning and utilization of newly acquired competencies is absorptive capacity (Cohen and Levinthal, 1990). Capability refers to the individual's capacity to complete a specific action in a clearly defined range of complex tasks, context and purpose. Capability results from learning and is often specified in terms of knowledge, skill, abilities and values (Cohen and Levinthal, 1990; Scarbrough *et al.*, 2004). People who are capable arguably have a higher propensity to transfer their knowledge to those who need it and to leverage on new knowledge. We classify the knowledge required by students to complete their projects successfully into two categories: (i) project related capabilities (which refer to the ability to perform designated tasks, activities and to fulfill specific requirements, e.g., getting team members to work together, designating member roles/tasks, meeting deadlines and so on as well as to achieve results), and (ii) project management know how. We argue that the extent of project-related capabilities (e.g., mental capacity to apply concepts to issue analyses) and management know how determine the amount of knowledge the transmitter transfers to recipients. In the light of the discussions concerning the importance of capability in team member knowledge transfer processes, we hypothesize the following:

H2: The extent of knowledge transfer between project team members is positively related to the capability (in the sense of application of concepts and concrete project management skills) of the team members.

Credibility (Joshi, Sarker and Sarker, 2005; Joshi and Sarker, 2006) refers to the quality of being dependable, believable, and genuine. It also has connotations of trustworthiness (Dirks, 2000; Dirks and Ferrin, 2001; Lee *et al.*, 2010). Credibility can relate to a statement, action, or source. It refers to the credibility of a person in terms of education, experience, performance, etc. The literature on knowledge transfer suggests that people will be motivated to engage in knowledge transfer activities with those who are perceived as credible (Gupta and Govindarajan, 2000; Zander and Kogut, 1995). Studies have documented the positive relationships between teacher immediacy and student perceptions of learning and credibility (Johnson and Miller, 2002). Therefore, we hypothesize the following:

H3: The extent of knowledge transfer between project team members is positively related to the credibility of the team members.

The other two variables of interest as potential drivers of knowledge transfer processes in teams are team cohesiveness and communication. Festinger *et al.* (1950, p. 64) define team cohesion as the "total field of forces causing members to remain in the group." According to Carron (1982, p. 124), it is "a dynamic process which is reflected in the tendency for a group to stick together and remain united in the pursuit of its goals and objectives." Cohesive groups have a shared set of values, appreciate the value and inputs of their fellow team members and thus enable knowledge transfer (Gross and Martin, 1952). Williams, Duray and Reddy (2006, p. 594) interpret group cohesiveness as "members" affinity for each other and their desire to remain part of the team." Members of cohesive teams are likely to have a positive attitude towards interactions with other team members, an attitude which supports the sharing of information and seeking knowledge. Where group cohesiveness is present, there is shared understanding, more interpersonal communication, a trusting atmosphere and greater potential for positive learning outcomes (Williams, Duray and Reddy, 2006, p. 607). Leidner and Fuller (1997) found that students working collaboratively were more interested in the material and perceived themselves to learn more than students working individually. Dineen's study suggests that active learning is easier in stable, cooperative teams rather than in fluid teams. Collaborative learning through teamwork is likely to enhance team processes (2005, p. 597). In the light of the discussions above about the role of cohesion in driving team member knowledge transfer processes, we hypothesize the following:

H4:   The extent of knowledge transfer between project team members is positively related to the strength of team cohesion experienced by team members.

Communication refers to the transmission and exchange of information so that the recipient understands what the sender intends (Kraut *et al.*, 1990; Uzzi, 1997; Reagans and McEvily, 2003). Communicative abilities represent essential soft skills in the field of management education (Halfhill and Nielson, 2007). Frequent and in-depth communication often lead to relationship building, trust and social capital which represent important preconditions for knowledge transfer and new knowledge creation (Cumming and Teng, 2003; DeLong and Fahey, 2000; Lee and Choi, 2005). Therefore, we hypothesize the following:

H5:   The extent of knowledge transfer between project team members is positively related to the extent of communication between team members.

In both types of individualist cultural patterns, knowledge transfer takes place with little difficulties due to the shared common belief system pertinent to social exchanges. Similarly, for members in VC and HC, there is mutual agreement and expectations on the transaction process and individual members interpret their message and content in the context of the relationships within the group membership (Bhagat *et al.*, 2002). Consequently, we expect to see a greater amount of knowledge transfer between VI and HI, and between VC and HC (Figure 1). The greatest challenges in terms of knowledge transfer are encountered by vertical individualists (VI) and horizontal collectivists (HC) as well as horizontal individualists and vertical collectivists (VC) as indicated by Figure 1.

Further to our interest in examining the potential moderating effects of each of the national culture sub-dimensions on knowledge transfer, we hypothesize that:

H6: The individualism dimension of national culture will moderate the relationship between the collectivism dimension and knowledge transfer outcomes.

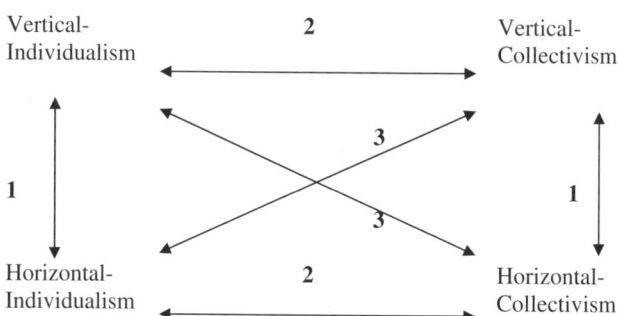

1 = less difficult to transfer knowledge in either direction
2 = more difficult to transfer knowledge in either direction
3 = most difficult to transfer knowledge in either direction

Figure 1. Knowledge transfer between cultural patterns
Note: Figure was adapted from Bhagat *et al.* (2002).

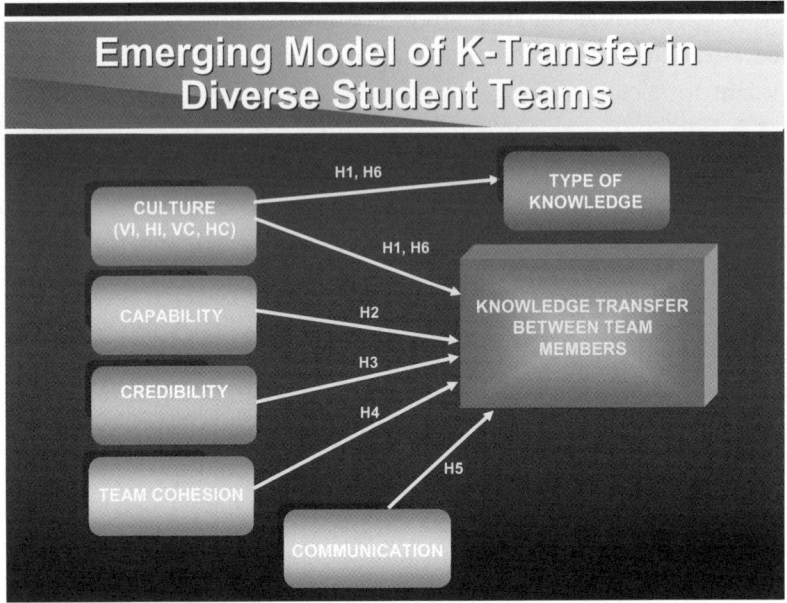

Figure 2.   Emerging model of K-transfer in diverse student teams

3. Method

3.1 *Research setting and sample*

Participants in this study are from undergraduate Leadership and Team Building (LTB) courses taught at a university in Singapore. All students enrolled at the university are required to take LTB as part of the University core. The course provides students with knowledge and skills about effective leadership and teamwork based on principles, concepts, application cases, exercises, and self-assessments that are designed to develop competencies around leadership and teamwork. Central to the course is a team-based Community Service Project aimed at making a positive impact in the country's social space. The project offers an opportunity for students to learn by doing in giving them hands-on experiences that facilitate the learning of leadership and team dynamics in real-life situations such as renovating flats or teaching a group of non-profit executives how to leverage on social media to enhance their outreach. The overall objective of LTB is to build students' competency base that will help them be more effective team members and leaders. Approximately 500 students enroll in this course each academic year. Each course is taught by one instructor together with six team advisors who are responsible for facilitating team sessions and discussions, helping students integrate and internalize core concepts and project-related issues, and ensuring that team projects are completed in a timely and professional manner. Each team comprises of 4–6 students which are diverse in terms of ethnicity, citizenship (there are about 20 percent foreign students in each course section), gender and age. All TAs are selected from a pool of students who have previously completed the LTB course successfully and with distinction.

To assess the various antecedents, several standard scales were identified, utilized and analyzed to measure knowledge transfer, cultural transaction patterns and so forth. In academic year 2007–2008, questionnaire surveys were developed and subsequently administered amongst diverse undergraduate student teams at the Singapore Management University (SMU). A total of 335 students responded to the survey, which assessed various demographic and knowledge-related variables as well as the cultural transaction patterns highlighted above. 54.7 percent of the respondents were male with 77.3 percent of Chinese ethnicity. Indians made up 4.8 percent, Malays 2.4 percent with the remaining 15.5 percent belonging to other ethnic races. The mean age of respondents was 21.55 years (sd = 1.59) with a range of 17.42 to 27.00.

3.2 *Measures*

The outcome measures were knowledge transfer, explicit knowledge and tacit knowledge.

Knowledge transfer. A 2-item measure adapted from Joshi and Sarker (2006) was used to measure the extent of knowledge transferred to a recipient. We explored to what extent (1 = not at all, 2 = a little, 3 = somewhat, 4 = a great deal) group members felt they had learnt or acquired course-related competencies from others.

Explicit knowledge and tacit knowledge. Explicit knowledge and tacit knowledge was assessed by means of a measure adapted from Liebowitz (ed. 1999, 2000) and Polanyi (1975). *Explicit knowledge* refers to knowledge stored in documents, databases, spreadsheets, e-mail messages, images, training materials and/or video material. *Tacit knowledge* refers to expertise and experiences of group members that has not been formally documented. It is shared through conversations, stories, etc. (e.g., during team sessions or over coffee). Respondents were asked to write down the name of each member in their team and to indicate the extent to which they felt that they had learnt or acquired *explicit/tacit* knowledge from him/her. Items are "I have received explicit knowledge from the following group members: ..." and "I have received tacit knowledge from the following group members:... ." A four-point Likert response format (1 = not at all, 2 = a little, 3 = somewhat, 4 = a great deal) was used.

Cultural patterns. Six items adapted from the scale developed by Triandis and Gelfand (1998) were used to assess each of the four cultural patterns (Soh and Leong, 2002). For example, sample items to measure vertical individualism are "When another person does better than I do, I get tense and aroused" and "It is important that I do my job better than others." Response options ranged from (1) strongly disagree to (5) strongly agree. The scale's alpha reliability in this study is 0.70.

Self-Report Capability. Students' absorptive capacity was measured by assessing their project related capabilities and (somewhat broader) in terms of their own project management ability using the response scale from 1 = not at all, 2 = just about satisfactory, 3 = above average and 4 = very strong indeed. *Project related capabilities* refer to students' ability to apply organizational behavior concepts in term projects. More specifically this includes their "general knowledge of LTB-related concepts," "competencies with regard to the practical applications of LTB concepts," the "ability to link their own pre-U practical experiences, concepts and project tasks to project requirements," "data collection competencies (e.g., mastery of interview techniques)," "analytical competencies" and "report writing skills." *Project management abilities* include "teambuilding skills," students' "overall understanding of how to communicate with team mates," "know how with regard to the management of the relationship with external parties," "project management skills," "understanding of the socio-psychological aspects of the project development process" and confidence "to apply conceptual skills in a "real" company project." The construct was a modified version of measures used by Joshi and Sarker (2006) which has been validated in other knowledge transfer projects. The scale's alpha reliability in this study is 0.76.

Credibility. A 4-item measure adapted from Joshi *et al.* (2005) was used to measure credibility. To examine the hypothesis that credibility is an antecedent of knowledge transfer, we examined the extent to which students agreed with related statements (e.g., "If I had my way, I wouldn't let this group member have any influence over project-related issues that are important to me"[1]) with regard to their various group members by using the scale 1 = strongly disagree, 2 = disagree, 3 = agree and 4 = strongly agree. Other items to measure the credibility of project group members in terms of trustworthiness included: "I would be willing to let this group member have complete control over my role and future in this project," "I really wish I had a good way to keep an eye on this group member[2]," "I would be comfortable giving this group member a task or problem which was critical to me, even if I could not monitor his/her actions." The scale's alpha reliability in this study is 0.70.

Team Cohesiveness and Communication. Using the scale from 1 = not at all to 4 = very strong indeed, group members were asked to evaluate their team's cohesiveness and the extent of communication with others. Measures adapted from Joshi and Sarker (2006) were used to assess team cohesiveness and the extent of communication with others. Cohesiveness-related items/questions included: "To what extent do you feel that you are a part of your group?," "If you had the chance to do the same kind of work in another group, would you move to another group?," "How does your project group compare with other teams you have worked with?." The scale's alpha reliability in this study is 0.77. In terms of communication, survey participants were asked to circle the response (1= not at all to 4 = a great deal) that most closely describes the extent to which their respective project group members have communicated with them. The scale's alpha reliability in this study is 0.72.

---

[1] Reverse-scored item.

[2] Reverse-scored item.

3.3 *Controls*

The data analyses were mainly concerned with examining first, the relationships between the potential antecedents of knowledge transfer, and second, the additive and multiplicative effects of the vertical-horizontal dimensions in predicting knowledge transfer. Hierarchical regression was used in performing these analyses.

Three demographic variables (gender, age, work experience) were employed as control variables. Gender was coded (0) "male" and (1) "female."

A three stage hierarchical regression model was used to examine the extent to which demographic characteristics and cultural dimensions predicted knowledge transfer. Explanatory (independent) variables were entered into the regression in a specified order as a means of determining their individual and joint contributions to explaining the outcome variable. In the first step, the demographic variables were entered into the regression. The "main effect" variables were entered as a single block in the next step of the regression procedure. In the final step, the interaction variables were entered into the regression model.

4. Results

The means, standard deviations and intercorrelations of the major study variables are presented in Table 2.

Overall, knowledge and explicit knowledge transfer showed significant correlations with vertical and horizontal collectivism, providing partial support for hypothesis H_1. The results of the correlation analysis also provide support for hypotheses H_2, H_3, H_4 and H_5. Certainly, knowledge transfer is positively related to the ability to manage a project, the perceived credibility of the individual sharing that knowledge, communication between team members, and team cohesiveness. A review of the collinearity statistics, that is, the tolerance and VIF values indicated no issues with multicollinearity.

The results of the regression analyses carried out to determine whether team credibility, team cohesiveness, capability and communication predicted explicit and tacit knowledge transfer between team members are shown in

Table 2. Correlations of major study variables (N = 330)

	Mean	SD	1	2	3	4	5	6	7	8	9	10	11	12	13
1. Gender	1.45	0.50	–												
2. Age	21.55	1.59	–0.45**	–											
3. Vertical Individualism	2.75	0.48	–0.14*	0.02	(0.74)										
4. Horizontal Individualism	3.11	0.42	–0.11*	0.08	0.29**	(0.73)									
5. Vertical Collectivism	2.84	0.40	0.05	–0.02	–0.11*	–0.09	(0.79)								
6. Horizontal Collectivism	3.16	0.42	0.05	–0.06	–0.13*	–0.12*	0.44**	(0.73)							
7. Capability	2.04	0.44	0.03	–0.18*	–0.14*	–0.04	0.16**	0.11	(0.76)						
8. Credibility	1.17	0.48	–0.02	–0.12*	0.06	–0.04	–0.17**	–0.14*	–0.04	(0.70)					
9. Communication	2.17	0.38	–0.02	–0.05	–0.12*	–0.01	0.20**	0.19**	0.62**	0.08	(0.72)				
10. Team Cohesion	2.76	0.35	–0.05	0.14	–0.06	0.05	0.14**	0.22**	0.34**	0.11	0.32**	(0.77)			
11. Knowledge Transfer	2.98	0.80	–0.03	–0.11	–0.03	–0.02	0.14**	0.20**	0.33**	0.18**	0.29**	0.34**	(0.78)		
12. Explicit K Transfer	2.84	0.85	0.09	0.05	–0.11	–0.08	0.22**	–0.15*	0.18**	0.24**	0.17**	0.19**	0.34**	(0.73)	
13. Tacit K Transfer	2.95	0.86	–0.03	0.06	–0.02	–0.03	0.05	0.10	0.26**	0.97**	0.34**	0.27**	0.59**	0.36**	(0.71)

* Correlation is significant at the 0.05 level (2-tailed). ** Correlation is significant at the 0.01 level (2-tailed).

α Reliability of factor scales (Cronbach's alpha) shown in parentheses.

Table 3. Regression model of the predictors of explicit knowledge transfer[a] (N = 330)

Variable	Model 1	Model 2
Intercept	0.36	0.69
Age	0.08	0.09
Gender	0.25	0.24
Work Experience	−0.05	−0.03
Capability		0.13
Credibility		−0.34***
Communication		0.15
Team Cohesiveness		0.42***
F	2.33	5.46***
R^2	0.027	0.135
ΔR^2	0.027	0.108

Dependent Variable: Explicit Knowledge Transfer
*$p < 0.05$
**$p < 0.025$
***$p < 0.01$

Tables 3 and 4. Credibility and team cohesiveness indeed predicted explicit knowledge transfer between team members. Similarly credibility, team cohesiveness and communication also significantly predicted tacit knowledge transfer.

The results of the regression analysis of explicit knowledge transfer on the Vertical-Horizontal dimensions of culture are shown in Table 5.

Vertical collectivism (VI) significantly predicted knowledge transfer outcome in the second step of the regression analysis (Model 2). Furthermore, horizontal individualism and vertical collectivism also jointly influenced explicit knowledge transfer outcomes (Model 3). This significant interactive effect is graphically presented in Figure 3.

Figure 3 graphically presents the joint influence of collectivism and individualism on explicit knowledge transfer. For individuals high on VC (1SD above mean), knowledge transfer remained relatively consistent irrespective of the level of the (HI) dimension. In contrast, this effect was very marked for high VC individuals (1SD above mean), reflected by the

Table 4. Regression model of the predictors of tacit knowledge transfer[a] (N = 330)

Variable	Model 1	Model 2
Intercept	2.07	−0.53
Age	0.04	0.06
Gender	0.01	0.04
Work Experience	−0.03	−0.03
Capability		0.24
Credibility		−0.30***
Communication		0.45***
Team Cohesiveness		0.37***
F	0.52	8.18***
R^2	0.006	0.191
ΔR^2	0.00627	0.184

Dependent Variable: Tacit Knowledge Transfer
$*p < 0.05$
$**p < 0.025$
$***p < 0.01$

steep gradient of the slope. The line representing low VC indicates that knowledge transfer is strongly and positively related to low HI; knowledge transfer is lowest for low VC and high HI individuals. Thus, low VC, high HI individuals are less likely to transfer their knowledge. This result suggests that information and knowledge exchange between vertical collectivists and horizontal individualists is indeed moderated by high and low levels of the VC and HI dimensions.

5. Discussion

A major objective of this study was to advance knowledge about the antecedents of knowledge transfer in culturally-diverse, knowledge-intensive student project groups in institutions of higher learning which are little understood at this point due to the lack of empirical research (Smith and MacGregor, 1992; Irvine and York, 1995; Appel *et al.*, 1996; King and Rowe, 1999). Our study is one of the first attempts to investigate the

Table 5.   Regression model of the predictors of explicit knowledge transfer (N = 330)

Variable	Model 1	Model 2	Model 3[1]
Intercept	0.89	0.92	5.16*
Age	0.08*	−0.08*	−0.09**
Gender	0.24*	−0.18	0.23
Work Experience	−0.04	−0.024	-0.03
Vertical Individualism		−0.11	3.09
Horizontal Individualism		−0.10	−2.35***
Vertical Collectivism		0.38**	−2.13***
Horizontal Collectivism		0.20	0.64
Vertical Individualism × Horizontal Collectivism			−0.14
Horizontal Individualism × Vertical Collectivism			0.81***
F	2.12	5.23***	4.44***
R^2	0.024	0.097	0.127
ΔR^2	0.024	0.073	0.030

Dependent Variable: Explicit knowledge transfer (with group members)
* $p < p$ 0.05
** $p < 0.025$
*** $p < 0.01$
[1] The β values are the unstandardized coefficients from the final regression equation, each term being corrected for all other terms.

relevancy of Triandis' cultural patterns and the specific links between related factors such as capability, credibility, communication and cohesion in the context of real knowledge transfer in team-based learning contexts at an "Asian" university. Such collaborative forms of learning have often been recognized as a value-added element of effective peer learning in higher education. However, empirical studies to support such claims are rare. Triandis' construct is useful because it helps us to measure and to make sense of both knowledge transfer and related difficulties between students with different cultural orientations and predispositions in an era of creating state-led regional educational hubs as practiced by Singapore (and Malaysia). Our findings are timely and important for both scholars and managers who

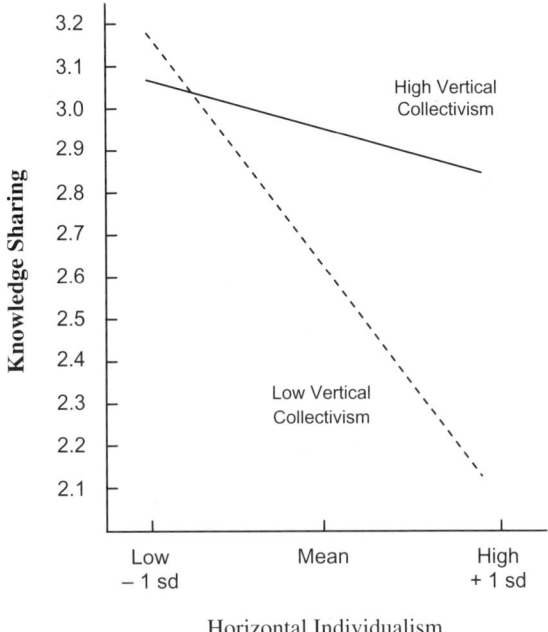

Figure 3. Relation between explicit knowledge transfer and horizontal individualism for high and low levels of vertical collectivism

want to understand knowledge transfer dynamics amongst university students in an era of increased cultural diversity, the setting up of more and more campuses across borders as well as sporadic attacks on Asian students on "shiny new campuses" in countries such as Australia.

Our data analyses indicate that cultural proclivities predict explicit knowledge transfer, that is, vertical collectivism and horizontal individualism predict knowledge transfer. However, this relation is qualified by a two-way interaction involving horizontal individualism x vertical collectivism. Consequently the main effects ought to be explained within the confines of the higher-order interaction. Horizontal individualists transfer less knowledge than vertical collectivists generally. The findings from our study corroborate this view and more interestingly, show that knowledge transfer tends to be stronger under the condition of low as opposed to high endorsement for vertical collectivism (Figure 3). The findings thus suggest that collectivism plays a critical role in moderating explicit knowledge transfer compared to individualism. This aspect is contrary to Triandis' propositions.

Observations of students' behavior in class and explorative interviews conducted with students prior to the survey suggest that transferring knowledge amongst students with individualistic and collectivistic tendencies can be a challenge. Perceptual differences between in-group and out-group members follow attitudinal, cultural and sometimes linguistic boundaries. For instance, Singaporean Chinese students experience difficulty in communicating in English with their foreign counterparts from Mainland China (PRC) although the latter typically possess a good working command of English. In contrast, PRC students' Mandarin is usually much better than that of the average Singaporean student although Mandarin is hardly the lingua franca even amongst students sharing a common ethnic-race background. Hence, there is the possibility that the exchange of explicit and tacit knowledge is hampered. Whether students from China are indeed more collectivistic compared to Chinese students from Singapore needs to be examined empirically in future studies.

Overall, our study underlines the critical role of cultural orientations in students' differing predispositions towards knowledge transfer in team-based learning contexts. Vertical collectivists who submit to the authorities of the in-group and are willing to sacrifice themselves for their in-group clearly transfer more knowledge than horizontal individualists who are inclined to do their own thing. Students with a predisposition towards vertical collectivism, strong project related capabilities, high credibility, frequent communication with other team members and membership in a cohesive group are able to effectively transfer knowledge to other recipients. However, competition and the lack of depth in relationships represent enormous structural knowledge transfer barriers amongst university students in Singapore, a country well known for its demanding quality curricula and competitive environment (Shaheen and Sim, 2009). Whether collectivism decreases knowledge transfer activities with out-group members as argued by Peltokorpi (2006, p. 144) represents an interest topic for further empirical research.

In practical terms, our findings indicate that knowledge transfer processes in culturally diverse student teams have to be nurtured, monitored and managed by instructors, e.g. through intercultural awareness building and training measures before the start of project work as well as evaluative focus group (after action review) discussions. Other requirements include imparting cross-cultural team-building and listening skills, diversity (language) training and inclusive curricula. Besides cultural intelligence (Earley and Mosakowski, 2002) and the ability to nurture a collectivist, robust culture in groups and teams (Joshi and Sarker, 2006), recent research suggests that leaders can influence the successful outcomes of knowledge transfer activities, e.g., by engaging in caring leadership behavior (O-Reilly and Chatman, 1986; Von Krogh *et al.*, 2001; Lee *et al.*, 2010) or brokering hidden knowledge between culturally diverse members (Baba *et al.*, 2004).

The results of our study are instrumental for practitioners in both education and business who are tasked with managing groups/high performance teams in culturally diverse settings. To achieve team-based, collaborative learning goals in diverse student teams, both educators and learners need to be equipped with knowledge about cultural value differences and how this impacts upon team member knowledge transfer. To influence team member knowledge transfer, both team building exercises and goal-oriented learning activities with a focus on imparting core team capabilities such as credibility development, persuasive communication and developing team cohesiveness are crucial to enable all team members to achieve learning objectives and to prevent cultural misunderstandings. If the latter occurs, interventions by the educator might be necessary to cope with related issues. Given the central importance of the knowledge transfer mechanism in the context of effective peer learning in institutions of higher learning, strategic team development measures are required to enable learners to transfer knowledge effectively in increasingly culturally diverse contexts. This can be achieved with the help of proven approaches such as learning-oriented conversations, authentic dialogue, after action reviews or knowledge café (Mazutis and Slawinski, 2008). The deployment of these tools can provide team members and educational leaders with a meaningful opportunity to share "diversity experiences" and to enhance personal learning. Cultural experts familiar with the cultural fabric of the respective institution and/or students' countries of origin as well as cultural peculiarities can be roped in to help novices to appreciate the impact of cultural diversity through mentoring.

Future attempts to examine the uniqueness of knowledge transfer processes in terms of sharing or knowledge hoarding behavior in multi-cultural contexts in "Confucian-influenced societies" have to consider the wide variations which exist both within Asia as a whole and within individual Asian countries. Singapore is an interesting example in this respect as it appears rather Westernized and modern from the outside (Ng, 2003). From the inside it is remarkably heterogeneous in terms of ethnic affiliations, religious beliefs and so forth[3]. While government policies with regard to language or housing (Wong and Yeh eds., 1985) have transcended intra- and inter-ethnic divisions over time, a visit of a traditional hawker stall or a sub-ethnic (e.g., Teochew) restaurant will convince the observer that ethnicity markers such as food continue to form an important part of the identity of many Singaporeans. Notwithstanding the dearth of empirical studies on ethnic conceptions of knowledge, knowing, knowledge sharing etc., it is theoretically possible that within Singapore's various ethnic communities certain barriers[4] exist which may make it challenging to ensure effective knowledge transfer, for example, between "Chinese-educated" Chinese Singaporeans and "English-educated" Chinese Singaporeans (Menkhoff *et al.*, 2007) or between "locals" and "expatriates."

Besides examining the influence of Singapore's particular location and governance dynamics on the diffusion of knowledge and the reality of intra-organisational knowledge transfer cum learning processes in higher education and industry, future research will also have to consider the impact of demographic shifts on cultural patterns. As Ng (2003, p. 223) has highlighted, in Singapore, the younger and English-educated section of the population is more individualistic, in comparison with their older counterparts. This may represent new challenges for intergenerational knowledge transfer activities which have gained in importance during the

---

[3]The ethnic Chinese population which forms the majority is subdivided into several sub-ethnic groups such as Hokkien, Teochew, Cantonese, Hainanese, etc.

[4]The creation of so-called "inter-racial confidence circles" in 2002 aimed at fostering greater interaction and understanding among the different ethnic (and religious) groups is a significant policy measure and indicates the benefits of transcending real or imagined borders in terms of cross-cultural cooperation and value creation.

last few years due to the rapid ageing of Singapore's population and related labor market issues.

More research is also needed to compare knowledge transfer processes in both online and face-to-face contexts. As Wei *et al.* (2007) found out in their study on the impact of Chinese cultural values on knowledge sharing in online communities of practice, the high degree of competitiveness among employees and job security concerns seemingly overrode collectivistic tendencies with the result of pronounced knowledge *hoarding* rather than knowledge transfer. From the perspective of the foreign student, fear and lack of confidence might prevent proactive interaction and integration efforts. Study demands can hinder integration as local students may prefer to leverage on their own friends and communities to achieve top grades rather than spending "costly" time to develop relationships to "foreigners" whose learning and working styles may differ from their own.

As far as the study's limitations are concerned, the reliance on self-report measures raises the issue of common method variance (Podsakoff, MacKenzie and Podsakoff, 2003), that is, the tendency for participants to respond to different questions in a similar way. Further studies using a multi-method approach (Eid and Diener, 2006) may be adopted to reduce such measurement errors and to examine the generalizability of the present findings to other settings. Given the nature of the student sample and the cross-sectional methodology, the results may not generalize to other settings and contexts. The present study has also focused on individualism and collectivism as individual traits rather than national attributes as in Hofstede's work. Clearly, other personality-cultural dimensions may also influence knowledge transfer (Mooradian *et al.*, 2006) and any inferences drawn from this study should be made with caution.

While this investigation provides preliminary insights into knowledge transfer activities in culturally diverse student project teams as well as the complex relationship between cultural dispositions and people's responses to the transfer of course-related competencies to others, our understanding of variations in individualism and collectivism within a particular national culture is still rather limited. More research needs to be conducted to better explain the predicting power of each of the cultural orientations in determining students' responses towards knowledge transfer. Additional qualitative research might help in contextualizing respondents and how they are embedded in their respective socio-cultural environment. The composition of the four cultural orientation groups by ethnicity and how that relates to knowledge transfer represents another important topic for further research.

References

Agarwal, R, R Echambadi, AM Franco, and MB Sarkar (2004) Knowledge transfer through inheritance: Spin-out generation, development, and survival. *Academy of Management Journal*, 47, 501–522.

Appel, M, D Cartright, SG Smith, and LE Wolf (1996). *The Impact of Diversity on Students: A Preliminary View of the Research Literature*. Washington, DC: Association of American Colleges and Universities.

Argote, L and P Ingram (2000). Knowledge transfer: A basis for competitive advantage in firms. *Organizational Behavior and Human Decision Processes*, 82(1), 150–169.

Argote, LI, P Levine, and RL Moreland (2000). Knowledge transfer in organizations: Learning from the experience of others. *Organizational Behavior and Human Decision Processes*, 1–8, 82–98.

Baba, ML, J Gluesing, H Ratner, and KH Wagner (2002). The contexts of knowing: Natural history of a globally distributed team. *Journal of Organizational Behavior,* 25, 547–587.

Berrel, M, M Gloet, and P Wright (2002). Organisational learning in international joint ventures — Implications for management development. *The Journal of Management Development,* 21(2), 83–100.

Berry, JW (2004). Fundamental psychological processes in intercultural relations. In *Handbook of Intercultural Training*, D Landis, JM Bennett and ML Bennett (eds.), pp. 166–184. Thousand Oaks, CA: Sage Publications.

Bhagat, RS, BL Kedia, PD Harveston, and HC Triandis (2002). Cultural variations in the cross-border transfer of organizational knowledge. *Academy of Management Review*, 27(2), 204–221.

Bhawuk, DPS (2001). Evolution of culture assimilators: Toward theory-based assimilators. *International Journal of Intercultural Relations*, 25(2), 141–163.

Brown, G and T Menkhoff (2008). Territoriality over knowledge: Toward a cross-cultural perspective. *Journal of Asian Business*, 22–23, 103–121.

Callahan, AL, JJ Callahan, and SJ Kischuck (1993). Intellectual property rights: Who owns knowledge?' *Industrial Management*, May–June, 6–9.

Carron, AV (1982). Cohesiveness in sport groups: Interpretations and considerations. *Journal of Sport Psychology*, 4, 123–138.

Chay, YW, T Menkhoff, B Loh, and H-D Evers (2007). Social capital and knowledge sharing in knowledge-based organisations: An empirical study. *International Journal of Knowledge Management*, 3(1), 29–48.

Chow, CW, GL Harrison, JL McKinnon, and A Wu (1999). Cultural influences on informal information sharing in Chinese and Anglo–American organizations: An exploratory study. *Accounting, Organizations and Society*, 24, 561–582.

Cohen, WM and DA Levinthal (1990). Absorptive capacity: A new perspective on learning and innovation. *Administrative Science Quarterly*, 35(1), 128–152.

Constant, D, S Kiesler, and L Sproull (1994). What's mine is ours, or is it? A study of attitudes about information sharing. *Information Systems Research*, 5(4), 400–421.

Cunming, J and B Teng (2003). Transferring R & D knowledge: The key factors affecting knowledge transfer success. *Journal of Engineering and Technology Management*, 20, 39–68.

DeLong, D and L Fahey (2000). Diagnosing cultural barriers to knowledge management. *Academy of Management Executive*, 14(4), 113–127.

Dirks, KT and DL Ferrin (2001). The role of interpersonal trust in organizational settings. *Organization Science*, 12(4), 450–467.

Dineen, BR (2005). Teamxchange: A team project experience involving virtual teams and fluid team membership. *Journal of Management Education*, 29(4), 593–616.

Earley, PC and E Mosakowski (2002). Linking culture and behavior in organizations: Suggestions for theory development and research methodology. In *The Many Faces of Multi-level Issues. Research in Multi-level Issues*, FJ Yammarino and F Dansereau (eds.), pp. 297–319. Oxford, UK: JAI Press.

Eid, M and E Diener (2006). *Handbook of Multimethod Measurement in Psychology*. Washington, DC: American Psychological Association.

Festinger, L, S Schachter, and K Back (1950). *Social Pressure in Informal Groups*. New York: Harper and Row.

Glaser, EM, HH Abelson, and KN Garrison (1983). *Putting Knowledge to Use*. San Francisco, CA: Jossey–Bass.

Gelfand, MJ, M Evez, and Z Aycan (2007). Cross-cultural OB. *Annual Review of Psychology on Cross-Cultural OB*, 58, 479–514.

Goh, SC (2002). Managing effective knowledge transfer: An integrative framework and some practical implications. *Journal of Knowledge Management*, 6(1), 23–30.

Gross, N and W Martin (1952). On group cohesiveness. *American Journal of Sociology*, 57, 546–554.

Gupta, AK and V Govindarajan (2000). Knowledge flows within multinational corporations. *Strategic Management Journal*, 21, 473–496.

Halfhill, T and TM Nielson (2007). Quantifying the soft side of management education: An example using teamwork. *Journal of Management Education*, 31(1), 64–80.

Hofstede, GH (2001). *Culture's Consequences: Comparing Values, Behaviors, Institutions and Organizations Across Nations,* 2nd Edition. Thousand Oaks, CA: Sage Publications.

Hornidge, AK (2007). *Knowledge Society*. Muenster: LIT-Verlag.

Hornik, S and A Tupchiy (2006). Culture's impact on technology mediated learning: The role of horizontal and vertical individualism and collectivism. *Journal of Global Information Management*, 14(4), 31–56.

House, RJ *et al.* (eds.) (2004). *Culture, Leadership, and Organizations — The GLOBE Study of 62 Societies*. Thousand Oaks, CA: Sage Publications.

Hutchings, K and S Michailova (2004). Facilitating knowledge sharing in Russian and Chinese subsidiaries: The role of personal networks and group membership. *Journal of Knowledge Management*, 8(2), 1367–3270.

Inkpen, AC (1996). Creating knowledge through collaboration. *California Management Review*, 39(1), 123–140.

Irvine, JJ and DE York (1995). Learning styles and culturally diverse students: A literature review. In *Handbook of Research on Multicultural Education*, JA Banks and CA McGee Banks (eds.). New York, NY: Macmillan.

Johnson, S and A Miller (2002). A cross-cultural study of immediacy, credibility, and learning in the US and Kenya. *Communication Education*, 51(3), 280–292.

Joshi, KD and S Sarker (2005). The impact of knowledge, source, situational and relational context on knowledge transfer during ISD process. Paper presented at the *38th Annual Hawaii International Conference on System Sciences (HICSS-38)*, January 3–6, 2005 HICSS-38 2005, *Conference Proceedings* RH, Sprague (ed.).

Joshi, KD and S Sarker (2006). Examining the role of knowledge, source, recipient, relational, and situational context on knowledge transfer among face-to-face ISD teams. Paper presented at the *39th Annual Hawaii International Conference on System Sciences (HICSS-39)*, January 4–7, 2006 HICSS-39 2006 *Conference, Proceedings*, RH Sprague (ed.).

King, IW and A Rowe (1999). Space and the not-so-final frontiers: Re-presenting the potential of collective learning for organizations. *Management Learning*, 30(4), 431–448.

Kogut, B and U Zander (1992). Knowledge of the firm, combination capabilities, and the replication of technology. *Organization Science*, 3, 383–397.

Kraut, RE, J Egido, and J Galegher (1990). Patterns of contact and communication in scientific research collaborations. In *Intellectual Teamwork: Social and Technological Foundations of Cooperative Work*, J Galegher, RE Kraut and C Egido (eds.), pp. 149–171. Hillsdale, NJ: L Erlbaum Associates.

Lee, W-N and SM Choi (2005). The role of horizontal and vertical individualism and collectivism in online consumers' response toward persuasive communication on the Web. *Journal of Computer-Mediated Communication*, 11(1), Article 15. Available at http://jcmc.indiana.edu/vol11/issue1/wnlee.html.

Lee, P, N Gillespie, L Mann, and A Wearing (2010). Leadership and trust: Their effect on knowledge sharing and team performance. *Management Learning*, 41, 473–491.

Leidner, DE and M Fuller (1997). Improving student learning of conceptual information: GSS supported collaborative learning vs. individual constructive learning. *Decision Support Systems*, 20(2), 149–163.

Li, W, A Ardichvili, M Maurer, T Wenting, and R Studemann (2007). Impact of Chinese culture values on knowledge sharing through online communities of practice. *International Journal of Knowledge Management*, 3(3), 46–59.

Liebowitz, J (ed.) (1999). *Knowledge Management Handbook*. Boca Raton, FL: CRC Press.

Liebowitz, J (2000). *Building Organizational Intelligence*. Boca Raton, Fla: CRC Press.

Loh, B, A-C Tang, T Menkhoff, YW Chay, and HD Evers (2010). Applying knowledge management in university research. In *Governing and Managing Knowledge in Asia, Series on Innovation and Knowledge Management*, T Menkhoff, H-D Evers and YW Chay (eds.), pp. 221–248. New Jersey: World Scientific.

Mazutis, D and N Slawinski (2008). Leading organizational learning through authentic dialogue. *Management Learning*, 39(4), 437–456.

Menkhoff, T, YW Chay, and B Loh (2004). Notes from an "intelligent island": Towards strategic knowledge management in Singapore's small business sector. *International Quarterly for Asian Studies*, 35(1–2), 85–99.

Menkhoff, T (2010). Creating value through knowledge management. *Business Times*, June 15, p. 24.

Menkhoff, T, H-D Evers, and YW Chay (eds.) (2010). *Governing and Managing Knowledge in Asia. Series on Innovation and Knowledge Management* 9, 2nd Edition. New Jersey: World Scientific Publishing.

Merritt, A (2000). Culture in the cockpit: Do Hofstede's dimensions replicate? *Journal of Cross-Cultural Psychology*, 31(3), 283–301.

Michailova, S and K Husted (2003). Knowledge sharing in Russian companies with Western participation. *Management International*, 6(2), 19–28.

Mills, J and MS Clarks (1982). Exchange and communal relationships. *Review of Personality and Social Psychology*, 3, 121–144.

Nemanich, L, M Banks, and D Vera (2009). Enhancing knowledge transfer in classroom versus online settings. *Decision Sciences Journal of Innovative Education*, 7(1).

Mooradian, T, B Renzl, and K Matzler (2006). Who trusts? Personality, trust and knowledge sharing. *Management Learning*, 37, 523–540.

Ng, AK (2003). A cultural model of creative and conforming behavior. *Creativity Research Journal*, 15(2–3), 223–233.

Nonaka, I (1991). The knowledge-creating company. *Harvard Business Review*, 69(6), 96–104.

Nonaka, I (1994). A dynamic theory of organizational knowledge creation. *Organization Science*, 5, 14–37.

Nonaka, I and H Takeuchi (1995). *The Knowledge-Creating Company — How Japanese Companies Create the Dynamics of Innovation*. Oxford, UK: Oxford University Press.

O'Reilly, C and J Chatman (1986). Organizational commitment and psychological attachment: The effects of compliance, identification, and internalization on prosocial behavior. *Journal of Applied Psychology*, 71, 492–499.

Osterloh, M and BS Frey (2000). Motivation, knowledge transfer, and organizational forms. *Organization Science*, 11(5), 538–550.

Peltokorpi, V (2006). Knowledge sharing in a cross-cultural context: Nordic expatriates in Japan. *Knowledge Management Research & Practice*, 4, 138–148.

Podsakoff, PM, SB MacKenzie, JY Lee, and NP Podsakoff (2003). Common method biases in behavioral research: A critical review of the literature and recommended remedies. *Journal of Applied Psychology*, 88, 879–903.

Polanyi, M (1975). Personal knowledge. In *Meaning*, M Polanyi and H Prosch (eds.), pp. 22–45. Chicago: University of Chicago Press.

Pratto, F, J Sidanius, LM Stallworth, and BF Malle (1994). Social dominance orientation: A personality variable predicting social and political attitudes. *Journal of Personality and Social Psychology*, 67, 741–763.

Reagans, R and B McEvily (2003). Network structure and knowledge transfer: The effects of cohesion and range. *Administrative Science Quarterly*, 48(2), 240–267.

Retna, KS (2001). The fifth discipline in a highly disciplined Singapore: Innovative learning organisations and national culture. *Innovation: Management, Policy and Practice*, 4(1–3), 215–226.

Rice, RE and EM Rogers (1980). Reinvention in the innovation process. *Knowledge: Creation, Diffusion, Utilization*, 1(4), 499–514.

Rogers, E (1983). *The Diffusion of Innovation*. New York, NY: Free Press.

Sassen, S (2001). *The Global City*. New York, London, Tokyo: Princeton University Press.

Saxenian Lee, A, Y Motoyama, and X Quan (2003). Local and global networks of immigrant professionals in Silicon Valley. *International Journal of Economic Development*.

Scarbrough, H, M Bresnen, L Edelman, S Laurent, S Newell, and J Swan (2004). The processes of project-based learning: An exploratory study. *Management Learning*, 35(4), 491–506.

Schwartz, SH (1992). Universals in the content and structure of values: Theoretical advances and empirical tests in 20 countries. *Advances in Experimental Social Psychology*, 25, 1–65.

Schwartz, SH and A Bardi (2001). Value hierarchies across cultures: Taking a similarities perspective. *Journal of Cross Cultural Psychology*, 32, 268–290.

Schwartz, SH (2004). Mapping and interpreting cultural differences around the world. In *Comparing Cultures, Dimensions of Culture in a Comparative Perspective*, H Vinken, J Soeters and P Ester (eds.). Leiden, The Netherlands: Brill.

Schwartz, SH (2006). Value orientations: Measurement, antecedents and consequences across nations. In *Measuring Attitudes Cross-Nationally — Lessons From the European Social Survey*, R Jowell, C Roberts, R Fitzgerald and G Eva (eds.). London, NY: Sage Publications.

Shaheen, M and MW Sim (2009). Perceptions and knowledge sharing practices of graduate students in Singapore. *International Journal of Knowledge Management*, 5(2), 21–32.

Shapiro, DL, S Furst, G Spreitzer, and M Von Glinow (2002). Transnational teams in the electronic age: Are team identity and high performance at risk? *Journal of Organizational Behavior*, 23, 455–67.

Sidanius, J and F Pratto (1999). *Social Dominance: An Intergroup Theory of Social Hierarchy and Oppression*. New York, NY: Cambridge University Press.

Smith, B and J MacGregor (1992). What is collaborative learning? In *Collaborative Learning: A Sourcebook for Higher Education*, A Goodsell, M Maher, V Tinto, B Smith and J MacGregor (eds.). University Park, PA: National Center on Postsecondary Teaching, Learning, and Assessment, Pennsylvania State University.

Soh, S and FTL Leong (2002). Validity of vertical and horizontal individualism and collectivism in Singapore. *Journal of Cross-Cultural Psychology*, 33, 3–15.

Starbuck, WH (1992). Learning by knowledge intensive firms. *Journal of Management Studies*, 29, 713–740.

Szulanski, G (2000). The process of knowledge transfer: A diachronic analysis of stickiness. *Organizational Behavior and Human Decision Processes*, 82, 9–27.

Szulanski, G (2003). *Sticky Knowledge: Barriers to Knowing in the Firm.* Thousand Oaks, CA: Sage Publications.

Tan, HH and D Chee (2005). Understanding interpersonal trust in a confucian influenced society: An exploratory study. *International Journal of Cross Cultural Management*, 5(2), 197–212.

The Economist (2010). Foreign university students — Will they still come? August 7, pp. 40–42.

Triandis, HC (1988). Collectivism vs. individualism: A reconceptualization of a basic concept in cross-cultural psychology. In *Cross-Cultural Studies of Personality, Attitudes and Cognition,* GK Verna and C Bageley (eds.), pp. 60–95. New York, NY: St Martins Press.

Triandis, HC (1990). Cross-cultural studies of individualism and collectivism. In *Cross-Cultural Perspectives: Nebraska Symposium on Motivation,* J Berman (ed.), pp. 41–133. Lincoln: University of Nebraska Press.

Triandis, HC (1995). *Individualism and Collectivism.* Boulder, CO: Westview Press.

Triandis, HC (1996). The psychological measurement of cultural syndromes. *American Psychologist*, 51(4), 407–415.

Triandis, HC and MJ Gelfand (1998). Converging measurement of horizontal and vertical individualism and collectivism. *Journal of Personality and Social Psychology*, 74(1), 118–128.

Tsui-Auch, LS (2003). Learning strategies of small and medium-sized Chinese family firms: A comparative study of two suppliers in Singapore. *Management Learning*, 34, 201–220.

Uzzi B (1997). Social structure and competition in interfirm networks: The paradox of embeddedness. *Administrative Science Quarterly*, 42, 35–67.

Von Krogh, GV, K Ichijo, and I Nonaka (2001). Bringing care into knowledge development of business organizations. In *Knowledge Emergence: Social, Technical, and Evolutionary Dimensions of Knowledge Creation,* I Nonaka and T Nishiguchi (eds.), pp. 30–52. Oxford and New York: Oxford University Press.

Williams, EA, R Duray, and V Reddy (2006). Teamwork orientation, group cohesiveness, and student learning: A study of the use of teams in online distance education. *Journal of Management Education*, 30(4), 592–616.

Wolff, K (1950). *The Sociology of Georg Simmel*. New York: Free Press.

Wong, AK and SHK Yeh (eds). (1985). *Housing a Nation: 25 Years of Public Housing in Singapore*. Singapore: Maruzen Asia for Housing and Development Board.

Zaltman, G, R Duncan, and J Holbek (1973). *Innovations and Organizations*. New York: Wiley.

Zander, U and B Kogut (1995). Knowledge and the speed of the transfer and imitation of organizational capabilities: An empirical test. *Organization Science*, 6(1), 76–92.

Part 4

Asian Business in Local Contexts

Chapter 16

Urban Property Development in Malaysia: The Impact of Chinese and Malay Conceptions of Space

Hans-Dieter Evers

1. Introduction: Defining the Issue

In the past 30 years, Peninsular Malaysia has undergone rapid urbanization from 34 percent urban population in 1980 to 71 percent in 2010. This has created an unprecedented building boom, leading to the rise of large construction companies. Population density in urban areas has increased and the townscape is now dominated by rows and rows of semidetached houses, high-rise buildings of over 20 stories high, and gated communities. High rise buildings have often been interpreted as symbols of modernity and progress (Goh, 1998, p. 168), but the question, by whom is grossly neglected. The housing estates and condominiums have been overwhelmingly designed and built by Malaysia's big property developers, huge companies with international connections and international capital. Government agencies, like UDA (Urban Development Authority) and government linked companies with Bumiputra part ownership like Paremba have also impacted on the cityscape. Though ownership and shares may be distributed between Chinese family conglomerates and Malay government connected elites, management and construction work is firmly in Chinese hands (Gomez, 2011; Evers and Nordin, 2012).

This chapter is going to argue that next to the political economy of ethnicity the cultural conceptions of space will have a decisive impact on the process of urbanization (Evers and Korff, 2000). The physical city-scape of Malaysian urban areas in turn will determine the everyday life and the employment opportunities of all Malaysians.

Malaysian society is multiethnic and countless observers have drawn attention to the unequal geographical distribution of its two major ethnic groups, Malays and Chinese. Overall population statistics of Peninsular Malaysia clearly show that the majority of Chinese live in urban areas, whereas Malays are still concentrated in rural areas. Malays have, however, increasingly migrated into urban areas. In Kuala Lumpur, there is now (Census 2010) an almost equal number of Malays and Chinese, but in Georgetown, Penang there are three times more Chinese than Malays. A few major towns, particularly on the east coast have a majority of Malays, but even here the central business district tends to be inhabited and owned mostly by Chinese. Those ecological areas of towns that convey a typically "urban" character are Chinese, whereas there are still Malay areas that maintain a typical "rural" appearance. It is not without justification that Malay areas within Malaysian towns are usually called *kampung*, whereas Chinese areas are given place names and street names, or are in some cases just called Chinatown. There are also Chinese villages with a predominantly agricultural population, and single Chinese families in Malay villages. But even then Chinese houses tend to have a more urban appearance. They tend to be built of stone more often than of timber and they sit squarely on the ground, whereas Malay houses are often raised on stilts, built of planks, and covered with corrugated iron sheets. Housing estates and high-rise buildings are increasingly dominating the urban landscape and tend to be ethnically diverse.

The rural character of the Malays and the urban mode of living of the Chinese have often been noted, described and explained. Malays always have been, so the argument goes, a rural people, who have adopted their style of life to the tropical climate of torrential rains and to paddy agriculture. Chinese are immigrants and had to find an ecological niche left by the Malays. They came into Malaya with the expansion of modern capitalism, partly even before colonial rule was firmly established. It was left to them to extend markets, to provide labor for tin mining and for the capitalist plantation economy, and to found and settle the communication centres of the new political and economic system, namely, the towns and cities. Thus, a colonial plural society emerged with a division of labor based on ethnic lines. All these reasons given for the unequal geographical distribution of Malays and Chinese are true, but not necessarily sufficient to explain present-day urbanization taking place under changed circumstances. This is because the cultural aspect has so far been neglected and the ideological superstructure disregarded. Even if the basic socioeconomic structure changes, even if the present development policy of rectifying the racial imbalance within the occupational and residential structure meets with success, Malays are unlikely to change their way of life immediately. Even those Malays that have been lured into the cities by the efforts of the Malaysian government to open up urban job opportunities for rural Malays appear to be still maintaining a rural ideology. Malay politicians are known to have admonished Malay civil servants to stay in town after retirement instead of returning to their home villages. Even within cities, areas with a concentration of a Malay population tend to preserve their rural character in at least a symbolic fashion.

It could be argued and statistically "proven" that the economic, educational, and occupational differences between Chinese and Malays are non-existent if one keeps place of residence (rural or urban) constant. Consequently, there are said to be no real differences between Chinese and Malays except place of residence. If Malays move to the city, differences between them and Chinese would disappear. This argument is, of course, nonsensical and based on a misunderstanding of both the political economy and the culture of Malaysia.

British colonial policy has created a socioeconomic base on which a cultural superstructure could flourish, creating, selecting, and maintaining traditional Chinese and Malay values that otherwise might have vanished. Soja (1971, pp. 9–10) has drawn attention to the fact that "conventional Western perspectives on spatial organization were powerfully shaped by the concept of property" and that "property has become rightly and territorially defined." This is certainly true though rigid territoriality is by no means an exclusively Western concept, as we are going to argue in the Chinese case.

In the following paragraphs, we will explicate an important aspect of Chinese and Malay cultural values, which appears to be a most relevant factor in shaping the process of Malaysian urbanization and the ecological structure of Malaysian urban areas.

2. Differing Conceptions of Space, Land and Landownership

The Chinese conception of space differs greatly from that of the Malays or other ethnic groups in the Nusantara (Evers, 1977). On entering a Chinese village one is sure where it begins and where it ends. Whereas Malay houses stand on stilts and are suspended above ground. Chinese houses sit squarely on the soil. There tends to be one main footpath or street passing through the village, which in most cases is usually clearly discernible even on a cadastre map because plots of land tend to be small but regular. Members of a Chinese family will be able to tell exactly where their land ends and the property of their neighbours begins. Quite often a fence is put up creating an inner yard attached to the house.

Whereas Malays tend to add the names of family members as owners of a plot of land on intestate inheritance, Chinese tend to subdivide or sell land. Working on land registry data we often came across plots of Malay-owned land that were divided into shares of one seventh, one twelfth, or up to several hundredth shares. Islamic law is partly responsible for this, but the fact remains that effective individual ownership is no longer possible. Though joint ownership is also common among Chinese, it seldom extends to unmanageable proportions.

Upon entering a Malay rural or urban kampung (village) one is faced with the problem of orientation. There is usually no main street. no plaza or main square, but only an apparently arbitrary system of winding footpaths leading from house to house becoming narrower at times or ending in blind alleys. There appears to be no clear pattern, no "readability" of the urban or rural scene, which according to Kevin Lynch's well-known study on "The Image of the City," is so important for the landscape of a town or settlement (Lynch, 1960). Malay houses themselves are built according to a clear pattern. They have a veranda (*serambi*), a main room (*ibu rumah*) from which one or two sleeping rooms may be divided (*bilik*), and a kitchen attached to the back of the house (*dapur*). The veranda usually (but not necessarily) faces the east or south to keep it cool in the afternoon, but in addition there are no rules or regulations about how houses ought to relate to each other. There appears to be a tendency to keep them apart as far as possible and in such a way that the view is never blocked by houses alone. This creates an impression of a wide-open space even if villages become more densely settled due to growing population and the rule of neo-local residence after marriage. Boundaries between the house lots are in no way demarcated, and residents find it difficult to point out the exact shape of the plot of land on which the house is built. Importance is only attached to the usufructuary rights to coconut trees or fruit trees; otherwise, boundaries do not seem to matter, though Malaysia has had, since British times, a fairly well-organized cadastre system. Malay villagers quite often do not bother to register changes in the ownership of their housing lots. If new settlers come in from other areas or new families are created by marriage, permission to put up a house is fairly easily granted by the owner and no rent is charged for the land (Evers and Goh, 1978). Houses, however, are rented or sold separately irrespective of the National Land Code which does not allow for a legal separation of land and building structures, except for newly introduced strata titles in high-rise buildings.

The nature of the conception of geographical space or land is demonstrated by a case from a village in which I resided for some time. A man moved into the village to earn a living as a sate vendor. He asked an absentee landlord whether he would be allowed to put up a house on his lot of land, and permission was easily granted. After the house had been built the absentee landlord visited the village and found to his surprise that the house was established on a lot adjacent to his. The actual owner on learning of the situation reacted only by exhibiting the common "never-mind attitude" (*tidak apa-apa*). Discussion with villagers to verify boundaries on cadastre maps proved to be very difficult and often futile. There appeared to be no clearly developed conception of bounded space and of clear-cut boundaries in general.

The same attitude is found when trying to delineate the boundaries of a kampong or village. A kampong is usually defined by the relationship of its inhabitants to the mosque or prayer house. As Clarke (1976, p. 63) pointed out in an analysis of the spatial order of Kota Bharu, Kelantan, "most areas have a central identifying physical feature and from this the area radiates in various directions. Boundaries are indistinct..." All those taking part in the election of the mosque committee belong to one kampong, irrespective of where they actually live. The kampung is therefore in essence not a residential group in the sense the term is defined in sociology text books. The definition of the village as a territorial group is based on the European image of a settlement and is strictly not applicable to the Malay situation.

Boundaries in the rice fields are more clearly defined, as rice fields are divided by dams and irrigation channels. But even here the conception of space or area is rather diffuse. Originally, the size of a paddy field was measured in sowing extent (i.e., according to a fixed measure of rice that was used to sow a plot of land, which could vary in size according to the availability of water and the quality of soil). Nowadays traditional Malay measures of rice land have their equivalent in English measures (acres, usually), but the equivalent acreage varies from area to area or from state to state. It is only in the area of small holding rubber plantations that fairly fixed conceptions of areas are maintained.

3. Conceptions of Religious Space

Among the Chinese the importance of the ownership of land and the concomitant clear-cut conception of geographical space is further emphasized by the fact that Chinese have developed a special science of boundaries, namely geomancy. The measures of a plot of land and the direction a house should face were traditionally determined by a ritual specialist, a geomancer. Though his services are not necessarily employed anymore, there is still a rudimentary knowledge of the science of geomancy (*feng shui*) and a clear understanding of the importance of spatial arrangements. Great attention is still paid to the direction of the main door and the positioning of houses in general. On occasion the outlay of cities and the fortune of their inhabitants are related to geomantic principles. One informant even tried to explain the initial success of British rule over Malaya by pointing out, in terms of geomancy, the most appropriate position of the living quarters of British residents and district officers, which tended to be located on hills turning their back to mountain range.

The difference between Chinese and Malay conceptions of space becomes particularly visible when comparing Chinese and Malay graveyards. Chinese attach a great importance to the exact location and the boundaries of a grave, which are as long as the family can afford it, indicated by strong walls surrounding the tomb. Ritual specialists are employed to measure and determine a good location for an ancestral grave. Chinese graveyards are therefore spatially highly structured and permanent. A Malay graveyard is in contrast very loosely structured. The two boundary stones put on each grave are scattered and extend into the surrounding areas as long as building regulations in cities have not made this impossible. No great importance is attached to the location of the grave. Wherever there is some space left the burial can take place. The only exceptions are graves said to possess magic powers (kuburan keramat), the graves of royalty and the mosques themselves, which have a clearly defined ritually pure area.

But even here the Malay conception of space has made inroads. A frequently found form of holy grave in Malaysia is the so-called *kuburan panjang* (long grave). The holy man buried here is said to have grown, thus pushing the boundary stones of the grave down. The grave stones have to be re-erected from time to time, extending the length of the grave in the process. Again, space is variable, has no permanent boundary and can be extended.

Even in the area of no orthodox religion the differences between the Chinese and Malay conceptions of space become apparent. The Chinese attach great importance to the earth goddess. Villages or town quarters tend to have a local guardian deity, a *Datuk*. Malay ghosts, however, are not attached to particular places of worship. Though the Malay also know guardian ghosts whose power emanates from a certain place, their power does not apply to a clearly defined area; they do not rule defined territories.

Our analysis of the differences between Chinese and Malay conceptions of geographical and religious space can also be extended to conceptions of social space.

4. Conceptions of Social Space

With very few exceptions the population of the Malay Peninsula consists of immigrants. This holds true both to Malays, many of whom originated from Sumatra, Java, or other Indonesian islands, and to Chinese and

Indians. Nevertheless, Malays would attach very little importance to their place of origin. Migrants from Sumatra or Java are quickly acculturated to a uniform Malay society. Second-generation migrants usually do not speak the dialect or language of their parents anymore and would claim, on being interviewed, that they are local people. On being questioned further, they might have some hazy conceptions of where their ancestors came from but will usually not know or be interested in the exact place of origin. Exceptions to this general rule tend to be people of Minangkabau origin, as long as they live together in close settlements and maintain a system of matrilineal descent (Evers, 1975a).

In contrast, Chinese tend to have a very clear conception not only of their general area of origin in China but even of the exact name of the village from which they originated. This knowledge is to a certain extent still transmitted from generation to generation. Whereas Malay identity is established by social and cultural facts — namely, by being a Muslim, speaking the Malay language, and being in very general, locally undefined terms a "*bumiputra*" (son of the soil) — Chinese determine their ethnic identity primarily by their dialect and their place of origin in China. A strict system of patrilineal descent, lineages, and clans defined by common ancestors, common geographical origin, and common localized places of worship is based on an identity between social and geographical space.

The localized bias in the Malay conception of social space could also be demonstrated in a study of the "mental maps" of Malaysian students in a northern town (Gould and White 1974, pp. 167–169). On being asked where they would prefer to find employment, most Malays gave the name of their current place of residence and to a lesser degree the surrounding area, whereas Chinese students preferred various urban centres along the west coast as far south as Singapore.

The Chinese mental map was clearly focused on major urban areas whereas the Malay one was cantered on the primarily rural home districts. These differing conceptions of space form in a general way the basis of another culturally defined complex, namely, the image of an urban area, a town, or a city. It is the combination of the conception of space and the image of an urban area that, I submit, still influences the urbanization process and the urban ecology of Malaysia.

5. Conceptions of Political and Urban Space

Though most Chinese immigrants to Malaysia came originally from rural areas in Southern China, they nevertheless brought with them the image of a rural life cantered on the city. As Skinner (1964) has pointed out in a lengthy study, Chinese rural social structure cannot be understood without reference to towns. Clusters of small villages surrounding a locally important town formed a discrete social and areal unit, which Skinner terms a "standard marketing area." Occupational and religious associations as well as kinship ties combined to turn this area into a tightly knit sociopolitical unit. Chinese social life, even in rural areas, was cantered on the city and it is likely that this image of the city was also brought over to Malaysia by southern Chinese migrants. At least Chinese secret societies that dominated Chinese society in the Straits Settlements and the Malay states perpetuated the urban image and enshrined it in their most important ritual, the initiation of new members. These rites were held in a Chinese temple, representing "an imaginary walled city through which the candidate was to take a symbolic journey" (Purcell, 1956, p. 165). A Chinese city itself was a highly structured spatial entity with definite boundaries, directions, and functional areas (Wheatley, 1971). Though no walled Chinese city was ever built in Malaysia (unless one wants to count the barbed wire-fenced "new villages" during the Communist uprising as such), the concept of dense urban living in bounded, and clearly defined space was certainly known and utilized as a "mental map" or blueprint to Malaysian Chinese urbanism.

In contrast, the Malay perception of political space and of the city was quite different. It seems to go back to, or at least to show great similarity to, Nusantara predecessors. In the empires of Majapahit and Mataram "territory was concerted as radiating in three concentric circles with the Kraton of the prince at the centre: (1) the *negaragung* or core regions, (2) the *mantjanegara*, or neighbouring regions, and (3) *thapasisir*, or coastal provinces" (Siddique 1977). The spatial perception is centrifocal and the centre is the palace of the ruler rather than the city. The Malay conception of political space appears to have been quite similar.

The centre of political power in the Malay states was the palace of the king or sultan. The istana was, and in some occasions still is, surrounded by royal villages, inhabited by retainers and craftsmen serving the royal court. Market places were usually physically separated from the palace by some distance. It is here that cities developed primarily through Chinese and Indian immigration. Up to recently the Malay image of the town (bandar) was one of the market place rather than a residential area. In fact, bandar means, strictly speaking, a port or harbor. *Kota*, another term frequently connected with town names in Malaysia, means fort or stockade. There is no precise Malay expression for town or city. Malays ideally live in villages (kampong), even if these villages now administratively fall within the boundaries of a municipality. Even if most urban Malays now live in terrace houses or flats, the kampong remains an ideal type of urban living. When a kampung is scheduled for destruction and to be replaced by high rise buildings, like Kampung Tanjung Tokong in Penang in December 2011, resistance and public protest flares up.

In contrast to Chinese conceptions of the spatial structure of society, Malay life was focused on the istana and the mosque, but not on the city. It is therefore not so much Kuala Lumpur, the capital city, but the national mosque, the Masjid Negara, and the king, the Yang di Pertuan Agong, elected from among the sultans of the Malay states that form the focus of Malay national sentiment and identity. In his effort of nation-building, Prime Minister Mahathir created a new Malay national capital, Putrajaya and a knowledge city Cyberjaya (Evers and Nordin, 2012), though he and his urban planners used Middle Eastern rather than Malay architecture to symbolize the new Bumiputra Malay image of a capital city. The move of the government from Kuala Lumpur, seen as a predominantly Chinese city to Putrajaya, the new Malay metropolis with Putrajaya and the new national university Universiti Kebangsaan Malaysia in its vicinity was a not entirely move to change the Malay conception of space.

In the ecological structure of some of the Malaysian cities the principles of an Islamized and Malayanized image of the Indian city of ancient Southeast Asia are still to be seen. A central square (padang) opens toward the sultan's palace (istana) and the living quarters of the sultan's extended family and their descendants. The main mosque is found next to the padang in the immediate proximity of the istana, whereas the market and the Chinese settlement are some way off the centre of religious and political power. Kota Bharu (Evers and Goh, 1976; Clarke, 1976) and Kuala

Trengganu conform very much to this pattern. But whereas some Javanese cities up to the 16ᵗʰ century were still surrounded by a wall, the Malayanized town consistently exhibits the centrifocal conception of space. The centre (padang, istana, and mesjid besar) is clearly defined, but beyond this area the spatial structures peters out and becomes less and less clear. The town is in cultural and social terms not a bounded area and it is absolutely undefined where the town ends and the villages begin.

Even among the modern Malay urban middle class, consisting of civil servants and professionals, the original conception of space and of the city is still maintained, whenever a chance is given. It is first of all expressed in a certain uneasiness and reluctance to move into the new middle-class housing estates and high-rise apartment blocks that are springing up in all Malaysian cities. A massive increase in Malay urban population living primarily in these estates has started in the Federal Territory surrounding Kuala Lumpur, but is extending into other urban areas and "new towns" as well. This may signal a change, but still the housing estates and condominiums are normally designed by Chinese architects, built by Chinese contractors, and conform to the Chinese cultural conception of space and housing. Most of these housing estates consist of modernized versions of the Chinese shop house, where the shop is replaced by a parking space for a small car. Mostly these houses are semidetached or row houses with a narrow back lane and very small backyards surrounded by a wall. The maintenance of boundaries is very important and clearly expressed in iron gates and stone walls. Not so in Malay areas designed and constructed by Malays themselves; here still kampong type houses are found, though the lower, formerly open part tends to be walled in and used by younger or newly married children of the family. But still, wherever possible, the boundary to the neighbour's house is not marked by a fence or a stone wall but is left open. If there are hedges or fences at all, they tend to have holes or passages, not so much from neglect, but maintaining such a visible boundary does not conform to Malay conception of space and reciprocal relations with neighbours.

This point is very clearly documented in a detailed ethnography of Kota Bharu, the capital city of the state of Kelantan. According to this study "a neighbour is one who makes himself available to other neighbours when he is at home. One of the most significant features of this is that a neighbour's house should be both visible and accessible to other neighbours who may wish to call. Informants frequently relate that persons they consider to be rich people (*orang kaya*) build houses which are surrounded by fences with bolted gates and lots of shrubbery. Persons classed as rich people are not neighbours" (Clarke, 1976, p. 167).

6. Conclusions

I have tried to demonstrate that Malays and Chinese exhibit two different concepts of space. Whereas the Malay conception of geographical, social, religious, and political space is centrifugal, the Chinese conception of space is bounded. Chinese, even rural Chinese, have a clear-cut image of the "city" and of urban life, whereas Malays centre their spatial attention on central institutions like the istana or the mesjid, both of which are not necessarily urban or connected with urbanism. Malay living quarters are still defined as kampung (villages) even if they happen to be part of a city.

I hope to have shown that the two differing conceptions of space are consistent and can be traced in different aspects of social organization and culture of Malays and Chinese (Evers and Nordin, 2012). Rather then essentializing Malay or Chinese culture, which has been criticized in the "orientalism" debate, recently summarized by Wan Zawawi Ibrahim and Noor Shaw (2012, pp. 165–200), I look at conceptions of space as a "*Tiefenstruktur*" of long-term cultural processes. Such consistent sociocultural patterns reinforcing each other account for the persistence of culture over long periods of time. This also means that they are difficult to alter even if the underlying socioeconomic system changes. This poses a dilemma.

The policy of the Malaysian government under the New Economic Policy (NEP) of the Second and Third Malaysia Plan has been to draw more Malays into urban occupations and to "urbanize" the Malay peasant. The 10th Malaysia Plan and the "Economic Transformation Programme" of 2010 stresses urbanization as a driver of growth (p. 125). As most urban centres have long been Chinese in terms of inhabitants and in terms of culture, the attempt to urbanize Malays could amount to a policy of Sinicization of parts of Malay culture. This is, of course, not the intention of the present Malaysian UMNO (United Malay National Organization) dominated government. What were the alternatives? The alternative was the development of an image of a Malay or at least Malaysian city in which Malay conceptions of space are translated into urban planning (Bunnel, 2002). The new administrative capital of Putrajaya appears to be a not totally successful attempt in this direction, neither is the image of Cyberjaya, the Malay–Malaysian knowledge city (Evers and Nordin, 2012). So far local and foreign architects and urban planners have either copied Western or Middle Eastern models or provided slightly modernized versions of the Chinese shop house city (Bunnell, 2004).

Legal provisions and building bylaws, enacted by local councils under the influence of Chinese developers, are usually detrimental to possible Malay types of buildings and Malay use of space. Thus the utilization of timber is often prohibited, subdivision is done to conform to the size of standard Chinese shop house lots, roads and back lanes are laid out (by Chinese city engineers) to conform to Chinese rather than Malay concepts of space. The Chinese concept of bounded space is furthermore turned upside down and has resulted in high-rise buildings often higher than 20 levels. Bounded conception of space is extended high into the third dimension. The highly speculative land market is, again, dominated by Chinese construction companies and low-cost housing schemes, promised by government authorities, tend to turn out to be again middle-class priced and built for a Chinese style of life.

Economic forces thus tend to maintain the present urban system in Malaysia, reinforcing the cultural superstructure of Chinese and Malay conceptions of space. It can thus be argued with some justification that the creation of a truly Malaysian city depends eventually on a change in the urban economy and a change in the urban political structure.

References

Bunnell, T (2002). Kampung rules: Landscape and the contested government of urban(e) Malayness. *Urban Studies*, 39(9), 685–701.

Bunnell, T (2004). *Malaysia, Modernity, and the Multimedia Super Corridor: A Critical Geography of Intelligent Landscapes*. London, UK: Routledge Curzon.

Clarke, RE (1976). Land and neighbourhood as features of Malay urbanism. PhD thesis, Department of Anthropology and Sociology, University of British Columbia. Vancouver.

Evers, H-D (1975a). Changing patterns of Minangkabau urban landownership. *Bijdragen tot de Taal-, Land- en Volkenkunde*, 131(1), 86–110.

Evers, H-D (1975b). Urbanization and urban conflict in Southeast Asia. *Asian Survey*, 15(9), 775–785.

Evers, H-D (1976). Urban expansion and landownership in underdeveloped societies. In *The City in Comparative Perspective*, J Walton and LH Masotti (eds.), pp. 67–79. New York, NY: Wiley.

Evers, H-D (1977). The culture of Malaysian urbanization — Malay and Chinese conceptions of space. *Urban Anthropology*, 6(3), 205–216.

Evers, H-D (1984). Urban landownership, ethnicity and class in Southeast Asian cities. *International Journal of Urban and Regional Research*, 8(4), 481–496.

Evers, H-D (2011). Urban symbolism and the new urbanism of Indonesia. In *Cities Full of Symbols. A Theory of Urban Space and Culture*, PJM Nas (ed.), pp. 187–196. Leiden: Leiden University Press.

Evers, H-D and BL Goh (1976). Urban landownership in Kota Bharu and Jeli, Kelantan. Project Paper Series No. 5, Centre for Policy Research, Universiti Sains Malaysia, Pulau Pinang.

Evers, H-D and BL Goh (1978). Urban development and landownership in Butterworth, Malaysia. *Journal of Southeast Asian Studies*, 9(1).

Evers, H-D and R Korff (2000). *Southeast Asian Urbanism: The Meaning and Power of Social Space*. Münster, Singapore, New York: LIT/ISEAS/McGraw-Hill.

Evers, H-D and N Ramli (2012). The Symbolic universe of Cyberjaya, Malaysia. ZEF Working Paper Series No. 95.

Goh, BL (1998). Modern dreams. An enquiry into power, cityscape transformations and cultural difference in contemporary Malaysia. In *Southeast Asian Identities. Culture and the Politics of Representation in Malaysia, Singapore, and Thailand*, JS Kahn (ed.). Singapore: ISEAS.

Gomez, ET (2011). *Chinese Business in Malaysia: Accumulation, Ascendance, Accommodation*. London, UK: Routledge.

Gould, P and R White (1974). *Mental Maps*. Harmondsworth: Pelican.

Ibrahim, Z and N Shah (2012). Indigenising knowledge and social science discourses in the periphery: Decolonizing Malayness and Malay underdevelopment. In *Social Science and Knowledge in a Globalising World*, I. Zawawi (ed.), pp. 165–200. Ibrahim. Kajang, Selangor: Malaysian Social Science Association.

Lynch, K (1960). *The Image of the City*. Cambridge, MA: MIT Press.

Purcell, V (1956). *The Chinese in Malaya*. London, UK: Oxford University Press.

Siddique, S (1977). Relics of the past? A sociological study of the Sultanates of Cirebon, West Java. PhD thesis. University of Bielefeld. Germany.

Skinner, GW (1964). Marketing and social structure in rural China. *Journal of Asian Studies,* 24, 363–399.

Soja, EW (1971). The political organization of space. Washington, DC: Association of American Geographers. Resource Paper No. 8.

Wheatley, P (1971). *The Pivot of the Four Quarters*. Edinburgh: University of Edinburgh Press.

Chapter 17

Informal Banking and Early International Entrepreneurs: The Case of the Chettiars

Jayarani Tan and Tan Wee Liang

1. Introduction

Though the Chettiars were not microfinanciers, as we understand it today, they were renowned for their mercantile and informal banking activities that took the form of moneylending in the pre-modern colonial era. With the emergence of 19th century colonialism their role as informal financiers changed to one of intermediary informal financiers, for example in British colonies of Asia and Southeast Asia where their financial activities played a key role in transforming and connecting rural sectors and other sectors to a colonial capitalistic economy. What is intriguing is their ability to establish international networks in the various overseas centers that proved to be a great advantage for their entrepreneurial endeavors across vast distances. This paper examines the various internal and external factors that facilitated such entrepreneurial internationalization that resulted in their success during the nineteenth century with the hope of providing some lessons for today's internationalization process of SMEs and entrepreneurs alike.

2. Who Are the Chettiars?

The Chettiars are a people of South Indian origin, whose homeland is located within the Indian state of Tamil Nadu. They belong to a trading sub-caste group and are among the most renowned of the twenty odd such groups in South India (Masters, 1957, p. 22).

Table 1. Overall population of Chettiars in India and overseas

Year	Population (people)
1891	7,851
1896	10,000
1969	80,000
1973	86,000
1980	100,000

They refer to their homeland as Chettinad, meaning "land of the Chettiars" and their territorial holdings consist of a cluster of relatively small villages in line with the community's historically relative small size compared to other ethnic groups in India. Their known overall population both in India and overseas are indicated in Table 1 below (the figures in Table 1 reflect the time period when the original research was done; see Pavadarayan, 1986, p. 2).

What is of particular interest is the entrepreneurial nature of the Chettiars as a people from very early on in their history to this day. Early in their history before the onset of colonialism, the Chettiars were known to venture overseas far from their homeland all the way from South Africa to Southeast Asia in pursuit of economic fortune. The following is a list of countries to which male members of the community set for sail (Pavadarayan, 1986, p. 1):

Mauritius
South Africa
Sri Lanka
Burma (now called Myanmar)
Thailand
Vietnam
Malaysia
Singapore
Indonesia

In this chapter, we shall be focusing on a particular economic activity, money-lending, they specialized in during what we now know as the colonial period in Southeast Asia, with emphasis on Singapore. The colonial period is marked by the following events:

- The British annexation of India, leading to the formation of the British Raj.
- The annexation of Burma, later governed by the British as a province of India.
- The founding of Singapore and later the Straits Settlements and full British control of Malaya.

The above events are noteworthy as they triggered changes in Chettiar economic activity in line with a series of events that opened up economic opportunities in the area of money lending in the British overseas holdings that led to their mercantile diaspora.

3. The Role of the Chettiars in the Colonial Economy

With the European colonization of Southeast Asian feudal kingdoms and the opening of Singapore as British port catering to international trade, word soon spread and the Chettiars, like many other trading communities, familiar with Southeast Asian maritime trade, were drawn to the new opportunities this turn of events presented.

The Chettiars had historically been traders in this part of the world, with money-lending only being an auxiliary business. In the following, we shall be focusing on the role the Chettiars played in Southeast Asia, including Singapore, where a demand for financing soared following the Singapore trade boom, cementing the Chettiar's place as informal bankers to world trade during this watershed period of Southeast Asian history.

The Chettiars were encouraged by the colonial authorities in Burma to provide financing to the indigenous peoples, especially peasants in order to increase production and link the rural informal economies to the world economy. Likewise, they were to do the same in Singapore but for those engaged in trade and other urban related economic activities. Where the colonial banks previously failed in making viable and recoverable loans, the Chettiars successfully took on the risk of lending and success-fully made a profit while achieving the aim of the colonial authorities, that was to "peasantize" or monetize the rural sector and trading sectors of the local economies of the colonies linking them to global markets (Pavadarayan, 1986; Rudner 1994; Turnell, 2005).

4. Drivers behind Chettiar Migration

The possible reasons behind Chettiar migration to Singapore and the other British colonies in Southeast Asia have been separated into the following push and pull factors to separate the impetus for departing Chettinad from the opportunities that attracted migrants to the colonies respectively.

4.1 *Push Factors for Internationalization*

Cultural impetus

Historically, the Chettiars have traded in Southeast Asia in addition to their money-lending activities. In fact, it is a source of cultural pride for a Chettiar male to leave family and home, that is, Chettinad to cross oceans in pursuit of economic success. This pride in venturing abroad to seek their fortune is comparable with the notion of "merantau," which can be interpreted as journeying, that is close to the hearts of the Minangkabaus of Sumatra (Naim, 1973, p. 3).

Social structures

Chettiar family structures, characterized by endogamous marriage rules at the community level, though not at the clan level, had both individualism and collectivistic characteristics in that the extended family structures had separate units of production and consumption. That is to say, each nuclear family was responsible for its own consumption in a setting of co-residence with the wider, collectivistic extended family that pooled economic resources (Pavadarayan, 1986). This paved the way for the development of some professional management practices though deeply entrenched or embedded in the Chettiar family systems that perpetrated norms of accountability and performance over nepotism as will be discussed below.

Sons were trained to work for others first before working for their respective fathers. Fathers shared best practices and sent their children for exposure at other firms before they were sent forth to represent the family firms.

Inheritance rules were also clearly spelled out. Assets were willed or distributed equally among the sons on the patriarch's sixtieth birthday but it was not uncommon for liquid assets like cash to be given to sons earlier. This was sometimes meant as provision for continued investments in the overseas centers (Pavadarayan, 1986).

Norms and values: Thrift, Accountability and Performance

The nature of Chettiar life and business reflect some elements of professional management principles that are embedded in their social and economic structures. The norms and value systems of the Chettiar community appears to shape the way in which they conduct their money-lending business which in turn affects the norms and socialization of their children from an early age. Pavadarayan (1986) wrote extensively on how values such as frugality and industry were inculcated from a very early age, and young boys in preparation for eventual participation in the money-lending business had their education centered on practical skills in bookkeeping before being eventually sent to the overseas centers for training and work.

Nuclear family units within the extended family household that are jointly owned ensured for greater self-dependence, responsibility and accountability for each family's economic performance. Values of thrift and hard work emphasized within the family and community also worked in tandem with the drive to perform in the economic realm. Hence, this type of family structures and value system lend themselves to the development of internationalization and elements of professionalization in their moneylending activities abroad.

Nepotism was kept in check as accountability was strongly emphasized and practiced. For example, any loan extended within the family or from the Chettiar temple there was notionally a "social contract" drawn up and repayment was expected. Accountability was both normative and institutionalized within the family structures (Pavadarayan, 1986).

The replication of home abroad vis-a-vis the overseas temple and overseas communes known as "kittingis"

The Chettiar males abroad who were engaged in the moneylending business lived in all-male communes known as "kittingis" that were exclusive to them. Here, the nexus between their communal distinctiveness and business networks was reinforced daily as the lines between work, community, religious and personal life merged.

Chettiars have been known to build their own overseas temples wherever they went, and the kittingis that were the centers of residence and places of conducting business. But these were not totally separated in some of the functions. While the temple was primarily a place of worship and fellowship among the migrant Chettiars, it was also the center of some business transactions. For example, interest rates would be determined and agreed upon at the temple premise and honorable borrowing from temple funds with interest was possible with such loans being repaid because it was believed that it would bring good business outcomes (Pavadarayan, 1986). Such religious practices served to connect and strengthen Chettiar financing activities to their internal social-cultural systems, the temple being one of them. The religious system served to reinforce their communal identity in the various overseas centers (Reid, 2005).

This Chettiar type of replication of home in the overseas centers lent itself to long distance internationalization of business. Having this social embeddedness enabled Chettiar internationalization as the "kittingi" provided the new entrants with cultural acclimatization. The local Chettiar community showed the new entrants the ropes. The new entrants co-located with the existing Chettiar moneylenders in the host countries like Singapore. They were able to learn from the "older" hands. Best practices can also be adopted since they sit next to each other at their desks.

The temple and their religious rites with the meals reduced the loneliness, homesickness and separation anxieties that new entrants to a host country would feel. The community and living in the same neighborhood meant that they were not living alone but as bachelors in a community within each city. There was access to help, advice and friendship just within reach.

Cultural affinity within the Chettiar clan provided the advantage of cultural similarities, principles and practices. With their community being tightly knit abroad, there was the added advantage that their network provided access to information about the respective parties to any business cooperation, information about new locales, etc.

Restriction of trade opportunities

With British control over India and increased pressure from British commercial interests, India's indigenous businesses found themselves hampered by the new order imposed by colonial authority. Whilst this created restrictions at home, British colonial expansion eastwards created new opportunities, especially in Burma, Malaya and Singapore. Reduced opportunities at home coupled with increased opportunities outside of home naturally pushed the Chettiars to look across oceans to lucrative opportunities there (Rudner, 1994).

Familiarity with overseas trading

The Chettiars were among the Indian communities with a history of trading in Southeast Asia. Overseas trading there was a viable, often chosen economic option. Hence, with the increased opportunities that arose from the political stability that followed the imposition of colonial authority, it only served to make it easier for the Chettiars to gravitate their economic activity abroad even further with the reduction of political risk.

4.2 Pull Factors

Political stability in the colonies

The Chettiars as a community have been known to be very risk-adverse, especially due to their relatively small numbers and nature of their economic activities. This fear, especially of political risks, can be attributed to their legends and folklore on incidents with ruling powers very early on in their history that have made them wary of the possible political repercussions towards them as a result of their outsider-minority status (Pavadarayan, 1986, p. 7). Their fears were well-founded as their money-lending businesses were the focus of political unrest in Burma which resulted in the seizure of their assets and them being forced to return to Chettinad or relocating to more politically stable overseas centers such as Singapore.

International monetization of rural peasant economies

In pre-colonial Southeast Asia, feudal peasant economies prevailed with the focus being on the sustenance of peasant farmers and the kingdoms' respective populations, and, of course, tribute that was a form of taxation, to the king of the state. The arrival of the colonial powers changed that as local economic production became reorganized to supply world demand for commodities fueled by the increasing demand of finished goods produced by industrial means.

For example, in the British colonies of Burma and Malaya, the British introduced policies to encourage export-oriented production. In Burma, land cultivation was reorganized and intensified leading to Burma becoming the "rice bowl" of the British Empire. Tin mining was intensified and rubber cultivation introduced into Malaya to meet the growing demand for finished goods of the industrial age such as tinned food and automobile tires.

To reach a sufficient level of production, the "peasantization" of indigenous farmers became necessary whereby their production would be geared through intensification of land cultivation to satiate global demand. To achieve that scale, financing was necessary and the Chettiars were brought in by the colonial authorities to act as financial intermediaries, lending to indigenous peasants and traders where the European banks were unwilling to do so.

Worldwide boom in trade

With the opening of the Suez Canal in 1869 coupled with the Industrial revolution, consumption became increasingly driven by European demand for now cheaper and cheaper finished goods. This in turn drove the demand for commodities produced in Asia such as cotton, rubber and tea necessary as raw materials. As a result, colonial interests and involvement in Asia rose leading to colonization and the subsequent introduction of market driven production. In the British Oriental possessions, Singapore and Hong Kong, which today are financial centers, emerged as hubs of entrepôt trade collecting and concentrating goods from all over the colonies before exporting them to Europe.

With this boom in trade came the need of financing of trade transactions. The indigenous and non-indigenous Southeast Asian traders needed credit, usually short-term though there were also long-term needs, often with little or no collateral on hand. Driven by world demand for commodities, indigenous and non-indigenous traders saw entrepreneurial opportunities by transforming hitherto subsistence-oriented loosely organized farm holdings into intensive commercial export-oriented agriculture as seen in colonial rice cultivation intensification in Burma and rubber plantation expansion in Malaya and entrepôt trade in Singapore.

Such enterprises required intense capital that is longer term in nature. Given their familiarity with conducting the money-lending business in Southeast Asia coupled with better ability to manage credit risks than the formal colonial banks, the Chettiars were well poised to finance emerging export businesses and profit from it.

5. Chettiar Trade Networks and Internationalization

Various factors contributed to the development and establishment of Chettiar networks and internationalization. Long before the onset on modern colonialism in Asia, Indian and other merchants have had a long history of seaborne trade in Southeast Asia dealing in salt, spices, finished goods, etc. Trading networks established across the waters of Southeast Asia and China have been evident long before nineteen century colonialism among various trading communities such as Jews, Arabs, Parsees, Indian Muslims and Chettiars from South India, Chinese traders, etc. Reid identifies three types of diasporic communities suggesting that internal structures and responses differed in the overseas settings of Southeast Asia (Reid, 2005, pp. 353–358).

5.1 *Familiarity as a Catalyst for Flourishing Networks*

The Chettiars, being historically familiar with conducting trade in Southeast Asia may not have possessed a trade network as we know it today. It can be argued that their first strong trade network emerged during the expansion of their overseas money-lending activities during the colonial period.

Their flexibility and experience led to their historical success as traders in Southeast Asia where they were known to have been able to acquire competence of the local languages, and being adaptive to the cultural sensitivities of the local communities they operated in. Prior to the arrival of Islam in Southeast Asia, the vast majority of Southeast Asian kingdoms along the Straits of Malacca, especially in Malaya and Indonesia were influenced by Hinduism and Buddism in nature. The imprint of these religions is still strongly present in both cultural practices and language that is evident today. To illustrate this point, many Malay words still in use to this day are of Tamil origin. Interestingly, the word "mudal" in Tamil which means capital, used in the Chettiars bookkeeping has an equivalent meaning in modern Malay financial terms, namely "modal."

Despite being a migrant community whose individuals operate temporarily in the overseas trade centers of Southeast Asia, individual Chettiars during their time overseas engaged themselves in local trade and commerce forming part of the local business culture. Although individuals eventually returned home, though not all at the same time, to Chettinad after completing their term of overseas economic activity, as a community they remained continuous and noticeable.

5.2 *Emergence of Informal Banking Network*

In engaging in the money-lending business, it was in the Chettiar community's common interest to mutually assist wherever possible given their precarious stranger and outsider minority status (Elias, 1965). In addition to possible political threats, money-lending is inherently a risky business commercially due to lack of available collateral of substantial value from clients and relatively high default risk.

By pooling together both capital and business acumen, they transcended the limitations as a minority outsider community turning their small yet close-knit ties of business and kinship into a strength. Lending and borrowing from one another was not an uncommon practice (Pavadarayan, 1986; Rudner, 1994).

This was taken one step further with the establishment of the Chettiar Chamber of Commerce in Singapore to protect their business interest as financial intermediaries in the island trade hub. It is interesting to note that the temple Trustee and temple committee members held key positions in the Chettiar Chamber of Commerce, creating a nexus between social, cultural and religious institutions with organized Chettiar commercial interest groups (Pavadarayan, 1986).

The above institutions facilitated the sharing of information and providing insights to individual Chettiar money-lenders on the state of affairs in the overseas centers, informing them of larger socio-political trends which may yield them threats or opportunities.

No matter how far from Chettinad they travelled or how long their overseas tour of enterprise was, the overwhelming majority of Chettiars desired to return home and when they did, succeeding generations of young men from the villages of Chettinad were already making the journey to take their place in the overseas centers. Hence, the focal point of Chettiar activity would always be Chettinad. This not only facilitates the sharing of information and trade network connections between generations operating in the same overseas centers but also across overseas centers.

For example, an adult Chettiar male departing from Chettinad to one overseas center, in principle could have the option, if he wanted to, avail himself to the business networks of his destination, for example, Singapore or that of another overseas center in Southeast Asia.

This informal Chettiar banking network between money-lenders of the various overseas centers and their homeland of Chettinad enabled both upside participation and downside mitigation. For example, the sharing of client credit information and economic risks specific to particular overseas centers implied that Chettiar moneylenders had possible avenues to collaborate across borders to provide joint-financing to clients, if necessary. In other words, if a Chettiar could not provide a loan to a client who intends to venture into an area of business outside that Chettiar's overseas center base, the network could facilitate or enable for the recommendation of the client to another Chettiar money-lender present at the client's investment destination. This practice was probably evident in cross-border transactions between British Malaya and Singapore.

In terms of downside mitigation, having access to their informal banking network made it somewhat easier for the Chettiars to get back on their feet when dealt with hard blows in times of crisis. Following the nationalization of their landholdings in Burma, which the Chettiars achieved through unplanned foreclosures on loan defaults, and later their expulsion from Burma, the Chettiars who had hitherto operated have been forced to return to Chettinad, financially broken. But the international network provided for opportunities to rebuild at the other overseas centers opened to them by the Chettiars who were already there as was the case in Singapore. The decline of Chettiar money-lending activity in Burma led to its increase in Singapore.

The movement of Chettiars from Chettinad to various overseas centers and between the overseas centers coupled with joint transactions within and across overseas centers where the Chettiar money-lenders cooperated with one another to fulfill the needs of clients while overcoming the constraints of working individually and domestically led to the development of an informal trade network focused on informal banking.

It was through this trade network that the Chettiars, despite being strongly-tied to their homeland, experienced internationalization as a business community becoming a force capable of shaping Asian finance that ultimately contributed to Singapore's development beyond entrepôt trade into an international financial center.

6. Discussion: Success Factors behind the Growth of Overseas Chettiar Moneylending

The following are suggestions on possible and very probable reasons for the success of the Chettiars in money-lending throughout Southeast Asia. It is more suggestive rather than exhaustive. We can clearly see the various external and internal dynamics at play that explain the success of the Chettiar economic ventures that spanned wide networks across Southeast Asia.

It was the larger external trends that largely set the stage for Chettiar economic activity expansion and would later dictate the story of its decline. However, had it not been for the robustness of the community's institutions shaping to the Chettiars *modus operandi* as money-lenders, the Chettiars would not have been able to fully avail themselves of the opportunities colonial expansion in Southeast Asia opened to all who were shrewd and able enough to capitalize on.

6.1 *External Factors*

External factors refer to the larger trends in the environment they operated in which would have been beyond the control of the Chettiars.

A key external factor that was an impetus for Chettiar expansion overseas was British patronage. The British, upon imposing their authority in the Southeast Asian colonies, e.g., Burma and Malaya, set forth to formalize the local economies. Realizing that the Chettiars could succeed where the colonial banks had failed in providing credit to local peasants and traders, the British actively encouraged and incentivized Chettiar moneylenders to set up shop in the colonies.

With British colonial authority came colonial law and order which was a source of protection and mitigation of risk. As mentioned earlier, the Chettiars were highly risk-adverse, especially toward the political risk their status as a minority outsider community entailed. The more formal colonial laws introduced by the British made the money-lending business less risky as the enforcement of loan repayments and foreclosures on pledged assets became more effective with government backing.

Global economic mega-trends resulting from the Industrial Revolution and colonial expansion in Asia and Africa led to a race which intensified economic production of commodities to meet the demand for increasingly cheaper finished goods in the West. Intensive capital injections were necessary to facilitate the intensification of land cultivation, opening of commercial plantations and expansion of mines.

There was no shortage of capital but a need for effective distribution via loans that were both profitable and recoverable given little or no collateral available from borrowers that implied high default risk. Given the Chettiar moneylenders' higher familiarity with local borrowers, they were more able to assess credit-worthiness. Being very risk adverse themselves, they were able to manage the risks associated with lending locally better than the European colonial banks, carving a niche for themselves as financial intermediaries between the formal sector and informal sectors of the colonial Southeast Asian economies.

Historically, the Chettiars have not shown keenness to venture very far for extended periods from Chettinad, desiring to be close enough to home to return with relative ease. Technological progress improved communications and logistics to the point that it led to accelerated production, reducing cost and increased demand for finished goods. As a result, the flow of goods and peoples eased not only between neighboring states but increased across continents.

With easier travel from Chettinad to the overseas centers, and direct communications through faster ship-borne mail correspondence coupled with telegraph services, the geographical distance constraints in the mind of Chettiars gradually evaporated leading them to intensify their economic activity in the overseas centers by both numbers and duration. Even so, they somehow consciously or unconsciously restrained themselves from venturing too far because settling overseas was rarely seen as an option, preferring to return home to Chettinad once they have accumulated sufficient personal wealth.

6.2 *Internal Factors*

Internal factors refer to community-specific elements that contributed to Chettiar success such as in-group values and institutions that enabled them to capitalize effectively on opportunities yielded by larger socio-macroeconomic trends.

The Chettiars of South India already had a history of trading, especially in Southeast Asia prior to British arrival. As mentioned earlier, South Indian trading communities were not only flexible and highly adaptable in their ability to do business in these foreign lands, but also left their mark in Southeast Asia.

By virtue of this historical link, the Chettiars were poised to operate in relative harmony with the local economies of Southeast Asia, being similar and familiar enough to the point that their outsider minority status would not be a serious impediment to commerce.

Among the communities of South India who have historically traded in Southeast Asia, the Chettiars were quite distinct culturally. Compared to their neighboring communities in Tamil Nadu, the Chettiars stand out in terms of sense of industry and nature of economic activity, especially moneylending. Pavadarayan (1986) has demonstrated that this cultural distinctiveness was maintained even in the overseas centers where

Chettiars actively differentiate themselves culturally even in the context of religious festivals from other communities originating from Tamil Nadu who practice the same religion.

With this cultural distinction and distancing from other South Indian communities and the local communities in the overseas centers they operated in, the Chettiars turned the small numbers from a disadvantage to a source of strength through social cohesiveness. This social cohesion was not only limited to groups of Chettiars in individual overseas centers but across borders linking them to their homeland of Chettinad and other overseas centers as well. This sense of community, mutual cooperation and trust became the foundation for their business network's success as discussed earlier.

The nexus between communal distinctiveness, e.g. social, religious and cultural, and business networks arising from social cohesion amongst the Chettiars across borders was key in creating synergy necessary to propel Chettiar money-lending activity far beyond Chettinad in a sustainable fashion for over a long period of time. Through time, the link was institutionalized as illustrated by the following examples of Chettiar life tied to their money-lending business contributing to their continued success. Their family ties characterized by endogamous marriages, that is, marriages within the Chettiar community, shared ownership of the ancestral house, rules of inheritance and the vital relationship between financial activities and the overseas Chettiar temples resulted in strong links within the overseas community (Reid, 2005) and also their homeland in Chettinad. In other words, though small in number their ethnic identity and distinctiveness abroad was preserved *vis-a-vis* the temples, the "kittingis," endogamous rules of marriage that prohibited intermarrying with the women overseas. This practice of remaining closely knit, and having strong affinity with social and religious institutions was also the case for other small diasporic mercantile communities, for example, the Jews, and Parsis of India. But the Chinese, primarily from Fujian province and other communities that were also active in Southeast Asia integrated with the overseas centers and readily intermarried with the women of these centers (Reid, 2005).

7. Lessons for SMES and Entrepreneurs

7.1 *Obstacles that SMEs and family businesses face and the Chettiar solution*

One of the key lessons that one can draw from the above study refers to the obstacles SMEs and family businesses may encounter that are presented in Table 2 below. The first column reflects the obstacles faced by SMEs while the second column indicates the obstacles of family businesses. Observations of how the Chettiars overcame these obstacles are also included. Needless to say, the observations made about the SMEs and family businesses are generalized depictions as there are many firms and organizations that may not encounter the obstacles listed or may have ways to overcome the obstacles.

Table 2. Possible lessons from the Chettiars

Obstacles facing SMEs	Family businesses	Chettiar Enabling Factors	Possible Lessons
Identifying & Sending expatriate staff	Identifying & sending Family or trusted employees	Sons	Expatriate selection, training and repatriation
Dealing with cross-cultural differences		Social structures extended overseas	Support systems needed
Lack of Organizational support	Lack of Organizational & family support	Chettiar community abroad	
Issues with control and consistency in business practice	Family businesses solve the obstacle of control & consistency by appointing a trusted family member or employee	Sons have been trained; Chettiars share best practices; accountability via extended family practices	Pre-deployment training Introduction of governances structures and control systems enhanced by accountability to others present in host country

Expatriate Selection, Training and deployment

Firms expanding their operations overseas tend to work through expatriate managers or family members in the case of family businesses unless the overseas operations are merely export, agency or distribution arrangements or transactions aided by electronic means. When internationalization involves actual physical presence in the host country, there is a need to engage personnel to run the business and this entails selection of home or host country nationals to manage the operations. The issues related to this are covered in the domain of international human resource management depicted in Table 2 (see first row).

It is common knowledge that the challenges most firms face in expatriation centre around the selection, pre-expatriation training, family adjustment, cross-cultural acclimatization, and repatriation issues. The Chettiars have been able to overcome these issues because it is an expectation that the men would go overseas. Training was part and parcel of the children's education. Hence there is no need to have specialized training to prepare them for overseas deployment. The presence of the social structures overseas in the host countries facilitates cross-cultural acclimatization and provides the equivalent of the organization support systems that expatriate managers need as mentioned below.

Social embeddedness Abroad: Extending Social Support Systems

SMEs or family businesses that internationalized often had to overcome obstacles mentioned in Table 2 (see second and third rows). Their expatriate staff or managers had to deal with new cultures that differed from their home countries. They often experienced difficulties adjusting to the new environments because they did not have the organizational and family support. Some SMEs and family businesses overcame the lack of family support by sending the expatriate managers with their families.

The Chettiars had advantages that enabled informal banking or moneylending across borders. There were strong community ties with cultural norms that support the necessary activities in the host countries. Outside the Chettiar community, non-Chettiar young men venturing overseas would not be able to establish independent businesses as individual moneylenders. The young Chettiar men readily did so with success. The replication of the Chettiar community overseas in each of the locations they ventured to facilitated this.

Shown as possible lessons in Table 2 (see column four), entrepreneurs embarking upon international entrepreneurship require cross-border ties. While the Chettiars had community ties, the modern day entrepreneurs would have to develop their own ties (Black and Gregersen, 1991; Osman-Gani, Tan and Toh, 1998).

Networks

While other internationalizing SMEs needed to resort to networks and networking activities to gain access to resources and other business people, the Chettiars relied on their own networks among their ethnic clan. This selection of business partners and co-location with others from the same ethnicity can be found among other Asians, although the Chettiars pre-date the rest. The establishment and reliance on business networks has played a crucial role for the emergence and success of many East Asian and Southeast business communities like the Japanese, Koreans, Taiwanese, etc. (Dumont and Lemaître, 2005; Kuznetsov, 2006; Park and Chang, 2005; Yeoh and Khoo, 1998).

Control and consistency

Non-Chettiar SMEs and family businesses venturing abroad had difficulties with control over operations and consistency of business practices as shown in Table 2 (see the fourth row). One way for SMEs to overcome this would be to deploy an expatriate manager and this means they would have to select the expatriates (Tan, Osman-Gani and Toh, 1999; Selmar, 2001) and train them for the overseas assignments (Osman-Gani, Tan and Toh, 1998). Family businesses could employ a family member or a non-family member.

In the Chettiar case, social institutions promoted and supported their economic ventures abroad. For example, the values and norms, such as accountability and performance, and how debts were to be dealt with were governing principles that undergird the international extension of their moneylending activities. Theirs was a unique mixture of family and business. While many other family businesses might have this mixture, the Chettiars had defined roles and principles that helped them obviate the conflicts and negotiations that were needed in other family firms.

SMEs with overseas operations can engage regional managers and internal auditors to check on the credibility of reports and on operations to ensure for compliance with the corporate policies of host countries. The Chettiar community at home and abroad operated on the same principles. These practices ensured consistency of practice and the accountability and the close proximity to other moneylenders made for peer review and assessment, reducing the need for formal external review or audit.

8. Conclusion

While the Chettiars are not the only ethnic group with successful internationalization, there are lessons that can be generalized from this study. It is clear that existing firms as opposed to born global firms, seeking to internationalize, need to make internationalization part of their DNA. Like the Chettiars through their culture, these firms need to make it part of their culture to have international operations. This culture would facilitate the deployment of staff overseas. The Chettiar story also demonstrates the importance of social embeddedness. This social embeddedness may not be possible for other firms but the development of organization support systems that can serve the same role for the expatriate managers abroad would be helpful. The Chettiar case demonstrates the value of cultural assimilation training for expatriate managers since other firms may not have communities into which their managers can be introduced. The Chettiar case supports the view that internationalizing firms should seek out communities of their own nationals in host countries. These communities could provide the advice, business practices and support that the expatriate managers would need.

Principles governed the accountability of the men sent out by their families. The norms of the Chettiars replace the need for corporate accountability policies and external audits. These norms together with the close proximity to peers who are able to observe and whom family members could resort to for feedback on what their men are doing.

Internationalizing SMEs, unless they are able to build strong corporate cultures that establish as clear accountability norms as the Chettiars, would need to rely on the external checks and reporting lines. It is not impossible to develop such organizational cultures but it requires effort and time. When firms are still small, it would be possible to establish such cultures where the incumbents realize that their actions contribute to the general welfare of the corporate body.

As the Chettiars internationalized as small operations, small firms may be able to emulate the Chettiars and be successful. The quest would be to identify institutional structures within their organizations that can play the same roles: communities of nationals in host countries to play the role of cultural assimilation, expatriation training for the Chettiar education, organization cultures for the Chettiar norms, and the external checks and systems that take the place of the overseas Chettiar community as means of peer review.

Clearly, from the case of the Chettiars we can draw relevant insights and lessons for the process of internationalization and the establishment of entrepreneurial networks for both SMEs and entrepreneurs today.

Chettiars in Southeast Asia are presently no longer engaged in moneylending as their main source of livelihood. Today they are employed in all kinds of professions and jobs, including small businesses.

References

Black, JS and HB Gregersen (1991). Antecedents to cross-cultural adjustment for expatriates in Pacific Rim assignments. *Human Relations*, 44(5), 497–515.

Dumont, J and G Lemaître (2005). Counting immigrants and expatriates in OECD countries: A new perspective. United Nations Expert Group Meeting on International Migration and Development, July 6–8. Available at http://www.un.org/esa/population/meetings/ittmigdev2005/P09_Dumont%26Lemaitre.pdf

Elias, N (1965). *The Established and the Outsiders*. London, UK: Frank Cass.

Evers, HD and J Pavadarayan (1993). Religious fervor and economic success. In *Indians in Southeast Asia*, KS Sandhu and A Mani (eds), pp. 847–865. Singapore: Institute of Southeast Asian Studies.

Evers, HD (1978). Chettiar moneylenders in Southeast Asia. *Asie de Sud, Traditions et Changements, Colloques' Scientifique*, 582, 635–645.

Kuznetsov, Y (ed.) (2006). *Diaspora Networks and the International Migration of Skills: How Countries Can Draw on Their Talent Abroad*. Washington, DC: World Bank.

Masters, A (1957). The Chettiars in Burma: An economic survey of a migrant community. *Population Review*, 1(1), 22–31.

Naim, M (1973). Voluntary migration in Indonesia. Working Paper No. 26, Department of Sociology, University of Singapore, Singapore.

Osman-Gani, AA, WL Tan, and TS Toh, (1998). Training managers for overseas business operations in the Asia Pacific region: A study of Singapore-based companies. *International Journal of Training and Development*, 2(2), 119.

Park, J and PY Chang, (2005). Contention in the construction of a global Korean Community: The case of the Overseas Korean Act. *The Journal of Korean Studies,* 10 (1) 1–27.

Pavadarayan, J (1982). Peasantization of a tribal society? A case study: Chimbu of *Papua New Guinea*. Diplomarbeit, Fakultaet fuer Soziologie, Universitat Bielefeld, Bielefeld.

Pavadarayan, J (1986). The Chettiars of Singapore: A study of an Indian minority community in Southeast Asia. PhD Dissertation, Universitaet Bielefeld, Bielefeld.

Reid, A (2005). Diaspora networks in the Asian maritime context. In *Diaspora Entrepreneurial Networks*, IB MacCabe, G Harlaftis and IP Minoglou (eds.), pp. 353–358. New York, NY: Berg.

Rudner, DW (1994). *Caste and Capitalism in Colonial India: The Nattukottai Chettiars*. Berkeley, CA: University of California Press.

Seibel, H (2005). From moneylenders to microfinance: Southeast Asia's credit revolution in institutional, eeconomic and cultural perspective. Workshop, Asia Research Institute, Department of Economics, and Department of Sociology, National University of Singapore.

Selmer, J (2001). Expatriate selection: Back to basics? *International Journal of Human Resource Management*, 12(8), 1219–1233.

Tan, WL and AA Osman-Gani (1999). Organisational and social supports for effective expatriate performance in Asia: A comparative study of Singapore based companies. Paper presented at the Eighth Annual World Business Congress, Monterey, California, USA.

Tan, WL, AA Osman-Gani, and TS Toh (1999). Selection of expatriates for regional business operations in Asia: A study of line managers in Singapore. Paper presented at the Academy of Management Conference, Chicago.

Turnell, S (2005, July). The Chettiars in Burma. Macquarie Economics Research Papers, No. 12.

Chapter 18

The Internationalization of Mainland Chinese Businesses

Hinrich Voss

1. Introduction

Thinkpad, the iconic American computer brand, belongs to the brand family of Lenovo, China since 2005. The British automobile marquee MG Rover changed into the Chinese hands of Shanghai Automotive Industry Corporation (SAIC) and Nanjing Automobile Group in 2005, while Sweden's Volvo followed in 2009 when Geely acquired it. Geely had also a production agreement with Mag, the producer of the classic black taxis of London. Weetabix, the British cereal producer, was partly acquired by China's Bright Foods in 2012.

These are but a few examples of an exciting development that will heavily influence and change the international business landscape. Mainland Chinese firms are internationalizing their business activities through direct investment in foreign markets. They acquire established firms, brand names, technologies and distribution channels in industrialized and developing countries to strengthen their international competitiveness and catch-up with the incumbents. Chinese firms also invest overseas to secure resources the Chinese economy is short off such as oil, minerals, timber and food. The rapid global increase in Chinese outward foreign direct investment (FDI) flows from US$2.9bn in 2003 to US$69.9bn in 2011 (MOFCOM, 2012), stimulates greater competition in markets previously thought to be the domain of Western firms and creates new ones in underdeveloped markets across the developing world. But, while FDI by businesses from industrialized countries and the "Asian Tiger Economies" are a common phenomenon and one that is sought after because of the positive economic growth impulses they bring to the host economy, the jury is still out on FDI from China.

FDI is generally welcomed by the host country's government. Long-term investments in real and productive assets ease the transfer of technologies and know-how, support competition and the increase of productivity of domestic businesses (UNCTAD, 2001). The United Nations Conference on Trade and Development (UNCTAD) therefore strongly supports the opening of economies to investment by foreign firms. Their support and related policies are based on observations on the impact of foreign investments by businesses from the US or Europe (Clegg and Scott-Green, 1999). Little is known yet about how Chinese investment will contribute to the host economy. Indeed, anecdotal evidence from Africa and Australia (Brookes and Shin, 2006; Alden and Davies, 2006; Fan *et al.*, 2012), and the fact that Chinese firms are not yet operating at the technological frontier (Economist, 2013), have let to assertions that Chinese investments can negatively effect the host economy. Chinese investments are argued to strip countries of the technologies that have made them competitive, relocate labor intensive activities to China, instil unfair competition through their "deep financial pockets," mistreat labor rights and discriminate against local workforces (Corkin and Burke, 2006; van der Lugt and Hamblin, 2011). Empirical studies in Southeast Asia paint a more positive picture of Chinese investments. The behavior and impact of Chinese firms is very similar to that of industrialized country investments (Kubny and Voss, 2010).

Before we turn to the outward internationalization of Chinese firms through FDI, it is important to consider where the Chinese firms are coming from and how they have created the capacity to internationalize. Internationalization describes, basically, that a firm is conducting business across borders. Firms can therefore internationalize through a number of modes of which exporting and direct investment are most commonly equated with internationalization. Other modes include a range of non-equity based relationships like contract manufacturing and agricultural business, licensing and franchizing and importing (UNCTAD, 2011). Some of the modes like exporting and FDI require that the firm gets actively involved in establishing a cross-border business operation while in, for example, contract manufacturing the manufacturing firm is often approached by a foreign firm that seeks a cheap and efficient production base. Firms pursue a number of these modes in parallel within the same country and across different countries, depending on how they strategically fit the development of the firm.

This range of modes is utilized by Chinese firms today as well. By the end of the 1970s, China was a closed economy and its businesses cut off from international production networks. This was reflected in the very low levels of trade and the virtually non-existing inward and outward FDI. Although the early reform and opening measures included references to support and increase the outward investments by Chinese firms (Voss *et al.*, 2009), it is reasonable to assume that Chinese firms were not in a position of doing so. They lacked the managerial skills, organizational structures and technological capabilities in pursuing overseas investments. Or, in the words of Fosfuri and Motta (1999), they were multinational enterprises (MNEs) without competitive advantage; a label that is still attached to Chinese overseas investors today. An upgrading and up skilling was required first.

2. Inward Internationalization of Chinese Firms

Following classical international business theory, a firm invests overseas from a position of strength. This strength arises from a dominant market position at home through which it can extract surplus rent, from the possession of a technological or organizational edge over its competitors and better utilization of given resources (Hymer, 1960). Such strength, or competitiveness, is required to help the firm offsetting the challenges and extra costs it will face when operating in a new and unfamiliar market that exhibits new business customs and regulations and new business networks (Johanson and Vahlne, 2009). Foreign investors that overcome these challenges and settle in a foreign market can bring substantial benefits to the host economy. They bring with them advanced technologies, organizational and managerial practices. These are shared with domestic firms intentionally, and unintentionally, through vertical linkages the foreign investor is establishing as it engages with local suppliers and distributors. Horizontally, domestic businesses with similar activities to the foreign investor have to react to increased and new forms of competitions.

These inward internationalizing stimuli add up to increasing levels of productivity across domestic businesses (Dunning and Lundan, 2008). In the long run, inward internationalization can support the outward internationalization of a firm later on as it has learned from its foreign partners and built an international business network (Dunning and Narula, 1996; Mathews, 2006).

Welch and Luostarinen (1993) coined the term "inward internationalization" which describes the internationalization of a firm's operations through, inter alia, imports, contract manufacturing for foreign clients, and the establishment of joint ventures with foreign partners in the home country. Inward internationalization is thus characterized by carrying out business activities across borders while remaining physically within the home country's boundaries and focusing the main business activities here. A company like Galanz, the Chinese microwave producer, is a good example of an inward internationalizing company. In an assessment of the internationalization of emerging market firms, Zeng and Williamson (2003) stated that Galanz was responsible for the production of 15 million microwave ovens for more than 200 brands worldwide. Thus, its products were not sold under Galanz' brand name and through its own distribution channels but contract-manufactured for foreign businesses who sold the microwaves under their brand name. Similarly, the Taiwanese companies Acer, Asus, or HTC started as contract manufacturers before they moved up the value chain and establishing themselves as serious end-consumer targeting businesses in their own right. While it is conceivable that a firm like Galanz might specialize in the manufacturing process and become the Foxconn of the white goods sector, the higher value added and high margin activities reside at the ends of the value chain, that is research and development and marketing (Bartlett and Goshal, 2000).

The Chinese government has supported the inward internationalization of domestic firms from early on in the reform and opening process that started in 1978. The establishment of Special Economic Zones enabled Chinese firms to experience and observe foreign firms' management and technology first hand, and to slowly build up the expertise to supply them. This has been supplemented with China's Foreign Investment Catalogue which specifies in which industry sectors foreign investment is welcome, the extent to which joint ventures have to be formed with local partners and technology has to be shared. The request for local content in the production of foreign invested companies was another cornerstone in the development and upgrading of the domestic industries. As a consequence of these policies, the typical foreign market entry mode in China was the one of a joint venture with a domestic firm. Over the years, the focus of the catalogue shifted allowing greater degrees of foreign ownership and opened more sectors to foreign firms (OECD, 2002). A good illustration of the supportive government policies is the automobile sector and Shanghai Automotive Industry Corporation (SAIC). SAIC has formed majority-owned joint ventures with Volkswagen in 1984 and General Motors in 1998. When Volkswagen entered the Chinese market, it was required to source an increasing share of inputs locally despite a lack of qualified suppliers at the time. To overcome the dilemma, VW engaged in the sharing of technology with SAIC and suppliers and the training of staff (Posth, 2008). In the food industry, multinational enterprises like Nestle and Mars work with Chinese suppliers on the knowledge and implementation of international production and quality standards. Although collaboration sounds fairly simple, in reality they involve complex and lengthy processes. The knowhow and expertise that needs to be shared in order to make the local operations more productive and efficient is only partially codifiable and easily exchangeable. A significant part of it is "sticky" and location-bound (Szulanski, 1996). These difficulties are offset by the potential advantages cooperation with foreign firms can bring. Arguably, the creation of the Chinese high-speed train infrastructure or the wind energy sector, among others, have benefited from international technology transfer (Liu *et al.*, 2011; Lewis, 2007).

3. Outward Internationalization of Chinese Firms

Against the backdrop of successful inward internationalization, Chinese firms have ventured abroad. They can choose between different modes of how to conduct business overseas. Exporting and direct investment are the most commonly discussed options due to the visible economic impacts on home and host economy.

3.1 *Exporting*

The Chinese economy has witnessed integration into the world economy at phenomenal speed after the national government embarked on reforms and gradual economic opening in 1978. At that time, China's exports in goods and services were valued at US$9.8bn or 0.6 percent of world exports (World Bank, 2012). In terms of share of global exports, this is comparable to the exporting might of Hungary in 2010. China, of course, has moved on from there. Over the period 1980 to 2010, China recorded an astounding compound annual growth rate of its exports of 16 percent. This progress briefly slowed down in the aftermath of the Asian Crisis of 1997 and dropped on three occasions (World Bank, 2012). The last year indicates the global impact of the Anglo–American financial crisis. China's export growth has had four main implications. First, in 2004 China overtook Japan to become the third largest exporting nation and in 2010 it surpassed Germany to move into second place behind the US. Looking at the stark drop of America's share in global exports since 2000 and China's continuous rise, it is conceivable that China will become the largest exporter shortly. Second, as a consequence of the first point, China has become a major trade partner for a number of countries and regions. For the EU, the US and China are the largest source country for goods and services. For Myanmar, Vietnam and Indonesia, China is the most important country to source products from. They imported about 40, 22, and 15 percent, respectively, of their total imports from China in 2011 (CIA Factbook, 2012). The level of dependency sits uncomfortable with some countries, foremost the US. But it has also contributed to the internationalization of Chinese firms. Despite the growth in China's exports, a large degree of it is carried either by or on behalf of foreign businesses. Third, China has constantly maintained a trade surplus. A trade surplus is achieved when the exports of a country are of higher value than its imports. 1993 is so far the last year in which China recorded an annual trade deficit. Since then, the surplus has averaged around US$100bn a year. The surplus contributes to the foreign exchange reserves which can be used to purchase government bonds and other debt obligations of other countries. The Chinese government is also using the reserves to fund its sovereign wealth funds (SWFs) China Investment Corporation, SAFE

Investment Company, and China–Africa Development Fund. The SWFs use the monies for portfolio investment in foreign infrastructure projects like Thames Water or to support financially the internationalization of Chinese firms in Africa. Fourth, Chinese firms learn. We have seen above that Chinese firms have benefitted from inward FDI and from becoming contract manufacturers for foreign firms. Through these activities, they learn about advanced production and management techniques, and how to comply with higher quality and safety standards. These learning processes help Chinese firms to develop internationally oriented businesses on their own. At the same time, these operations give Chinese firms an insight into customer preferences and demands. Similar learning processes are supported by exporting activities whereby the exporter has to adhere to the quality and environmental standards of the host country (Christmann and Taylor, 2001).

3.2 Drivers of Chinese outward FDI

Chinese firms are investing overseas for a number of reasons. Some of which don't sit easily with classic international business theories that emphasize the monopolistic advantage a firm needs to possess when investing overseas (Hymer, 1960). As described above, Chinese firms have had opportunities to learn from foreign investors and business partners for a number of years about the customer and regulatory demands in overseas markets, observe how foreign operations can be established and generally upgraded their operations. However, the greater levels of productivity and efficiency only partially prepared Chinese firms for the increasing levels of competition that came along with China's accession to the World Trade Organization (WTO) in 2001. The removal of investment barriers and the lowering of import tariff with the WTO accession were accepted by the Chinese government in order to keep the pressure on Chinese firms to reform and modernise. So, one reason for Chinese firms to internationalize is a negative change in the home environment which pushes them overseas. In other words, they seek to escape from an increasingly competitive market in which they are not very competitive and receive little governmental support (Witt and Lewin, 2007). At the time of the WTO accession, the Chinese government announced the "Go Global" policy in support of a strategic internationalization of Chinese firms rather than as escape mode.

The "Go Global" policy was set to encourage and support Chinese firms to internationalize through the reduction of domestic barriers to overseas investments and the establishment of specific institutions (Voss *et al.*, 2009; Buckley *et al.*, 2011). Implicitly, the policy was therefore one instrument in the government's toolkit to modernize Chinese firms. Up until the Go Global policy, overseas investments were treated very restrictively and FDI approached from a learning perspective by the government administration and related businesses. At this time, only state-owned enterprises were allowed to apply for overseas investments which required the approval from the Ministry of Commerce, the State Administration of Foreign Exchange, and other administrative bodies. This process was lengthy which meant that foreign acquisition targets could be snatched up by faster moving competitors. All this changed, successively, with the new policy which has since been restated and re-emphasized in the five year plans. Administrative decisions about individual investment projects have been decentralized from the national government organizations to the province- and city-level and the investment value threshold below which firms can decide over investments have constantly increased. Private firms are now allowed to invest overseas and are encouraged to do so. The institutional environment that has been developed to support the internationalization of Chinese firms includes the creation of an outbound investment catalogue that indicates sectors of interest for particular host countries (hereby mirroring in spirit the Foreign Investment Catalogue); the establishment of fora to communicate and exchange overseas experience and learn from successful investors; the provision of funds for the acquisition of strategic assets, among others (Voss, 2011). Firms that internationalize against this backdrop follow a different, strategic purpose in comparison to the Chinese outward investors pushed out of China.

Chinese firms invest overseas in order to close the gap in international competitiveness, develop new or secure established markets, and secure raw materials which are in short supply within China (Buckley *et al.*, 2007; Buckley *et al.*, 2008; Kolstad and Wiig, 2012). China's Wanda

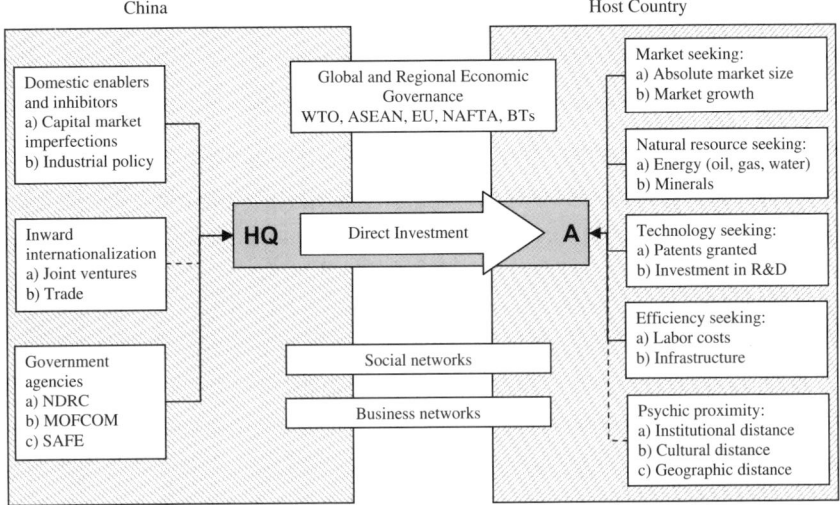

Figure 1.   Chinese outward foreign direct investment

Notes: Solid lines indicate direct effects while broken lines indicate indirect effects.

HQ: Headquarters, A: Foreign affiliate, BTs: Bilateral treaties.

Source: Buckley *et al.* (2011).

Group acquired the US based cinema chain AMC in 2012 and Wanxiang has purchased a number of smaller car part businesses over the years in order to expand their position in the American market. Market developing investments are not constrained to acquisitions but are also reflected in Greenfield activities. Huawai and ZTE, the Chinese telecommunication equipment manufacturers, have established new operations across the EU and Great Wall Motors has established an assembly line in Bulgaria for the European market. Other firms pursue so-called strategic asset seeking activities. Strategic asset seeking activities are those investments that target the acquisition of brand names, distribution channels, and technologies. TCL's acquisition of Thompson's TV business and Haier's attempt to take over Maytag are examples of this. The range of motives for international expansion described here for Chinese firms are common to businesses from all countries. What makes Chinese investments different is the perceived focus on strategic assets and natural resources and that both these activities receive government support.

Buckley *et al.* (2007) and Wang *et al.* (2012) indicated that Chinese investments could be driven by government support. They found that Chinese firms tended to invest in countries that are perceived to be fairly risky by Western analyses. At the same time though, a firm with significant financial and political support could endeavour investing in such a country as the potential rewards are high. Similarly, strategic asset seeking investments can take a long time to pay off. Sources of appropriate technologies in the host country have to be identified, accessed, absorbed and transferred to the parent company in China. The difficulties of international technology transfer have been mentioned above. To this, it has to be added here that Chinese firms come from a challenger position. They seek technologies to become more competitive in order to challenge the position of the incumbent businesses. Firms, therefore, need the financial strength for a lengthy process that is likely to make significant losses in the beginning.

Another level of support for the internationalization of Chinese firms derives from international business and social networks. The inward internationalization has created links between Chinese firms and their foreign partners. Over time, these have contributed to a deep understanding of each other's businesses and high level of trust. Building on this, we observe that the European countries most successful in attracting Chinese investors are also the Europe's largest traders with China (Clegg and Voss, 2012). The existing linkage supports the identification and integration of European acquisition targets (Klossek *et al.*, 2012; Voss *et al.*, 2010).

3.3 *Chinese business activities in ASEAN*

The Association of Southeast Asian Nations (ASEAN) is part of the home region of Chinese firms and its member states Myanmar, Laos and Vietnam border China. If Chinese firms were to follow a regional pattern of internationalization as identified for MNEs from Europe and the US by Rugman and colleagues (Rugman, 2005; Rugman and Li, 2008), the ASEAN member states should be attractive host countries for Chinese firms. Indeed, the Chinese FDI stock in these countries has grown significantly from 2003 to 2011. In 2003, it was valued across all members' states at US$0.59bn. This has increased to US$21.5bn in 2011 which, in terms of percentage of China's OFDI stock is an increase from 7 to 14 percent (MOFCOM, 2012). Up until August 2011, Chinese investment in ASEAN totalled U$22.3bn which accounts for about a third of China's outward FDI flows recorded in 2011 (Roman, 2012). The rise of Chinese investments is particularly pronounced in a small number of ASEAN countries. In Cambodia, Laos, and Myanmar, more than 20 percent of the inward FDI stock in 2011 was attributed to mainland Chinese investors (UNCTAD, 2012; MOFCOM, 2012; see also Figure 2); increasing from 3.0, 1.5 and 0.2 percent respectively eight years earlier. This marks not only a huge relative increase of Chinese investment. It also suggests a growing dependency of these countries on Chinese business activities for the creation of employment, and their transfer of technologies and

Figure 2.   Chinese OFDI stock in ASEAN

Notes: White: less than 1 percent; Grey: 1–5 percent; Black: more than 20 percent.

Source: Author's illustrationbased on MOFCOM (2012) and UNCTAD (2012).

knowhow. China finances and constructs numerous agricultural, hydro-power, housing, railway, roadworks and mining projects in the region, particularly in Cambodia, Laos, Myanmar, the Philippines and Vietnam (Hodal, 2012). It takes advantage of lower labour costs than at home by relocating labor-intensive production facilities (Wu and Sia, 2002). In Cambodia, for example, Chinese firms have invested significantly in the textile industry. In Thailand, Chinese firms seek to tap into the local market and secure natural resources (Suvakunta, 2007). SAIC has agreed with the Charoen Pokphand Group to jointly produce and sell "MG" cars MG 3, MG 5 and MG 6 in Thailand for the local and international markets by 2014. The firms have enjoyed a business relationship for more than 25 years which reflects the importance of long-term ties in international business (CPThailand, 2012). Fujian Industry is to set up a special economic zone for heavy industries in Maluku province jointly with its partner Seram Jaya Perkasa (China.org.cn, 2012). Overall, Frost (2004) argues that Thailand has benefitted from the free trade agreement with China which has resulted in an increase in direct investments.

Considering a key mode of cross-border investments, merger and acquisitions (M&As) of local firms, a different regional distribution emerges. Businesses in Singapore, Indonesia and Malaysia are the main takeover targets (see Table 1). The focus on these countries is not too

Table 1.   Chinese mergers and acquisitions in ASEAN

	All sectors	Oil, Gas, Mining	High technology	Financials	Infrastructure & construction
Indonesia	21	12	1	2	—
Laos	1	1	—	—	—
Malaysia	14	—	8	2	1
Philippines	5	1	1	1	—
Singapore	85	8	20	15	23
Thailand	12	3	3	3	—
Vietnam	8	1	2	—	1
Total	146	26	35	23	25

Notes: No data is available for Myanmar and Brunei; - denotes no recorded data is available.
Source: Thompson Reuters (2012).

surprising. They represent large domestic economies with significant sales potential for Chinese firms. Across the ASEAS member countries, they also represent the most technological advanced economies, hosting a large number of subsidiaries from industrialized economies and therefore offer potential for Chinese firms to upgrade their technological profile. This is reflected in its concentration on the oil, gas and mining, high technology, financials and infrastructure and construction sectors. However, a grand total of 146 recorded acquisitions (across seven countries and twenty years) is by all means a modest number.

One of the most active Chinese outward investor is Haier, the Qingdao-based white goods manufacturer. Over the last years it has successively acquired the regional washing machine, consumer use refrigerator and other consumer electric appliance operations of Sanyo in Indonesia, Philippines, Thailand and Vietnam. Through the acquisitions, Haier has reinforced its end market penetrating operations in Southeast Asia. It now enjoys greater flexibility in the selection of production locations which allows Haier to take full advantage of the trade benefits that came with the establishment of the China–ASEAN free trade agreement in 2010. The focus on the regional consumer market is also reflected in the acquisitions by the Industrial and Commercial Bank of China (ICBC) of the ACL Bank PCL in Thailand and the Bank Halim Indonesia PT in Indonesia. These acquisitions provide ICBC with access to large and well developed markets in which it can gain knowledge and further gain experience about investing internationally. Other major Chinese acquirers in the region include the China National Offshore Oil Corporation (CNOOC), PetroChina and China Ocean Shipping (Group) Company (COSCO). CNOOC and PetroChina have engaged in the acquisition of oil fields and related products and now have stakes in the oil and gas exploration and exploitation in Indonesia. COSCO's activities have concentrated on Singapore.

The increase in Chinese investments in ASEAN does not come without tensions. In Myanmar, Chinese firms seek to exploit the mineral and metals wealth of the country and develop its transport and energy infrastructure (ERI, 2008). Bordering to the Chinese province of Yunnan, Myanmar offers an interesting prospect for Chinese firms that seek to expand markets and secure raw materials. In 2011, the government of Myanmar suspended the construction of the US$3.6bn Myitsone dam across the Irrawaddy River by China Power Investment, a state-run Chinese company, because of relocation and environmental concerns as well as public anger about the transfer of generated energy to China (Fuller, 2011; Moe, 2012). In late 2012, social protest against the expansion of a copper mine by a Chinese-Burmese consortium, including Wanbao Mining Ltd, a subsidiary of Norinco, had to be stopped by local security forces (Fuller, 2012). For Chinese firms, these problems partially arise from a lack of understanding of how to identify and manage multiple stakeholders in a foreign country (Bi, 2012). Chinese firms will possess stakeholder management capabilities but these are developed and tuned for the Chinese business environment.[1] If costly mistakes are to be avoided, revision and adaption of these capabilities for any new host market is required.

3.4 *The role of tax havens and offshore financial centres*

Tax havens and offshore financial centres play undoubtedly an important role in the internationalization of Chinese firms. Hong Kong, Cayman Island, and British Virgin Islands account for 74 percent of China's outward FDI stock in 2011. In their respective regions, Asia and Latin America, they are important host countries for Chinese investments. What attracts Chinese firms to these territories?

The dominant feature that is used to characterise tax havens is their low tax rates. In countries like the Cayman Islands firms actually have to pay no tax at all but merely an administrative charge. Incorporating here and, formally, conducting all international operations, or the least the most value adding ones, allows firms to legally channel profits to low tax countries. Tax havens are of strategic value as well. They offer a foreign identity to businesses, secrecy, access to external funding, and opportunities to restructure international operations.

China, like other host countries that seek to attract foreign investors, offers investment incentives to investors. To this end, common benefits investors can receive include tax breaks or holidays, preferred access to

---

[1] The failed acquisition of Unocal by CNOOC in 2005 is partially attributable to CNOOC's lack in understanding the American stakeholder landscape.

scarce resources, and one-off welcome payments. In the Chinese case, such benefits were not available to domestic firms but foreign investors only. It was therefore a sensible strategy for Chinese firms to incorporate in, for example, Hong Kong or the Cayman Islands and gain the host country's identity in order to be recognized as a foreign invested entity when the Chinese firm reinvests in China. These so-called "round tripping" arrangements obscure FDI statistics in two ways.[2] The degree of genuine inward FDI into China, that is FDI by non-Chinese firms, is lower than the official Chinese statistics indicate. The extent to which round tripping is lowering official data is contested. However, according to UNCTAD (2007), round-tripping accounts for about 25 percent of inward FDI. Following on from the earlier discussed notion of FDI bringing advanced technologies and skills, this needs to be revisited in cases where the validity of official data needs to be doubted.

At the same time, the other side of the coin is that the outward FDI data might be exaggerated. By 2011, nearly 80 percent of Chinese FDI was directed towards the well-known tax haven British Virgin Islands, Cayman Islands and Hong Kong. All of which are important home countries for investments into China. If outward FDI might be smaller than officially stated, the real regional distribution of Chinese investments has to be regarded as conservative. Investments that are channelled through tax haven into the EU or ASEAN might not be identified as originally Chinese and therefore attributed to another home country. Such "onward journeying" can be supported by better access to external finance than would have been possible in China. Private firms in China are suffering from a financial system that is skewed towards state-owned enterprises. Lack of capital is hampering the domestic and international development of the private businesses. Tax havens are tightly embedded in the international financial network of banks, venture capital and stock exchanges whereby the Caribbean havens functions as an entrepôt to the North American financial market, and Hong Kong to Asia markets (Sutherland *et al.*, 2010; Sharman, 2012).

---

[2] Analyses of "round tripping" have focused on China although it is not unique to it. Indian investments are channelled through Mauritius, Russian through Cyprus and British ones through the Channel and Caribbean islands.

4. Conclusion

The internationalization of Chinese firms has come a long way since the beginning of the Open Door policy. During the early stages, with the support of the Chinese government, Chinese firms focused on absorbing skills from foreign businesses. This mainly occurred through the international technology transfer attached to international trade and inward investment into China. Inward FDI has supported the upgrading of the Chinese economy and led to increases in firm productivity. Since the early 2000s, Chinese firms are increasingly venturing abroad through foreign direct investments. These investments are motivated by a desire to develop overseas markets, secure natural resources, and strategic assets like distribution channels, technologies and brand names. Strategic assets are important to sustain the competitiveness of Chinese firms domestically and globally. These investments are not uncontested. CNOOC, Huawei and ZTE all have faced difficulties in the US. Some resistance is also building up in Australia, New Zealand and African countries where a too great a dominance of Chinese firms is feared. Although Chinese firms are not dominating yet any industry sector in the way Nestle, Google or Microsoft do, Chinese firms that seek to upgrade along the value chain and become internationally successful investors need to address these concerns and improve their communication in and with host countries as well as with other international stakeholders. As Chinese outward investment is here to stay and likely to grow further, Chinese MNEs have to anticipate and address possible resentments.

References

Alden, C and M Davies (2006). A profile of the operations of Chinese multinationals in Africa. *South African Journal of International Affairs*, 13(1), 83–96.

Bartlett, CA and S Ghoshal (2000). Going global: Lessons from late movers. *Harvard Business Review*, March–April, 132–142.

Bi, S (2012). Respect helps ease firms' way in Myanmar. *Global Times*, October 14. Available at http://www.globaltimes.cn/content/738207.shtml.

Brookes, P and JH Shin (2006). *China's Influence in Africa: Implications for the United States*. Backgrounder No. 1916, February 22, Washington DC: Heritage Foundation.

Buckley, PJ, LJ Clegg, AR Cross, X Liu, H Voss, and P Zheng (2007). The determinants of Chinese outward foreign direct investment. *Journal of International Business Studies*, 38(4), 499–518.

Buckley, PJ, AR Cross, H Tan, X Liu, and H Voss (2008). Historic and emergent trends in Chinese outward direct investment. *Management International Review*, 48(6), 715–748.

Buckley, PJ, H Voss, AR Cross, and LJ Clegg (2011). The emergence of Chinese firms as multinationals: the influence of the home institutional environment. In *China and the Multinationals: International Business and the Entry of China Into the Global Economy*, R Pearce (ed.), pp. 125–157. Cheltenham, UK: Edward Elgar.

Christmann, P and G Taylor (2001). Globalization and the environment: Determinants of firm self-regulation in China. *Journal of International Business Studies*, 32(3), 439–458.

CIA Factbook (2012). *Imports — Partners*. Available at https://www.cia.gov/library/publications/the-world-factbook/fields/2061.html.

Clegg, LJ and SC Scott-Green (1999). The determinants of new foreign direct investment capital flows into the European Community: A statistical comparison of the USA and Japan. *Journal of Common Market Studies*, 37(4), 597–616.

Clegg, LJ and H Voss (2011). Inside the China-EU bilateral foreign direct investment bond. EU–China investment relationships. *China and World Economy*, 19(4), 92–108.

Corkin, L and C Burke (2006). *China's Interest and Activity in Africa's Construction and Infrastructure Sectors*. Stellenbosch University: Centre for Chinese Studies.

CPThailand (2012). Charoen Pokphand Group and "Shanghai Automotive Industry Corp" (SAIC) to jointly produce "MG" cars in Thailand for the local and international market. *CP Group Press Releases*, December 12, Available at http://www.cpthailand.com/Default.aspx?tabid=68&articleType=ArticleView&articleId=1397

Dunning, JH and R Narula (1996). The investment development path revisited: Some emerging issues. In *Foreign Direct Investment and Governments: Catalyst for Economic Restructuring*, JH Dunning and R Narula (eds.), pp. 1–40. London, UK: Routledge.

Dunning, JH and SM Lundan (2008). *Multinational Enterprises and the Global Economy*, 2nd Edition. Cheltenham, UK: Edward Elgar.

The Economist (2013). How innovative is China? Valuing patents. January 5.

ERI (2008). *China in Burma: The Increasing Investment of Chinese Multinational Corporations in Burma's Hydropower, Oil and Natural Gas, and Mining Sectors*. Chiang Mai and Washington: EarthRights International.

Fan, D, CJ Zhu, and C Nyland (2012). Factors affecting global integration of Chinese multinationals in Australia: A qualitative analysis. *International Business Review*, 21(1), 13–16.

Fosfuri, A and M Motta (1999). Multinationals without advantages. *Scandinavian Journal of Economics*, 101(4), 617–630.

Frost, S (2004). Chinese outward direct investment in Southeast Asia: How big are the flows and what does it mean for the region? *Pacific Review*, 17(3), 323–340.

Fuller, T (2011). Myanmar backs down, suspending dam project. *New York Times*, September 30. Available at http://www.nytimes.com/2011/10/01/world/asia/myanmar-suspends-construction-of-controversial-dam.html

Fuller, T (2012). Violent raid breaks up Myanmar mine protest. *New York Times*. November 29. Available at http://www.nytimes.com/2012/11/30/world/asia/myanmar-security-forces-raid-protest-camp.html?_r=0.

Hodal, K (2012). China invests in south-east Asia for trade, food, energy and resources. *The Guardian*, March 22. Available at http://www.guardian.co.uk/world/2012/mar/22/china-south-east-asia-influence.

Johanson, J and JE Vahlne (2009). The Uppsala internationalization process model revisited: From liability of foreignness to liability of outsidership. *Journal of International Business Studies*, 40(9), 1411–1431.

Klossek, A, BM Linke, and M Nippa (2012). Chinese enterprises in Germany: Establishment modes and strategies to mitigate the liability of foreignness. *Journal of World Business*, 47(1), 35–44.

Kolstad, I and A Wiig (2012). What determines Chinese outward FDI? *Journal of World Business*, 47(1), 26–34.

Lewis, JI (2007). Technology acquisition and innovation in the developing world: Wind turbine development in China and India. *Studies in Comparative International Development*, 42(3–4), 208–232.

Liu, X, Cheng, P and A Chen (2011). Basic research and catch-up in China's high-speed rail industry. *Journal of Chinese Econ omic and Business Studies*, 9(4), 349–367.

Mathews, JA (2002). *Dragon Multinational: A New Model for Global Growth*. Oxford, UK: Oxford University Press.

Moe, KZ (2012). Letpadaung protests to test the limits of reforms. *The Irrawaddy*, December 4. Available at http://www.irrawaddy.org/archives/20528.

MOFCOM (2012). *2012 Statistical Bulletin of China's Outbound Foreign Direct Investment*. Beijing: MOFCOM.

OECD (2002). *China in the World Economy: The Domestic Policy Challenges*. Paris: OECD.

Posth, M (2008). *1,000 Days in Shanghai: The Volkswagen Story — The First Chinese–German Car Factory*. London, UK: Wiley.

Romann, A (2012). China's small stake in ASEAN going to pick up soon. *China Daily,* February 17. Available at http://www.chinadailyapac.com/article/chinas-small-stake-asean-going-pick-soon.

Rugman, AM (2005). *Regional Multinationals*. Cambridge, UK: Cambridge University Press.

Rugman, AM and J Li (2008). Will China's multinationals succeed globally or regionally? *European Management Journal*, 25(5), 333–343.

Sharman, J (2012). Chinese capital flows and offshore financial centers. *Pacific Review*, 25, 317–337.

Sutherland, D, A El-Gohari, PJ Buckley, and H Voss (2010). The role of Caribbean tax havens and offshore financial centres in Chinese outward foreign direct investment. 2nd Copenhagen Conference on *Emerging Multinationals: Outward Investment from Emerging and Developing Economies*, Copenhagen Business School, Copenhagen, November 25–26.

Suvakunta, P (2007). China's go-out strategy: Chinese foreign direct investment in Thailand. *Thammasat Review*, 12(1), 116–146.

Szulanski, G (1996). Exploring internal stickiness: Impediments to the transfer of best practice within the firm. *Strategic Management Journal*, 17, 27–43.

UNCTAD (2001). *World Investment Report 2001: Promoting Linkages*. Geneva and New York: UNCTAD.

UNCTAD (2007). *Rising FDI Into China: The Facts Behind the Numbers*. UNCTAD Investment Brief No. 2. Available at http://unctad.org/en/Docs/iteiiamisc20075_en.pdf [5 January 2013].

UNCTAD (2012). *UNCTADStats*. Available at http://unctadstat.unctad.org.

van der Lugt, S and V Hamblin (2011). *Assessing China's Role in Foreign Direct Investment in Southern Africa*. Stellenbosch University: Centre for Chinese Studies.

Voss, H (2011). *The Determinants of Mainland Chinese Outward Foreign Direct Investment*. Cheltenham, UK: Edward Elgar.

Voss, H, PJ Buckley, and AR Cross (2010). The impact of home country institutional effects on the internationalization strategy of Chinese firms. *Multinational Business Review*, 18(3), 25–48.

Voss, H, PJ Buckley, and AR Cross (2009). An assessment of the effects of institutional change on chinese outward direct investment activity. In *China*

Rules: Globalization and Political Transformation, I Alon, J Chang, M Fetscherin, C Lattemann and JR McIntyre (eds.), pp. 135–165. London, UK: Palgrave Macmillan.

Wang, C, J Hong, M Kaforous, and M Wright (2012). Exploring the role of government involvement in outward FDI from emerging economies. *Journal of International Business Studies*, 43, 655–676.

Welch, LS and RK Luostarinen (1993). Inward-outward connections in internationalization. *Journal of International Marketing*, 1(1), 44–56.

Witt, MA and AY Lewin (2007). Outward foreign direct investment as escape response to home country institutional constraints. *Journal of International Business Studies*, 38(4), 579–594.

World Bank (2012). *World Development Indictors*. ESDS International, University of Manchester. Available at http://dx.doi.org/10.5257/wb/wdi/2012-04.

Wu, F and YH Sia (2002). China's rizing investment in Southeast Asia: Trends and outlook. *Journal of Asian Business*, 18(2), 41–61.

Zeng, M and PJ Williamson (2003). The hidden dragons. *Harvard Business Review*, 81(10), 92–99.

Index

Abdul Razak   83
Accounting Standards Act   200
Adelaide Casino   85
Advertising X   318, 327, 328, 331,
    332, 334, 338, 339
affirmative action   76
affirmative policy   74, 95, 102
Africa   3, 15
Alex Au   207
Ali-Baba   97, 99, 100, 102
Ananda Krishnan   90
anti-Chinese violence   120, 122
Asian financial crisis   88, 91, 103
Asian leadership   280
Asian-centric   158
Asia-Pacific   86
Asiatic Development Sdn Bhd   86
assimilation   238, 247
    Assimilation Programme
        236
    politics   246
Australia   85, 86
Australian State   85

Baba   99
Bahamas   85, 86
Bailieu Myer   90

Bak Foong pills   221
Ban Hin Lee Bank   94
Bank Central Asia (BCA)   251, 252,
    256
Banking Act   200
banking industry   77
benevolence   103
Benny Santoso   260, 263
Berjaya Group   78
Bhd, Sdn   76
Boon Siew   76
British Malaya   75
Buddhist perspective   283
Bumiputera   73, 75, 78, 95, 99
Bumiputera Commerce Bank
    (CIMB)   77, 90
Bumiputera Commercial and
    Industrial Community (BCIC)   74,
    103
Bumiputera partners   95, 96, 100–102
Bumiputeras   74, 93
Bursewood Island Resort   85
business conduct   231–234, 238, 243,
    245, 247, 248
business network   141
business partnerships   102
business practices   239, 240, 242–248

Campaign Asia   328
Capitol Theatre in Sydney   87
casino   85, 86
casino business   103
casino resort   86
Central Bank   94
Central Bank of Malaysia   92
Chamber of Commerce   406
change leadership style   160
change management (CM)
  behavior   47
change measure   166, 167
Chettiar migration   400
Chettiar trade networks   405
Chettiars   397–399, 402–406,
  408–416
Chinese banks   76
Chinese business groups   74, 78, 95,
  102
Chinese-educated   45, 48, 49, 59
Chinese family business   194, 197,
  208
Chinese family enterprise   51
Chinese firms   420, 421, 423, 425,
  426, 428, 431–434
Chinese Indonesians   107, 108, 116,
  117, 120, 124
Chinese partners   95, 99, 101
Chinese traditions   236, 243
Chinese way   232, 233, 240, 242, 244
Chinese-Bumiputera   100
Chineseness   23, 24, 27, 29, 30,
  37–39, 41, 107, 109, 110, 114, 119,
  123, 236–239, 246
Christian perspective   288
Code of Corporate Governance   200,
  202
coercive style   160, 169
Coles-Myer   90

collaborative style   159, 160, 168
collaborative-coercive   184
collaborative-consultative   163, 168,
  174
colonial economy   399
communists   114, 115
Como Hotel in Melbourne   87
Company's Act   200
conceptions of space   384
condominium (Kudalari)   87
Confucian perspective   286
Confucian values   231, 234
construction   76, 88, 101–103
consultative style   159, 160, 168
corporate ownership   78
critical perspectives   231
cultural and critical
  perspectives   248
cultural context   236
cultural orientations   345
culturalist   231, 233, 234

Dato' Lee Kong Lam   92
Desa Angkasa   87
diligent (qin)   90
directive style   160, 169
directive-coercive   171, 174,
  184
discursive-contextual approach   232,
  246–248
    expression   239, 247
    practices   242, 245
Djuhar family   258

Early International
  Entrepreneurs   397
Economic Planning Unit   92
education   232, 238, 241, 244, 245,
  247

effective communication   305
English-educated   45, 48, 49, 59
entrepreneur   96
ethnic Chinese business   193, 199
ethnic group   234, 237, 238
Eu family   215–217
Eu Yan Sang (EYS)   213–215, 217, 219, 222, 224

family-controlled firms   196
Fang Yen San   82
Finance Minister   93
First Pacific Company   258
Forbes Asia   90
Foxwoods Casino   85, 86
frames of reference   232, 236
Fujianese migration   3, 4

Ganqing   134
Garden, Ipoh   76
generation   235
    generational approach   248
    generational change   233, 247
    generational encounters   235
    first generation   232, 238
    second or third generation   102, 231, 234
Genting   86, 91
    Genting Berhad   79
    Genting Group   78, 79, 84, 86, 102
    Genting Highlands Hotel Berhad   84
    Genting Highlands Hotel Sdn Bhd   83, 84
    Genting Hong Kong Limited   79
    Genting International   84
    Genting Malaysia Berhad   79
    Genting Plantations Berhad   79

Genting Sanyen Industrial Paper Sdn Bhd   86
Genting Sanyen Newsprint Sdn Bhd   86
Genting Sanyen Power Sdn Bhd   86
Genting Singapore PLC   79
Genting Ulu Kali Mountain   83
Gleneagles Hospitals   87
Global Leadership and Organizational Behavior Effectiveness (GLOBE)   280, 281
Goldis Berhad   87, 88
government   81, 93, 100, 102
government-link   91
government-linked banks   94
guanxi   93, 133–135, 137–139, 141, 146, 149

hamper sales   221
high urgency and high resistance   163
Hindu perspective   284
Hock Hua Bank   94
Hokkien   6, 9
Hong Kong Stock Exchange   79, 86
Hong Kong's Asia Commercial Bank (ABC)   94
Hong Leong Bank   77
Hong Leong Group   76, 78
huaqiao   10
human smugglers   3
Hussein Onn   83
Ibrahim Rishad   258

identity   235, 236, 238
IGB   88, 91
    IGB Corporation   88
    IGB Corporation Berhad   87

IGB Group   78, 87, 102
IGB REIT   87
illegal migrants   3
incremental   163
    incremental change   184
    incremental change
        strategies   170
individualism-collectivism   349,
    352
Indonesian Bank Restructuring
    Agency (IBRA)   251
Informal Banking   397
Institute of Strategic and International
    Studies (ISIS)   89
intangible knowledge   102, 103
inter-ethnic ownership   102
internationalization   405
intra-ethnic   95
    intra-ethnic networks   231
    intra-ethnic ownership   102
    intra-ethnic ties   233
IOI Group   78
Ipmuda Berhad   87
Ipoh Garden   87
Islamic perspective   289

Japanese company   85
Japanese government   82
JCG Finance   94
jian (thrift)   88
jinqian (cash or capital)   88
joint-venture   83

Kenny Yap   175, 186
Kerry Group/Kuok Group   78
Kien Huat   76
Kien Huat Private Limited   80
Kim Yeow   87
kinship   136, 137, 141

KL Mutual Fund Berhad   94
KLSE   87
know-how   75, 103
knowledge   73, 74, 79, 80, 89, 91–93,
    95–97, 100, 102
knowledge leadership   178, 179
knowledge management (KM)   73,
    91, 299, 302–306, 313
knowledge transfer   345, 346, 348
knowledge-based   96
know-who   74, 99, 102, 103
KrisAssets Holdings Berhad   87
Kuala Lumpur   79, 80, 83, 87
Kuala Lumpur Stock Exchange
    (KLSE)   75, 84
Kuala Lumpur–Kepong Bhd
    (KLK)   75
Kuala Lumpur Kepong Group   78

land and landownership   384
Las Vegas Sands Corp (LVS)   86
leadership approaches   184
leadership development   293
Lee Foundation   302, 312
Lee Kong Chian (LKC)   205–313
Lee Loy Seng   75
Lee Pineapple Company Private
    Limited   301
Lee Rubber Company Private
    Limited   301, 310
Lee Rubber Group   301–303
Lee Seng Wee   206, 207
Liem family   258
Liem Sioe Liong   252–254, 258
Lim Goh Tong   76
Lim Kok Thay   84
Lion Group   76, 78
Loanpac Insurance Bhd   90
local SMEs   47, 156

Loh Boon Siew 76
Loy Hean Heong 75
low urgency and low resistance 163
Lucayan Beach Resort 85

Mainland Chinese Businesses 419
Malaya 74–76, 80, 82, 96, 99, 100
Malayan Banking 77, 79, 90, 94
Malayan Borneo Finance
 (MBF Berhad) 75
Malayan Mining Limited 82
Malayan Sugar 76
Malaysia 84, 88
Malaysian Business Council 89
Malaysian Stock Exchange
 (KLSE) 79
management 91, 92, 101, 103
manufacturing 96
maritime 6
market-dominant minorities 107,
 108
Mashpee Wampanoag 86
MiCasa Hotel Apartment 87
Mid-Valley City 88, 90
migration 235, 241, 242, 247
migration networks 4
mindfulness 282–284, 286
Ministry of Finance 92
Ministry of International Trade
 and Industries 89
modern organizational
 structure 310
modern Western 52, 61
Mohamad Noah Omar 83
Monetary Authority of Singapore
 (MAS) 200
multinational corporation
 (MNC) 23, 25
Myanmar 94

Nam Aik 301, 302, 304, 307,
 310–312
 Nam Aik Company 299, 308,
  309, 311, 312
 Nam Aik Rubber Company
  300
narratives 236, 243
nation building 74
National Development Policy 102
Native American tribe 86–86
network 93–95, 101, 233
New Economic Policy (NEP) 76, 91,
 93, 96, 102
New Order 236–238, 246, 247
Niagara Falls 86
Nissan Sugar Manufacturing 76
non-Chinese 245, 246
non-governmental linked
 company 90

Old Chang Kee 182
older and younger generation 239,
 247
older generation 238
older and younger 232
one-man rule 159
One-man show 159
Onn, Tun Hussein 89
or medium 238
Oriental Group 78
Oriental Holdings Berhad 76
Outsiders 139
Overseas Chettiar
 Moneylending 408
Overseas Chinese Banking
 Corporation (OCBC) 91, 199,
 205–207
Overseas Chinese
 entrepreneurship 132

Overseas Chinese Trading
  Networks   133
owner-managers   165

Pahang Government   83
Parkway Parade   87
partnership   95, 97–100
PB   93, 94
people-oriented   56
people-related   60
peranakan   109, 110–113, 118, 119
personal networks   240–242, 246,
  247
Petaling Garden   87
Petaling Jaya   80
Pipa Limited   146–148
plantation   75, 86
political and urban space   389
post-independence period   75
President Suharto   252–258, 263
pribumi   110–124
proactive   183
property development   76, 88
Public Bank (Hong Kong)
  Limited   94
Public Bank (PB)   77, 90
Public Bank Berhad   90
Public Bank Group   78, 90, 94, 102
Public Finance   92
Public Finance Limited   94
Public Mutual   94

Qian Hu   175–178, 182, 318,
  335–337, 339
Quanzhou   7, 9
Queen Victoria Building   87

RAV Bahamas   85
reactive   183

Real Estate Investment Trust
  (REIT)   87
relationship   97, 96, 102
religious space   386
remittances   4
ren (recognize, know, make
  out or identify)   90
resort casino   86
Resort World Berhad (RWB)   84,
  85
Richard Eu   213, 216, 217, 219,
  221–223, 226
Rimbunan Hijau Group   78
riots   237
Robert Kuok   76, 90

Salim family   258
Salim Group   251, 253, 254,
  256–258, 260, 262–265
    Anthony Salim   251, 252, 254,
      256–258, 260, 262–265
Seafood Restaurant   318, 319, 322,
  323, 325, 326, 336
Second World War   80
Securities and Futures Act   200
Selangor government   83
Selangor Hardware Dealers'
  Association   82
Seneca Nation of Indians   86
Seng Kee Dredging   83
Sentosa Integrated Resorts (IR)
  85
Shanghai   94
Shangri-La Hotel   87, 90
Shenyang   94
Shenzhen   94
Sime Darby   90
Sime Merchant Bank   94
Singapore   10, 84

Singapore Chinese Chamber
of Commerce & Industry
(SCCCI)   49
Singapore Exchange (SGX)   200
Singapore Land   198
Singapore Stock Exchange   79
Singaporean Chinese Trading
Networks   143
Singapore-based company   226
Sino–Bumiputera partnership   96
Sino-Thai Rice   87
Siok San   320, 324, 325, 326
sleeping partners   77, 99
small and medium enterprises
(SMEs)   50, 96, 102, 155, 177, 178,
182, 238–239, 245–247, 315
small and medium sector   232
smart partnership   95, 103
SME Master Plan   185
SME owner-managers   179,
183
Social Space   387
Soedono Salim   252
South China   6
South China Sea   9
Southeast Asia   6, 9
Southern Bank   77, 94
SPRING   322, 334, 338
Sri Lanka   94
Stanley Leisure Ltd.   84
Star Cruises Limited   86
Star Cruises'   86
state social engineering   25, 33
strategic partnerships   96, 102
Sudwikadmono   258
Sunway Group   78
Sutanto Djuhar   258
Suzukawa   143–146
Swedish cruise ships   86

Tan & Tan Development   87
Tan Chin Nam   76, 87
Tan family   88
Tan Kah Kee   301
Tan Sri Dato' Thong Yaw Hong   92
Tan Sri Lim Goh Tong   79
Tan Sri Nik Ahmed Kamil   93
Tan Sri Teh Hong Piow   90
team-oriented style   281
Tedy Djuhar   258
tin mining   75, 83
TKK   301
totok   109, 112, 113, 117–119
traditional Chinese   52, 61
Traditional Chinese Medicine
(TCM)   213, 215, 217, 219, 226,
228
transformative change   184
transnational (TNC)   96, 98
transnationalism   3
tribute trade   6
trust   233, 240–242, 245, 246
trustworthiness   240, 245
Tunku Abdul Rahman's   83
Tun Abdul Razak   89

United Industrial Corporation
(UIC)   198
United Malay National Organization
(UMNO)   93
United Overseas Bank (UOB)   198
United Overseas Land Limited
(UOL)   198
Urban Property Development   381

vertical-horizontal   351, 352

Wah Seong   88
Wah Seong Corporation Berhad   89

Wah Seong Corportion   87
Wah Tat Bank   94
Wee Ee Cheong's   209
Wee family   198
Western-centric   158
William Cheng   76

Xiao Yao Wan   221

Yap Lim Sen   89
Yogyakarta   238
YTL   *78*, 91

Zhangzhou   9
Zheng He   6, 7
zhi (wisdom or resourcefulness)
   90